WACO-McLENNAN COUN
1717 AUSTIN A\
WACO TX 7670₁

FIRST FALLEN

The Life of Colonel Elmer Ellsworth,
the North's First Civil War Hero

Meg Groeling

SB

Savas Beatie
California

Library of Congress Cataloging-in-Publication Data

Names: Groeling, Meg, author.
Title: First Fallen: The life of Colonel Elmer Ellsworth, the North's
   First Civil War Hero / by Meg Groeling.
Other titles: Life of Colonel Elmer Ellsworth, the North's First Civil War Hero
Description: El Dorado Hills, CA : Savas Beatie LLC, [2021] | Includes
   bibliographical references and index. | Summary: "Elmer Ellsworth was
   the first Union officer killed in the American Civil War. He is a
   perfect historical lens through which to examine the fresh face of
   America that responded to the Union's call. That he is not well-known
   today is a tragedy. His intriguing personality, his remarkable life—so
   tightly bound to the history of his time and to President Lincoln—and
   his contributions to the war efforts of the North make him too important
   to be forgotten"— Provided by publisher.
Identifiers: LCCN 2021001212 | ISBN 9781611215373 (hardcover) | ISBN
   9781611215380 (ebook)
Subjects: LCSH: Ellsworth, E. E. (Elmer Ephraim), 1837-1861. | United
   States. Army. New York Infantry Regiment, 11th (1861-1862)—Biography. |
   Lincoln, Abraham, 1809-1865—Friends and associates. | United States.
   Army.—Officers—Biography. | United States—History—Civil War,
   1861-1865—Biography. | Alexandria (Va.)—History—Civil War, 1861-1865.
Classification: LCC E523.5 111th .G76 2021 | DDC 973.70973 [B]—dc23
LC record available at https://lccn.loc.gov/2021001212

First edition, first printing

SB
Savas Beatie
989 Governor Drive, Suite 102
El Dorado Hills, CA 95762
Phone: 916-941-6896 / (E-mail) sales@savasbeatie.com

Savas Beatie titles are available at special discounts for bulk purchases in the United States. Contact us for more details.

Proudly published, printed, and warehoused in the United States of America.

For Bree Meerjans, who was there at the beginning,
and Robert Groeling, who is here at the end

Table of Contents

Table of Contents (continued)

Photos and maps have been distributed
throughout for the convenience of the reader.

Introduction

No comprehensive biography of Colonel Elmer Ellsworth has been published since Ruth Painter Randall wrote hers in 1960. I thought it was about time for another one. Ellsworth was one of those historical personages that never made it to the "A" list for some reason. Had he lived, he may have, but we will never know. Most people, including some Civil War historians, do not even know who he was. This book contains what we *do* know about him.

Elmer Ellsworth was the first Union officer killed in the American Civil War. Myths abound about him, but they are just that—myths. Ellsworth came from a working-class background, not poverty. He could have attended West Point had he chosen to do so, but he decided instead to join the legions of young Yankee men who left the family homestead and moved westward to make their own futures. Young Ellsworth not only worked in Abraham Lincoln's law office, he passed the Illinois bar exam before leaving Springfield for Washington. He neither smoked nor drank, and he expected the same of his companions. He was handsome and sophisticated enough to charm the men (and women) of the moneyed class, gathering around himself influential political figures who moved and shook the North in the time immediately before the Civil War.

It was the influence of his performance group, the United States Zouave Cadets, and their tour of the Northeast that paved the way for the militia movement, which exceeded the quota of 75,000 volunteers that Lincoln called for after Fort Sumter was fired upon in Charleston Harbor. One might go so far as to suggest that it was Ellsworth's military efforts that readied the North for the eventuality of the war itself. Although rarely mentioned, it was Ellsworth who provided military-themed entertainment at the Republican Convention in Chicago in 1860. Ellsworth, John Hay, and Ward Hill Lamon worked together to create enough interference at the "Wigwam" to move support from William Seward and other contenders to Abraham Lincoln, who finally won the nomination on the third ballot of a brokered convention. The use of marching militia members influenced the growth of the "Wide-Awakes," a group of young men that wore distinctive black capes and carried oil lanterns. At first, they escorted stumping politicians to and from the trains to the hustings, but later they held late-night parades supporting Republican candidates.

The self-made men of the North who had experienced 1850s politics saw the return to slave laws and Southern congressional control as a return to the past, erasing the progress of the Missouri Compromise. They saw themselves as "wide awake," aware of the purposes of union and politics. Elmer Ellsworth is a perfect historical lens through which to examine this fresh face of America. He espoused discipline, self-reliance, and confidence, and he showed that there was indeed a chance for someone not born to wealth to exercise power at higher levels of politics and society. The example he set was followed by many, including those involved in numerous militia organizations.

During his short life—he died when he was just twenty-four—Elmer Ellsworth became "the most talked-of man in the country," according to John Hay. Ellsworth was welcomed into the best houses in Illinois, including the Lincolns'. Mary Todd Lincoln loved Elmer much like a son and was heartbroken at his death. President Lincoln trusted the young man so much that he was put in charge of crowd control during the "Inaugural Express" train trip to Washington. When Lincoln realized his life was threatened and chose to leave the train early, he asked Elmer to take care of Mary and their sons.

When Lincoln called for volunteers in April 1861, Elmer Ellsworth was one of the first to leave Washington and travel to New York City to recruit a regiment. Ellsworth wanted the New York firemen in particular; he felt that the strength and discipline of the job of fighting fires would give these men an advantage in any imminent battles against Southern volunteers. If Ellsworth had done nothing except bring his regiment to Washington, that would have been as much as many. But he did more. He uniformed his men, armed them, and immediately began to teach them his French Algerian-inspired Zouave drill. This drill had some significant differences from the one that was currently used by the army, which had not changed much from the Mexican War era. Had Ellsworth lived long enough to continue this training, his units might have become forerunners of the elite forces used by our current military. After his death, many of the 11th New York Fire Zouaves, as Ellsworth's men were known, complained that this training had been abandoned.

Even Ellsworth's death helped the Union war effort. He was seen as the quintessential "Boy of '61," and newspapers in many Northern cities ran black-banded headlines when his killing was announced. "Remember Ellsworth" was a rallying cry throughout the war. It rang out in Irish brogues on the battlefield of First Bull Run. Francis Brownell, the private who shot the man who shot Colonel Ellsworth, became identified as "Ellsworth's Avenger." He was awarded the first Medal of Honor of the Civil War. Even the love story of Ellsworth and his young fiancé, Carrie Spafford, furnished a captivating tale to the nation, one illustrated most sadly when I paged through Miss Spafford's scrapbook and found an assortment of funeral flowers pressed between its pages.

That Elmer Ellsworth is not more well-known today is a tragedy. His intriguing personality, his remarkable life—so tightly bound to the history of his time and to Abraham Lincoln—and his personal contributions to the war efforts of the North make him, I feel, too important to be forgotten. I have tried to present Ellsworth, along with his friends John Hay and John George Nicolay, the Lincoln family, and those early years in Chicago as clearly as possible. I have also included a chapter on James Jackson, the Virginia secessionist who killed Ellsworth. I am hopeful that my dedication and that of those who joined me in this process will help a new generation remember Ellsworth. "Never," said the *New York Times*, "has a man of Ellsworth's age commanded such national respect and regard in so short a space."

Acknowledgments

No project like a full-length book is finished without the help and encouragement of many. I hesitate to try to list all the beautiful people who helped me—I know I will forget someone, probably many someones. If I leave you off, call me. I will brew you a cup of coffee, and we can sit on the porch and pet the cats.

I particularly want to thank the former principal of Brownell Middle School, Greg Camacho-Light. Brownell Middle School is named for early California educator E. E. Brownell. Randomly, during an open house, Greg asked if I knew what the "E. E." might stand for. Without thinking, I answered that it probably stood for Elmer Ellsworth. I added a comment about the name "Brownell," who was known as "Ellsworth's Avenger" for shooting James Jackson almost instantly after Jackson killed Ellsworth. We both started laughing. I had no idea my principal/boss was a Civil War buff, and he had no idea his new 7th grade math teacher was one as well. Over the next few years, Greg supported my effort to get a master's degree in military history and to write the first iteration of this book. Nothing he did was necessary, but everything he did was much appreciated.

I would also like to thank my "family" at the *Emerging Civil War* blog, especially Chris Mackowski. They gave me my first chance to write history for the public. I've never looked back! My professors at American Public University helped hone my writing and research skills. They were very supportive of on-line students, especially those of us who are women. No special treatment, just the same grueling study schedule for all. Huzzah!

Research! There are so many who deserve my thanks, especially Doug Dammann and Gina Radandt, the lovely folks who welcomed me to the Kenosha Civil War Museum in Wisconsin and helped me sort things out. Also, the people at the New York State Military Museum in Saratoga, who talked to me for hours about the restoration of the Marshall House Flag and offered to help me in any other way I wished. They have curated the flag and the uniform in which Elmer met his death with much skill and care! Finally, I would like to thank Brown University and my research assistant, Kathryn Samp. She not only found Ellsworthy things, but she also located information about Elmer's connection to the Wide-Awakes, creating my next project. Her best find was the writing Elmer did of his name using soldiers as letters. It was a perfect match for the one he did for Carrie. Nice catch, Kathy!

The on-line community, especially Facebook's *Civil War Faces*, was of incredible help in identifying and sourcing images. *Ancestry*, *Fold3*, and *Newspapers.com* are valuables sources that were not available even ten years ago. What a difference technology has made for all of us who toil in the history mines. The internet also allowed me to find and stay in touch with individuals whose interests in things Elmer Ellsworth in nature have kept me going when I thought I'd never solve a problem or uncover any meaning in my work. Thanks also to Allen Cebula, Mike Maxwell, Stephen Restelli, Harry Smeltzer of *bullrunnings. wordpress.com*, and the second version of the 11th New York Fire Zouaves: Shaun Grenan, Marc Hermann, Patrick Schroeder, and the late Brian Pohanka.

I owe a massive debt to publisher Theodore P. Savas, Managing Director of Savas Beatie Publishers, and his staff. They gave me my first chance to be published, with *The Aftermath of Battle* and have done so again with *First Fallen*. Ted introduced me to my editor extraordinaire, Mitchell Yockelson. Editing is hard enough, but editing during the time of Covid was about as much as I could handle. Mitch, thank you so much. Thank you, all.

There are more: all the powerful, determined women who are writing Civil War history now and never had to wait until they retired; I feel like their grandmother. Then there are the friends who never laughed at my efforts to do this work and kept me going when I just wanted to quit—Terry, Bree, and Gregory. Finally, there is the helpful, anonymous docent at the National Portrait Gallery who asked me what was wrong and handed me a real cotton handkerchief to dry my eyes when I imploded at the 2011 exhibit, "The Death of Colonel Ellsworth." That exhibit was the catalyst for this book. Somehow, I knew my life was changing, right there in the gallery.

Lastly, I want to thank my family. My sister Martha never loses faith, no matter what, and Robert, my husband, keeps the home fires burning when I am writing all night. Both assure me that my parents, John and Yvonne, would be proud.

The East Room: May 26, 1861, 3:00 a.m.

THE Washington night was utterly still. The two-story white house where the Lincolns now lived sat far enough off Pennsylvania Avenue that little noise penetrated its thick walls. For a third night, the moon remained so bright that no other light source was needed to illuminate the dark city.[1] Washington's early spring humidity had dropped only slightly since midnight, and a faint feeling of sticky staleness hung in the comatose air.[2]

Although it had rained in the early afternoon, the thunderstorms that regularly freshened the atmosphere along the Atlantic coast were not yet, by late May, a regular occurrence.[3] In a vain attempt to cool the big mansion, someone had left one window slightly ajar in the East Room, but there was no breeze to tinkle the crystal swags on the Andrew Jackson chandeliers or ruffle the lace that fell beneath the maroon velvet drapes hanging from ceiling to floor. The cloying scent of lilies, roses, and white trillium hung heavy in the motionless air of the aging, formal room.

---

1 John A. O'Brien, www.lincolninwashington.com/2012/07/16/he-has-probably-gone-to-mr-sewards-house/, accessed August 28, 2017.

2 Special Correspondent, *The New York Times*, May 26, 1861, www.nytimes.com/ 1861/ 05/26/news/death-col-ellsworth-full-particulars-assassination-eye-witness-zouaves-swear.ht ml?pagewanted=all&mcubz=3, accessed August 28, 2017; *The Olathe* [KS] *Mirror*, June 13, 1861. Many eyewitness and newspaper accounts note the brightness of the full moon on May 24-25 and 25-26, and its reflection on the Potomac River.

3 James M. Gillis, *Meteorological Observations Made at the United States Naval Observatory During the Year 1861* (Washington: United States Government Printing Office, 1873), 444; Robert K. Krick, *Civil War Weather in Virginia* (Tuscaloosa, AL: The University of Alabama Press, 2007), 25.

Mary Todd Lincoln had first set foot in the of disrepair and shabbiness left by previous occupant James Buchanan. Mary intended to commence refurbishment right away. Two months had passed, however, and the house still looked the same or worse. In mid-April, the East Room had been a temporary bivouac for General James Lane's rough Frontier Guards, one of the many volunteer militia companies pouring into the nation's capital. Soldiers tracked mud on the floor and left bits of equipment scattered about. Yesterday, May 25, 1861, the room had served only one purpose.[4] It had held the coffin of Colonel Elmer Ellsworth.

Over the last twenty-four hours, White House staff had rapidly planned for the arrival of Ellsworth's remains—scurrying about for flowers, coaches, and funeral cerements.

Although the once-elegant East Room had hosted presidential funerals, this was the first time a military officer lay in state within its walls. Thousands of people had read about Col. Ellsworth in the newspapers. Many had watched his regiment of New York Fire Zouaves become both the toast and, for some, the terror of the capitol, or had seen the United States Zouave Cadets during their 20-city tour in 1860. Mourners arrived to stand in line, then stand in respect, at Ellsworth's coffin, which was covered in a large bouquet of white lilies, all except for the small, oval glass window over his face. Shortly after eleven in the morning of May 25, the funeral service itself began.

President and Mrs. Lincoln entered the East Room and sat near the foot of the bier. Both were openly tearful, heartbroken by the sudden death of their friend.[5] Elmer Ellsworth had fit so easily into the Lincolns' life, both in Springfield and now here in Washington. He was handsome, cheerful, always reliable, and, at twenty-four, so very young. Ellsworth, along with Lincoln's private secretaries, John George Nicolay and John Hay, had been the heartbeat of Lincoln's presidential campaign and election. These three young men, best friends, had served as Lincoln's bodyguards on the train trip from Springfield to Washington, and in that dreary, muddy city, their bright exuberance and energy had been indispensable to the entire Lincoln family, from their youngest son, Tad, to the President himself.

Nicolay and Hay, along with Simon Cameron, Salmon Chase, and other members of Lincoln's cabinet, were seated close to the President and First Lady. So

4 Margaret Leech, *Reveille in Washington: 1861-1865* (New York: Carroll and Graf Publishers, 1949), 59.

5 Charles M. Segal, ed., *Conversations with Lincoln* (New Brunswick, NJ: Transaction Publishers, 2013), 122-123.

was General Winfield Scott, senior commander of the United States Army. Newspaper reports on the funeral specifically mentioned the general, now seventy-four years old and in poor health.[6] They told how difficult it seemed for Scott to look upon the coffin of a soldier as full of military promise as he himself had once been, and now taken early in his career. What a loss to the Union cause, Scott must have thought.[7] One soldier at the end of his career, general-in-chief for President Lincoln, trying to build an army out of three-month volunteers; another, dead before the beginning of his, trying to develop and enact a plan to quickly put the various militias of the North into full military service.

At noon, the minister, Reverend Dr. Smith Pyne of Saint John's Episcopal Church, gave the funeral oration.[8] Reverend Pyne only knew Ellsworth by reputation, but spoke about the young officer as though they had been long-time acquaintances. Elegantly, Pyne told about the gallant and brave actions of Col. Ellsworth and the way in which he had been able to instill an almost instant affection for himself in his troops. Using the power of love as the theme for his sermon, Pyne closed by intoning, "The Scripture tells us of a man who approached our Divine Savior, and when He looked upon him, He loved him."[9]

Members of Ellsworth's regiment, the 11th New York Fire Zouaves, walked past his casket in silent tribute, weaponless, heads bowed in grief. Military officers and diplomats joined them. Julia Taft, the sixteen-year-old sister of Holly and Bud Taft, neighbors and playmates of the Lincoln boys, described the scene in her memoirs. She laid a wreath of white roses among the lilies on Col. Ellsworth's rosewood bier. The sight of his pale features, seen only days before at Camp Lincoln, where Ellsworth had been cheerful and full of plans for the future, made young Julia feel faint.[10]

---

6 *White Cloud Kansas Chief,* June 20, 1861.

7 Ibid. The thoughts expressed in the article in the *Chief* are from the pen of Colonel John W. Forney, who owned the *Philadelphia Press,* among other things. His piece on Ellsworth's funeral, which was printed in many papers, pointed out the irony of the old general and the young colonel "meeting" in such a manner. Though a Democrat, Forney was a favorite journalist of the Lincoln administration.

8 "St. John's Episcopal Church," Abraham Lincoln Online, showcase.netins.net/web/creative/lincoln/sites/stjohn.htm, accessed, June 1, 2011.

9 Charles P. Poland, Jr., *The Glories of War: Small Battles and Early Heroes of 1861* (Bloomington, IN: Authorhouse, 2004), 24.

10 Michael Burlingame and John R. Turner Ettlinger, *Inside Lincolns White House: The Complete Civil War Diary of John Hay* (Carbondale, IL: Southern Illinois University Press, 1997), 23; Julia Taft Bayne, *Tad Lincolns Father* (Lincoln, NE: University of Nebraska Press, reprint, 2001), 15.

Mrs. Lincoln herself, weeping, placed a photograph of Ellsworth surrounded by a wax wreath of laurel at the foot of the coffin. She spoke of the dead colonel's great energy on behalf of her husband and the Union.[11] "He looks as natural as though he were sleeping a brief and pleasant sleep," she commented sadly. Doctor Thomas Holmes, the mortician who volunteered to perform the arsenic embalming, then a new science, had done an excellent job; he would have ample opportunity to hone his craft over the next four bloody years.

By the end of the afternoon, a multitude of tears had been shed. Attended by mourners, the coffin was taken, in procession, to Washington's Union Station. Rare was the Washington citizen, regardless of political sympathies, who failed to turn out to witness the public spectacle of Ellsworth's funeral parade. At Union Station, his remains were placed on a special train and transported to New York. Double lines of spectators filled the streets of Capitol Hill, waiting in silence for the funeral cortege. Companies of soldiers marched in slow procession with arms reversed, drums muffled, banners furled. Four white horses pulled the glass carriage containing Ellsworth's coffin. Its pall was the American flag. Six bearers walked beside the hearse, followed by a small, representative band of Fire Zouaves. Ellsworth's entire regiment could not be spared at one time, as Alexandria, just across the Potomac in Virginia, was still under martial law. After the Zouaves came Ellsworth's riderless black warhorse.[12]

The huge Confederate flag from the Marshall House, stained by Ellsworth's blood, followed. It was carried by Private Francis E. Brownell, who would be accompanying the body of his colonel to its final resting place in Mechanicville, New York. During this sad procession, Brownell had angrily stabbed the flag with his bayonet and hoisted it into the air.[13] As a part of the small group of soldiers and

---

Camp Lincoln was just one of the many impromptu "camps" created to contain the thousands of soldiers who had responded to the president's call for volunteers. They ringed the city of Washington and mostly bore patriotic names. Camp Lincoln was situated near the Potomac to the southeast of the city, and the 11th New York, Ellsworth's Fire Zouaves, was ordered to camp there.

11 Margaret Leech, *Reveille in Washington, 1860-1865*. New York: Carroll and Graf Publishers, Inc., 1949, 81-82.

12 Harry E. Pratt, ed., *Concerning Mr. Lincoln: In Which Abraham Lincoln is Pictured as he Appeared to Letter Writers of his Time* (Springfield, IL: The Abraham Lincoln Association, 1944), 81.

13 William Eleazar Barton, *The Life of Clara Barton: Founder of the American Red Cross*, 2 vols. (Boston: Harvard College Library, Theodore Roosevelt Collection, Roosevelt Memorial Association, 1943), 1:116-117.

reporters that had accompanied Ellsworth to Alexandria that fatal morning, Brownell had been the one who fired the shot that killed Marshall House hotel proprietor James Jackson seconds after a blast from Jackson's double-barreled shotgun fatally struck Ellsworth near the heart. Brownell was now "Ellsworth's Avenger."[14] He was followed by coaches carrying Washington government officials and led by President Lincoln and his cabinet. One story says that the flag was returned to the White House. Mary Lincoln, sickened by its sight, folded it up and put it in a bureau drawer. She never wished to see that flag again.[15] This is just one of the Marshall House flag myths that endures, even now. There are several more.

Carrie Spafford, Ellsworth's eighteen-year-old fiancée, did not journey to Washington for the funeral. She remained at her family's house in Rockford, Illinois, having returned from her New York boarding school for the summer. A severe ankle injury and the quick turnaround between Ellsworth's death and his funeral kept her at home. Devastated by the sadness of these events, she wouldn't attend any of the ceremonies, including the interment in Mechanicville. Carrie spent the next few years grieving in isolation, mourning Ellsworth in death longer than the two and a half years she had known and loved him in life.[16]

Ellsworth's parents were to meet their son's remains when the train reached Grand Central Station in New York City. From there it was to be moved to lie in state in City Hall. Later in the day, the Astor House Hotel had scheduled a private viewing for the Ellsworth family and close friends. In continuing tribute, a steamer draped in both black and bunting would then take the casket to Albany, where the body again would lie in state. Lastly, another funeral train would bring Ellsworth to his boyhood home of Mechanicville, for burial on May 27.[17]

President Lincoln's exhaustion was visible. Ellsworth's passing was a bitter, personal blow. Everything had taken its toll—the attack on Fort Sumter, the parade of secessions in the South, the need to build an army for a war he did not want, and

---

14 *Harper's Weekly*, June 8, 1861, 357-358, www.harpweek.com www.harpweek.com, accessed July 6, 2013.

15 *Olathe* Mirror, June 13, 1861.

16 Bayne, *Tad Lincolns Father*, 15-16.

17 Kathi Kresol, "Voices from the Grave: Carrie Spafford, a life of sorrowthe tragedy of one of Rockford's founding families," *The Rock River Times* [Rockford, IL], October 8, 2014; "Her Summons Comes Sunday: Mrs. Carrie Spafford Brett Expires Without Warning in Her Sister's Arms," *Rockford* [IL] *Daily Register-Gazette*, October 9, 1911; Ruth Painter Randall, *Colonel Elmer Ellsworth: A Biography of Lincoln's Friend and the First Hero of the Civil War* (Boston: Little, Brown Publishing, 1960), 270.

now . . . this death. Abraham Lincoln loved the young man in the coffin. Elmer Ellsworth was like another son to him, a glimpse of Lincoln's hopes for his own children, Robert, Willie, and Tad. The young soldier could be counted on to do anything he could for the Lincolns: tease Mary into a smile, play with the younger Lincoln boys, and graciously accept whatever came his way as far as military employment. Ellsworth came into Lincoln's life unexpectedly during a militia practice, brightened it, and had now, just as unexpectedly, left it.

After tossing and turning, around 3:00 a.m., Lincoln rose from his bed. Walking the presidential mansion at night would become a familiar ritual to Lincoln, but he had only lived there two months, and no one habit was yet a routine. Quietly, so he would not wake Mary or Tad and Willie, he walked down the two short flights of stairs from his bedroom to the first floor, then turned right. The worn marble muffled his steps as he entered the East Room. The lack of light dulled the red, orange, and gold carpet, and the long velvet drapes looked black. The chandeliers were lit with the lowest of gaslights, left on, perhaps, so the darkness would not dishonor Ellsworth's memory.[18] Lincoln walked to the hastily-created plank and barrel bier, where the coffin had lain, and bowed his head. "My boy! My boy! Was it necessary this sacrifice should be made?"[19] Then he turned and sought a chair from the several left after the funeral, still scattered in a semicircle around the edges of the room.

The President folded his tall body into the same seat he had used earlier in the day and put his hands on the armrests of the worn and creaky furniture. The low light of the chandeliers threw the top of Lincoln's hands into deep relief. Veins stood out prominently, and the skin stretched, then fell into wrinkles. He looked down at his well-worn hands that had held an ax, a pen, a book. Now they lay on the chair arms, limp and ineffective. Over the next four years death would be a

---

18 Undated, unspecified newspaper clippings describing Ellsworth's various funerals found in Carrie Spafford's personal scrapbook, Civil War Museum, Kenosha, WI (Lake Forest Academy). Hereafter cited as KCWM/LFC.

19 www.mrlincolnswhitehouse.org/washington/mr-lincolns-white-house-maps/, accessed August 18, 2017. This site is dedicated to chronicling the changes that occurred to the Executive Mansion during the Civil War.

constant presence, and the President took every war casualty to heart. At this moment Lincoln closed his eyes, remembering Ellsworth.[20] [21]

20 Owen Edwards, "The Death of Colonel Ellsworth," *Smithsonian Magazine* (April 2011), http://www.smithsonianmag.com/history-archaeology/The-Death-of-Colonel-Ellsworth.ht ml accessed July 5, 2012.

21 This last paragraph, inspired by the statue at the Lincoln Memorial in Washington, is, admittedly, fictional. Lincoln was very affected by Ellsworth's death, and may very well have sat quietly in the East Room, contemplating the future. There are several accounts of his nightly wanderings given by his secretaries, John Hay and John Nicolay, especially during times of personal emotional stress.

CHAPTER 1

Inauspicious Beginnings

"I have been advised to prepare a memorandum of events occurring in the life of my
son Elmer, that would serve to illustrate his peculiar cast of character in order that
they may be available hereafter should his biography be written."

"I know that mothers are partial judges of their children, even whilst they live, and that
death hallows and beautifies to them what to others may seem faulty; yet, I trust in
view of my great bereavement, I shall be forgiven if I have given too much weight
to small things; the more especially as I shall confine myself to facts, and leave
it to the historian to make selection of what he shall think proper."[1]

— Phebe Ellsworth's *Memoranda*

NINE-YEAR-OLD Elmer Ellsworth had a new project
in mind: he would turn two of his
drawings of military heroes into full-fledged oil paintings. After all, he loved
looking at martial artwork, and he spent a great deal of time sketching. His parents
had never discouraged this tendency and were usually on hand to admire his
efforts—which generally consisted of soldiers in fanciful uniforms. The drawings
in question were of General George Washington and his staff, and General
Andrew Jackson and his staff. Elmer's immediate problem was to gather supplies
to complete his project. He had already decided that the fabric of his mother's
window shade would make a perfect canvas for his work. Now all he needed was
paint. He cast about Malta and found he could get industrial paints at a carriage
shop, talked the shop owner out of a small number of various colors, brought them

1 Phebe Ellsworth, "Memoranda—Diary, Letters, and Poem," dictated manuscript, written
by Charity Louisa (Steadwell) Mabbitt, New York State Historical Society photostat copy,
KCWM/LFAC, 1.

home, and went to work. His mother, Phebe, was left with a most unusual window shade.[2]

The America of 1837, the year Elmer Ellsworth was born, bore little resemblance to the America that had won its independence from Great Britain just fifty-four years previously. After the Treaty of Paris, which had ended the Revolution in 1783, the new country scrambled to create workable systems to allow each newly minted state to govern within its borders; but it also had to devise a way to encourage a viable, united effort for the country as a whole to pay for the war it had just won. By the time the Constitution was ratified in 1788, the states were already in profound disagreement as to how this should take place; they made progress, however, over the next four decades. With the construction of the Erie Canal in 1825, New York's Hudson River towns, some of which had previously consisted of only two or three buildings, boomed. The trail of candle glow along the canal route lit up like a string of Christmas lights as small towns became more substantial, and the resultant small cities grew in population and economic importance. Almost every place along the length of the Erie Canal became prosperous, providing the inns, restaurants, shops, and entertainments necessary to support the Canal trade. Malta, where Elmer Ellsworth was born, was one such town.

Located in Saratoga County, New York, Malta is rich in colonial and revolutionary history. At least two of Elmer's relatives participated in the American Revolution. His paternal grandfather, George Ellsworth, fought in the battle of Saratoga at only fifteen years old. He was present at the surrender of Burgoyne after the subsequent battle, at Bemis Heights.[3] Another relative, Peter Ellsworth, is listed as an officer in a New York unit, and he received a pension for his services in the Continental Army.[4]

---

2 Ibid.

3 Ibid., 1; Pension File of Charles Ellsworth, no. W19226, National Archies and Records Administration (hereafter cited as NARA); "Revolutionary War Pension and Bounty-Land Warrant Applications Based on Revolutionary War Service, compiled ca. 1800-1912, documenting the period ca. 1775-1900," M804, 300022, New York State, online version: www.fold3.com/image/17125638?terms=George%20Ellsworth, accessed June, 2011.

4 William Thomas Roberts Saffell, *Peter Ellsworth—Records of the Revolutionary War* (Phoenix, AZ: Heritage Books Reprints, 2007), 418, online version: www.fold3. com/ image/1/171 25534, accessed June 2012.

Elmer's father, Ephraim Daniel Ellsworth, came from a large family. He was born on May 22, in either 1809 or 1810, one of fourteen brothers and sisters.[5] As an adult, Ephraim Ellsworth learned and practiced the tailor's trade at Waterford, New York. He moved his business to Malta in 1836, the same year he met and married Phebe Denton. Elmer's mother descended from the large, relatively well-off English-Scottish Denton family. Many of her half-brothers and sisters resided near Malta. In the 1840 census, Ephraim Ellsworth's occupation is not listed.[6]

A year after his parents married, Elmer Ephraim Ellsworth was born on April 11, 1837—the same year that the nation's most significant financial panic (up to that time) occurred. New York was struck especially hard. Within two months, the state lost nearly $100,000,000 in value.[7] During the first three weeks of April, 250 business houses also failed. No one was left untouched, from the wealthiest bankers to the mechanic, the farmer, or the basest laborer. Financially, eight states partially or entirely failed, and the central government could not pay its debts. Trade ceased almost completely, and there was no confidence in business. The impact of this disaster lingered until 1843.[8]

Young Elmer's father suffered along with other businessmen. Tailoring is the creation of new clothing, not the repair of old. In a stressed economic environment, getting a new suit of hand-tailored clothes might not be as high a priority as it was before the financial downturn. Ephraim Ellsworth lost his business in the ensuing panic and turned to other ways to support his family. He peddled oysters and netted then-abundant (now extinct) passenger pigeons to sell as meat. According to John Hay, the Panic of 1837 "ruined" Ellsworth's father, but there is evidence to the contrary. Ephraim may have lost his tailoring business, but

5 McAbee, Ephraim Daniel Ellsworth Family Tree, March 23, 2009, www.geni.com/people /Ephraim-Ellsworth/6000000003288068328#/tab/media, accessed September 5, 2017.

6 1850 Census for Malta, New York, United States Census; www.censusrecords.com/ record?id=usc%2f1840%2f005154829%2f00449&parentid=usc%2f1840%2f005154829%2f0 0449%2f009, accessed September 3, 2017.

7 The Lehrman Institute, "Andrew Jackson," accessed June 4, 2016. (Specific cite/article?).

8 Ibid.

according to the census of 1850, he made a decent living as a butcher in Mechanicville.[9]

Ephraim, Phebe, and their little son lived in a "low-browed cottage," so-called for the two small, rectangular windows on the upper half-story, which suggested eyes peering out from under the eaves. The baby was named for his father (Ephraim) and a family friend (Elmer) and was christened "Ephraim Elmer," but when he was fifteen or so, young Elmer decided to reverse the names so he would not be confused with his father.[10] They were joined by Elmer's little brother Charley, born in 1840.[11]

A few stories concerning young Elmer Ellsworth survive. The source of these anecdotes is Phebe Ellsworth's forty-three-page manuscript, "Memoranda—Diary, Letters and Poems." Some of it is questionable—what mother would make her son sound anything less than perfect? Her manuscript was composed in response to many requests after her son's death:

> I have been advised to prepare a memorandum of events occurring in the life of my son Elmer, that would serve to illustrate his particular cast of character, in order that they may be available here after should his biography be written.[12]

Phebe, seriously afflicted with a palsy that made writing impossible for her, dictated her stories to a family friend, Charity Louisa Steadwell Mabbitt.[13] One of the more interesting of these is the one wherein Elmer, then about three years old, "purchased" his newborn brother, Charley. Elmer, as an older brother, was fascinated by and very fond of the new baby. Elmer paid his debt in good faith, although Phebe does not tell how he earned the money:

9   1850 United States Census, "The Town of Half-Moon, Saratoga, NY," uscensus.gov, accessed June 8, 2016.

10 Birth certificate for Elmer Ellsworth, online version: search.ancestry.com/search/category.aspx?cat=123, accessed June 9, 2016); Charles Anson Ingraham, *Colonel Elmer E. Ellsworth, First Hero of the Civil War*, reproduced by the War College Series (February 2015), 4; Ellsworth, "Memoranda," 1.

11 Malta, New York, Census of 1850, www.newyorkfamilyhistory.

12 Ellsworth, "Memoranda," 1. KCWM/LFAC

13 Mrs. Ellsworth may have suffered from Parkinson's, for she is described as having shaky hands in her later life. She was physically unable to write out her memoirs herself and asked a friend for help.

Before long Elmer had his 'moments of disillusionment' about babies, finding out that they cried a great deal and had other disconcerting and irresponsible habits which made for a lot of work. Then he would say that 'he had got cheated,' and made 'a poor bargain.'[14]

Mrs. Ellsworth adds that Elmer assumed a sort of supervision over his little brother, which grew into paternalistic care in time. Charley, however, never developed the sense of responsibility that made itself evident in Elmer from an early age. As Charley grew to adulthood, he was in danger of becoming a financial liability to his parents. Several years later, while he was living in Chicago, Elmer sent for his brother in order to relieve the burden of upkeep for his parents and to attempt to instill in Charley some sense of adult responsibility. Elmer tried to find employment for his brother and, of course, promptly enrolled him into the militia group begun by Elmer himself, the Chicago Cadets. Because of Ellsworth's own abilities, Charley was readily accepted by the group.[15]

Phebe Ellsworth's "Memoranda," written on foolscap and tied at the top, in the center, by a faded ribbon, offers several specific examples of times when young Elmer was bullied or teased by others because of his short stature and what he referred to as his "limited means." His mother wrote about one time in particular, "the day he came home fighting mad because another boy had twitted him with the fact that his mother wore *patched shoes*." Another such occasion involved Elmer having been called "oyster keg."[16] Elmer's father told his wife that youngsters are often thoughtless and cruel, and that lean economic times stress children as well as adults. These were painful experiences for the youngster, and no doubt, created ugly memories. Still, none of this sounds much different from the general run of bullying, which seems to increase on the schoolyard whenever the economy is fragile. Phebe Ellsworth matter-of-factly narrated these events, mentioning twice that she felt this was merely typical childhood behavior.[17]

Mentioned within Phebe's "Memoranda" are several instances in which her son used poor judgment, resulting in punishment. Elmer was not a naughty child but, like all little ones, he sometimes needed to be reminded that behavior has

14 Ellsworth, "Memoranda," 3. KCWM/LFAC.

15 Grave of Charley Ellsworth, author's collection; Randall, *Colonel Elmer Ellsworth*, 164.

16 Ellsworth, "Memoranda," 15.

17 Ibid.

consequences. Mrs. Ellsworth used terms like "great energy" and "indomitable pride" to describe her son's early character. Occasionally, those attributes earned him a reprimand:

> I used sometimes for punishment to sit him on the floor requiring him to sit there still and unemployed. He would beg me to whip him and release him, for that he could bear, but to sit in disgrace on the floor in constant expectation that some of the neighbors would come in and see him there, was more than his philosophy could cope with.[18]

Phebe Ellsworth's oldest boy often took things literally. Whatever someone told him was taken at face value, although young Elmer often attempted to test the truthfulness of what he heard. At about four years of age, his mother had told him, "in order to make him more sensible of the nearness and supervision of the Almighty," that God knew and saw everything he thought and everything he did. She explained that when God caught him being naughty, he would put down a black mark next to his name. Phebe warned Elmer that too many black marks would result in punishment. His mother claimed that she erred by making the impression "rather too material and tangible," because Elmer sat down next to six-week-old Charley's crib to put the whole idea to the test.[19]

Elmer looked innocent enough, watching his baby brother and peering out the window, but as soon as his mother turned away, Elmer pinched Charley. His wounded sibling gave a sharp cry, but Elmer reassured his mother that nothing was wrong. A few minutes later, Elmer repeated his pinch. This time Mrs. Ellsworth asked him, "What are you doing to your brother?" Elmer replied that little Charley was saying his prayers. Elmer then pinched the unsuspecting baby again, but this time he decided his experiment was over:

> There, Mother. The Lord has told a lie himself—for I have been naughty—I've pinched my little brother, and I've told a lie, 'cause I told you I hadn't done anything to him—and the Lord hasn't seen me nor done anything to me for it, so he's lied himself for you say he says he will punish naughty boys.[20]

---

18 Ellsworth, "Memoranda," 7.

19 Ibid.

20 Ibid. 9.

This story made the rounds in Elmer's hometown. Soon afterward, a neighbor decided he would have some sport with the budding agnostic. Young Elmer went alone to pick up the mail, and, in the front room of the post office, the neighbor—Stephen—lifted a book from the counter. Stephen told Elmer that the book was the Bible, and "the Lord said that Elmer Ellsworth must die and go to hell!"[21] Elmer, truthful himself, did not suspect that he might be being "made sport of." He asked the man if he knew his letters and if he could spell. The rascally neighbor answered "yes" to both questions.

Elmer thought for a moment and then asked the postmaster, "Would you call Stephen a good reader?" after which the postmaster vouched for Stephen's literacy. Elmer grabbed the mail and ran for the door. He came "flying in" to the Ellsworth house and looked directly at his mother. "Ma, get the Bible and read it through quick for I want to know what the Lord says about me."[22]

She explained that God did not put down individual names but only said good and bad boys. Elmer was not satisfied. He asked his mother for some paper and told her he would write a letter "to the Lord himself."[23]

Mrs. Ellsworth continued:

> To keep him from teasing, I gave him some paper, and he climbed up to the desk and soon marked it full on both sides, and started once more for the office, where he presented his *letter* with the request that they should send it to the Lord;—they told him there was no mail ran there and they couldn't send it. The bystanders seeing his perplexity, began to tease him, and asked him what he was going to do in such a case. He seemed purrled [sic] for a moment, and then replied, 'I'll go and ask a lawyer—he will tell me.' [24]

Young Elmer attended Malta's public schools and mastered his lessons quickly. Another story from Phebe Ellsworth concerns his love of reading. One day the adult Ellsworths had to attend a funeral.[25] They planned to be gone from about eight in the morning until four in the afternoon. Elmer was left at home with specific instructions to feed the pigs at noon, and was very excited at the idea of

21 Ibid.

22 Ibid.

23 Ibid, 9-10.

24 Ibid.

25 Ibid," 16-18.

both the freedom and the responsibility. He pulled down the window shades, found a comfortable seat, and began to read a book he had brought from school. His parents returned at four to a house that looked deserted. When his mother opened the door, Elmer looked up, gasped, and asked, "Why Ma, what are you back for?" She told him it was already four, just when they said they would return. At this point, Elmer jumped up, laying his book aside, and exclaimed, "I didn't even think it was noon! Let me run and feed the pigs." It must have been a good book, for Elmer had read for eight hours straight.[26]

Elmer was interested in much more than school, drawing, and reading. He was cheerful by nature and enjoyed the variety and wealth of his surroundings. Elmer loved to be active and outdoors as much as he loved to read. He was athletic, and enjoyed sports and team competitions. This was something Elmer carried with him into adulthood. He also liked water. There were many lakes near Malta, including Lake Saratoga and Round Lake; it was here that Elmer learned to row and to become fascinated by the mysterious ebb and flow of waterways. When he was twenty-one, he wrote a description of the ideal home he wanted to provide for both his parents and for himself. It would be a large house near a town or city, "situated on the banks of a fine river or lake."[27] He felt that life somehow would be incomplete without the charm of a nearby waterway. Elmer liked to draw and paint pictures with water in them. One of his works of art is painted in pigments of the type found in a carriage shop. It shows a wide river with a sailboat in the foreground; hills rise on the far side of the river. On the hills are castles with turrets and flying flags, looking as if they have come right out of Malory's *Le Morte d'Arthur*. The Hudson probably served as the model for this river.[28]

As a family, the Ellsworths had habits—they were quiet, sober, and religious—that made them valued members of the community. As such, their sons were playmates of the children of Robert Sears, a well-to-do merchant living close by in Mechanicville. Elmer, Chester Denton (Phebe's half-brother), and Charley played with the Sears children, Charles and his sister, Mattie. With Mattie's help, Ellsworth learned to ride Mink, the family's working horse.[29]

---

26 Ibid. 17.

27 Elmer Ellsworth to parents, November 15, 1858, KCWM/LFAC.

28 Elmer Ellsworth to "Friend Parks" (Henry Parks), December 12, 1858, KCWM/LFAC.

29 Randall, *Colonel Elmer Ellsworth*, 27.

"In his tenth year," according to Mrs. Ellsworth's dictation, Elmer went to work and "live with a man who kept a saloon and grocery together," which presented a difficult choice for the youngster. According to his mother, Elmer was very distressed about such matters as the consumption of alcohol. As a small boy, he had been taken to a temperance lecture and listened attentively. Within a day or so, he asked to borrow a "gun and 'cussion cap." When asked why he needed such items, he informed his parents that he was going to "shoot the Devil." More questions followed, including just where he thought he would find the Devil, to which young Elmer replied that the temperance man had said the Devil was in a cider barrel, and he knew just where he could find one.[30]

When he was nine, Elmer had managed to join a local temperance society, at which point he informed his mother that he would never drink. This earlier pledge made it difficult for Elmer to work in a general store that sold liquor and sundries.[31] However, he wanted that job! Should he accept the living arrangements and the responsibilities that went with them? Elmer and his employer, Mr. DeGoff, finally arrived at an agreement that satisfied everyone's concerns: Elmer would not serve alcohol, wait on alcohol customers, wash their glasses, or in any way have anything to do with liquor. Working for DeGoff was Elmer's first job as a clerk and storekeeper. Moreover, he kept his temperance pledge until the end of his life.[32]

About a year later, Elmer had to quit his job at the general store when his family moved to Mechanicville, not far away. When Ellsworth was older and had a personal financial setback that shook his faith in people, he confided to a diary his longing for the times of his boyhood, when the world was still a perfect place and his thoughts free from disillusionment:

> With mind free from care, I wandered away into the green old hills, or in my boat drifted slowly down the Hudson and dreaming of the future built castles in the air and longed for the time to come when I could commence the battle with the world. And I . . .with the generosity of boyhood peopled the world with the brave, the good—the noble hearted.[33]

30 Ellsworth, "Memoranda," 10.

31 Ibid, 11.

32 Ibid, 11-12.

33 Ellsworth to "Friend Parks," December 12, 1858.

There can be little doubt that Ellsworth's proximity to Saratoga, his having direct relatives who had fought with Washington, and the fact that many men and women of the Revolutionary period were still living in the area, created a powerful, compelling influence over him as a youngster. The intense feelings of those who actively participated in the struggle for liberty from England, and the energy that possessed them to engage in the "great experiment" of democracy, provided a template for Ellsworth's sense of patriotism, military duty, and his love of country. Early in his life, he gave evidence of a propensity for things military. His mother pointed out that he did not play "soldier, but "officer." He was usually in command, but his playmates showed no objection to his skillful leadership. Phebe's manuscript quotes Elmer's maternal grandfather, himself a veteran, as saying, "'That child will be a great military character if he lives,'—adding impressively 'remember what I tell you.' . . . I thought it the childish fondness of the grandfather, but since then it has assumed the shape of prophecy."[34]

Various sources have influenced history's perception of the Ellsworth family's precarious financial position, including Ruth Painter Randall's biography of Ellsworth, *Colonel Elmer Ellsworth*, and Charles Ingraham's *Elmer E. Ellsworth*. Unfortunately, these works rely only on the collection of Elmer Ellsworth's letters to his parents and how he talked about his parent's finances to friends like John Hay. Both of Ellsworth's parents objected to this portrayal during their son's lifetime: Phebe's "Memoranda" mentions that Elmer's constant concern about his parents' "poverty" so annoyed his father that Ephraim claimed such concern was "proof of insanity."[35] Nevertheless, Elmer always maintained a genuine affection for his family. From an early age, he informed his mother that "when I'm a man I'll work and earn money, and you shall ride in a carriage."[36]

*   *   *

Living in Malta put young Elmer in direct contact with the road that ran through the little town on the way to Saratoga Springs and Ballston Spa, two of the most fashionable resorts in New York. During "the season," coaches driven by

---

34 Ellsworth, "Memoranda," 1-2.

35 Ibid, 18.

36 Ibid, 18-23.

liveried drivers would pass along the road, carrying expensively dressed ladies and top-hatted gentlemen representing another world entirely to a small boy who saw himself as very poor. As Elmer got a little older and left home, these fanciful images continued to haunt his thoughts, and became responsible for his ideas concerning the trappings that indicated wealth. His working-class parents may have seemed, by comparison, poverty-stricken.

Elmer repeatedly mentioned his promise to his parents that he would, somehow and somewhere, amass enough money to alleviate the perceived "hardships of his early life."[37] Several points of information argue, however, that, although certainly not wealthy, the Ellsworth family was at least working class. The psychological underpinnings of Ellsworth's fixation on his parents' financial state—always undervaluing their monetary worth and exaggerating their efforts to subsist—is not clearly defined. One could speculate that he needed to create his own mythological beginnings. Elmer Ellsworth was a complicated man, and speculation is usually a waste of time in these cases. The facts concerning the Ellsworth finances are, on the other hand, undeniable. Both the house in Malta and the later one in Mechanicville were purchased outright by Ephraim Ellsworth. The Mechanicville home was a working farm, complete with the usual assortment of domestic animals such as cows, dogs, pigs, poultry, and Mink, the farm horse.[38]

By 1838, the Ellsworths had taken in a boarder of sorts. Phebe Ellsworth's younger half-brother, Chester Denton, came to live with the family. As Mrs. Ellsworth explains, the offer to care for her brother was made to help out a family member, not to improve finances.[39] Phebe and Ephraim worked hard to help the family make ends meet, but the ends always met. The national economy was challenging for everyone, but there was still a safe, loving home and plenty of food on the Ellsworth table—hardly the poverty that dutiful son Elmer talked of and wrote about to his friends.

37 John Hay, diary, undated, John Hay Collection, Brown University, Providence, RI. Hereafter cited as BU/JHC.

38 Malta, New York, Census of 1850; Ellsworth, "Memoranda," 2.

39 Ibid.

Elmer's parents, Ephraim (above) and Phebe (below). *Chicago History.org*

Later, as commander of the 11th New York Fire Zouaves, Colonel Ellsworth proudly rode a large, handsome black horse called "Joseph."[40] This horse was such a source of pride to Ellsworth that, upon his death, Elmer's father went to a great deal of trouble and expense to bring the animal back to Mechanicville. In a letter to "Friend Jackson," dated January 26, 1862, Mr. Ellsworth wrote:

I have been to Washington and got our son's horse at last. The first time I went there after him I could not find him. They said they had sold him for his bill but could not tell where he was nor who had him. But I put a man on watch and he said he was down in Sickles' Brigade and then I started again and maid [sic] out to find him but I had to give one hundred and fifty dollars for him before they would give him up. I paid them for him and got him home safe.[41]

40 "Introducing Our Own Authors: Dr. Charles Ingraham Tells Us More of Colonel Ellsworth Whose Life We Have Just Published," *Press Impressions for December* (Chicago: The University of Chicago Press, 1925), 3; Ingraham, "Ellsworth," 28.

41 Ephraim Ellsworth to "Friend Jackson," January 26, 1862, The Rosenbach of the Free Library of Philadelphia, "Portraits of Civil War Heroes," www.rosenbach.org, accessed July 27, 2011.

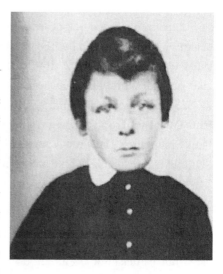

A young Elmer Ellsworth
Chicago History.org

Today, that amount of money would be worth over $2,000.00, further evidence that the Ellsworth family was not in the dire financial circumstances described continuously by their son.[42]

Although John Hay did not know Ellsworth's family, he wrote after Ellsworth's death, "His parents were plain people without culture or means. One cannot guess how this eaglet came into so lowly a nest."[43] In retrospect, the nest was not so lowly. The Ellsworths recovered from the Panic of 1837, owned their houses, and were able to keep their sons healthy and in school. It took his father working outside the home and his mother taking in boarders, but the Ellsworths were not poverty-stricken. After all, Abraham Lincoln himself came from a humble log cabin that would have made the Ellsworth homes look almost palatial.

Fortunately, a trio of ambrotypes from J. W. Blanchard's Photographic Gallery in Troy, New York, is in the photographic archives of the Chicago History Museum. Two of them are of Mr. Ephraim D. Ellsworth and Mrs. Phebe Ellsworth.[44] The third is an image taken of Elmer Ellsworth when he appears to have been about five or six years old. It shows a handsome little boy with large eyes and a sensitive mouth. His full head of dark hair appears combed into place, but a couple of stray curls may be seen above the boy's forehead. Elmer is dressed neatly in a dark suit with the white collar of his shirt showing at the neckline. The buttons

42 "Introducing Our Own Authors: Dr. Charles Ingraham Tells Us More of Colonel Ellsworth Whose Life We Have Just Published," Press Impressions for December, (Chicago: The University of Chicago Press, 1925), 3 and Ingraham, "Elsworth (sic)," 28.

43 John Hay, "A Young Hero: Personal Reminiscences of Colonel E. E. Ellsworth," *McClure's Magazine* (1896), volume 6, books.google.com/books, accessed August 10, 2013.

44 www.chsmedia.org:8081/ipac20/ipac.jsp?session=1504LW5Q31048.61805&source=~!h orizon&profile=public&page=5&group=0&term=Ellsworth&index=.GW&uindex=&aspec t=subtab112&menu=search&ri=1&ts=1504565279471&deduping=, accessed Sept.1, 2017.

on the front of the coat appear to be brass, and the boy within the jacket looks healthy and confident. In the 1840s, when these images were taken, an ambrotype's average cost was about twenty-five to sixty-five cents per picture.[45] In today's currency, this would be between $20.00 and $50.00, a significant amount for a working-class family to spend.[46] Ephraim and Phebe felt it was important to travel from Malta to Troy to have their images captured, perhaps to share with other family members. The simple, honest faces in the ambrotypes make it easy to see that these were likable people and a family of which to be proud.

Looking at the evidence available, Elmer's parents worked hard, provided well, and gave their sons as much love and gentleness as was possible in the 1840s. They offered examples of sustaining religious faith, integrity, and patriotism. Elmer absorbed these values and made them his own. Financially, the family was working class, but Elmer grew up in emotional and intellectual abundance. The grinding fear that real poverty brings with it as surely as we all have shadows was, thankfully, not often a visitor to the "low-browed" cottage.[47]

In such an atmosphere, it is not difficult to feel that an earnest little fellow with curly brown hair and hazel eyes could continue to kick at the dust along the tow road next to the Champlain Canal. Young Elmer Ellsworth was assured of safety and love, and free to dream his childish daydreams of martial glory.

---

45 www.loc.gov/pictures/collection/lilj/ambrotypes.html, accessed August 25, 2017.

46 www.measuringworth.com/uscompare/, accessed August 28, 2017.

47 Ellsworth, "Memoranda"; John Hay's various letters and diary entries; Census information from New York; George Nicolay's letters and diary entries, *et al.*

CHAPTER 2

Portrait of the Colonel as a Young Man

"'No', said Heron, 'Dedalus is a model youth. He doesn't smoke and he doesn't go to bazaars and he doesn't flirt and he doesn't damn anything or damn all.'"

Portrait of the Artist as a Young Man by James Joyce

As an adult, Elmer Ellsworth would write that his early life seemed to him to be nothing more than "a curious jumble of strange incidents."[1] Why the events of his childhood should seem disconnected is not known; maybe it is that way for all children. Even as a youngster, however, Elmer seemed able to divide his world into three convenient packages: the reality of his working-class parentage, the serene beauty of his physical surroundings, and the interior fantasy world of soldiers and uniforms, castles and flags. Elmer Ellsworth compressed much experience into his short life and an understanding of his early adolescent years is important for building a complete image of him as an adult. An exact chronology of this part of his life is difficult to reconstruct due to the inevitable incompleteness of the historical record, but the American male society of the 1850s, into which young Ellsworth had to find his place, was becoming increasingly well defined.

From the end of the 1780s onward, America had been incubating an idea: that of the "Self-Made Man." The phrase allegedly originated from the reference to "a nation of self-made men" in Henry Clay's Senate oration in February 1832, but it was an idea that had been part of the American male mind ever since colonial society did away with standard European stereotypes of "effeminate

---

1 Peter Cozzens and Robert I. Gerardi, eds., *The New Annals of the Civil War* (Chicago: Stackpole Books, 2004), 3.

foppishness."[2] By definition, a self-made man left the comfort and safety of his birthplace—often a family farm or a small town—to pursue economic and social opportunities through individual advancement, usually in larger towns and cities. Marriage, the classic coming-of-age experience, was frequently delayed. Often a man "on his own" did not wed until his mid-to-late thirties, when he could reliably provide a secure future for a wife and family of his own. Many young men in the Northeast sacrificed the protection and stability of family for a more personal definition of identity. This large influx of young, single men put stress on cities such as San Francisco, New York, and Chicago, but each place developed a variety of ways for single men to deal with the necessities of life, such as food, shelter, and employment.[3]

Where did Ellsworth's journey to manhood start? He left his early childhood behind in Malta, and it is known that his family moved to Mechanicville in 1847 or 1848. This was a distance of less than 9 miles, but Mechanicville, unlike "sleepy little Malta," was considered an up-and-coming place—one of the now-steady lights in the string of cities that followed the path of the Erie Canal. The city's railroad was an additional draw, connecting Mechanicville to Troy, New York. Nevertheless, it was still a town of only about 800 inhabitants.[4] Elmer was ten or eleven by this time. After settling into their new home, his parents enrolled him in a Mechanicville public school. Phebe Ellsworth reported that he did well, just as he had done in Malta.[5] The Ellsworths, like most working-class parents of any century, knew that education was one of the keys to success for their children. They tried to keep young Elmer in school, but early on he felt that he should be employed in some manner to help support his hardworking parents. Elmer could not rid himself of the phantom specter of poverty, although his family had moved to a larger home

2 Henry Clay, "The American System," speech made on Senate floor, February 2-3 and 6, 1832, from Wendy Wolf, *The Senate, 1789-1989: Classic Speeches, 1830-1993*, ed. Wendy Wolf, (Washington, DC: United States Government Printing Office, vol. 3, Bicentennial Edition), online version: www.senate.gov/artandhistory/history/resources/pdf/American System. pdf, accessed August 23, 2017.

3 Winkle, (accessed August 2011).

4 John Homer French, *Gazetteer of the State of New York: Embracing a comprehensive View of the Geography, Geology, and the General History of the State, and a Complete History and Description of Every County, City, Town, Village and Locality. With Full Table of Statistics.* (London: Forgotten Books, 2016,) 593, online version: books.google.com/books?id=R_zHwh4xByQC&printsec=frontcover&dq=gazetteer+new+york#v=onepage&q=saratoga%20county&f=false, accessed August 23, 2017.

5 Ellsworth, "Memoranda," 14.

and his father's butcher business was becoming well established. By the age of twelve, Elmer once again secured a job, this one on weekends. The railroad that ran between Mechanicville and Troy offered an opportunity to young men who wished to sell newspapers to train patrons. The newsboys had to pay for their papers in advance, and then attempt to recoup their investment and make a profit by hawking their wares up and down the passenger cars during the train's journey. Elmer was very successful at this enterprise, and he worked in this manner, weekends and summers, for at least two years.[6]

One interesting anecdote about young Ellsworth centers on this period of his life. There seems to be some truth to this story, based on actions Ellsworth took in order to contact the man in question a few years later. Elmer enjoyed his time selling papers; it kept him physically busy, and he was able to meet people outside his family circle. Elmer Ellsworth was a charming man, but he must have been an equally charming boy. Both a paying customer and Ellsworth identically remembered a chance meeting. The customer was John Moore Corliss, Jr., owner of Corliss & House: Ready Made Linnen (sic) Manufacturing. Corliss was in his mid-thirties at this time and was attracted by Elmer's "frank, bright, and manly appearance."[7] The gentleman engaged Ellsworth in a long conversation. Because Corliss owned a mercantile/dry goods store in Troy, perhaps he saw in the youngster, so intent on selling newspapers, the makings of an exceptional clerk. They discussed Elmer's future goals, and the gentleman brought up the possibility of Elmer relocating for employment as a clerk in Corliss & House. They made no immediate plans, however, and did not exchange personal information. Still, Elmer Ellsworth did not forget the meeting. Opportunities were scarce, and this one seemed promising in the future, if not immediately.[8]

The other important event in young Elmer's life at this time concerns the creation of his first military drill team, the elegantly titled "Black Plumed Riflemen of Stillwater," named for a book written by Newton Curtis in 1846.[9] Ellsworth was fourteen or fifteen years old at this time. No one remembered if the "Black Plumed Riflemen" had real rifles, or even real black plumes. What is known is that the small town of Stillwater was just outside Mechanicville, and Elmer Ellsworth organized a

6 Ingraham, "Elsworth," unpaginated notes, timeline, KCWM/LFAC.

7 Ibid.; www.familyrecord.net/getperson.php?personID=I3301&tree=Corliss Ord way, accessed July 13, 2018.

8 Ibid.

9 Adam Goodheart, *1861: The Civil War Awakening* (New York: Alfred A. Knopf, 2011), 190.

group of his friends into a pseudo-military company, serving as its drillmaster. Ellsworth, young as he was, had memorized the most popular version of the manual of arms—General Winfield Scott's *Infantry Tactics, or Rules for the Exercise and Maneuvre of the United States Infantry*, published in 1835. He later memorized the manual of arms written by William J. Hardee.[10] Although short and slight of build, Elmer was able to execute both types of drill with apparent ease and rapidity using the old family musket.[11] Some history concerning the manual of arms is necessary, not only to understand drill as the heartbeat of the military, but to see how Ellsworth's own manual of arms for his Zouave units, *Complete Instructions for the Recruit in the Light Infantry Drill*, compiled just a few years later, differed in comparison.

By 1855, the United States Army had adopted a new, percussion-fired rifled musket, with a 33-inch or 40-inch barrel, depending on the gun's use. The manual of arms then popular had been written by Gen. Scott in the 1830s. It was based on French army tactics, which emphasized masses of men concentrated together on the march and on the battlefield. These formations were necessary when older-style muskets were in use, as they were relatively inaccurate. By the 1850s, however, this type of movement had become slow and outdated. Revisions in the manual of arms were necessary to bring infantry tactics into line with modern, long-range rifles. Lieutenant Colonel William Joseph Hardee was chosen to write the new manual. Hardee drew extensively on his knowledge of the French military, as well as his own experiences in the Mexican War and on the Texas frontier. Hardee attempted to modernize the American infantry into a faster, lighter force capable of taking advantage of the more accurate rifle. Versions of Hardee's drill were in use several years before the U. S. Army formally adopted Hardee's *Rifle and Light Infantry Tactics* in 1855.[12] Just how any version of a military drill maneuver looked when executed by a group of young teenagers in 1851 is open to the imagination. Nevertheless, the boys were enthusiastic about performing physical stunts to show off their talents; this was another trait Ellsworth would later include with his Zouave drills.

---

10 Louis E. Laflin, unbound, unpaginated, hand-written notes concerning Ellsworth's early militia involvement, KCWM/LFAC

11 Ellsworth, "Memoranda," 12.

12 William J. Hardee, *Rifle and Light Infantry Tactics; For the Exercise and Manœuvres of Troops When Acting as Light Infantry or Riflemen* (Philadelphia: Lippincott, Grambo & Co., 1855), online version: babel.hathitrust.org/cgi/pt?id=hvd.hn6fre;view=1up;seq=1, accessed August, 2011.

In her biography of Ellsworth, Ruth Painter Randall tells a particularly colorful anecdote, claiming an "old-timer of Mechanicville" related it.[13] Mr. F. D. Hatfield, the teller of the story, owned a general store in Mechanicville and may have embellished this tale of Ellsworth and his "plumed riflemen." After all, he told it many years after the incident occurred. Ellsworth, however, did work for him as a store clerk in the early 1850s, and as an employee, Ellsworth knew the physical layout of Hatfield's store very well.[14] The business itself was on the street level, but there was also a large door on the second floor that opened to the outside. Through this door, boxes of goods were taken up the side of the building by tackle, to be disassembled and then sold downstairs. Although Mr. Hatfield was not personally informed ahead of time, the Black Plumed Riflemen of Stillwater had chosen to make an appearance in Mechanicville that day, and the group needed to find a place for breaks and food. No doubt Elmer thought the uninhabited second floor above the store would make a good place for this, but he had not asked permission of the owner before he made this decision. Once the boys were in town, Ellsworth realized that walking into the store through the street entrance and then up the stairs might cause a bit of concern to Mr. Hatfield. Someone, perhaps the fearless leader of the Riflemen himself, thought this concern could be avoided if the "men" formed a human ladder and climbed over each other to the door on the second floor.[15]

Mr. Hatfield did not remain ignorant for long. He heard a loud and curious thumping on the outside wall of his store, followed by a rush of footsteps, encouraging laughter, and jubilant shouts directly above him. He ran into the street to investigate, arriving just in time, according to the version he told of the story after Ellsworth's death, to see the last of the Riflemen being pulled through the upstairs door. Historian Randall wrapped up the tale this way: "His dumbfounded

13 Randall, *Colonel Elmer Ellsworth*, 31.

14 Paul Loatman, "Elmer E. Ellsworth—Citizen Soldier," from an address given May 21, 2000, www.mechanicville.com/history/ellsworth/citizensoldier.htm, accessed August 4, 2011.

15 Ellsworth, "Memoranda," 13. A film of such a maneuver by a group called Devlin's Zouaves, who performed in Buffalo Bill's Wild West Show in the early 1900s, can be viewed at www.youtube.com/watch?v=IA7Dlyf2JK0, and a review of the show can be found in the California Digital Newspaper Collection, *Los Angeles Herald* (September 28, 1908), "Zouaves to be Seen in Coming Wild West Show," http://cdnc.ucr.edu /cgi-bin/cdnc?a=d&d= LAH19080928.2.90&dliv=none&st=1&e=en—20—1—txt-txIN—1.

expression doubtless added the final glee to what the Riflemen felt had been a most successful day."[16]

With young Ellsworth's propensity for all things military, it would seem that West Point might be in his future. In fact, there is a historiographical mystery concerning Elmer Ellsworth's desire to attend the United States Military Academy, and his inability to do so. Nothing has been found concerning Ellsworth's feelings on the matter at the time, but his attendance, or lack thereof, is still a topic of historical conjecture.[17] Various sources claim that the Ellsworth family was too poor to pay his tuition, room, and board, although West Point provides an education at no cost to the student other than an enlistment in the army after graduation.[18] Others claim that Mechanicville had no existing school that would give Ellsworth the preparatory education he would need to enter an institution that was, even then, primarily an engineering school. Mechanicville's schools, however, were good enough to advance Elmer's future in business. Considering young Ellsworth's energy and his overwhelming desire to be on his own and no longer a financial burden to his parents, there is a good case to be made for his choice not to attend West Point (or any other college) rather than not being wealthy or well-educated enough to do so.

In the 1850s, a congressional appointment was the only way to attend the Military Academy.[19] It was necessary, therefore, for a potential cadet to have some sort of relationship with a person who was politically connected. One might assume that the Ellsworths had no such connections, but they were good friends with the Sears family. Robert Sears was a prominent banker and farmer in Mechanicville, and his young sons and daughter played with the Ellsworth boys. Evidence of the enduring friendship of both families can be found in the fact that it was Robert Sears who volunteered to accompany and emotionally support the

---

16 Randall, *Colonel Elmer Ellsworth*, 32.

17 When Ellsworth was casting around for militia jobs, he often wrote his own third-person press reviews. In one he claimed that he had, in fact, attended West Point. This was an outright lie on Ellsworth's part and is one of the few times he can be considered guilty of such egregiousness.

18 The pattern concerning the presentation of both an ignorance of West Point as well as an ignorance of Ellsworth occurs in short articles mentioning Ellsworth in passing, as opposed to primary sources or Randall's and Ingraham's biographies.

19 Entrance to West Point today can occur in a variety of ways, but still must include nomination by the candidate's representative in Congress, by either of the senators from the candidate's home state, or by the vice-president of the United States.

grief-stricken parents on their sad journey to New York City to claim their martyred son's remains and escort them back to Mechanicville for final burial.[20] Although the small township of Mechanicville had little to recommend it to the greater part of New York, perhaps, if asked, Mr. Sears might have pulled a string or two to help recommend Elmer to West Point. Neither Elmer's correspondence nor his diary indicates that anything like this occurred. In fact, by the time he was fifteen, the earliest age to be considered for possible admission to the Military Academy, Elmer Ellsworth had already left home. In his opinion, Mechanicville had exhausted its possibilities for providing a viable future.[21] By 1852, Ellsworth had moved to Troy, New York.[22]

Ironically, within a few years Ellsworth himself would touch on the subject of his attendance at West Point. As his own publicist, Elmer was often the author of newspaper articles about militia groups with which he was involved. He usually spoke of himself in the third person, and was never reticent in his praise of himself and his doings. One manuscript example in particular claimed, "He developed a remarkable taste for military studies at a very early age and prepared to enter the U. S. Military Academy, but after obtaining an appointment was forced to abandon it."[23] No evidence has been found to substantiate Ellsworth's claim.

*   *   *

The contacts Elmer Ellsworth made on the train between Mechanicville and Troy provided him with the opportunity to secure employment as a clerk in John Moore Corliss's Troy-based firm, Corliss & House, which dealt in cloth and other linen goods. Few documents remain concerning Ellsworth's time in Troy, but he was listed in the 1852 Troy city directory.[24] Based on his later habits of economy, he must have lived simply, as he was able to save enough money to leave Troy by the summer of 1853. In one of Ellsworth's rare letters describing this time of his life, it is clear that he was no longer satisfied to merely "plod along," but was now thinking

20 Ingraham, "Elsworth," KCWM/LFAC.

21 Elmer Ellsworth to Charley Ellsworth, December 1858, KCWM/LFAC.

22 Ingraham, "Elsworth," unpaginated notes, timeline, KCWM/LFAC.

23 Elmer Ellsworth, from an autobiographical manuscript entitled "Tribune No. 3," BU/JHC. Several extant manuscripts, written in Ellsworth's hand and bearing his signature, are in the third person, and appear to be intended for newspaper publication.

24 Ingraham, "Elsworth," KCWM/LFAC.

about making "a bold push for fortune" in the West.[25] Perhaps there he would be able to find more gainful employment so that he might lessen his parents' "toil and privation."[26]

In the early 1900s, when Ellsworth biographer Charles Ingraham began the research for his book *Elmer Ellsworth and the Zouaves of '61*, he exchanged letters with an elderly gentleman named Charles H. Goffe. Goffe, a former resident of Kenosha, Wisconsin, responded to Ingraham's requests for memories and personal anecdotes regarding Elmer Ellsworth during the 1850s. On August 2, 1917, Goffe's letter to Ingraham appeared in Kenosha's *Telegraph-Courier*. Goffe wrote that he had met the sixteen-year-old Ellsworth in Kenosha, in the summer of either 1852 or 1853:

> There was also boarding at Mrs. Bell's at this time, a young man of handsome features and fastidious ways, accentuated by a repelling hauteur and exclusiveness, so often found peculiar to genius. His associates were few, and his disposition was not calculated to make intimates of those he came in contact with. No one seemed able to penetrate the mystery of his personality and yet there was something about the youth that arrested the attention of all. But he was obsessed with a penchant or habit, born perhaps of idle vanity, of writing (or scribbling) his name in a bold, flowing, and not ungraceful hand, upon every scrap of paper, on the weatherboards of the house, and on gate and fence posts, a name which a few years later was on every tongue, flashed in the headlines of the daily press, and stamped in deathless lines upon the history of his country—the name of Elmer E. Ellsworth . . .[27]

If this anecdote is to be believed, Goffe and Ellsworth were not good friends. According to Goffe's memory, a rivalry began concerning all this "writing business." There was an ongoing contest between the two young men to see who had better penmanship. Goffe, in his eighties when interviewed by Ingraham, still prided himself on his cursive skills, claiming that he had "followed penmanship

---

25 Elmer Ellsworth to Edwin Williams, April 18, 1855, KCWM/LFAC.

26 Ibid.

27 Charles H. Goffe to Charles Ingraham, *Kenosha* [WI] *Telegraph-Courier*, August 2, 1917; Randall, *Colonel Elmer Ellsworth*, 33; Charles A. Ingraham, *Colonel Elmer E. Ellsworth: First Hero of the Civil War* (Charleston, SC: Nabu Press Reprint, 2014), 9. Both Charles Ingraham and Louis Laflin have read the original newspaper article, written by Charles Goffe many years after Ellsworth's death. Both have concluded that the article was probably not to be believed. In Ingraham's notes, he considers that Ellsworth may have gone to a year (or less) of high school in Milwaukee, but as of this writing, there has been no evidence of an Elmer Ellsworth being enrolled at any school in or near Kenosha.

teaching while yet in my teens." Ellsworth, too, had developed a beautiful writing hand. Written communication was very important to Ellsworth, as evidenced by the advice he gave to his younger brother in a letter:

> . . . devote yourself to the study of arithmetic and grammer [sic], and pay particular attention to your spelling and writing; for Heaven's sake brother, understand the importance of these things and work, as you can work, when you have a mind to. . . . Write as handsome a letter as possible without aid from any one, be careful of your spelling.[28]

Ellsworth later earned his living copying legal papers, but at this time he was in the process of perfecting his "art." Both young men bragged about their penmanship, and Ellsworth challenged Goffe to a contest. Each had to write the name "Elmer E. Ellsworth" without taking the pencil off the paper. Sixty years later Goffe was still relishing the fact that Ellsworth "was forced to admit I could lay over him."[29]

Ingraham also included another of Goffe's memories in his biography of Ellsworth. Goffe claimed that, at this same time, Ellsworth had travelled up to Muskegon, Michigan. While there, he was "adopted" by the Ottawa Indians and "made a chief among them," given high honors, and adorned with native dress. Goffe's story continued:

> But, alas, when the novelty of barbaric glory and display had become stale, and the craving for other conquests and other scenes, and perhaps dreams of awaiting glories had disturbed his vision, this eccentric child of genius suddenly disappeared from his tribe and had gone no one could tell where. His people waited long, but he returned no more, and the red-skinned maidens of the tamarack swamps waited and sighed in vain for the handsome young chief on whom they doted, and for whom they had hoped and dreamed. And the seasons came and passed, and the moons had filled their horns many times only to wane, and the white chief came no more.[30]

Little of this "Indian" nonsense got past even such a Victorian romantic as Charles Ingraham. He followed the quote with a polite disclaimer: "[I]t is probable that

---

28 Elmer Ellsworth to Charley Ellsworth, November 15, 1858; Ellsworth, "Memoranda," 6.

29 Goffe to Ingraham, *Kenosha Telegraph-Courier*. With respect to Ellsworth's propensity for writing his name, during the research for this book, the author discovered several examples of this tendency. One in particular, from the Ellsworth Collection at Brown University, is a very fancy rendition of his name. "ELLSWORTH" is spelled with drawings of men posed individually or in groups, forming the letters of his name.

30 Ibid.

Ellsworth visited Kenosha, and it is likely, too, that on his way home he stopped at Muskegon to view the Ottawa Indians living there, but that he remained a year or more . . . is highly improbable."[31] All that can be currently established concerning Elmer Ellsworth argues against the truthfulness of this anecdote. Ellsworth had little interest in "barbaric glory," and he certainly did not treat women in the manner indicated by Goffe. Elmer was concerned with personal honor, and was prudish in his relationships with women. At the time Ingraham established contact with Goffe, Ellsworth's fame was undergoing something of a renaissance, especially in Wisconsin. Goffe may have "improved upon" his memories to create the sense of having shared a deeper relationship with Ellsworth than may have actually existed. This sort of behavior is not uncommon when the people concerned are of unequal importance. Historically, it is fairly easy to establish an authentic timeline for Ellsworth's activities during this period; it is harder to fill in the details. What seems most probable is that Elmer Ellsworth worked for about a year at Corliss & House—and did not write many letters home. "Elmer Ellsworth" was not registered at any schools in Kenosha, and his name does not appear in any census lists. The tales are compelling, but they may be exactly that: tales. They were told sixty-five years after the incidents allegedly occurred. They muddy the waters and are probably untrue. They do, however, remind historians that even a lie will get repeated, especially if the person under discussion is famous enough.

By the fall of 1853, Ellsworth had returned to Mechanicville in order to visit his parents and look for a new job. Elmer quickly remembered the persistent fact that, in Mechanicville, there was no opportunity for getting work with interesting or successful prospects. Elmer was ambitious to make something of himself and refused to continue to work at jobs that denied him the sort of future he desired. His personal dreams eclipsed what Mechanicville could offer. Elmer said goodbye to his parents and brother, and took the train east, then south from Albany, to the New York City branch of Corliss & House, where he worked for another seventeen months.[32] One of the advantages of living in New York was that Elmer had an opportunity to attend the drills of the 7th Regiment of the New York Militia. This was the "Silk Stocking" regiment, so named due to its disproportionate number of members from the city's social elite. Ellsworth did not make enough money to join the group but—as always—he was eager to learn as much as he

---

31 Ingraham, *Ellsworth: First Hero*, 10.

32 Elmer Ellsworth to "Friend Alfred" (Alfred J. Cobb), April 18, 1855, KCWM/LFAC; Randall, *Colonel Elmer Ellsworth*, 34, Ingraham, *Ellsworth: First Hero*, 7.

Ellsworth in mufti—a rarely seen image of Elmer Ellsworth out of any kind of uniform. *Wisconsin Historical Society*

could about military tactics. He attended the drills and practices of the 7th every chance he got.[33]

33 Elmer Ellsworth to "Friend Alfred," April 18, 1855; Randall, *Colonel Elmer Ellsworth*, 34; Ingraham, *First Hero*, 11.

After a year and a half of sales work in New York City, Elmer began looking for other employment. He was soon hired by a group of engineers whose project was the improvement of the ocean channel at Hellgate, a narrow tidal strait in the East River. These improvements were accomplished using divers who placed explosives on the surface of the surrounding rocks. The explosives were then detonated by electricity, widening the channel. Exactly what Elmer Ellsworth did on the engineering team is unknown. Perhaps, considering his drawing skills, he was employed as a draftsman. Young, strong, and agile, he may have done any number of odd jobs.[34] At least it got him out from behind a counter.

For Ellsworth, especially at this time in his life, the need to exercise some control over his future was necessary. Self-made men must constantly prove themselves against all comers, and the forces pulling Elmer Ellsworth westward, at least as far as Chicago, were irresistible. Not only did he need to "do battle with the world on my own account," as he wrote to his brother Charley in a letter, but Elmer had to prove to his parents that he could help them out of their perceived poverty.[35] The West was young and new, untried and untamed. America was promising a bright future for those fearless enough to heed the counsel of the editor of the *New York Tribune*, Horace Greeley. "If any young man is about to commence the world, we say to him, publicly and privately, 'Go to the West.'"[36]

Ever since he was a child, Elmer had heard the tantalizing stories of the gold strikes in California, where a man could wash incredible wealth right out of the streams. He had sold newspapers with headlines about glittering, sophisticated cities like Chicago and San Francisco. He had hawked daily news about Mexico, its riches and land there for the taking after the United States won the Mexican War. He had read about the "filibusters," or freebooters, who conducted unauthorized military expeditions into Mexico, the Caribbean, and Central America, claiming land and taking control of it by force of arms. If anyone was primed to go west and try his hand at finding his personal "Manifest Destiny," it was young Elmer Ellsworth, and thousands of men like him.

The team of engineers with whom he had worked on the channel at Hellgate decided to take a job offered to them in the Chicago area. Elmer promised to join

---

34 Elmer Ellsworth to "Friend Alfred," April 18, 1855; Randall, *Colonel Elmer Ellsworth*, 34; Ingraham, *Ellsworth: First Hero*, 7.

35 Elmer Ellsworth to "My Dear Brother," November 15, 1858, KCWM/LFAC; Ellsworth, "Memoranda," 3.

36 Horace Greeley, *The New Yorker*, August 25, 1838.

them, but he wanted to visit his parents and brother in Mechanicville once again.[37] It was 1854. Ellsworth was seventeen. He stayed home for a week or so, burning into his memory the faces of those he loved. Then, amid sad goodbyes, he was gone again. Charles Ingraham claims Charley went with him, only to return soon after. Ruth Painter Randall does not mention Charley at all during this period. It is difficult to imagine both boys leaving home at the same time. Perhaps Charley went a little way with his brother, and then returned. Much about this time in Ellsworth's life is unknown. What *is* known is that he would not return to Mechanicville or see his parents for four years.[38]

37 Elmer Ellsworth to "Friend Alfred," April 18, 1855; Randall, *Colonel Elmer Ellsworth*, 34; Ingraham, *Ellsworth: First Hero*, 7.

38 Ingraham, "Elsworth"; Ellsworth, "Memoranda," 18-19.

CHAPTER 3

"Under the terrible burden of destiny . . . "

Hog Butcher for the World,
Tool Maker, Stacker of Wheat,
Player with Railroads and the Nation's Freight Handler;
Stormy, husky, brawling,
City of the Big Shoulder

"Chicago" by Carl Sandburg[1] from Phebe Ellsworth's Memoranda

ELMER Ellsworth may have been a small man with narrow shoulders, but he found his first real break in the growing industrial giant of Chicago. In 1850, Chicago was a small city of 30,000 people, but within ten years her population had more than tripled to over 109,000. Illinois had become the fourth most populous state in the Union; its explosive growth during the 1850s was unparalleled anywhere else in America, and its biggest city had become a transportation and commercial center almost overnight. A British visitor referred to Chicago as "the lightning city," writing that, "the growth of this city is one of the most amazing things in the history of modern civilization."[2]

Only one railroad passed through Chicago in 1850, but by 1852, that number had increased to five. By 1856, ten railroads and over 3,000 miles of track enlarged Chicago's rail system. This transformation in status brought with it life-altering changes in employment opportunities. Jobs associated with the railroad were

---

1 Carl Sandburg, "Chicago," Chicago Poems (New York: Henry Holt and Company, 1916), 3.

2 Harold M. Mayer & Richard C. Wade, Chicago: Growth of a Metropolis (Chicago: University of Chicago Press, 1969), 35; Benjamin Dreyfus, The City Transformed: Railroads and Their Influence on the Growth of Chicago in the 1850s, 1995, online version: file:////The%20City%20Transformed.webarchive, accessed July 2012.

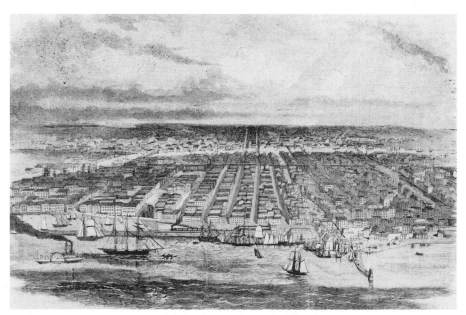

Elmer Ellsworth may have been a small man with narrow shoulders, but he found his first real break in the growing industrial giant of Chicago, pictured here in an 1860 sketch for *Harper's Weekly* on the eve of Republican nominating convention. *Harper's Weekly/Library of Congress*

plentiful, but so were positions in commerce and manufacturing. This increase in employment made an increase in service jobs necessary as well, especially for the thousands of young men who came looking for work.[3] Chicago was a raw, young city, well on its way to the top of the social and economic pile. Only three urban areas, San Francisco, Chicago, and New York, were vying for the honor of being *the* modern nineteenth century city, and all three were bustling with commerce, culture, and opportunity. San Francisco, whose growth was hastened by the California Gold Rush of 1849, was on the far western end of a huge continent. It was only accessible in one of two time-consuming ways: by boat around the Horn of South America, or across land by wagon or on horseback. It was not until May 10, 1869 that the "Golden Spike" connected the Central Pacific and Union Pacific rail systems to become the First Transcontinental Railroad. New York City was already the oldest, biggest, and most economically successful of the three cities. Its harbors and business opportunities were legendary, as was its wonderful array of entertainments. It had the drawbacks of a big city as well as the advantages,

3 Ibid.

however. Disease, poverty, corruption, and lawlessness were the other side of the glitter of success and prosperity. Where San Francisco was establishing itself and New York was bound by its past, Chicago was closer to Mechanicville, and had nothing ahead but the future. It was the perfect city for a restless adolescent—it was the perfect city for Elmer Ellsworth.[4]

One may speculate that Ellsworth was clerking at this time, although no one has yet discovered where. Clerking was an occupation with which he had experience in both Troy and New York City, and there were plenty of such positions available in Chicago. He remained conflicted, however. In a letter to his friend, Henry Parks, he wrote:

> My life has been a constant struggle between duty and inclination. My parents . . . should ever be my first care. I want to see them placed beyond the reach of want-relieved from the necessity of future exertion. Now how am I to accomplish this, is it my duty to settle down to some business and plod along till I can realize the accomplishment of my desires or shall I follow my inclination and make a bold push for fortune where I can experience but one of two things—success or death.[5]

Ellsworth's first "bold push" came when he went to the patent office, seven dollars in hand, to register an invention. Elmer Ellsworth's life at this point presented a picture of someone fully determined to make his mark without the benefit of family name or money. Young men of like ambition quickly became Ellsworth's friends. One such acquaintance was Merritt Hutchins. After Ellsworth became famous, many people came forward with stories to tell about their relationships with him. Hutchins claimed to have known Elmer during that first year in Chicago, in 1854. He recalled that, at one point, Ellsworth came to see him about an appliance he had invented. It was a catch or spring that held a train window open at the exact height the passenger wished. This was preferable to "up," which was closed and let in no fresh air, or "down," which was completely open and let in plenty of fresh air, as well as smoke and coal smuts that ruined clothing and choked any passengers who had not been nearly blown away by the rushing outside breeze. Ellsworth saw a need for this convenience early in his life as he rode back and forth from Mechanicville to Troy on the local passenger train. He gained further experience by riding trains in the New York area and from

---

4　Dreyfus, *The City Transformed*, accessed May 14, 2016.

5　Elmer Ellsworth to "Friend Parks," December 12, 1858, KCWM/LFAC.

Mechanicville to Chicago. His travels convinced him that this idea was one whose time had come. Now, all Ellsworth needed was seven dollars. Mr. Hutchins graciously loaned his friend the money with which to register the patent for the window catch.[6]

Cash in hand, Ellsworth went to a patent-soliciting business run by Arthur F. Devereux, another young man in his early twenties. Devereux, a native of Salem, Massachusetts, had attended Harvard and West Point, but had dropped out of both. He then came to Chicago to seek his fortune by pursuing a career in business.[7] Ellsworth and Devereux liked each other immediately. Not only did Ellsworth become Devereux's friend and business partner, but both men loved the pageantry of the military and enthusiastically joined the newly burgeoning militia movement in Chicago. Both Devereux and Ellsworth eventually became members of the Illinois National Guard, where Devereux served as adjutant to Major Simon Bolivar Buckner, later a Confederate general during the Civil War, and eventually governor of Kentucky.[8] In 1854, however, Elmer and Arthur were simply two young men who were captivated by all things military, including the flashy, exciting Zouave method of drill inspired by the French army units of the same name that fought in North Africa clad in elaborate uniforms influenced by Algerian fashions.

To support his military habit, Devereux began a patent-soliciting business in which he filled out the legal forms and provided the footwork between the inventor and the United States Patent Office. On that day in 1854, Devereux processed Ellsworth's forms, and then, after a little more conversation, offered the Mechanicville entrepreneur a position as a clerk in his business. Within weeks Devereux offered Ellsworth a partnership. Their business prospered, as Chicago was teeming with inventors who needed their services. Ellsworth had high hopes of being able to make enough money to help his parents and to make an agreeable home for himself: " . . . if I possessed today ten thousand dollars, I would give every cent to my parents, bid them goodbye, and go abroad to earn the right to come home and make *myself* and *another* happy," he wrote to Henry Parks two years later.[9]

---

6 Elmer Ellsworth, diary, undated entry, KCWM/LFAC.

7 George W. Nason, *History and Complete Roster of the Massachusetts Regiments, Minute Men of '61* (Boston: Smith and McCance, 1910), 250-252.

8 Nason, *History*, 251.

9 Elmer Ellsworth to "Friend Parks," December 12, 1858, KCWM/LFAC.

More immediately, however, Ellsworth was finally able to support a military habit of his own.

Before the mid-nineteenth century, as the need for armed protection grew less pressing, militias began to serve another purpose, one having little to do with fighting for and defending citizens. For most Americans, according to Adam Goodheart, "Volunteering for military service was more like joining a weekend bowling league than enlisting in the army as we know it."[10] There had not been a mobilization since 1812, and the military state of local militias was poor. Most units were trained to walk (not march!) in a Fourth of July parade, and little else. Many were not armed, but drilled with sticks or cornstalks, especially those from small country settlements. The brave and gallant "minutemen" of 1775 had become little more than social organizations, providing a place for young men to gather, away from the prying eyes of home.

In the mid-century North, such quasi-military militia organizations became more common in both larger cities and small towns. They attracted young men of prominent families who could afford the uniform, weapons, dues, and travel required of unit membership. In turn, social contacts were made, which could lead to profitable business or political alliances. The recognition of the abilities of nineteen-year-old Elmer Ellsworth, from Mechanicville, New York, by a man of Devereux's background indicates a great deal of social progress on Ellsworth's part, which could only have been made by someone presenting a level of sophistication that comes from being raised in a family far from poverty. Within a box labeled "MS. E. Ellsworth" in the Kenosha Civil War Museum there exists a dance program, a fancy, ornamented card with now-tarnished gilt tassels, saved from the First Grand Military and Civic Ball given by "the Cadets" on November 12, 1856. Listed on the inside front of the program are the names of those responsible for the dance: the "Committee of Arrangements." Among the names are two business partners, A. F. Devereux and "Captain" E. E. Ellsworth. After less than two years in Chicago, the impecunious patent clerk had already become a captain of a city militia group.[11]

Unfortunately, no one's path is that smooth, and Elmer Ellsworth's was about to take a severe downward turn. In another letter to Henry Parks, Ellsworth poured out the story of an economic upset that almost destroyed him. He had been

---

10 Goodheart, *1861*, 191.

11 "The Fiery Trial," exhibit, KCWM/LFAC. Viewed August 16, 2016, Kenosha Civil War Museums Archives.

working hard. "How I labored, what I suffered, and what privation I endured God and myself only knew."[12] He had been saving his money to help his not-exactly-helpless parents and had almost saved enough to "place them in circumstances which would leave me at liberty," when financial disaster struck.[13]

Little is known about the specific details of the situation, but enough information is available to be able to piece together an idea of the problem. By 1857, Ellsworth was twenty years old and had worked in the patent business for three years, when "[i]n an evil hour I placed confidence in an infernal scoundrel. I was robbed of everything in a moment, saw the reward of three years' toil fade from my eyes when about to grasp it."[14] The "infernal scoundrel" was not named, but simply referred to as an "agent." One may gather from Ellsworth's letters and from the nature of shady business practices, which have changed very little, that both Devereux and Ellsworth made a poor arrangement with this man, entrusting him with a large sum of money to invest on their behalf. The money and the man disappeared, the firm was ruined, and Elmer Ellsworth found himself with no position, no means, and worst of all, in debt.

Ellsworth was a person who compartmentalized his views of the world. If he treated people fairly, it should follow that he would be treated fairly in turn. Professional betrayal was a terrible shock to him. Losing money was only part of the blow. In the immediate aftermath of this reverse, he became bitterly disillusioned, depressed, and very suspicious of everyone:

> I hardly dare to trust myself to form an ardent friendship. I acknowledged no friend, and within myself held all at defiance, and goaded on almost to madness by disappointment and misfortune, bid fate to do its worst. This was not the result of trivial disappointment or trouble, but in consequence of suffering most terrible rendered more poignant by a pride which forced me to bear in silence and alone, what now seems utterly impossible.[15]

For someone of Ellsworth's temperament, the fact that he was now seriously in debt was intolerable and humiliating, even if the condition was no fault of his own. His correspondence at the time indicates that his creditors "treated him roughly." Although the amount of the debt has never been revealed, and no more

12 Elmer Ellsworth to "Friend Parks," December 12, 1858, KCWM/LFAC.

13 Ibid.

14 Ibid.

15 Ibid.

information as to his creditors has been uncovered, Ellsworth's writings indicate that the problems he and Devereaux were undergoing had become public knowledge. Ellsworth complained that he had to endure "the insults and infernal stare of those who do not know me, who thought I had no right to hold up my head or look like other men."[16] He claimed his creditors "attacked . . . like a pack of hungry wolves."[17] Purple as Ellsworth's prose might have been, the problem was real, as was the effect it had on him. Some saw him as part of the dishonesty involved in the loss, as he claimed he had to fight personal, slanderous attacks on his values and behavior.

Elmer Ellsworth was always concerned with his public image. It was during this time that he felt he was being accused of a host of vices, including drinking and gambling. Ellsworth had signed a temperance pledge when he was only nine years old, and no one has unearthed any proof that he ever broke that vow.[18] In fact, there is evidence to the contrary, as seen in this August 1860 letter to Ellsworth from Isabelle G. Duffield, of Detroit, Michigan:

> I write to thank you and every mother ought to unite with me in thanking you for the noble example you have set to young men, in forming and keeping up a military company under such strict temperance rules. . . . What an achievement!! Had such a thing been told us two years ago, we should not have believed it, but it has been done by the noble "Chicago Zouaves," who will always have the greatest glory, because they were the first to set the example.[19]

Earlier, in a missive of brotherly advice, Elmer had warned Charley not to run around with people of a bad reputation, or else he may be thought of as the same sort of man.[20] This period in Ellsworth's life was anxious and frightening, and there seemed to be no end in sight. He had debts to pay, a reputation to restore, and no clear way of doing either. In later years, when he wrote of this bitter experience, Ellsworth said he felt like he had been "the sport and foot-ball of fortune."[21]

---

16 Ibid.

17 Ibid.

18 Ellsworth, "Memoranda," 10.

19 Ibid; 11-12.

20 Elmer Ellsworth to Charley Ellsworth, November 15, 1858, KCWM/LFAC.

21 Ibid.

Twenty years old, broke, in debt, and bitter, Elmer Ellsworth faced his future. It looked bleak, but not entirely hopeless. The patent business had introduced him to the intricacies of law, and to a variety of Chicago patent attorneys. In addition, Ellsworth wrote clear, legible, and sophisticated cursive. He obtained a job as a clerk in the law office of J. E. Cone, who offered his new employee only a subsistence wage. Elmer was forced to give up his hotel room and slept on the floor of the law office for several months. He was often hungry, as much of his pitiful remittance went to pay down his debts.[22]

Heartbroken, he gave up the expense of belonging to a military company. He was too proud to admit that he was in such dire straits. In his diary, sporadically kept, he entered this on April 12, 1859:

> . . . two years ago, when I was so poor—one day went into an eating house on some errand. While there, Clybourn and several friends came in . . . as I started to go out they stopped me and insisted upon my having an Oyster stew with them. I refused—for I always made it a principle never to accept even an apple from any one because I could not return like courtesies—while they were clamoring about the matter and I trying to get away from them, the waiter brought on stews for the whole party—having taken it for granted that I was going to stay.[23]

At this point, "Clybourn" told Ellsworth that it was fine if he went without eating, but the stew was already paid for. Ellsworth continued:

> . . . so to escape making myself any more conspicuous by further refusal I sat down. How gloriously every morsel tasted—the first food I had touched in three days and nights.[24]

The "Clybourn" of the story was James A. Clybourn, who later became a member of Ellsworth's U. S. Zouave Cadet company. When Ellsworth approached him later that year to repay him for the oyster stew, Clybourn initially refused to take the fifty cents, but Ellsworth successfully pressed the money upon his friend.[25]

There were, however, some bright spots for Ellsworth during this time. Although it was not widely known at the time, he apparently was the special friend

22 Elmer Ellsworth, diary, April 12, 1859, BU/JHC.

23 Ibid.

24 Ibid.

25 Ibid.

of a lovely woman in Chicago. The story is found in his diary and was written about two years after he had become acquainted with her. True to Victorian literary conceits, the lady was identified only by a long dash, and not her name. In this manner she could never be identified, and never has been. She was beautiful, older than he, and married. Ellsworth was in the habit of going to see her when he was ill or tired from working in the law office, or discouraged about life in general. "Mrs._____" had made inquiries and discovered Elmer's true living circumstances. At one point, she attempted to give the young man money:

> She found out how I was situated and then she said she wanted me to accept money. That if I did not, she would certainly find out all that had transpired, [about the original swindle] and perhaps place herself in a dangerous position, for she was determined to aid me and force me to accept it. I gently but firmly refused; she would not listen for a long time. At last I made her understand my scruples and she put up her money. God bless her for her kindness. I left with a lighter heart. I had the sympathy of a true friend and had successfully resisted temptation.[26]

He continued to see "Mrs. _____," although she was married to, in the opinion of Ellsworth and a friend who also admired the lady in question, "a brute who did not appreciate his wife."[27] They discussed her often, no doubt justifying their mutual infatuation with this married woman. Ellsworth's diary sheds a little more light on the true nature of his "friendship" with her:

> There are but few such women as she was living. The wildest description of beauty and fascination I ever read would not do her justice.[28]

He then came as close as he ever did to admitting that she was something more than a friend:

---

26 Elmer Ellsworth, diary, April 13, 1859, KCWM/LFAC. "Mrs. _____" is all that is written in Ellsworth's diary. This was a conventional Victorian way of explaining something without using an identifiable name. It was quite common, but it leaves us wondering. I have found nothing more to enlighten me except a small cardboard note card, upon which is written, in Ellsworth's hand, the words "I can be discrete." Thanks to Doug Dammann of the Kenosha Civil War Museum for sharing it, and for a good discussion of including such a scandalous tale in this book.

27 Ibid.

28 Ibid.

A dapper Chicago gentleman—Elmer Ellsworth. *Chicago History.org*

She lived to acknowledge that she who had reigned [as] undisputed queen of the hearts of some of the noblest and most talented men in this country loved me, a poor, unknown boy, who she had fondled, petted, and told her heart's secrets. . . . But when I was absent from her a year, a year of suffering which has shortened my life by many a bright year, I am afraid—I returned, no longer a boy, but a man. I thank God that I came safe from the ordeal to which I was exposed without doing what would have brot [sic] unhappiness to more hearts than one—verily life is full of romance and reality is much more startling than fiction.[29]

29 Ibid.

No doubt her affection gave Elmer some comfort in his times of trial.

Not every young man left his family and went to "the city." Many were already there, with some hailing from well-to-do households that were only too happy to provide their sons with advanced educations and entry-level jobs in business upon graduation. They joined the ever-growing group of young men who had come to places like Chicago and New York from the farms and small towns of the Northeast, and the male immigrants from Ireland and Germany. This new bachelor class created demands on the moral and social structure of larger cities, which were met in many ways and with varying degrees of success. Boarding houses, offices with a back bedroom, or the family home provided little for a young man to do after work. Besides going out to meet friends for supper, most of the evening activities available to single males involved alcohol, gambling, or sex. Of course, a young man could take in a play or see a concert, but this usually entailed some cost, and entry-level jobs were notoriously low-paying, then as now. Gymnasiums, often free of charge, were open in the evenings, and fraternal orders and men's clubs were formed to combat the allure of the saloon and pool hall. This situation created the beginnings of such fraternal orders as the Odd Fellows and the Knights of Pythias, as well as the Young Men's Christian Association and similar organizations.[30]

Since Ellsworth had little money and thus had been forced to give up his membership in the Cadets of the National Guard, he chose to join the YMCA in order to continue to have a place to exercise. With the deluge of young, single, self-made men upon cities all over the Northeast and West, facilities that catered to them became much more common. Single gender boarding houses, inexpensive restaurants, saloons with free lunches for paying patrons, barber shops, cafes, pool halls, billiard parlors, and a variety of seedier establishments could be found in every neighborhood, and sometimes on every corner. The first American location of the YMCA was established in 1851; it provided housing, rooms in which to read and talk, and access to facilities for exercise and camaraderie.[31] It was at such an establishment in Chicago that Elmer Ellsworth met the intriguing Dr. Charles A. DeVilliers.

Historian Adam Goodheart has written that if Elmer Ellsworth's life were a movie, it could not have had more perfect characters or better timing. A native of

---

30 Howard P. Chudacoff, *The Age of the Bachelor: Creating an American Subculture* (Princeton, NJ: Princeton University Press, 1999), chapters 4 and 5, *passim*.

31 Chudacoff, *The Age of the Bachelor*, 106-145, 156-165.

France, Dr. DeVilliers had served with a French Zouave unit as an officer and a surgeon during the Crimean War, and had then immigrated to America, ending up in Chicago. The former Zouave doctor was also a master swordsman, and plied his trade as a teacher of the art of fencing at various gyms around the city, including the YMCA. Ever the romantic, Elmer Ellsworth was immediately captivated by the idea of flashing blades and became his pupil. Elmer learned to fence so quickly and so well that he soon began assisting DeVilliers in his YMCA classes. With the older, exotic, and experienced DeVilliers as his mentor, Ellsworth flourished. This relationship expanded Ellsworth's love of all things military. Under the tutelage of DeVilliers, within a matter of months Ellsworth mastered fencing, and added to his list of accomplishments an interest in an entirely new type of military drill.

DeVilliers held Ellsworth in thrall with his exciting descriptions of the Algerian Zouaves, with their unusual uniforms and graceful military movements. Ellsworth scrimped to get enough money together to send to France for a set of books, in French, which explained the dramatic, colorful, and new (to America) Zouave drill. While he waited for the books to arrive, Ellsworth worked with DeVilliers to perfect both Scott's and Hardee's military drill and tactics, attempting to improve on both in style, if not in substance. Ellsworth sought to bring speed and grace into all military drill movements without compromising the movements themselves. Ellsworth began to attract attention for his "lightning drill," which he demonstrated in the YMCA gymnasium.[32]

When the books arrived from France, Ellsworth, with the help of Dr. DeVilliers, learned enough military French to be able to read them. The doctor was able to answer various questions for Ellsworth: Why were those scarlet trousers so loose and baggy? Why did the dark blue, gold-trimmed jacket have no collar? The answer was that no one could perform the exacting Zouave drills in a stiff, tight uniform; a Zouave had to have complete freedom of motion to go through his maneuvers.[33] Just as he had mastered, then improved upon, the drills of Scott and Hardee, Ellsworth worked with DeVilliers to perfect the intricate Zouave drill as well.

"Intricate" does little justice to the complicated moves and gymnastic performances required to execute this drill, which has been compared to a

32 Goodheart, *1861*, 193.

33 Edward G. Longacre, "Elmer Ephraim Ellsworth," American National Biography, eds., John A. Garraty, Mark C. Carnes (New York: Oxford University Press, 1999), VII, 454.

combination of the modern *Cirque de Soleil* and SEAL Team 6.[34] It features a unit of four soldiers, backs together, each one facing a cardinal direction.

> The Manual of Arms will be taught to four men, at first in one rank . . . After causing the squad of four men to execute one command several times, until they comprehend it, cause another squad to take their place, and in turn execute the same command.[35]

The Zouave drill taught soldiers to load and fire on the run, while lying down, or when kneeling. When seen in exhibition, these individual maneuvers were performed while the entire company was also forming double crosses, revolving circles, pyramids, and intersecting lines, all with incredible speed and accompanied by a system of precise verbal commands and responses. The abbreviated exhibitions of this new drill style, performed in the gymnasium under Ellsworth's direction, began to be a hot topic of conversation among the local militias. Ellsworth tried hard to keep himself attentive to his employment in the Cone law office, but his heart lay elsewhere. His friend John Hay, whom he met in 1859 in Springfield when he was there to drill the Springfield militia, and who later became one of Abraham Lincoln's personal secretaries, wrote that any occupation that was not military in nature was not one that would hold Ellsworth's complete attention.[36]

When Devereux finally was able to talk Ellsworth into rejoining the Chicago National Guard Cadets, Elmer had already begun teaching the Zouave drill to small groups, and his reputation as a drillmaster had grown. His military skills, along with the fact that he was from upstate New York, added sparks to the rumor that Ellsworth had attended West Point for a while but had been expelled for some unknown infraction. Ellsworth himself did nothing to silence such gossip, but he did not—at this time—add to it.[37] The mystery surrounding this man of five feet, six inches, with long, dark, curling hair and merry hazel eyes deepened. He was

34 Goodheart, 1861, 194; Adam Goodheart, Center for the Book Presents "The Book and Beyond" Series, May 11, 2011, transcript, Library of Congress, www. loc.gov/today/cyberlc/transcripts/2011/2011nbf/agoodheart.txt, accessed October 13, 2017.

35 Elmer Ephraim Ellsworth, *Manual of Arms for Light Infantry: Adapted to the Rifled Musket, With or Without the Priming Attachment* (Charleston, SC: Nabu Press Reprint, 2011).

36 John Hay, "Ellsworth," *McClure's Magazine* (July 1861), 122.

37 Jeremiah Burns, *The Patriot's Offering; or, the Life, Services, and Military Career of the Noble Trio, Ellsworth, Lyon, and Baker* (New York: Cornell University Library, 1862), 9.

handsome, well dressed, dynamic, smart, and accomplished. No one needed to know anything more.

Devereux talked up Ellsworth's reputation and promised the militia company that his much-expanded talent would reinvigorate the moribound unit. On April 27, 1859, Ellsworth took over. Their uniforms were shabby, and the company was deeply in debt, but Ellsworth, who was then twenty-two and full of military ardor, determined not to let the opportunity pass him by.[38] This task, however, was much more easily hoped for than accomplished. A new uniform was adopted, which consisted of light blue pants with a buff stripe, a dark blue frock coat with buff trimmings, and a tall cap of dark blue crowned by a red, white, and blue pompon. White crossed belts and a knapsack with a red blanket neatly rolled and strapped on top completed the "infantry uniform" outfit.[39]

Along with the new uniform came new rules governing its wearing: members were prohibited from entering drinking saloons or other disreputable places when representing their company. Other changes were made, including altering the name of the company to the "Chicago Cadets of the National Guard." The unit rented a new, more substantial armory, and three drills a week were instituted. In less than a month over fifty recruits were added to the roster. Finally, a still-unidentified person stepped forward to assume the debts of the old company. As promised, Ellsworth had been able to breathe new life into this dying organization.[40]

As with so many aspects of Elmer Ellsworth's life, the timing of events had once again fallen favorably in his direction. By the end of 1858, he was in an excellent position to become an officer and drillmaster of a militia unit. Ellsworth "knew that God had made him a soldier," and the available place at the head of a local Chicago militia unit seemed to be a perfect fit.[41] He quickly attracted the attention of important men. Congressman John Pope Cook, commander of the Springfield Greys, had already recognized Ellsworth's skills. Through Cook, Ellsworth would eventually come to the attention of Brigadier General Richard

38 Alfred Theodore Andreas, *History of Chicago: From the Earliest Period to the Present Time, Volume II: From 1857 Until the Fire of 1871* (Chicago: The A.T. Andreas Company, Publishers, 1885), 187-190, online version: play.google.com/books/reader?id= iKE4AQAAMAAJ&printsec=frontcover&pg=GBS.PP6, accessed October 5, 2017.

39 Andreas, *History of Chicago*, 188.

40 Ibid. Andreas claims that many of his facts concerning Ellsworth's Chicago Zouaves were taken from the text of an address delivered by Colonel E. B. Knox at a reunion of the cadets.

41 John Hay, *McClure's Magazine*, 1895/96, vi, 356.

Kellogg Swift, a wealthy Chicago banker and the commander of the Illinois State Militia. Swift appointed Ellsworth to be an aide on his staff, with the militia rank of major, when he rejoined the company.[42] In 1856, Ellsworth had helped Swift organize other military companies in and around the Chicago area. Because of these efforts, Swift always included Ellsworth in his plans concerning the state militias.[43] Ellsworth was also writing his own manual of arms, which, when published, was quickly adopted by militia companies across the state of Illinois.[44] Ellsworth began to train members of the former Chicago Cadets of the National Guard in his new French Zouave drill, with surprising success.

42 Ibid. Local militias had a ready-made structure, and most of them maintained an armory of some sort. An armory was traditionally a place where weapons were stored and where volunteer soldiers were trained, but by the 1850s, armories also functioned as a sort of social hall for single men. There were reading rooms, sometimes a card room, and a place to drink within the safety of a well-known, locally established "clubhouse." The militia unit usually charged annual dues to maintain the armory, and each volunteer was responsible for his own uniforms and weapons. Membership could be gained in one of two ways: as a legacy, usually through a male relative, or through an application process wherein the applicant had to have appropriate local recommendations. By joining a militia company, a young man on his own could meet and mingle with other young men, many of whom came from the better families in the city. Militia membership provided a chance for a man to make contacts and open doors in business, and was an opportunity to be seen by the social community, including families with eligible daughters, as being something other, something better, than the usual fellow on the Chicago streets.

43 First Brigade Illinois Volunteers, "General R. K. Swift. https://sites.google.com/site/1stbrigadeil/general-r-k-swift, accessed June 2011. John Cook was an Illinois politician who became a general in the Union army during the Civil War. His father was Daniel Cook, a member of the U.S. House of Representatives. John Cook was elected mayor of Springfield in 1855, and also was the captain and commander of the Springfield Grays, a militia group. Cook went on to serve as quartermaster general of the Illinois State Militia. Brigadier General Richard Kellogg Swift, originally from New York, moved to Chicago in 1835 and began a loan and pawn broking business. He commanded an artillery unit in the Illinois State Militia from 1846 to 1853, purchasing uniforms and maintaining the guns at his own expense. In 1855 the governor of Illinois, W. H. Bissell, appointed Swift to the position of brigadier general of the Second Brigade, Sixth Division, of the Illinois Militia. His first command assignment was when Mayor Boone of Chicago requested help from the state to have the militia (now called the State National Guard) quell the unrest in Chicago during the "Lager Beer Riot" in 1855. In 1856, Elmer Ellsworth, now considered a major, aided Gen. Swift in organizing military companies in the city and surrounding area. At the outbreak of the Civil War, loyal states were called upon by President Lincoln to provide troops to help enlarge the federal army. Governor Yates of Illinois instructed Gen. Swift to take command of the river town of Cairo, Illinois. His force of approximately 595 militia members boarded two trains and occupied of Cairo. General Swift later returned to Chicago and was instrumental in recruiting volunteers in Illinois for the rest of the war.

44 Andreas, *History of Chicago*, 187-190.

As has been discussed, the militia companies enjoyed entertaining, often holding banquets as well as formal dances. In December 1857, the Rockford City Greys issued Ellsworth an invitation to attend a dinner at the Holland House in Rockford, Illinois, a small city about 90 miles south of Chicago. Luckily, there is an account of the event, which describes Maj. Ellsworth, standing with other militia officers at the Holland House on that occasion, over 160 years ago. A Rockford Grey named Frank E. Peats attended the banquet and later wrote about it. In typical Victorian prose, Peats mentioned the "brave men and fair women" who were "tripping the light fantastic" and enjoying a "flow of soul."[45] Peats wrote affectionately of Ellsworth, for he would come to know him well. "Let me present him as he appeared to me that evening," mentioning his "boyish figure" topped by:

> . . . a well-balanced head crowned in a wealth of dark brown hair that fell in careless, clinging curls around his neck, eyes of dark hazel, that sparkled and flashed with excitement or melted with tenderness, and a generous mouth with lips full and red, and teeth of dazzling whiteness that were revealed by his quick, winning smile or laugh. Thus stood Major Ellsworth as I saw him then.[46]

Peats recorded several interesting incidents that occurred at the banquet. According to "ancient precedent," the leader of the Greys was to turn over the command of his men to one of the guests from another group. Each one declined the honor, saying, "We beg to be excused while Major Ellsworth is present." When Ellsworth's turn came, he accepted the commander's invitation. He then faced the Rockford Greys, who were lined up in readiness, and began to drill the rival group. His power of voice astonished the gathering, as they had not heard it in command before. Peats remembered that it "could have been distinctly heard at a distance of four blocks away." If this was a test of Major Ellsworth's skills, he passed it admirably. The Greys invited him to come to Rockford the following summer and be their drillmaster. In this way, Elmer Ellsworth moved to Rockford, where he would meet a young woman who would change his life. The "terrible burden of destiny" was about to be lightened considerably.[47]

45 Longacre, "Elmer Ephraim Ellsworth," 454.

46 Ibid.

47 Ibid.

CHAPTER 4

Ellsworth, Triumphant

When our Zouaves go through their splendid manual, in a three-hours' drill, with a precision
like clockwork, moving limbs and pieces as if each was a part of a complicated and nicely
adjusted machine, when they come swooping down in a gallant charge of bayonet, or
to follow their complex evolutions in perfect harmony of movement, they elicit
more than the admiration of ladies clapping their delicately kidded hands.
Grim old military men allow their features to grow sunny with delight,
and the marvel initiated by the young volunteer soldiers of Chicago,
is accepted and praised by all.

Chicago Tribune, October 2, 1860[1]

WITH pleasure, Ellsworth accepted Rockford's offer to bring the
Greys home to drill during the summer of 1858. He drilled
the militiamen, according to contract, almost every night of the week. But Elmer
spent most days in the company of the lovely Carrie Spafford. At fifteen, Carrie was
the eldest of the three children of Charles H. Spafford, a well-to-do banker in
Rockford. Carolyn, called "Carrie" by all, was about five feet, two inches, which
made her a perfect size to walk beside her new beau in his flashy militia uniform.
Her hair was a deep, lustrous brown and her long-lashed eyes were hazel, like
Elmer's. Ellsworth met Miss Spafford at the December festivities to which he had
been invited the previous winter. The reception, held on the grounds of the
Rockford Seminary, had been attended by the elite of the city, including the
Spafford family and their eldest daughter. Ellsworth saw much of Carrie that

1 *Chicago Tribune*, October 2, 1860, online version: www.chicagotribune.com/tribune-archives/, accessed October 16, 2017.

Carolyn "Carrie" Spafford.
Wisconsin Historical Society

summer. He came frequently to the Spafford home, a large, comfortable house with a cupola on its roof. By the time a fourth Spafford baby was born in April 1860, Elmer Ellsworth would be so much an accepted member of the family that he was given the privilege of naming the little girl: Eugenia.[2]

Courting was never a private matter in the mid-1800s, and Ellsworth had to "court" Carrie's family as well as Carrie herself. Initially this was a comfortable arrangement for Ellsworth, as the Spaffords had the kind of home he wished he could provide for his parents. According to Ruth Painter Randall's biography of Elmer Ellsworth, written at a time when people who had known the family were still living, the Spaffords were "sterling, warmhearted, interesting people who had all the privileges of money, culture, social position, and everything that makes up a gracious mode of living."[3]

One of the many facts that throw the "poverty" of Ellsworth's upbringing into question was the ease with which he moved into the social stratum occupied by

---

2 Elmer Ellsworth to Carrie Spafford, April 15, 1860, KCWM/LFAC. In this somewhat-disjointed letter to Carrie is a passage that refers to the birth of Carrie's new sister, named "Eugenia" by Ellsworth:

Baby in the house—it completely unnerved me. It was equivalent to a cry—of fire, murder, thieves, etc., etc. . . . Lady friend of mine came along looking radiantly happy—spoke to me and I unconsciously asked if she had a baby? she flew of[f] in a passion and a sympathetic friend asked what was the disturbance? I replied a baby. Friend came up with a Theatre bill in his hand; asked me if I'd seen "The Object of Interest?" told him no, but was going to, he immediately handed me two Theatre tickets and asked whom I would take. I answered the baby. Gentleman said he would like to join my company—asked what were the qualifications? I answered—a baby. He said something about—babies, and I strolled into an eating house, being hungry, meek looking waiter inquired what would I have? told him, a dozen fried; waiter impudently asked, 'fried what?' and I replied babies.

3 Elmer Ellsworth, diary, undated, KCWM/LFAC.

Carrie's family. Both families shared distinguished Revolutionary War ancestors, Ellsworth was well thought of by important people in Rockford, and the Spaffords found him an acceptable suitor for their daughter. Ellsworth soon began to refer to Mr. and Mrs. Spafford as "Father" and "Mother."[4] Among the facets of an agreeable life at the Spafford house, which charmed Ellsworth, was the unusual fact that they believed in a complete education for the girls in the family as well as the boys. Carrie was a student at the Rockford Seminary when she met Ellsworth, and there were already plans to send her to New Hampshire to attend school, which Ellsworth approved of completely. College education did not start for students at a particular age, but rather after the student finished with the teaching available at local schools. Ellsworth's letters to Carrie when she was away at her eastern academy were very supportive and encouraging, if a bit "of the day" in their recurrent theme of "personal improvement":

> Don't forget about exercise—first thing you know I shall send you a pair of dumb bells to exercise with if nothing better happens. . . . Why, when I have an opportunity I am going to make a perfect amazon of you. I shall teach you how to ride, skate, shoot, fence, and an endless variety of accomplishments not usually found in the list of studies embraced in the catalogues of our seminaries.[5]

Elmer was aware of her youth when he wrote, "I pictured to myself what you *might* become," even as he warned her against "tight lacing."[6]

Life could not have been more perfect that summer in Rockford, and Maj. Ellsworth was delighted. He had a job he loved—drilling a militia unit and seeing its daily progress. He had the respect of the important men of the Springfield-Rockford area, including John Cook, Gen. R. K. Swift, and Charles Spafford. And he had the growing attention of a lovely young woman and the approval of her parents. Ellsworth's glorious summer needed a grand finale to set it off as truly memorable.

When an antebellum military company perfected an unusual and exciting new drill, the next part of the plan was to show it off to the local community and invite

4 Ellsworth's letters to the Spaffords frequently use the salutation "Dearest Mother."

5 Elmer Ellsworth to Carrie Spafford, May 9, 1859, KCWM/LFAC.

6 Elmer Ellsworth to Carrie Spafford, May 18, 1859, KCWM/LFAC.

Major Ellsworth of the Rockford Greys.
Wisconsin Historical Society

other companies to come, observe, and celebrate. The Rockford Greys were to go "into camp" at the local fairgrounds from September 22 to 25, 1858, and had invited the National Guard Cadets of Chicago (Ellsworth's "home" unit) and the Washington Continental Artillery, from Elgin, to join them. Nestled in tissue paper in a sentimental cardboard box at the Kenosha Civil War Museum, among a collection of Carrie Spafford's personal effects, is a paper and cardboard program entitled "Camp Sinnissippi." It is embossed with an image of the American eagle against a background of eight banners. The dates of the encampment are listed, and underneath, in now-scuffed gilt, is the name "Major E. E. Ellsworth, Commanding." The arrival of the "Companies from Abroad" was to be celebrated on the first day by a "Grand Full-Dress Parade Through the City." The "Battalion Drill" was scheduled for Thursday, September 23, and the final celebration was planned for Friday, September 24. In large red letters, the program announces that the Rockford City Greys were to present the "Zouave Drill of the Chasseurs de Vincennes of the French Army."[7] The entire town of Rockford must have looked forward to this event, making plans for picnics and gatherings, meeting friends and watching the precise, exciting drills of the local militias, made up of handsome young men considered to be the "flower" of Illinois manhood.

The four-day military celebration ended with a party. A formal, handwritten note remains folded into the program addressed to "Major E. E. Ellsworth, Commander of Camp Sinnissippi." It "respectfully" invites Ellsworth and his company to a gathering "to be given by the Ladies of this City at Metropolitan Hall on Friday evening, at eight o'clock."[8] What a beautiful, festive picture this paints: the young ladies in their hoop-skirted finery, white shoulders bared to the evening

7 Exhibit, "The Fiery Trial," KCWM/LFAC.

8 Ibid.

breezes and carrying small, ineffective fans, useless for cooling off but perfect for completing the picture of fashion in 1858; handsome men in splendidly tailored military uniforms of blue, red, and gold, polished boots, shining hair, smelling of Bay Rum, all smiling gaiety and romance. One of the visiting companies was honored in a special ceremony that evening. The Spafford family is the source of this story, wherein Miss Carrie herself presented a flag to the Chicago Cadets of the National Guard, Maj. Ellsworth's Chicago unit. The story creates a charming scene, entirely complementary to the rest of the images of these last days of September 1858. It is easy to picture the lovely girl, with her hoops and tiny waist, making her "graceful little speech of presentation" to the handsome, dashingly uniformed Maj. Ellsworth, who no doubt gave an appropriately eloquent reply.[9]

It was heartbreaking to Ellsworth when fall arrived and his contract with the Rockford Greys ended. The town had welcomed him, his men had drilled and performed flawlessly, adding to his growing reputation in militia circles, and he had met a wonderful young woman who might just be the person with whom he hoped to share a life. The Rockford Greys were not eager to say goodbye to Ellsworth. Being under his command had helped spread word of their proficiency, and many new volunteers were waiting to join the ranks of such an illustrious troop. To show their appreciation of his efforts—for other than room and board, Ellsworth had not yet been paid for his work—the unit presented him with a fine gold watch, "as a token of their regard for him as a gentleman and a soldier."[10]

Sadly, a dejected Maj. Elmer Ellsworth left Rockford in October 1858. He now was to report to Madison, Wisconsin, where he had taken another job drilling a militia company. Had Ellsworth known just how much Rockford still had to offer, he would not have accepted the proposition made by the prestigious Lake Forest Academy and the Governor's Guards. He was concerned, however, with making a living and building his reputation as a drillmaster. He and Carrie were courting, if only by mail. If the words had not yet been said in person, his letters reflected interest in a long-term relationship.[11]

Carrie and Elmer wrote constantly. At first Ellsworth's letters were tentative. In one of his early attempts, he addressed her three ways: "Miss Carrie Spafford, Miss— Carrie—," and finally "My Dearest Friend." Elmer informed her of his

9 Ibid.

10 Elmer Ellsworth, diary, September 24, 1858, KCWM/LFAC.

11 Elmer Ellsworth to Charley Ellsworth, November 15, 1858, KCWM/LFAC.

whereabouts, explaining that he was supposed to be in Wisconsin, as he had "received a proposition, so advantageous to myself, that it would have been folly to refuse."[12] He said that he had been offered the opportunity to drill the Wisconsin Governor's Guards, a cavalry company, and to give them daily fencing lessons. In addition, he was to drill a company of young cadets at Lake Forest. He mentioned being bothered by a law in Wisconsin that made the rank of company commander dependent upon political appointment. This was the first time Ellsworth had dealt with the practice of patronage, the power of a politician to control appointments to office. He hated the practice, but it would not be his last experience with it. Ellsworth never grew to see patronage as anything but a form of political corruption. He was able to proudly tell Carrie in another letter that, despite his refusal to presume upon anyone's name other than his own, he had been offered full command of the Madison encampment.[13]

Carrie Spafford was not the only person to whom Ellsworth wrote. It had been over four years since he had been back to Mechanicville to see his parents and younger brother Charley. His mother's letters of this time take Elmer to task concerning his long absence. Ellsworth responded with placating letters in which he described how he would make his "neglect" up to them. He again told them how he planned to give his parents "a neat, comfortable, unpretending house, such a one as would please and content you, dear mother, and tickle father so hugely that he would not speak for a month." It was to have "two nice parlors, a generous, old fashioned hall and a pleasant family room, fitted up with every appliance for comfort that could be procured, well-stocked with books and pictures." There would be a "nice cozy sleeping room . . . a good kitchen, dining room, washing room, wood shed, etc. . . . last though not least I would find a couple of middle-aged colored people, to whom I would promise a home for life on condition of their serving you faithfully." He did not specifically mention Carrie by name just yet, but described the Spafford family as "some kind friends . . . who, could you know them, you would love with your whole heart."[14]

He also wrote several letters to his sometimes-ne'er-do-well brother, warning against such "vices" as smoking, drinking, and consorting with a "fast" set of

---

12 Elmer Ellsworth to Carrie Spafford, November 1858, KCWM/LFAC.

13 Ibid.

14 Elmer Ellsworth to Phebe and Ephraim Ellsworth, undated, winter, 1858-59, BU/JHC, Box 2.

young men. Elmer promised Charley that he would help him get out of Mechanicville, but until he could do so, Charley was to devote himself to his studies. Ellsworth promised his family that he would see them all soon, but not in the immediate future.[15]

As the winter weather worsened in Wisconsin, he lamented the fact that he and Carrie were separated. On December 2, 1858, Carrie celebrated her sixteenth birthday without her sweetheart at her side. His birthday letter did not arrive until December 13, but it is very different from his earlier, tentative attempts at a love letter. He told her he was sorry to have missed her party, but offered his best wishes upon the occasion:

> I will not wish you a life of unclouded happiness, for that I fear can hardly be realized by any of us. But I will wish, dear Carrie, what may, and I trust will be realized—that your life may be that of a true hearted, noble woman; unmarred by a thought or deed to which in after years you cannot refer with pleasure—an ornament not only, but a blessing to society and your friends.[16]

He then quoted a sentimental verse, which, though a bit cloying to the modern reader, was trendy in the mid-1800s:

> Angels attend thee! May their wings
> Fan every shadow from thy brow;
> For only bright and lovely beings,
> Should wait on one so pure as thou.[17]

Professionally, Ellsworth did well in Wisconsin. He marched with the Governor's Guard in a parade on December 26, as historian Charles A. Ingraham mentioned in his short book, *Colonel Elmer E. Ellsworth, First Hero of the Civil War*. A Madison newspaper noted that the Guard was "much improved in a military point."[18] His contract completed, Elmer left Wisconsin in early January 1859 and went directly to Rockford. During this visit Ellsworth spent a great deal of time with Mr. Spafford, pleading his case to Carrie's father to accept him as Carrie's

---

15 Ibid.

16 Elmer Ellsworth to Carrie Spafford, February 26, 1859, KCWM/LFAC.

17 Ibid.

18 Ingraham, *Ellsworth: First Hero*, 14.

fiancée. The Spaffords approved of Elmer Ellsworth as a person, and there was no way to deny that he and Carrie seemed to be genuinely in love, but as any father must be, Mr. Spafford was concerned by how Ellsworth planned to support a wife on his small salary as a poorly paid militia drillmaster. No doubt Ellsworth wondered about this himself. The military was his love, his ideal profession, but he was not a West Point graduate, or even a regular in the army. Mr. Spafford suggested that Ellsworth enter a law office and study under the sponsorship of that attorney until he should be able to gain admittance to the Illinois Bar on his own. Then he and Carrie could be married, if that was still what they wished to do.[19]

Ellsworth was deeply disappointed, although he did persuade Carrie's father to let them be engaged. He had enough experience in law offices to know that he did not want to become a lawyer. To be tied to a desk and office was the opposite of what Ellsworth enjoyed—being outdoors, in action, and personally in charge of his destiny. He loved Carrie, however, and the acceptance the Spaffords had shown him was compelling. By January 1859, he had decided to at least investigate the possibilities of becoming a lawyer. He sent a few letters of inquiry, kissed his sweetheart, put her picture in his breast pocket, and left Rockford. The break between contracts allowed Elmer the opportunity to see his parents in Mechanicville.[20]

He stopped overnight in Chicago to visit his old friend Gen. R. K. Swift, who was then commander of the Chicago Cadets of the National Guard. Swift had been a supporter of Ellsworth from the beginning of the latter's time in Chicago. In addition to utilizing Ellsworth's military knowledge to organize militia groups, Swift had helped his protégé financially by giving him legal work to copy. Swift always paid in advance, encouraging Elmer in every way possible to work hard and do well. Swift had introduced Ellsworth to Judge John T. Morgan, who had recently begun practicing law in Monmouth, Illinois.[21] Swift gave Ellsworth good references, and within the space of a day, Ellsworth had secured a position in

19 Elmer Ellsworth to Charles Spafford, January 20, 1859.

20 Ibid.

21 Judge John T. Morgan practiced law in Monmouth, Illinois. He graduated from Lombard University in Galesburg, Illinois, then read for the law with General Eleazar A. Paine. He left Paine's office after three years to continue his studies at Albany University in New York. In 1856 he graduated from the New York State Law School in Poughkeepsie, and returned to Monmouth to open his own law office. Online version: www.accessgenealogy. com/ idaho/ biography-of-judge-john-t-morgan.htm, accessed October 18, 2017.

Morgan's office as a law student, with access to the judge's extensive legal library. In exchange, Ellsworth was to clerk for him and do office work. The job was to begin when Ellsworth returned from his visit to New York.[22]

On January 26, 1859, Ellsworth reached Mechanicville, "by Canada," with stops in Detroit and Albany. His letters to Carrie mention that he spent an afternoon in Albany visiting the adjutant general of New York, who gave him some books, before he finally reached his boyhood home. Ellsworth had left Mechanicville when he was seventeen, and this was the first time he had returned in five years.[23] Perhaps he walked the old familiar places with his brother, kicking up gravel on the canal trace next to the Hudson River, or stood in the barn, looking up at the dust motes and remembering Mink, the family horse. His parents may have looked older, and he could not have helped but notice the tremors in his mother's hands, as her Parkinson's disease was beginning to manifest itself. Long talks, simple meals—a good homecoming, everything considered.

He had gotten used to being addressed as "Major Ellsworth," but instead he was just "Elmer." All his life Ellsworth was concerned with his name accurately reflecting his identity. He had flipped names with his father because he did not want to be confused with him. The situation bothered him so much that Elmer wrote to Carrie, after being known as "Major Ellsworth" to his cadets and "Ellsworth" to his closer friends: "It seems odd to be called *Elmer* by old and young." He was uncomfortable with his family and friends thinking of him as the little boy they had once known. The tone of his letter to Carrie indicates that Elmer found it challenging to be "merely" the son of Ephraim Ellsworth, and not the dashing, fawned-upon Chicago militia officer he was used to being.

By the middle of March, Ellsworth was on his way back to Chicago, and then on to Rockford to spend a few more days with the Spaffords. Seemingly resigned to studying law, the rest of Ellsworth's vacation had only one vexing problem: Carrie would be leaving soon to continue her schooling at the Tilden Seminary in West Lebanon, New Hampshire. Elmer suspected an underlying reason for sending Carrie so far away. His letters contain a couple of remarks that indicate he was aware of Mr. Spafford's reservations about him as a potential son-in-law. With no profession and no income, and with every sign of being a wanderer and a dreamer,

22 Elmer Ellsworth to Carrie Spafford, April 20, 1859, KCWM/LFAC.

23 Elmer Ellsworth to Carrie Spafford, January 17, 1859, KCWM/LFAC.

maybe temporarily separating Elmer from his daughter seemed like a good idea. In his letter to Carrie of April 2, 1859, he dramatically complained:

> I returned to my hotel, went to my room—canvassed the whole matter over thoroughly—considered the chances and contingencies—thought of you, dearest, and my determination was made. God only knows what a struggle it cost me to forsake a profession for which I have prepared myself with so much labor, and in the face of so many difficulties—I have done this for your sake, dear Carrie, and I have now before me am arduous task, which will have to be pursued under many disadvantages, and I shall need all the encouragement which your rapid progress towards that noble womanhood, which I anticipate for you will afford me.[24]

Carrie began her trip east in early April. She stopped for a day in Chicago to meet with Ellsworth and say goodbye, then continued onward with a token of his love clutched gently in her hands. Ellsworth had made a sentimental scrapbook for her entitled *Album of Love*.[25] It contained drawings, lettered mottos, and three pages of a carefully composed love letter, reminding her to study and work hard for the next two years, remembering always that this was the way in which she could "prove the extent of your affection for one whose whole happiness is centered in the hope of your future excellence." Ellsworth felt that he would "prove the extent of his affection" in the same manner, by working hard at the study of law.

His plans to work with Judge Morgan had fallen through, as Morgan had suddenly moved from Monmouth to Elgin, Illinois. Ellsworth once again worked in the law offices of his former employer, J. E. Cone. As before, he found the work monotonous. He lived in the back room of the law office, and this time things were financially much worse. On April 11, he celebrated his twenty-second birthday by beginning a diary. It is within a transcribed copy that one finds these words: "I enter the second year of my manhood with my heart filled to overflowing with gratitude for the many and undeserved mercies for which I am indebted to God."[26]

24 Elmer Ellsworth to Carrie Spafford, April 2, 1859, KCWM/LFAC.

25 *The Album of Love* is one of the Ellsworth pieces that has not come to light. Again and again, Elmer Ellsworth closed his missives to Carrie with the admonition to "burn or destroy this letter." Luckily she did not, and most of the other things—the diary, Charity Mabbett's manuscript—eventually were found. But the *Album of Love* is still missing. It may have been destroyed by a heart-broken Carrie Spafford after Ellsworth's death.

26 Elmer Ellsworth, diary, early April 1859, KCWM/LFAC.

Unfortunately, his heart was the only thing about Ellsworth that was anywhere near full.

As an engaged man, Ellsworth cut his socializing to a minimum, and tried to save as much money as he possibly could. He wrote frequently to Carrie that he was alone and did not leave his room except to go to the post office. Elmer complained about the difficulty of reading Blackstone's *Commentaries on the Laws of England,* the required course of study for nineteenth century law students, and he got a little depressed when he thought of her apparently happy and carefree life in New Hampshire:

> Darling, did you ever go out of a morning when the mist had just cleared sufficiently for you to distinguish a faint outline of surrounding objects, without any distinct idea of their location or character? If you have, you may know just my position and sensation, when I asked myself what I had learned of the law, in that first book of Blackstone. . . . I read a sentence or paragraph that contains an idea or definition of the meaning of some part of the law,—then I read and re-read that portion aloud, then lay aside the book—repeat the ideas in my own language—apply it to some common ordinary occurrence of every day life—get it firmly fixed in my mind—& then write it in a blotter or commonplace book—without any reference to the language used by Blackstone.[27]

The diary, in which Ellsworth was far more candid than he was in his love letters, explained why. Most entries ended with the curious annotation, "1 doz. Bist to day—sleep on office floor to night." Sometimes this was relieved by "2 lb Crac." Ellsworth was living—literally—on bread and water and sleeping on the hard, wooden floor of the Cone law office. He had convinced himself that this was not only possible but preferable. It freed up the small amount of money he had for buying items such as a desk, for which he paid fourteen dollars to "indulge my idea of order in the arrangement of my papers etc. to their fullest extent."[28]

One must suspect that, then as now, young men abused their bodies in all manner of ways, thinking that it would never make any difference to their later health or well-being. Ellsworth was stoically convinced that enduring such deprivations would strengthen his character, enabling him to rise above such mundane needs as hunger or rest. His diary, kept sporadically until August 25,

---

27 Elmer Ellsworth to Carrie Spafford, April 17, 1859, KCWM/LFAC.

28 Elmer Ellsworth, diary, early April 1859, KCWM/LFAC.

1859, told another story. Starvation is never a good choice, even for an otherwise-healthy young man. Sleeping on a wooden floor has drawbacks as well. His normally dramatic letters to Carrie soon included complaints of blinding headaches, a severe cold and cough, and light-headedness. His physical condition did not help his studying. He complained of not being able to understand or retain the law he was reading. Sick and starving, Ellsworth quickly became depressed as well. Nevertheless, his now-lean appearance and hunger-brightened eyes proved irresistible to women. He wrote in his diary of "close escapes" involving General Swift's daughter, who flirted with him when he was visiting the Swifts, and of a young woman (allegedly of a respectable family) who stalked him at a photographer's studio. He had also renewed his "friendship" with "Mrs. _____." This time, however, Ellsworth had promised to marry another woman. He quickly realized that the older, married lady was still interested in him as more than a friend. After a binge-eating episode involving a plate of buckwheat pancakes, he went to "Mrs. _____'s" home. His own words explain it best:

> I told her that it was not right for me to see her and I would not call there again as I was convinced that it would only work us both harm, told her I loved a young lady and was engaged to be married to her. She said that [the engagement] could make no difference to her feelings toward me, she is most persevering in her love. . . . She had found out nearly the extent of my resources and insisted upon my accepting money. To do her justice, she was as delicate about it as possible. I bid her good bye and came home in a perfect shower of rain. I dared not stay any longer.[29]

Again, Ellsworth's preferred occupation—the military—appeared in time to rescue him from complete despair. When he had returned to Chicago the previous fall, he renewed his friendship with some of the members of the Chicago National Guard Cadets. By mid-April, Ellsworth was informed that he had been elected captain of the Cadets, although he did not know he was even being considered for the position. The Cadets had disintegrated as a militia unit during the time Ellsworth had been away. They had continued to drill in the standard way, according to the West Point drill manual. The men were bored, and their efforts attracted neither interest nor audiences. Ellsworth was unsure about accepting the captaincy. He wrote in his diary that, as he was involved in his law studies, he would only be able to give the struggling group his attention one night a week. He was not

29 Elmer Ellsworth, diary, April 23 to May 28, 1859, KCWM/LFAC.

sure this would be enough to "build them up," and he did not want to be blamed if the group disbanded permanently. He had also decided that, if he took on this responsibility, it would be with the agreement that the militia team would learn his Zouave drill.

He chose not to refuse the offer outright and agreed to meet with the entire company a week later, on a Tuesday, when he would give them his final decision. One may imagine the temptation of this opportunity for Ellsworth. He was torn between his sense of responsibility to Carrie and her father to stay at his studies, and his need to get out of the hated law office and onto the parade ground, doing what he loved best with a group of men he already knew and respected. The outcome of the meeting was certain before it even occurred. He met with the unit, looked them over, made a rousing twenty-minute speech, and took the job. The very next day, to the detriment of his law work, he copied a "Pledge of Consent for the Cadets," and arranged a subscription plan to raise some much-needed money.

By Friday of the same week, he had met with unit representatives several times and was actively engaged in drilling the men. Unfortunately, rumors were begun claiming that Ellsworth had "pulled strings" to be elected to his post as head of the Chicago Cadets. These attempts to blacken Ellsworth's good name with slandering rumors got as far as Rockford. Mr. Spafford was upset to find that his future son-in-law had abandoned the study of jurisprudence and returned to the specious work of teaching grown men how to walk in a straight line. Ellsworth found himself explaining his actions in letters to Carrie and her mother, hoping each would intercede on his part to smooth things over with Mr. Spafford. To make things even more complicated, Ellsworth was severely plagued by body aches, headaches, a sinus infection, and finally, a completely decayed back tooth.[30]

Only one aspect of Ellsworth's condition had improved. He bought a "lounge" for $3.75, which now gave him a place to sleep other than the floor of Mr. Cone's office. He added an overcoat to the skimpy blanket under which he had been unsuccessfully trying to sleep, although pain due to the toothache kept him awake. None of this changed his determination to continue along his appointed course. On May 6, he wrote and tacked up an inspirational message to himself:

30 Elmer Ellsworth, diary, April 30 into mid-May 1859, KCWM/LFAC.

So aim to spend your time, that at night when looking back upon the disposal of the day, you will find no time misspent no hour no moment even that has not resulted in some benefit no action that had not a purpose in it.[31]

Below this he listed his weekly schedule. On Monday, Thursday, and Saturday he got up at 5:00 a.m., studied law until 10:00, copied for Mr. Cone from 10:00 until 1:00 p.m., studied (again) from 4:00 until 7:00, and then exercised from 7:00 until 8:00. On Tuesday, Wednesday, and Friday he slept in for an extra hour, rising at 6:00 a.m. He studied until 10:00, worked for Mr. Cone until 1:00 p.m., studied and copied from 1:00 until 7:00, and drilled the Cadets from 7:00 until 11:00 p.m.[32] No place in the schedule had been allowed for meals, so perhaps hunger had made Ellsworth delirious enough to believe he could keep to such a program.

Just as he followed his own strict regimen, he expected the Cadets to obey certain rules as well: "I told the Cadets if they wanted a company of soldiers in every sense of the word and were anxious to make that company a source of improvement morally as well as physically then I would command them and commanding them would enforce the strictest discipline."[33] The Cadets had to be willing to be governed by Ellsworth's wishes, which included the rule that any member would be promptly expelled if he were found entering a saloon in uniform or otherwise indulging in conduct unbecoming a gentleman. If they did not agree to work hard to place their militia group in a top position by perfecting the Zouave drill, he would have nothing to do with them. In a testament to his abilities to lead groups of men, he was "unanimously elected" as their captain. From this time forward, the Cadets were, to a man, his.

By June 4, he felt he had them where they needed to be in order to achieve his lofty goals. "What a glorious thing it is, to feel that you control the minds of men," Ellsworth wrote.[34] Eight days later, at a rousing meeting in which he praised the progress the unit had made, he enumerated their advantages. They now possessed "the best Armory, the finest uniform, and . . ." when suddenly a Cadet shouted out, ". . . and the gayest Captain in the country!" There was loud applause, and

31 Elmer Ellsworth, diary, May 6, 1859, KCWM/LFAC.

32 Ibid.

33 Elmer Ellsworth, diary, April 29, 1859, KCWM/LFAC.

34 Elmer Ellsworth, diary, June 10, 1859, KCWM/LFAC.

Ellsworth stood, smiling and proud.[35] No one knew that the "gayest Captain in the country" was also the hungriest.

Ellsworth's health continued to deteriorate, which made it difficult for him to work to capacity at Cone's office, build the militia, and continue to write loving letters to Carrie. Mr. Spafford's objections to Ellsworth's apparent lack of concern about his promise to study law were a continual worry. Letters from this period portray Ellsworth in a defensive posture, continually trying to justify his decisions to the Spaffords and to Carrie. It became evident that he was exhausted and ill, as his letters were often cranky, disorganized, and self-serving. On May 13, he wrote of attempting to buy some dried meat, being "so sick of crac." The clerk apparently noticed that Ellsworth seemed ill. He tried to give the meat to him for free, as it was a small amount. Ellsworth still had his pride and refused the offer, then went into a "segar store" and bought a "dozen segars" which added up to about the same cost as the meat. A trade was made, and Ellsworth was able to eat something besides "crac" that evening and keep his ego intact.

On May 14, he complained to his diary that his tooth was worse than ever. Two days later he wrote, "My health has never been so bad as at present, my catarrh of which I thought myself completely cured has returned and when I study an hour steadily my head becomes like a furnace."[36] His diary continued with similar complaints until June 12, when he fell victim to a fainting spell. The next day he wrote, "I have not the slightest idea how or when I wrote the preceding page."[37] During the time he was ill, he continued to drill his Cadets, worked to open a new armory, and won fencing matches. Perhaps Gen. Swift helped the struggling young man as he had before, or perhaps Ellsworth abandoned the starvation diet, sold the desk, and got his tooth pulled. There is no way to know, as the diary concludes soon afterward, with no other mention of health matters. The only clue in existence to Ellsworth's mindset at this time is a passage from a letter to Carrie on May 9:

> Yes, Carrie, I have changed my mind and have taken command of the Cadets for a limited time. . . . I have an object in view, which would justify me even in laying aside my studies

35 Elmer Ellsworth, diary, June 4, 1859, KCWM/LFAC.

36 Elmer Ellsworth, diary, May 14 and 16, 1859, KCWM/LFAC.

37 Elmer Ellsworth, diary, June 13, 1859, KCWM/LFAC.

entirely untill [sic] after the 4th of July, (the time for which I have accepted the command). ... I have changed the company entirely and in every particular, uniform and all.[38]

As with anything innovative, the idea of the Zouave drill was not readily accepted among local militia groups. Not every organization wanted to learn it and, considering its physicality, some members were no doubt unable to perform the athletic tumbling runs and intricate positions. But Ellsworth's group—*his* men—was eager to learn the drill. Independence Day would introduce them as the United States Zouave Cadets, masters not only of the traditional military drill, but of the new and exciting Zouave drill as well.

As June ended and July began, Chicagoans grew excited about the upcoming militia presentation. General Swift sent letters of encouragement, and Ellsworth began to receive (and refuse) offers to drill other companies. Militia groups from surrounding cities, having heard the "buzz" about Ellsworth's new Zouave drill, were writing to ask permission to join the celebration planned for the Fourth. Even the Chicago Volunteer Fire Brigade wanted to be part of the excitement. This was especially meaningful to Ellsworth; in June his name had been presented for membership in the Brigade, but he was rejected. Now things had come full circle, and the Fire Brigade was forced to ask Ellsworth for a favor. Graciously, he allowed them to be part of the parade, which took place in front of Chicago's luxurious Tremont House.[39]

Two of Ellsworth's diary entries, one for July 3 and the other for July 5, describe this exciting time:

> July 3—Tomorrow will be an eventful day to me, Tomorrow I have to appear in a conspicuous position before thousands of citizens an immense number of whom without knowing me except by sight are prejudiced against me. Tomorrow will demonstrate the truth or falsity of my assertions that the citizens would encourage military companies if they were worthy of respect. It is a trial I have courted let it come, tho' it is scarcely a pleasant thing to place yourself in a position where men who think you are a devil or a fool are to decide upon your merit and make or mar your reputation.[40]

38 Elmer Ellsworth to Carrie Spafford, May 9, 1859, KCWM/LFAC.

39 Elmer Ellsworth, diary, July 3, 1859, KCWM/LFAC.

40 Ibid.

July 5—Victory, and thank God a triumph for me. This day has well nigh established my reputation . . . our Boys looked very handsomely in their new uniforms and equipment and marched like old veterans . . . we commenced our movements first in quick time, then on the run . . . a chalk line could have been drawn across the front of the company and touched every man alike, we cleared the crowd like chaff and such a cheer as we recd, I never heard given to a military Co before. From that time until the close of the drill, the crowd was absolutely enthusiastic, applauding every new movement and cheering alternately the company and myself.[41]

After the Cadets performed their Zouave drill, no other company would take the field. Ellsworth's dominance, and that of his Zouaves, was complete.

The *Chicago Tribune*, which had not been a "fan" of militia companies, gave the United States Zouave Cadets a long, positive review, ending with the observation that "all who saw the drill yesterday morning . . . say the company cannot be surpassed this side of West Point. The regulation in regard to liquor &c was rigidly enforced. The effect on the boys has been excellent, it has given them a name to be proud of and upheld and they will conduct themselves accordingly."[42]

From all the personal disappointments of 1857 and 1858, by the summer of 1859 Elmer Ellsworth had emerged triumphant. "Victory and thank God!," he wrote.[43] No one realized at the time that this would be Elmer Ellsworth's penultimate July 4.

---

41 Elmer Ellsworth, diary, July 5, 1859, KCWM/LFAC.

42 Ibid.; *Chicago Tribune*, July 5, 1859, *et al.* Online version: ProQuest Historical Newspapers: *Chicago Tribune*, sfx.carli.illinois.edu/sfxuiu?rft.object_id=63750000000000183&ctx _ver= Z39.88-2004&rfr_id=info%3Asid%2Fsfxit.com%3Aazlist&sfx.ignore_date_threshold=1, accessed July 1, 2016.

43 Elmer Ellsworth, diary, July 4, 1859, KCWM/LFAC.

Chapter 5

1-2-3-4-5-6-7-8-Tiger! Zouaves!

"... he required the greatest sacrifices of his men & secured their compliance by performing twice as much himself. He possesses remarkable power of controlling and animating his men, which is one secret of his success, as an instructor & disciplinarian. For four months previous to the trip he would attend to business during the day—drill the company from 7 till 12 oclock, then study & write until 4 or 5 oclock in the morning—lie down anywhere, on a bench or sofa sleep until 9 & then work again."

Elmer Ellsworth, from an autobiographical manuscript entitled "Tribune No. 3."[1]

THE sparkle of Elmer Ellsworth's Independence Day triumph began to dim immediately. On July 7, 1859, he wrote in his diary, "Attempted to work, but failed. I can do nothing with the same energy that I could bring to bear when I was living like a human being."[2] He knew he had to continue with both his law study and the militia drilling, but was also terribly concerned that his bright success on the parade ground might have a more sinister, personal aspect to it. The dreaded letter finally arrived on July 11. The Spaffords wanted to see him.

Ellsworth was torn between the promises he had made to the girl he loved and her family, and the sadly irrefutable fact that he hated law, the study of law, law offices, and everything about the whole legal business, except perhaps lawyers themselves. What happened next was pivotal for Elmer Ellsworth. His life, until this point, had been without real purpose. He had accomplished small goals one by

---

1 Elmer Ellsworth, "Tribune No. 3," BU/JHC. There exist several manuscripts in Ellsworth's writing and signed by him that are written in the third person and appear to be intended for newspaper publication.

2 Elmer Ellsworth, diary, July 7, 1859, BU/JHC.

one, with no larger schema in which to fit them. His next two weeks would be filled with disappointment, reflection, and self-pity. By the end of that time, however, he would emerge the dynamic, focused man he needed to be in order to become the first military hero of the Union. In little more than a year, he would pin upon the breast of his United States Army colonel's uniform a gold circle pin bearing the motto *Non Solum Nobis sed Pro Patria* ("Not for Ourselves Alone, but for Country"), words which many would come to know in the years to follow.[3]

On July 14, just ten days after his Chicago triumph, Elmer Ellsworth arrived in Rockford. It is easy to imagine his discomfort. The Spaffords, disapproving; Ellsworth, nervous, worried that he was in danger of being denied his fiancée. Nowhere in Ellsworth's history were there any recorded incidents of parental confrontation. He had been his own man since he was fifteen, if not before, and his compartmentalized thinking made it impossible to consider letting another person take charge of his future. Ellsworth's personal scruples remained inflexible. He wrote in his diary that night:

> . . . had some conversation with Mrs. S [Spafford] in regard to my relations with the family, told her as long as people chose to listen to the stories of my enemies [concerning his law future] I felt that it must annoy her and Mr. S. and I should release Mr. S. from his promises to me and [they] need feel under no further obligation to treat me other than a stranger until time and my exertions had caused a change in the minds of those who now misunderstood and malign me. Mrs. S. insisted that I should dismiss the matter from my mind and do nothing about it. I felt, I had done and was about to do my duty, the highest and strictest sense of honor could demand nothing more, though in doing so I was about to dismiss so to speak my best almost my only friends. Then a sense of my utter lonelyness [sic], of my embarrassing position, of all that I have to contend with swept across my mind and for once I could not help it, I indulged in a real womanish cry. . . . after it, I was calmer and more resolute. I fancy, Mr. S., although I believe he respects me, likes me when I am present, yet when he thinks of my position and that his daughter might have married some person of greater wealth he must feel in his own mind that he would have been better pleased had I never met Carrie. This was what determined me to release him from his promises or permission rather. Had something to eat to day, and sleep on a bed to night.[4]

---

3 Ashley M. Byrock, *Embalming in Memory: Mourning, Narrativity, and Historiography in the Nineteenth-century Unites States* (Seattle: Northwest University, 2008), 168, online version: www.worldcat.org/title/embalming-in-memory-mourning-narrativity-and-historiography-in-the-nineteenth-century-united-states/oclc/607112261, accessed July 5, 2016; Randall, *Colonel Elmer Ellsworth*, 190, 254.

4 Elmer Ellsworth, diary, July 14, 1859, KCWM/LFAC.

"Doesticks" often accompanied his humorous
articles with illustrations.
Harper's Weekly

Because, for all his experience, and for all his perseverance, Elmer Ellsworth was still a young man, just twenty-two years old.

Eight days later, a happier but no less dramatic Ellsworth, feeling renewed by his visit and with his engagement still in place, left Rockford on July 22. He was accompanied by the memory of the soft strains of a cornet band. He had been awakened the night before by the sounds of a small group of musicians who had come to present a serenade to Mrs. Spafford. His diary records the moon as being bright, a soft breeze coming off the river, and the sound of the band playing sweetly to his host's wife:

> . . . it pictured in my mind such scenes of happiness as I fear I may never enjoy. I almost think I have two natures separate and distinct, following the promptings of one. I would want my parents comfortably and happily situated, my brother an honest high-minded man, a house adorned and beautified by the presence of such a noble woman as I could love with my whole soul, an honorable and respected name. This would constitute happiness, my ambition would extend no further although distinction at the hands of the public would give me pleasure the absence of it would cause me no regret. The other, freed from all care, giving free rein to an ambition as boundless as the air we breathe, not for personal advancement merely, but to do good to my fellow man, making everything consistent with honor subservient to this. To estimate this latter or secondary peculiarity of my disposition I must have some powerful incentive.[5]

When he returned to Chicago, the details of Ellsworth's vision for his militia company were complete. By August 13, the United States Zouave Cadets had been drilled back to their July 4 excellence. They gave an exhibition drill that was

5 Elmer Ellsworth, diary, July 22-23, 1859, KCWM/LFAC.

The U. S. Chicago Zouave Cadets and the Light Guard Band—Ellsworth is center-right, facing forward. *Frank Leslie's Illustrated Newspaper*

well-attended and well-reviewed. They wore, for the first time, their new Zouave uniforms, which were soon to change military uniform styles all over the Northeast. People began to come to the new armory and watch the evening drill practices. With its hall and two parlors, Brussels carpet, oversized mirrors, and piano, the armory itself was undoubtedly a sight worth seeing. Ellsworth had already begun to add a series of songs and distinctive call-response yells to the Zouave performance. Plans were in place for the introduction of this revised, more stunning drill at the Illinois State Agricultural Fair. Humorist Mortimer Thomson, a journalist who signed himself "Q. K. Philander Doesticks," began writing a series of newspaper articles about being a Zouave, with a great deal of good-hearted exaggeration concerning the sorts of skills the group was acquiring. He wrote, "I generally walk on my hands around the table [of his boarding house] and give each of the boarders a patronizing shake of my slipper."[6]

6 Q. K. Philander Doesticks, P. B. (Mortimer Thomson), "The Progress of My Zouave Practice," *The Saturday Evening Post*, Spring 1859, online version: misterron. libsyn.com/ mister_ron_s_basement_1758, accessed July 5, 2016.

Word spread rapidly about the U.S. Zouave Cadets. Major Ellsworth would not ease up on the rules he set for his men concerning gambling and other less-than-sterling activities, especially while in uniform. He also made sure he still had their unquestioned obedience. He had to reprimand at least two men for drinking in public, and he made sure that the actions of a few did not besmirch the reputation of the entire group. Later, John Hay would write that Ellsworth's men "feared him as a colonel should be feared and loved him as a brother should be loved."[7] Ellsworth was still living in John Cone's law office, but Cone experienced financial difficulties that made it necessary for him to shutter his practice. Ellsworth thus had to find another place to live. In a letter to Carrie dated August 29, he indicated that he was not particularly upset about the matter. In a well-known quote from this correspondence, he told Carrie about an imaginary, dreamlike episode that had occurred to him at some point:

> This is a very extensive world sweet one and there are in it many people among them undoubtedly is some aged and obese gentleman possessed of a fabulous fortune, in his own right, and a gold headed cane, who only awaits a convenient opportunity to pat me on the head and adopt me as his own. I expect to meet this individual about the same time my fortune changes and I can see in the future something else than mis-fortune and disappointment. . . . at the 'U. S. Agricultural Fair' there is to be a prize of a handsome stand of colors given to the best drilled military company. We are to compete, but unfortunately, owing to the short notice and the fact of having a larger number of new members who will not be fully posted in the drill, we shall not be able to take the Colors.[8]

Elmer Ellsworth may have been prescient by imagining the help of an older man in forming his future, but about everything else his assessment of the situation was woefully inaccurate, particularly about the outcome of the drill competition.

Seventy thousand people attended the Agricultural Fair the night the U.S. Zouave Cadets won the "Prize Stand of Colors." For the first part of their exhibition, the team performed the Hardee drill, and after a brief intermission, they returned and presented their now even more spectacular Zouave drill. The only other military group to compete was the Highland Guard of Chicago. When the

---

7 John Hay, "Ellsworth," *The Atlantic Monthly*, July 1861, Vol. 8, number XLV, 125, online version: play.google.com/store/books/details?id=OFkCAAAAIAAJ&rdid=book- OFkCA AAAIAAJ&rdot=1, accessed June 2012.

8 Elmer Ellsworth to Carrie Spafford, August 29, 1859, KCWM/LFAC.

winner was announced, a stunned Maj. Ellsworth stumbled through a short speech, received the championship colors, and handed them to his Zouaves. The six-foot main flag was two-sided, with blue silk on one side and white on the other. Embroidered on the white side were the arms of the United States, the inscription "Champion Flag," and "September 15, 1859." On the blue side, along with the words "U.S. Agricultural Society," a massive white star was appliquéd in the center of the flag. On the star was an American shield with a tiger head in the center. From this point on, the tiger became the symbol of the U.S. Zouave Cadets. Almost every newspaper in Illinois carried the story the next day.

The Zouaves' triumph quickly changed Elmer Ellsworth's life. In August, before the competition, he had met with the Illinois Adjutant General's Office about the possibility of an appointment to the staff, based on his legal experience. While there, he found that the position of state paymaster general was also vacant, as were posts such as adjutant of the 60th Regiment and state brigade inspector. Nothing had come of the interview, but just after the Zouaves made headlines with their triumph at the Agricultural Fair, Ellsworth received a large envelope containing information concerning his appointment as assistant adjutant general and paymaster general of Illinois. The envelope also contained his state militia commission. He was no longer *Major* Ellsworth—he was now *Colonel* Ellsworth.[9] He took on more work drilling other militia groups, such as the young boys at Linds University (later renamed Lake Forest Academy), a private school for the sons of the wealthiest men in Chicago. The students called themselves the "Ellsworth Guards."[10]

Winning the Championship Colors had given Ellsworth a valuable public relations opportunity, but the fact that only one other company had drilled against them created some degree of dissatisfaction among other militia companies throughout the Northeast and the South. The militia companies from the East Coast cities, some of which had been established before the American Revolution, laughed at the idea that a group of pretentious "prairie boys" would have the gall to call themselves champions when there had been no real competition involving an older, more established company—such as one of theirs. Rather than seeing this as a problem, Col. Ellsworth leaped into the fray, immediately issuing an international

9 William H. Bissell, O. M. Hatch, commission, September 1, 1859, BU/JHC.

10 Randall, *Colonel Elmer Ellsworth*, 149.

challenge to any drill company in the United States or Canada to compete against his U.S. Zouave Cadets, and he put the now-famous stand of colors up as the prize. He even offered to pay the competitors' expenses to Chicago and back. "Having received the Colors, and not caring to wear honors until fairly and unquestionably our own, we [have] determined to give opportunity to all . . . to contest our right to this honor."[11]

While waiting for responses to his challenge, Ellsworth drilled his Zouaves, and invitations to perform their exciting maneuvers in their fanciful, brightly colored uniforms continued to pour into Chicago. They received a trophy from Fond du Lac, Wisconsin, as well as a ribbon bouquet made up of ribbons donated by over two hundred women for drilling at a celebration to honor the opening of the North Western Railroad in October 1859. Also during this time, Mr. and Mrs. Ellsworth had put up with enough of brother Charley's drinking and poor work record, and asked Elmer to send for his brother. Elmer had always felt a large amount of responsibility for the sibling he had "purchased" so early on. When Charley arrived, Elmer, hoping to make some changes in his brother's bad habits, enrolled him in the Cadets.[12]

An event in the fall of 1859 had nothing personally to do with Ellsworth, but much to do with the poor condition of both the northern and southern states in the area of military preparedness. On the evening of October 16, abolitionist John Brown and a total "force" of twenty-one men, including three of his sons, thirteen other white men, three free black men, one freed slave, and one fugitive slave, attempted to take over the army's arsenal at Harpers Ferry, in western Virginia. After a dramatic capture by Captain Robert E. Lee and his troopers, Brown was tried, and then executed on December 2.[13] The nation was approaching a time when people often spoke of armed conflict between its northern and southern regions. That local militias should not consider themselves ready or able to respond to a direct call for service was not a possibility for Elmer Ellsworth. He knew he

11 Elmer Ellsworth to Carrie Spafford, October 9, 1859; "Challenge" issued to local newspapers, September 30, 1859, KCWM/LFAC. Funding for local militias, including the Zouave Cadets, was achieved by subscriptions and donations from private individuals and local businesses.

12 Elmer Ellsworth to Carrie Spafford, February 5, 1860, KCWM/LFAC.

13 Oswald Garrison Villard, *John Brown 1800-1859: A Biography Fifty Years After* (Gloucester, MA: 1910, Peter Smith Reprint, 1965), 678.

must do whatever he could to build up the military strength of the North. Although not first on his list of concerns, letters from this time indicate this broader point of view.[14] A year later, the election of Abraham Lincoln and the reaction of the South would put this concern directly on the front burner of those in the northern states.

In a letter to Carrie dated December 13, 1859, Elmer casually mentioned a plan to go to Springfield, Illinois, to drill the Springfield Greys for an exhibition performance.[15] On Sunday, December 18, Col. Ellsworth took the train to Springfield, anticipating only a quick look at the town, a meeting to firm up the plans to drill, and then a return to Chicago. The man with whom he met to complete arrangements concerning the Springfield Greys was Colonel John Cook, commander of the Greys and Ellsworth's friend from earlier militia activities. Cook was also a good friend of Abraham Lincoln, a Springfield lawyer and potential candidate for president of the United States. Lincoln read newspapers and knew what was happening in his hometown. He also had plenty of contacts in Chicago, who kept him informed of people and events that were beginning to create energy in the popular mind in that metropolis. Lincoln was aware of Ellsworth and wished to meet him. John Cook introduced the two men, and Lincoln was, according to Cook, very impressed with Col. Ellsworth. A little later, after Ellsworth had left Springfield, Lincoln and Cook discussed the young man. In Cook's personal reminiscences, he wrote that he was "in a position to know that Mr. Lincoln had a very special interest in Ellsworth and was making every effort to have him settle down in Springfield to study law in the Lincoln law office."[16] It was this informal, almost casual, meeting with Abraham Lincoln that changed the trajectory of Elmer Ellsworth's life, although it would take him a while to realize it.

By January 15, 1860, Ellsworth had already moved to Springfield (temporarily, he thought) and was drilling the Greys. He had been invited to stay with Cook's family, which welcomed and quickly accepted him. Elmer had the opportunity to see the Lincolns often, as they and the Cooks socialized together. Ellsworth became friends with the immediate Cook family, and with the Lincolns as well. In a letter to Carrie dated January 15, 1860, he mentions Abraham Lincoln to her for the first time. Ellsworth told Carrie he had broken his gold watch. Cook offered to take

---

14 Elmer Ellsworth to Carrie Spafford, January 29, 1860, KCWM/LFAC.

15 Elmer Ellsworth to Carrie Spafford, December 13, 1859, KCWM/LFAC.

16 C. A. Tripp, *The Intimate World of Abraham Lincoln* (New York: Free Press, 2005), 113.

the watch in for repair, and when he returned it, it had a new, fifty-dollar gold watch chain attached. "I felt some hesitation about accepting it, but he forced me to keep it. He is very anxious that I should come to Springfield next spring and study with Abram [sic] Lincoln if satisfactory arrangements can be made."[17] Cook certainly seemed to be the driving force behind the budding friendship between Ellsworth and Lincoln.

Two weeks later, on January 29, Ellsworth mentioned Lincoln to Carrie again:

> I don't know what I shall decide in reference to Mr. Lincoln's proposition, or rather Mr. Cook's. Mr. Cook told me that Mr. L especially desired him to leave no means untried to induce me to come to Springfield. . . . I cannot but regard that as a very great compliment.[18]

Ellsworth took Lincoln up on his offer soon afterward, but with one restriction—he would agree to work in the Lincoln-Herndon law offices *after* his obligations to the U.S. Zouave Cadets were met. On January 16, the exhibition drill in which the Greys took part was held, and Ellsworth returned to Chicago a few days later. He was now ready to give his full attention to drilling the Zouave Cadets in preparation for the competitive drill contests he anticipated, based on his earlier-issued challenge to compete with any other drill team for the title of "champion."

His friendship with Lincoln ensured that Ellsworth and his Zouaves would play an integral part in the presidential campaign of 1860, and also that Ellsworth would successfully pass the Illinois Bar.[19]

*   *   *

Just what was it about Zouaves that so enthralled the northeastern United States during the summer of 1860? Zouaves were anything but American. Their military clothing was based on that of the ferocious native Algerian fighters of the Zouaoua tribe, who resisted France's attempt at the colonization of North Africa in the 1830s. French army units styled themselves "Zouaves" and adopted versions of

---

17 Elmer Ellsworth to Carrie Spafford, January 15, 1860, KCWM/LFAC.

18 Elmer Ellsworth to Carrie Spafford, January 29, 1860, KCWM/LFAC.

19 John A. Lupton, "Forsaking the Law to Save the Nation: Elmer Ephraim Ellsworth, Attorney," *For the People: A Newsletter of the Abraham Lincoln Association*, Vol. 39, No. 1, 6-7.

the baggy pantaloon-style trousers, white leggings, colorful waist sashes, and short, embroidered jackets as their uniforms. Headgear ranged from the Algerian fez to Turkish wrapped turbans. In this era of intensely romantic Orientalism, when painters like Jean-Leon Gerome and Eugene Delacroix and writers like Lord Byron and Victor Hugo were creating exotic, sensual, violent, and voluptuous fantasies in word and image, the colorful "Zouaves d'Afrique" were romanticized as swashbuckling military elite.[20]

As part of an alliance of the British Empire, the Ottoman Empire, and the Kingdom of Sardinia, these French units took both their unusual uniform and their fast, furious, athletic, and gymnastically stylish drill with them when they entered the Crimean War, part of a long-running contest between the major European powers for influence over the territories of the declining Ottoman Empire. "wikipedia,org/wiki/Decline_of_thr_Ottoman_Empire". Most of the fighting occurred on the Crimean Peninsula, but smaller campaigns took place in western Anatolia (modern-day Turkey), the Caucasus, and on the Baltic Sea.

In 1855, a year before the Crimean War ended, British adventurer and writer Richard Burton published his *Personal Narrative of a Pilgrimage to El-Medinah and Meccah* in London. Photos of Burton in Muslim dress illustrated this chronicle of his journey to the holiest city of Islam. Burton's book helped reinforce the fascination of Europeans with the Zouave uniform and culture. In America, travel author Bayard Taylor entertained audiences with tales of his adventures in the Orient dressed in traditional Arab costume. So, American audiences were already primed for Col. Elmer Ellsworth's United States Zouave Cadets. As the fame of the Cadets grew due to the "challenge for the colors" and because of Ellsworth's personal charisma (and undaunted publicity grabs like writing his own third-person newspaper interviews), by 1859-60 all things Zouave became a fad in the northern and midwestern United States. Elmer Ellsworth did not create the Zouave interest all by himself, but he was where he needed to be, with all the right information and accouterments, when Zouave lightning struck.

As no militia companies had up taken Ellsworth's challenge to compete against his troops for the Illinois Championship Colors, Ellsworth decided to bring it to twenty of the largest cities in the Northeast. He raised the funds to do so by

---

20 Jerry Wasserman, *Transnational Cross-dressing, Intercultural Pageantry: Zouave Costume in Performance*, 22-23, online version: www.inter-disciplinary.net/wp-content/uploads/.../jwasser manpaper.pdf, accessed summer 2011.

soliciting donations. He got free passes from the railroads in exchange for the promise of publicity. Additionally, each city agreed to provide a place for the Cadets to stay for the duration of their performance.[21] With this in mind, Ellsworth again rewrote rules outlining the demands he would make of the Cadets. This time he called them the "Golden Resolutions," and they expanded the earlier promises he had exacted of his men. Each Cadet had to pledge, under penalty of expulsion and public humiliation (created when the name of the offender and a list of his alleged misdeeds would be published in all the Chicago papers) that he would not enter a drinking establishment, a house of ill fame, or a gambling saloon. Even going into a public billiard hall was forbidden due to the attendant drinking therein. Cadets were to wear their company corps badge at all times when in public, so that society could "judge for themselves of the manner in which the foregoing resolutions are observed."[22] It is a testament to Ellsworth's leadership and personal charisma that he was able to convince his Zouaves to sign the pledge and hold to it for the duration of the tour.

On January 23, 1860, the Zouave Cadets were appointed to be the Governor's Guard of Illinois. The tour had added the services of the Chicago-based Light Guard Band, and the morale of the group was high. Ellsworth, however, was again beset by worry. He was still considering Lincoln's offer, and wrote to Carrie, away at boarding school, in mid-January:

> I don't know what I shall decide in reference to Mr. Lincoln's proposition. I cannot but regard this [the offer to come to Springfield and study law] as a very great compliment. I believe that the influence of Mr. L—would do me great service. I mean the influence of his early example. He earned his subsistence, while studying law, by splitting rails, and it is said that at the age of twenty he could neither read nor write, so you perceive, Carrie, I have a greater advantage than he possessed. I can read.[23]

21 William C. Davis, Brian C. Pohanka, and Don Troiani, eds., *Civil War Journal: The Legacies* (Nashville, TN: Thomas Nelson, Inc., 1998), online version: books.google.com/books?id= rO2utXnI41oC&pg=PT212&sig=4f31en4hB7SwKuo2-RRXBpsYMX4&hl=en#v=onepage &q&f=false, accessed summer 2011.

22 Elmer Ellsworth, "Golden Resolutions," March 9, 1860, published in a variety of newspapers, including the *Chicago Press & Tribune*.

23 Elmer Ellsworth to Carrie Spafford, January 29, 1860, KCWM/LFAC.

Although Ellsworth was incorrect about Lincoln's reading and writing abilities, Lincoln inspired him. He wrote to Mrs. Spafford about the opportunity. "I was offered very great inducements to remain at Springfield, and still stronger ones to go there in the spring and complete my studies with Hon. Abram Lincoln. What think you?"[24]

In March, John Cook told Ellsworth, "My conviction that this is the place for you to commence life as a public man is unchanged." Later Cook wrote:

> You ask me if I have seen our friend Lincoln. I answer yes repeatedly and never without the conversation turning upon you and his expressing an ernest [sic] desire that you should make this place your home and his office your headquarters. He has taken in you a greater interest than I ever knew him to manifest in any one before.[25]

At this time, two young men, John Hay and John George Nicolay, became part of Ellsworth's inner circle. Hay, at twenty-two years old, was just a year younger than Elmer Ellsworth. He had attended prestigious Brown University, gaining a reputation as a good student and an excellent writer. Hay composed poetry (he had been named "class poet" at Brown), experimented with hashish, and received his master of arts degree in 1858.[26] After graduation, Hay returned to Springfield, where his uncle had moved his law practice. He became a law clerk in his uncle's firm so that he, too, could study law.[27] The firm was one of the most prestigious in Illinois, and its offices were across the hall from that of William Herndon and Abraham Lincoln.[28] Hay was only about two inches taller than the five-foot, six-inch Ellsworth. Both were very handsome, elegant men with charming dark eyes. Hay wanted to be a poet, but his family had put the same default plan to him as the Spaffords had pushed on Ellsworth: become a lawyer. He and Ellsworth became close friends, exchanging their innermost thoughts and hopes for the future. Nicolay had been born Johann Georg Nicolai in Bavaria. In 1838, his family

---

24 Elmer Ellsworth to Mrs. Abigail Spafford, January 31, 1860, BU/JHC.

25 John Cook to Elmer Ellsworth, March 15, 1860, BU/JHC.

26 John Taliaferro, *All the Great Prizes: The Life of John Hay, from Lincoln to Roosevelt* (New York: Simon & Schuster, 2013), 22-23; Howard I. Kushner and Anne Hummel Sherill, *John Milton Hay: The Union of Poetry and Politics* (Boston: Twayne Publishers, 1977), 11, 15-16.

27 Kushner and Sherill, *John Milton Hay*, 23-24.

28 Ibid.

settled in Cincinnati, Ohio, where he attended school and learned English.[29] Hay and Nicolay met in Pittsfield, the seat of Pike County, in 1851.[30] Nicolay worked for the *Pike County Free Press*, within three years, he was running the newspaper, and wrote many editorials favoring lawyer and politician Abraham Lincoln. Later, when Lincoln began to consider running for president, he asked Nicolay to come to Springfield as his secretary.[31] It was in the Lincoln-Herndon Law Office that the three men met. Nicolay was taller than Hay, and older by seven years. He was slender, with blue eyes and thinning brown hair. He wore a goatee, and his mien was much more severe than that of Hay or Ellsworth. Like Hay, Nicolay was fond of Ellsworth, writing, "I felt almost a direct personal pride and interest in his success."[32] All three young men, friends and companions, were to be a large part of the events that have become important in American history.

As May, the month decided upon for the 1860 Republican Presidential Convention, loomed closer, Hay, Nicolay, and Ellsworth volunteered their services to Lincoln's campaign manager, Judge David Davis. The Lincoln campaign team was new, and was working together on the national stage for the first time. Davis, a 300-pound man of determination, grit, and creativity, ably headed this slightly unorthodox group. Davis had ridden Illinois' 8th Circuit with Lincoln for many years and knew him like a brother. Lincoln's selection of Davis as his campaign manager was a masterstroke of political know-how. The judge knew that practical politics, seasoned with a touch of audacity, won nominations, and he worked tirelessly for his candidate.[33]

John Nicolay held down the office in Springfield and aided candidate Lincoln, who honored the tradition of the candidate not attending the convention. Nicolay made countless trips across the square to the Western Union office, supplying

---

29 Taliaferro, *All the Great Prizes*, 23.

30 Ibid.

31 Ibid.

32 John Nicolay to Therena Bates, May 25, 1861, in Michael Burlingame, ed., *With Lincoln in the White House: Letters, Memoranda, and Other Writings of John G. Nicolay, 1860-1865* (Carbondale, IL: Southern Illinois University Press, 2000), 43.

33 David Davis and Jesse DuBois to Abraham Lincoln, telegram, May 15, 1860, Abraham Lincoln Presidential Library Collection, Springfield, IL (hereafter "ALPLC"); Kenneth D. Ackerman, *Abraham Lincoln's Convention: Chicago, 1860—The First Reports* (Falls Church, VA: Viral History Press, 2012), 37-38.

Lincoln with telegraph updates all through those excruciating days in mid-May. Lincoln's order to Davis was "Make no promises!" Davis responded, in Chicago and safe from Lincoln's wrath, "Lincoln ain't here!"[34] Coming to the convention from Springfield with his uncle, a Republican delegate, was twenty-two-year-old John Hay. As soon as he arrived in Chicago, Hay left his uncle and volunteered his services to Davis. He was not yet an enthusiastic Lincoln supporter, but by the time Lincoln was nominated he had been won over.[35] Elmer Ellsworth was already in Chicago, finalizing various plans for the Zouave Cadets. He had volunteered not only his services, but those of his Zouaves, to Davis.

At 12:20 p.m. on Wednesday, May 16, 1860, the convention was called to order. The "Wigwam," the vast wooden building erected especially for the Republicans' gathering, was filled to capacity with 10,000 delegates, most of whom were supporters of William Seward of New York. An additional 20,000 to 30,000 people crowded the streets outside. That evening, the Lincoln team realized that they needed to have a more substantial showing of support for their candidate. Davis knew the right people for the job, and Elmer Ellsworth was one of them. The Zouave Cadets had already been the entertainment part of the festivities on the convention's first day, which was devoted to the acceptance of delegates and other organizational business. Their "exhibition drill" had been received with cheers and huzzahs, none more vociferous than those for twenty-three-year-old Col. Ellsworth himself. Ellsworth had been pleased to bring his men to the convention and was eager to help Lincoln in any way possible.[36] He was informed by Illinois lawyer Ward Hill Lamon, another good friend of candidate Lincoln, and Davis's resident dirty trickster, that there was something else he could do: bring on the local brass bands and marching units. Ellsworth knew every militia unit in Chicago, and the bands that supported them. It was Ellsworth, after all, who was giving Chicago—indeed, all Illinois—such a good name in the militia world, so he had a few chips he could call in. He assured Lamon that there would be plenty of marchers available, and music as well.

34 Michael S. Green, *Lincoln and the Election of 1860* (Carbondale, IL: Southern Illinois University Press, 2011), 57.

35 Taliaferro, *All the Great Prizes*, 31-35.

36 Green, *Lincoln and the Election of 1860*, 648.

Elmer Ellsworth and John Hay made the rounds of every militia armory in greater Chicago that evening. Ellsworth had promised Lamon that he would bring the flower of Chicago manhood—and their brass bands—to the streets surrounding the Wigwam to march and play for candidate Lincoln. Seward had brought only one band; Ellsworth would bring many more. The newly formed Chicago "Wide-Awake" club joined Ellsworth's marchers. Wide-Awake groups, which had sprung up all over the North in support of Lincoln's candidacy, were uniformed, well organized, and fearsome in their demeanor. The next day, the noise outside the Wigwam was second only to the din inside. Finally, as Lincoln's name was put into nomination, the "uproar was beyond description . . . a concentrated shriek that was positively awful and accompanied [by] stamping that made every plank and pillar in the building shake."[37]

On May 18, 1860, Abraham Lincoln won the nomination to be the Republican candidate for president of the United States. Elmer Ellsworth and John Hay were present for the event, as they would be for many others, and they cheered enthusiastically.[38] Lincoln did not attend, as was the current practice; but to make sure now-candidate Lincoln knew that Ellsworth and his Zouaves were firmly "in his camp," Elmer decided to take a howitzer to the roof of Chicago's famous Tremont Hotel. There he and his men fired off a blank cartridge. To avoid an accident, as if the entire undertaking were not risky enough, they decided to remove their boots while working around the black powder necessary to fire the charge. After the cartridge was in the howitzer, Ellsworth put his boots back on, and it was lucky for him that he did. According to storyteller James M. DeWitt, Ellsworth slipped while moving the howitzer into position, and only the heel of his boot kept poor Elmer from falling off the roof.[39] Perhaps this was the moment when Elmer Ellsworth permanently decided he was going to be one of "Lincoln's men."

*   *   *

37 Murat Halstead, *Caucuses of 1860: A History of the National Political Conventions of the Current Presidential Campaigns* (Reprint by Inman Press, 2008), 145; L. F. Anderson (?) to Elmer Ellsworth, August 24, 1860, BU/JHL.

38 Taliaferro, *All the Great Prizes*, 32.

39 Randall, *Colonel Elmer Ellsworth*, 174-175. A howitzer is a short cannon for firing shells with high trajectories at low velocities.

By October 1859, Elmer's younger brother Charley had joined him in Illinois. A year earlier, Elmer had written a long, admonishing letter to his brother reprimanding him for such offences as not improving his education or freeing himself of "all bad habits and low associations":

> In a word, if I come in a few months, and say 'brother, our parents have toiled, and suffered for us, until they are broken in health if not in spirit, now let us (as far as possible) discharge this great obligation; are you ready and capable of rendering me any efficient aid? Or, on the other hand, are you permitting yourself to associate yourself and mingle with that class, who lounge about, with no aim or ambition beyond keeping themselves supplied with segars and tobacco, and with opportunities for the indulgence of their low propensities?[40]

Upon his arrival, Charley was immediately mustered into the militia, as no position of employment was available to him at the time. In the early spring of 1860, Charley travelled with the Cadets to Springfield for a martial exhibition and, while there, became ill. He was diagnosed with typhoid fever, although Elmer's letters also show concern about smallpox. Ellsworth managed to get his brother back to Chicago and nursed him there. His correspondence to Carrie Spafford during this period detailed the progression of Charley's illness. In a letter dated April 1, he wrote:

> I am watching by the bedside of my brother . . . it is now nearly twelve o'clock. You must not look too closely at the remainder of this letter as I have just been compelled to turn the gas down until I can scarcely distinguish the lines, in order to let Charley sleep.[41]

Preparations for the departure of the Zouaves on their twenty-city tour were nearly complete when, on June 11, Ellsworth wrote the terrifying news to Carrie that his brother had taken a serious turn for the worse. Nine days later he wrote, this time from Mechanicville, that young Charley had died. Elmer explained to her that he had brought Charley's body back to his parents' farm for burial and would be leaving as quickly as possible. He did not even plan to attend the funeral. His concern for the health of his father and mother was intense, and Elmer was worried that he might be contagious. After leaving the body, in its lead-lined coffin, in Mechanicville, Ellsworth went to the Astor House in New York City to quarantine

---

40 Ellsworth, "Memoranda," 3-4.

41 Elmer Ellsworth to Carrie Spafford, April 1, 1860, KCWM/LFAC.

until he was sure he did not have typhoid fever or any other disease. He planned to return to Chicago as soon as possible, provided he did not get sick.[42]

Again, circumstances crushed Ellsworth's spirit. He had not only lost his beloved younger brother to disease; he also had failed to take care of Charley, breaking his parents' trust as well as their hearts. Charley had died on June 16, just days before the Zouave tour was to begin, and now Ellsworth was in New York, waiting to see if he was going to die as well. The waiting must have been devastating, but it was necessary. When he realized he was free of contagion, he rushed back to Chicago to get the tour back on track. The Zouave craze was building nationally, and Ellsworth was determined to ride its crest.

On July 2, Chicago gave its favorite militia commander, his team of U.S. Zouave Cadets, and the eighteen-piece Light Guard Band a grand sendoff; they were escorted to the railroad station by two other companies, the Light Guards and the Highland Guards. Ellsworth's fifty hand-picked men had signed the "Golden Resolution" pledge and were ready to defend their title of "the finest militia unit in the Midwest."[43] The Cadets would bring their precisely-executed Zouave drill to

42 Elmer Ellsworth to Carrie Spafford, March 25, 1860; April 1, 1860; June 20, 1860; KCWM/LFAC.

43 Edward Gay Mason, *Fergus' Historical Series* (Minnesota: Fergus Printing Company, 1882), 75, online version: books.google.com/books?id=jdcNAQAAMAAJ&pg=PA75&lpg =PA75 &dq=George+Harris+Fergus+Elmer+Ellsworth&source=bl&ots=T0mUpX4-tp&sig=-bsJ IcpJw4oGCm7v8s10SgFhaVk&hl=en&ei=LdXdTbj0M4eisQOpwfSXBw&sa=X&oi=book _result&ct=result&resnum=1&ved=0CBsQ6AEwAA#v=onepage&q=George%20Harris% 20Fergus%20Elmer%20Ellsworth&f=false, accessed September 2012; Ingraham, "Elsworth," KCWM/LFAC.

Below is a list of the fifty Cadets who signed Ellsworth's Golden Resolution:
Officers:
Commander: Colonel Elmer E. Ellsworth
2nd Lieutenant: H. Dwight Lafflin
Surgeon: Charles A. DeVilliers
Commissary: Joseph R. Scott
Paymaster: James B. Taylor
1st Sergeant: James R. Hayden
2nd Sergeant: Edward Burgin Knox
Quartermaster: Sergeant Robert W. Wetherell
Color Sergeant: Bennet B. Botsford

Privates: Frederick J. Abbey, Gerrett V. S. Aiken, John Albert Baldwin, Joseph C. Barclay, Merritt P. Batchelor, William Beherand, Augustus A. Bice, Samuel S. Boone, Edwin L. Brand, James Alexander Clybourn, Edwin M. Coates, Freeman Conner, William H. Cutler, William Newton Danks, James M. DeWitt, George Harris Fergus, George W. Fruin, Harry H. Hall, Louis B. Hand, Charles H. Hosmer, William Innis, Louis L. James, Ransom Kennicott, Lucius

twenty northern cities in Illinois, Michigan, Ohio, and New York. They would perform before President James Buchanan and at West Point, and then would travel through Pennsylvania, Ohio, and Missouri, before finally returning to Chicago. Their first stop was in Adrian, Michigan. They were met, in pouring rain, by the local militia, the Adrian Guards. The Guards accompanied the Cadets to the newly named Camp Ellsworth, where they were to stay during their time in Adrian.

How an entire town could be so excited about a military drill team is challenging to understand in the twenty-first century; the U.S. Zouave Cadet tour might compare to a concert tour undertaken by one of today's popular music groups. People flooded into Adrian to see the Cadets' exhibition, which took place at the grand marquise diamond during the town's July 4 celebration. Adrian was awash in stirring martial music, glittering brass band instruments, waving flags, draped bunting, and handsome soldiers in colorful, exotic uniforms—it was all irresistible. The show was sold out; there was standing room only, and even that was crowded. The audience was mesmerized by the bright, swiftly moving spectacle, which required much skill and grace. Quickly changing, intricate movements punctuated by the staccato call-response between the Cadets and their star commander, Col. Elmer Ellsworth, held everyone in thrall. Just like the Zouaves themselves, the spectators quickly fell under the magnetic spell Ellsworth had woven.

John Hay, who knew that, unless feeling it himself, no one would truly understand the magnetism Ellsworth could create, wrote:

> No man ever possessed in a more eminent degree the power of personal fascination. That faculty . . . 'of winning, . . . moving, and commanding the soul of thousands till they move as one,' he enjoyed in a measure, of which the world will forever remain ignorant. He exercised an influence almost mesmeric, upon bodies of organized individuals with whom he was brought in contact. I have seen him enter an armory where a score of awkward youths were going sleepily through their manual, and his first order, sharply and crisply given, would open every eye and straighten every spine. No matter how severe the drill, his men never thought of fatigue. His own indomitable spirit sustained them all.[44]

S. Larrabee, John Conant Long, Waters W. McChesney, Samuel J. Nathan, William M. Olcott, Charles Crawford Phillips, Robert D. Ross, B. Frank Rogers, Charles Scott, Jr., Charles H. Shepley, Charles C. Smith, Clement Sutterly, Ira G. True, Smith B. VanBuren, Henry S. Wade, Sidney P. Walker, Frank E. Yates.

44 Michael Burlingame, ed., *Lincoln's Journalist: John Hay's Anonymous Writings for the Press* (Carbondale, IL: Southern Illinois University Press, 1999), 67.

Only someone with such a degree of charisma could make the summer of 1860 a "Zouave summer." What happened on that tour was described as almost magical. The handsome young commander and his company of men, built around the high ideals of the Golden Resolutions and the patriotism of nineteenth-century America, were taken into the hearts of the nation. When the U.S. Zouave Cadets left a city, spirits rose, hope refreshed itself, people made plans, and, perhaps, a few hearts broke. Each stop added its voice to those of the others, so that by the time the tour was barely underway, anticipation ran at breakneck speed for the Zouaves' arrival at the next town.

The Cadets usually arrived on a patriotically decorated train or steamboat, and were met by the local volunteer militia company. This extension of politeness was a standard way to welcome dignitaries and others of importance at the time. From there both groups paraded to the campgrounds where the Cadets were to stay. Whenever possible, Ellsworth preferred his men to set up camp. In this way he could keep a better eye on them, and it gave him a place from which to extend his own hospitality. Politicians, businessmen, and their families were invited to tour the camps, watch practice drills, and ask questions of the Cadets, guided by their charming host and often accompanied by the soft strains of the Light Guard Band. Both sides made graceful speeches, and the company received a huge variety of trophies, bouquets, flags, and other gifts of welcome. The pre-program activities always included a parade through the town by the Zouave Cadets, in their striking red, blue, and gold uniforms, in anticipation of the main event, the exhibition drill. The Cadets were certain to perform for their hosts the cheer that was quickly becoming famous: "One-two-three-four-five-six-seven-eight-Tiger-Zouave!" They played to enthusiastic reviews and Carrie, as evidenced by her scrapbook, kept track of her fiancée's whereabouts by collecting newspaper articles about the Zouaves' performances. Friends and relatives mailed them to her, and she trimmed them to fit the pages of her book.[45]

The Zouave drill itself was largely theatrical and heavily choreographed, with routines not included in any military drill book. The displays of agility were impressive, but not meant to be used on a field of battle. But one of the differences between the Cadets and other drill teams who did versions of the Zouave drill was that Ellsworth's men were proficient in both Hardee's and Scott's strictly military

45 Carrie Spafford Scrapbook, KCWM/LFAC.

drills as well. Ellsworth's exhibition included Zouave versions of such common drill maneuvers as "double quick," "lunging," "thrusting," and "leap to the rear."[46] The Zouaves humbled their competitors and awed thousands who came to watch their superbly choreographed performances, and their elegant young commander became an overnight celebrity. Although the intricacies of the Zouave drill were not appropriate for training a group of men to fight in an actual battle, the patriotic enthusiasm helped to provide the impetus that would soon be necessary to the buildup of the United States army.

Elmer Ellsworth could not have undertaken this tour at a more crucial time. What was shaping up to be the most important presidential election to date was going to be held in the fall. The Republican platform included limiting slavery to those states wherein it was already legal, but several southern states had let it be known that they would secede from the Union should Abraham Lincoln, the Republican candidate, win the election. Lincoln was personally opposed to secession, and the chances for war were increasing. The U.S. Zouave Cadet tour was patriotically effective in motivating thousands of men who would be serving in that war within a year. Their vigorous, highly practiced drill encouraged young men in, towns and cities all over the Northeast to form local militia groups and encouraged those units already in existence to attain greater proficiency. Newspapers consistently described Ellsworth as "the most talked-of man in the country."[47] The United States Zouave Cadet tour reminded citizens that depending on unprepared volunteers might have its drawbacks. This explosion of patriotism would prove to be a catalyst for the upcoming Northern war effort.

46 E. E. Ellsworth, *Complete Instructions for the Recruit In the Light Infantry Drill*, viewed on *The Authentic Campaigner: A Web Site For the Authentic Civil War Living Historian*, online at www.authentic-campaigner.com/forum/showthread.php?2614-Zouave-Drill, accessed summer 2011.

47 Burlingame, ed., *Lincoln's Journalist*, 68.

CHAPTER 6

Celebrity Summer

Here's luck to the boys who never say die,
The boys of the Tiger Zouaves;
The world, the flesh, the devil at once they defie
The boys of the Tiger Zouaves.
The Tiger Zouaves, the Tiger Zouaves,
The boys of the Tiger Zouaves.[1]

"Song of the Tiger Zouaves," author unknown

No important public occasion in the nineteenth century was complete without a glorious exhibition drill from the local militia, coupled with rousing patriotic music from an accompanying military band. Elmer Ellsworth can be given credit for increasing the popularity of these local militia companies throughout the Northeast in the summer of 1860. After the Zouave Cadets left a city, an instantaneous rise of imitators began. Homegrown militias adopted versions of the Zouave drill and towns that had never had them before suddenly boasted militia units. The public excitement was palpable as the Zouaves' twenty-city tour began. The *Chicago Press & Tribune* wrote just days before the tour:

> We beg leave to commend the Zouave Cadets of this city to the press of the east as young gentlemen whose military skill and discipline, and whose correct deportment and good habits entitle them to esteem and respect. They are about to visit a few of the larger Eastern cities; and if during their absence they teach other volunteer companies that the dissipation which too frequently accompanies amateur military exercise is only a detraction from the good name of the corps in which it is practiced, their visit will not have been in vain. We

---

1 Unknown, "Song of the Tiger Zouaves," KCWM/LFAC. This is the first of six verses found in the manuscript boxes at the Kenosha Civil War Museum, which contain some of Ellsworth's personal papers. It is written in pencil and, according to the notation accompanying it, should be sung to the tune of "Vive la Compagnie."

Alfred Waud sketched Ellsworth's Chicago Zouaves, bringing them additional notoriety. *Frank Leslie's Illustrated Newspaper*

believe we are not mistaken when we say there is not an unworthy young man in the company.[2]

After the July performance of the U.S. Zouave Cadets in their home city of Chicago, the press could not stop praising them. Was it the insistence of obedience to the "Golden Resolutions," which set a high moral standard for the members of the Cadets, or their athletic, organized, and beautifully executed Zouave drill? Was it the Zouave uniform with its gold flashes against red and blue, or the charisma of Ellsworth himself, evident by the unusual loyalty of the men to their leader? Perhaps it was everything. The Chicago press was charmed and supportive from the beginning:

Cadets on Tuesday evening last gave an exhibition drill in their splendid gymnasium in the Garrett Block (southeast corner of Randolph and State streets) and notwithstanding the

2 *Chicago Press & Tribune*, "The Zouave Cadets," June 30, 1860, online version: chicagotribune. newspapers.com/image/27626781/?terms=Chicago%2BZouaves, accessed October 23, 2017.

Cover sheet for the Cady & Root "Zouave Cadet" March showing the variety of uniforms worn by the cadets. *Library of Congress*

intense heat a splendid audience, among whom were many of the F.F.s of Chicago, attended it. The Cadets appeared for the first time in the Zouave uniform, which is of course just the dress portrayed in the illustrated newspapers, and is adopted by the Cadets as a fatigue suit. . . . There is nothing in it to impede the movements as there is in the stiff dress of the British soldier and the scarcely more conventional attire of our own regulars. If the Chicago cadets do no other good, they may lead to important dress reform. . . . As for the evolutions of the Cadets, we do not exaggerate when we say that even their most sanguine friends were surprised at the wonderful precision, rapidity, and difficulty of their drill. They cheered loud and long as one splendid evolution succeeded another, each in turn something that we had never seen before, or so perfectly performed that no one could recognize the old exercise. Major Ellsworth has done nobly and received well-merited applause.[3]

The Zouave Cadets wore three distinct uniforms. The full Zouave dress uniform consisted of a short, dark blue coat, blue pantaloons with buff trimmings, and a red kepi. The drill uniform consisted of loose, short scarlet trousers, high gaiters with leggings, a short blue jacket, and a red kepi, with the various articles trimmed in blue, orange, and red. The Zouave jacket had no collar—the neck was left free from the "choking process so common in . . . infantry dress." The brass buttons had a back shank, called at that time "bell" buttons. The jackets and vests were lined and faced with moiré. The fatigue, or "chasseur" uniform, consisted of neatly trimmed red pants and a blue sack coat. Ellsworth was determined that his men should cut a good sartorial figure no matter what the martial circumstance.[4]

With the good wishes of Chicagoans still ringing in their ears, the Zouave Cadets performed in Adrian, Michigan, on July 4, 1860. The cannon smoke and fireworks had barely cleared the air in Adrian when the Cadets arrived in Detroit on the 7:00 a.m. Toledo train for the second stop of the summer. Even at that early hour, they were met by the Detroit Light Guard, given an escort to the Michigan Exchange, and treated to breakfast. The rest of the day the Zouaves toured the city, again in the company of the Light Guard. Cheers of support and excitement followed them wherever they went. At 3:00 p.m., the Cadets and their band joined forces with the Detroit Light Guard and their musicians. Then both units marched to the Cricket Ground, an enclosure of about five acres. This "parade" attracted

3   Charles A. Ingraham, *Elmer E. Ellsworth and the Zouaves of '61* (Chicago: The University of Chicago Press, 1925), 32; Ingraham, "Elsworth," KCWM/LFAC; Robert Leibling, "America's Zouaves," *AramcoWorld*, March/April 2017, online version: www.aramcoworld.com/ ko-KR/ Articles/March-2017/America-s-Zouaves, accessed November 1, 2017.

4   "THE MILITARY FURORE; Arrival and Reception of the Chicago Zouaves Exhibition Drill in the Park Our Militiamen Astonished. THE RECEPTION OF THE ZOUAVES. EXHIBITION DRILL IN THE PARK," *The New York Times*, July 16, 1860, online version: www.nytimes.com/1860/07/16/news/military-furore-arrival-reception-chicago-zouaves-exh ibition-drill-park-our.html?pagewanted=all, accessed October 31, 2017.

over 5,000 men, women, and children, all eager to see not only the performance of their own Light Guard, but also that of the famed Zouave Cadets.[5]

The city of Detroit was not disappointed. The Cadets drilled for an hour and a half, going through "thirty different evolutions amid the applause of the spectators."[6] The only sour note, which was not made public, was the expulsion of a single Cadet for breaking one of the Golden Resolutions. Exactly which member is not known, but he was promptly stripped of his uniform, given a cheap suit of citizen's clothing, and a railroad ticket back to Chicago. All it took was one example—there were no more discipline problems.[7] The Zouave Cadets were enthusiastically appreciated, and when the company left Detroit at 7:00 a.m. the next morning, many new supporters were at the depot to cheer them on.[8]

After eight hours on the train, sleeping wherever and whenever they could, the Cadets arrived in Cleveland on the afternoon of July 6. They were met once again by the local militia company, the Cleveland Light Guards, who were accompanied by the Hecker Band. Artillery Company E, under the command of Captain Louis Heckman, fired an artillery salute in their honor. The entire group marched to the Cleveland Armory, where Ellsworth made a short speech, and the Cadets thrilled their audience with a performance of the Zouave cheer. Doffing their kepis and jerking them up and down in unison, the Cadets counted sharply from one to seven (the number varies in different accounts), ending with a shouted, "Tiger! Zouaves!," and the crowd went wild.[9]

The colorful, exotic uniforms always got good press, as did the look of the unit as a whole. Most of the Cadets were muscular and compact. Their rifles and backpacks were heavy, and all the men needed to be able to meet the physical standards for the tour, which required each one to perform the entire drill carrying his equipment. They had similar haircuts, a bit shorter than Ellsworth's own long curls, and many had grown mustaches, goatees, and what might today be termed "soul patches." At the Weddell House, where the Zouaves were staying, the Light Guard Band favored the crowd with several popular, patriotic selections. The

---

5 Doug Dammann, "All Glory and No Gore: Elmer Ellsworth's 1860 Militia Tour Helped Prepare the North for War," *Civil War Times* (December 2010), online version: www.historynet.com/civil-war-timeselmerellsworthand his zouaves, accessed fall 2011; Ingraham, *Zouaves of '61*, 70; Ingraham, "Elsworth," KCWM/LFAC.

6 Dammann, "All Glory and No Gore."

7 Elmer Ellsworth to Carrie Spafford, July 9, 1860, KCWM/LFAC.

8 Ibid.

9 *Cleveland Morning Leader*, July 9, 1860); Ingraham, *Zouaves of '61*, 70; Ingraham, "Elsworth," KCWM/LFAC.

company left Cleveland on Saturday evening, July 7, for Buffalo, New York, where they took some time for a well-deserved rest. Ellsworth wrote to his fiancée Carrie:

> We left on Saturday Evening escorted by an escort of Horsemen bearing torches and loaded with fireworks with which they kept the street blazing along the line of march. By the time we reached the Depot, at least half our men had boquets. [sic][10]

The *Cleveland Morning Leader's* review of July 9, 1860, ended as follows:

> We heartily bid the Zouaves good-speed . . . and if these two columns do not convince our readers that we go for the Zouaves . . . then let them call on us and ask us what we think of the United States Zouave Cadets of Chicago. One, two, three, four, five, six, seven, Tiger! Zouave![11]

Niagara Falls is about 20 miles north of Buffalo. Originally, the Cadets had not planned to visit the popular tourist destination, so no preparations had been made to receive them; but the men, many of whom had never been far from Chicago, were so enthusiastic to see this "wonder of the world" that the itinerary was changed. According to one of Ellsworth's letters, dated July 8, 1860, the group went first to Buffalo, where they were met by a small contingent of the Spaulding Guards, who were wearing civilian clothes rather than uniforms.[12]

The Guards, as a company, had prepared to receive the Cadets the day before. When they heard that the Cadets had been delayed and were arriving the next morning, they went down to the depot to personally offer their welcome. Ellsworth invited the Guards to eat with his men before they left on the next train for Niagara Falls. During breakfast, two gentlemen approached Ellsworth: Colonel Harrison Stiles Fairchild and Adjutant George W. Avery, surgeon of the 54th Regiment from Rochester.[13] Fairchild and Avery urged Ellsworth to bring his cadets to Rochester after the trip to the "Falls," and Ellsworth agreed to another change in the schedule. The Cadets, as usual, presented a handsome appearance during their visit

10 Elmer Ellsworth to Carrie Spafford, July 8, 1860, KCWM/LFAC.

11 Editorial, *Cleveland Morning Leader,* July 9, 1860, online version: chroniclingamerica. loc.gov/ lccn/sn83035143/1860-07-09/ed-1/seq-1/#date1=1860&index=0&rows=20&words=1860 +9+JULY+July&searchType=basic&sequence=0&state=Ohio&date2=1860&proxtext=July +9%2C+1860&y=6&x=15&dateFilterType=yearRange&page=1, accessed August 14, 2013.

12 Elmer Ellsworth to Carrie Spafford, July 8, 1860, KCWM/LFAC.

13 Patrick J. Egan, ed., "Rochester's Militia: 54th Infantry Regiment NY National Guard" (Rochester, NY, 2009), online version: www.scribd.com/document/16449496/ Rochester-NY-54th-Regiment, accessed October 20, 2017.

to Niagara Falls. They left on the 5:00 p.m. train for Rochester, arriving three hours later. To their surprise, all the local militias welcomed them with a parade and then accompanied Ellsworth and his Cadets to the local armory, where they spent the night.[14]

On Monday, July 9, the Cadets were escorted to Jones Square by companies of the Rochester 54th Regiment, with drums beating and bugles blaring. At 3:00 that afternoon, the Zouaves gave their much-heralded exhibition to over twelve thousand spectators. The audience was treated to a series of company movements from Ellsworth's *Manual of Arms*, then the chasseur drill, which consisted of skirmishing, deploying from geometric formations, firing, and retreating, as well as a demonstration of remarkable skill in the execution of the French bayonet drill. Cheering and applauding, the audience found the young Cadets irresistible.[15] At 8:00 p.m. the Zouaves accompanied the Lyons Light Guard to the east bank of the Genesee River, where all were seated to enjoy a tremendous firework display organized in their honor, which took place both in the air and on the river. The Cadets left for Utica, New York the next morning at 7:35. The Union Guards and thousands of cheering fans followed them to the Central Depot.[16]

Delayed another day because of rain, the Zouave Cadets pulled into Utica at 10:00 a.m. on Wednesday, July 11. The small city gave them a large reception at the train station. The 45th Regiment, in full-dress uniform and under the command of Major H. R. White, met and marched with the Cadets to city hall, accompanied by the stirring notes of the Utica Brass Band. Later in the day, the Zouaves performed their drill to the enthusiastically shouted huzzahs of thousands of Utica citizens. The *Auburn Daily Union* specifically mentioned "Colonel Ellsworth giving his orders with startling emphasis and energy—orders which were obeyed with marvelous rapidity and precision." The tired-but-satisfied men left for Troy the next morning.[17]

Troy—once home of "Elmer Ellsworth, paper boy and shop clerk"—now welcomed "Colonel Elmer Ellsworth and his nationally acclaimed Zouave drill

14 *New York Herald*, July 20, 1860, online version: chroniclingamerica.loc.gov/lccn/ sn83030313/1860-07-20/ed-1/seq-1/#date1=1860&index=2&date2=1860&searchType=a dvanced&language=&sequence=0&words=Cadet+Cadets+ZOUAVE+Zouave+Zouaves& proxdistance=5&state=New+York&rows=20&ortext=Zouave+Cadets&proxtext=&phrase text=&andtext=&dateFilterType=yearRange&page=1, accessed September 2, 2017; Ingraham, *Zouaves of '61*, 73-75; Ingraham, "Elsworth," KCWM/LFAC.

15 Ibid.

16 Ibid.

17 *Auburn* [NY] *Daily Union*, July 13, 1860; Ingraham, *Zouaves of '61*, 76-77; Ingraham, "Elsworth," KCWM/LFAC.

team . . . on their triumphant tour of the Northeast United States." Ellsworth's personal and professional reputation grew everywhere the Zouaves went. He was seen as the quintessential self-made man, brought to public attention only by his own efforts. Some of the most powerful political men in the North now called him their friend.[18] After each demonstration and drill, for which not a penny was charged, Ellsworth's Zouaves were escorted to the local train station by military companies and firefighters. Young girls ran to them as they marched down the streets of the small towns of the Upper Midwest, New York, and New England, bearing bouquets and charming letters proclaiming heartfelt, undying love. From a few hundred interested onlookers to massive throngs of many thousands, the crowds grew in size and enthusiasm as the tour chugged on.

In Troy, at 9:00 a.m. on Thursday, July 12, the Cadets were once again met at the depot by the local militia group, the Troy 24th Regiment, and its officers. They all marched to the Troy House, where a late breakfast awaited them. Several of the men in the 24th had also been members of Stillwater's Black Plumed Riflemen, Ellsworth's first military drill team, and their former commander greeted them enthusiastically. By 3:30 p.m., the Zouaves formed up in front of the Troy House and marched to Camp Wool, named for General John E. Wool, a citizen of Troy and a hero of the Mexican War. General Wool himself joined the audience that day to watch the maneuvers of the Cadets. Again, they demonstrated the Zouave drill, whirling from squares to crosses to pyramids to revolving circles and back. When they finished, amid the accolades, thrown flowers, and ribbons, Wool addressed the company, complimenting them, and stating that he had never seen their drill excelled anywhere.[19] By 7:00 p.m. the Cadets were entrained and on their way to Albany.

If the tour was going to be subjected to any bad reviews or criticism in the future, it likely would start in Albany, the capital of New York. Then, as now, New York audiences were tough and demanding, and the caravan had already experienced a one-day rain delay. Albany's own militia drill team, the famous Burgesses Corps, was the idol of the city, and they were not ready to give up their place in the public sphere to a group of Chicago yahoos. The train pulled into an oddly quiet depot. Earlier, Ellsworth had wired ahead concerning the delay, but perhaps no one had received the message, as no one was there to meet them. The Cadets marched about a mile to the Bleeker House gymnasium to spend the night.

---

18 Ellsworth was pleased that Chicago politicos such as David Davis, Abraham Lincoln, and Mayor John Wentworth were men upon whom he could call both socially and politically. As the U.S. Zouave Cadet tour moved across the Northeast and down the Eastern seaboard, Ellsworth's circle of powerful friends grew.

19 Ingraham, *Zouaves of '61*, 78-79; Ingraham, "Elsworth," KCWM/LFAC.

The lack of support initially concerned Ellsworth, but the next day, a lucky Friday, July 13, the story was considerably different. Albany Mayor George Thatcher hosted the rescheduled reception at city hall where the welcome was warm and sustained. By the time the Zouave Cadets got to the Washington Parade Ground, the crowd had swollen to 25,000 people, "including one-half of Troy," which had followed Ellsworth and his men to Albany.[20] The *Albany Journal* editorialized on July 14, 1860:

> Our citizens enjoyed a rare treat yesterday. The drill of the Zouaves, interesting to all, was to military eyes most exciting. Twenty five thousand people at least were attracted to the Parade Ground, and were charmed with the spirit, discipline, and perfection of the corps—a corps which, in the language of the veteran founder of our excellent Burgesses, was "an honor to the Drill Officer and to themselves." And the perfection of this company in military education is the more surprising from the fact that the officers and men are self-instructed. We do no injustice to the numerous and excellent military companies by whom we have been visited, in saying that the Chicago Zouaves, in thorough, effective knowledge and discipline, surpass them all.[21]

The famed Burgesses Corps treated the Zouaves to dinner at the American House. By 8:30 p.m., the Cadets were on board a boat, heading down the Hudson River to New York City. The places in which they had performed quickly recruited men for their own militia units, and Albany's Burgesses Corps now had to share their glory with the newly formed Albany Zouave Cadets.[22]

The press had begun to use the word "mania" in their reviews of the drills of the U.S. Zouave Cadets. Washington diarist, Crimean War correspondent, and current reporter-at-large for *The Times of London*, William Howard Russell, wrote:

> The Zouave mania is quite as rampant here as it is in New York, and the smallest children are thrust into baggy red britches and are sent out with flags and tin swords to impede the highways.[23]

20 Ibid.

21 *Albany Journal*, July 14, 1860, newspaper microfilm 2497; *Albany Evening Journal* (Albany, NY: B.D. Packard & Co., 1830-1925), online version: catalog.loc.gov/vwebv/search? search Arg=Newspaper%20Microfilm%202497&searchCode=CALL%2B&searchType=1&recCount=25, accessed October 15, 2017, Goodheart, *1861*, 205.

22 Dammann, "All Glory and No Gore."

23 William Howard Russell, *My Diary North and South* (Boston: T. O. H. P. Burnham, 1863), 129.

The crowds were building at every stop, firing cannons and waving banners. Historian Adam Goodheart quotes a satiric poem from the *New York Atlas*:

> They have come!
>   Who?
>   Again every man, woman, and child echoes the cry.
>   They have come!
>   Who?
>   Upon lightning wings the words reach the uttermost bowels of
>   the Union, and millions reiterate them:
>   They have come!
>   Who?
>   The far-famed military organization, the Tan Bark Sheiks
>   from Little Egypt, is in town.[24]

On Saturday, July 14, at 6:00 a.m., the Cadets arrived aboard the steamboat *Isaac Newton* at New York City's Cortland Street Pier along the Hudson. Cannons boomed in salute, and the local 6th Regiment stood in wait to escort Elmer and his Cadets to the Astor House for breakfast. Crowds of enthusiastic New Yorkers followed them along the line of march, up Broadway, around Union Square, and down the Bowery to the 6th's armory at Center Market.[25]

As Ellsworth called out commands, readying his troops for their first New York City exhibition drill at City Hall Park, he may have thought back to the first time he had seen the city, as a teenaged dry goods clerk. He must have remembered going to the drills of the 7th Regiment of the New York Militia, standing against the wall of their elegant armory, watching the sons of New York's "first families" drill as members of the "Silk Stocking Regiment." How gratifying it must have felt to return in such triumph.

At this particular performance, the Zouaves went through their maneuvers without any music or drum beat—a version referred to as a "command drill." There was no break in the line. Their speed and agility were uniformly perfect, guided only by Ellsworth's powerful voice. An examination of Ellsworth's *Instruction Manual* makes clear the intricacy of their drill. Even the operation of stacking arms seemed a feat of magic. Maneuvers first completed in quick time were repeated in double-quick time, and each movement demanded extreme

---

24 *New York Atlas*, unidentified clipping, July 1860, Library of Congress; Goodheart, *1861*, 201.

25 *New York Times*, July 18, 1860, online version: newspaperarchive.com/new-york- times-jul-18-1860-p-8/, accessed April 10, 2015; Ingraham, *Zouaves of '61*, 81-82; Ingraham, "Elsworth," KCWM/LFAC.

athletic agility. The Zouave Cadets performed perfectly. The subsequent dinner at the LaFarge Hotel, given in their honor on Saturday evening by the officers of the 6th Regiment, was a tribute to their collective skill and prowess, but surely Ellsworth felt a touch of personal satisfaction.

On Monday, July 16, the Cadets gave another exhibition, this time outdoors at Madison Square. The crowd began cheering the moment they heard the Light Guard Band marching to the Twenty-fourth Street Gate at 2:45 p.m. Ellsworth's men had just begun their drill when a violent thunderstorm interrupted the show. The Zouaves enveloped themselves in the red blankets they carried over their shoulders, quietly waited out the rain, then returned to the field amid cheers louder than the earlier ones. The drill exhibition was a resounding success.[26]

The next morning, Tuesday, July 17, the Cadets marched to Brooklyn, where they had promised to perform at Fort Greene. The level parade ground at the foot of a broad but gentle rise gave the Cadets a perfect field upon which to present their drill. The slope of the hill was filled by thousands of men, women, and children, cheering them on. Ellsworth's troops made such a positive impression on Brooklyn that later, when Ellsworth returned to New York City to recruit soldiers, the citizens gave him gracious support and a good number of volunteers.[27]

There followed a couple of days of rest and leisure for the Zouaves, who were encouraged to remember their "Golden Resolutions" as they toured the city. They were welcomed everywhere they went. On Thursday evening, July 19, the Cadets gave the only performance for which they charged money. They had promised to perform one exhibition indoors at the Academy of Music. Initially, Ellsworth was against charging an entrance fee, but when checking his funds, he realized that purchased tickets were a necessity if the trip was going to continue. The tour had already had some delays and donations were running low. Although Thursday evening was hot and muggy, the Academy's chairs were filled, and crowds stood wherever a place could be found. Along with the Zouave flourishes for which they were known, the Cadets added a "tap drill," wherein all the exercises in the manual of arms were executed to drum taps rather than verbal commands. Their grand finale, even more impressive in the confines of a theater, was an all-out charge to the edge of the stage, right up to the footlights. The result was "uncontrollable, and

26 *New York Times*, July 18, 1860, online version: newspaperarchive.com/new-york- times-jul-18-1860-p-8/, accessed April 10, 2015; Ingraham, *Zouaves of '61*, 83; Ingraham, "Elsworth," KCWM/LFAC.

27 *Boston Post*, July 21, 1860, online version: newspaperarchive.com/boston-post-jul- 21-1860-p-2/, accessed on October 31, 2017; Ingraham, *Zouaves of '61*, 85-86; Ingraham, "Elsworth," KCWM/LFAC.

loud, prolonged cheering, shouting, whistling and huzzahing" from the audience.[28] By the end of the evening, the glittering Academy crowd rose to its feet and gave the U.S. Zouave Cadets a standing ovation. Instead of looking like country cousins, the Cadets had made New York City their own. This performance generated no bad press reviews, and no criticism. In addition, they raised over $2,000.00, putting them on a secure financial footing for the rest of the tour.[29]

The following evening, Friday, July 20, the 6th Regiment (the "Governor's Guard"), in full dress as ordered by their captain, escorted the Zouaves to Vanderbilt Avenue. There, from a railroad building known as Grand Central Terminal (which was enlarged and renamed "Grand Central Station" in 1871), they left New York for Massachusetts. Although he must have been both busy with and distracted by his success in New York, Ellsworth found time to send a brief, affectionate note to Carrie Spafford. They had discussed the possibility of meeting while he was in Buffalo, but nothing came to pass:

> I have only time to express my intense disappointment at not meeting you at Buffalo. This is actually the first leisure moment I've enjoyed since we started. You can easily keep track of our movements by the papers—see the *New York Herald, Times, Tribune,* and *World,* from the 26th to the 20th of July. Write me at Baltimore, care of Capt. J. Lyle Clark. Don't fail to write me! I can write no more at present. Goodbye.[30]

The men's spirits felt renewed when the Cadets arrived in Boston on Saturday, July 21, at 6:00 a.m. The 2nd Battalion, a local militia group, was waiting for them. The 2nd had assembled at the Armory of the Corps earlier and proceeded to the Worcester Depot, along with the nationally famous brass band of Patrick Sarsfield Gilmore. From there, the Zouaves were escorted back to the city's armory. Later in the day, the Cadets gave a short exhibition, had supper at the Parker House, and attended a promenade concert at the Music Hall as guests of bandleader Gilmore. On Monday morning, July 23, the Zouaves were escorted to the parade ground at Boston Common. There, in front of an assembled crowd of 15,000, and announced by a thirty-three-gun salute, the Zouave Cadets performed their now-famous drill. The crowds had to be held back by a contingent of one hundred police officers, but the enthusiastically cheering fans followed the Cadets back to

---

28 Dammann, "All the Glory and No Gore."

29 *Boston Post,* July 21, 1860, online version: newspaperarchive.com/boston-post-jul- 21-1860- p-2/, accessed on October 31, 2017; *The Essex Institute Historical Collection,* vol. XXV, (Salem, MA, 1888), 222-223; Ingraham, *Zouaves of '61,* 86.

30 Elmer Ellsworth to Carrie Spafford, July 20, 1860, KCWM/LFAC.

the Armory. Later in the morning, the Charlestown City Guard and the Brigade Band escorted Ellsworth's men to Charlestown, where they spent the early afternoon sightseeing.

While visiting at the Navy Yard and the Bunker Hill monument, a familiar-looking young man walked up to Ellsworth. As he extended his hand in greeting, Ellsworth found himself looking into the welcoming face of Arthur F. Devereaux, his former Chicago patent company business partner.[31] They embraced and talked about the changes time had brought to them both. Ellsworth did not have to be reminded that it had been Devereaux who had initially introduced him to the Chicago National Guard Cadets. Devereaux was now a captain in the Salem Light Infantry. Salem was less than sixteen miles south of Boston, just an hour's ferry ride away, so when Devereaux invited the Cadets to visit the city, Ellsworth agreed instantly. They were met at the ferry dock by Devereaux's company, which escorted them to the armory. Equipment was deposited, speeches were made, and then both companies marched to the Essex House for supper.[32] When the Zouaves returned to Boston the next day, they gave one more indoor performance, at the Boston Theater. The audience was made up mostly of women, for the Boston belles were not willing to be shut out of the national excitement. From donations, the Cadets raised another $1,300.00 to add to their "war chest," but because so many had been turned away from the first performance, the company gave another one the following day, July 25. At the end of this performance, the spectators called for Ellsworth to return to the center of the stage. They stood and gave him three rousing cheers. The press considered this an unusual demonstration for a "sophisticated" Boston theatre audience.[33]

---

31 After he and Ellsworth lost their patent business in Chicago, Devereaux moved back to his birthplace of Salem, where he became captain of the Salem Light Infantry in 1859. After the fall of Fort Sumter, the Salem Light Infantry journeyed to Washington, where it was assigned to the 8th Regiment Massachusetts Volunteer Infantry for three months of service. The 8th Massachusetts was mustered out of service on August 1, 1861, but Devereaux immediately sought a place in a new regiment. On August 22, 1861, he was commissioned lieutenant colonel of the 19th Massachusetts, attached to the 3rd Brigade, 2nd Division, of the II Corps, Army of the Potomac. Devereux and the 19th Massachusetts played a significant role in the battle of Gettysburg on July 3, 1863.

32 *Essex Institute Historical Collection*, 222-223; Ingraham, *Zouaves of '61*, 87-88; Ingraham, "Elsworth," KCWM/LFAC.

33 *New York Times*, "The Zouaves at West Point: The Chicagoans Entertained by the Second Company, National Guard Exhibition Drill at Cozzens' Hotel," July 27, 1859, online version: www.nytimes.com/1860/07/27/news/zouaves-west-point-chicagoans-entertained-second-company-national-guard.html?pagewanted=all, accessed November 1, 2017; Ingraham, *Zouaves of '61*, 90; Ingraham, "Elsworth," KCWM/LFAC.

Throughout the well-planned tour, one particular incident stood out as a possible harbinger of a coming war. On Thursday, July 26, the Zouave Cadets performed for the staff and cadets of the United States Military Academy at West Point, New York. Lieutenant General Winfield Scott, the general-in-chief of the U.S. Army, and Commandant of Cadets William Hardee, both of whom had written well-respected military drill manuals, viewed the performance. The Zouaves went through their now-famous French drill, but Hardee's reaction to it was critical; he felt the maneuvers were showy and not at all practical. When Ellsworth heard about Hardee's reaction, he sent his men back out to the parade ground. In front of Scott and Hardee, the Zouaves performed the "Scott drill" and the "Hardee drill" flawlessly, "in strict adherence to the manuals." This time, both officers warmly received the perfectly executed performance. Even the West Point cadets were surprised that "a civilian militia corps could have attained such proficiency."[34]

Traveling aboard the steamer *Kennebec*, the Cadets reached Philadelphia on Saturday, July 28, at 6:30 p.m. An immense crowd had started gathering at the wharf as early as 3:00 that afternoon, but strong winds delayed the boat. The masts and decks of nearby harbor craft were filled with spectators, listening for the signal, "Here she comes!" Though half an hour late, the *Kennebec* finally arrived. The Washington Grays, Philadelphia's finest militia company, stood in a double line, waiting to welcome the brilliantly clad Zouaves. The Cadets gave their enthusiastic "Tiger! Zouave!" cheer, and the Grays marched with them to Jones's Hotel, where Ellsworth and his men would be quartered during their Philadelphia visit. The young men were exhausted by this time. They ate little, drank little, walked or marched everywhere possible, and were thin, tanned, and tired.[35]

The next day, Sunday, was a badly needed day of rest and recuperation, but on Monday the Zouaves marched to Independence Hall, where they were "received as representative of the citizen soldiery, not of Illinois alone, but of the entire Union."[36] Stretching back almost a hundred years to the Revolution, citizen soldiers had played a significant role in Philadelphia; no one realized precisely how important they would once again become in 1861. The Zouaves outdid themselves in the City of Brotherly Love. They did a drill demonstration in Fairmont Park that afternoon to an immense and welcoming crowd. The next day, Tuesday, July 31,

---

34 Elmer Ellsworth to Carrie Spafford, July 28, 1860, KCWM/LFAC; Dammann, "All Glory and No Gore."

35 Elmer Ellsworth to Carrie Spafford, July 28, 1860, KCWM/LFAC.

36 *Nashville Tennessean*, August 10, 1860, online version: www.newspapers.com/ image/ 119267441/?terms=Chicago%2BZouave%2BCadets, accessed on October 15, 2017; Ingraham, *Zouaves of '61*, 95; Ingraham, "Elsworth," KCWM/LFAC.

they gave another exhibition in Point Breeze Park and still another that evening at the Academy of Music. The exhausted men left for Baltimore that night.

The performance in Baltimore was a little different from the others. It was to be held at the Base Ball Grounds. The Cadets arrived Wednesday, August 1, and were met by the Baltimore Grays, Maryland Guards, Law Grays, and the City Guard Battalion militias. Ellsworth wanted to show his appreciation for such a grand welcome. When he saw the open-air stadium, he decided to make an addition to the planned program. This was not the first time he had done so on the tour, and his men were ready when the drill began at 4:00 p.m. They ran through their usual exciting, athletic skirmishes and performed the manual of arms in the Zouave manner, but then Ellsworth gave the command to "Fire at Will." The men fired blanks, of course, but they fired by file, by platoon, and as a company.[37] They fired while kneeling, reloaded on their backs, and fired again. One can imagine that last rifle shot, then silence, the field and the Cadets wreathed in ghostly trails of fragrant black powder smoke. As the haze slowly lifted, the U.S. Zouave Cadets were standing at attention, all eyes on their colonel, whose own eyes in turn were on the Baltimore citizens. The audience of 30,000 stood, clapping and shouting its approval. Baltimore would never again be so kind to Elmer Ellsworth, but upon that warm summer evening, the city was his.[38]

On Saturday, August 4, the Cadets, accompanied by the Baltimore Grays, left for their next performance, on the lawn of the "President's House" in Washington. This most anticipated performance of the summer was held on Sunday, August 5. President James Buchanan and his niece, Harriet Lane, reviewed the drill with delight. Buchanan declared:

The people in this country must be prepared, themselves, to defend their own rights and liberties, and their own firesides and their own altars; and whatever tends to induce a military spirit among the people, and render them capable of standing erect against a world in arms—that is surely patriotic—that is surely beneficial to the nation, to the whole country.[39]

37 In this instance, "fire at will" refers to a series of maneuvers designed by Ellsworth to showcase the abilities of his cadets to fire in a variety of positions. The Regular Army drill differentiated firing by battalion, by company, and by file. Ellsworth based his program on the drills practiced by the Regulars, but it was basically a series of choreographed moves.

38 *Baltimore Sun*, August 2, 1860, online version: www.newspapers. com/ image/214330582/? terms=Chicago%2BZouave%2BCadets, accessed November 1, 2017.

39 Doug Dammann, "Elmer Ellsworth and His Zouaves," *Historynet*, October 10, 2010, www.historynet.com/elmer-ellsworth-and-his-zouaves.htm, accessed May 30, 2017.

Cheering crowds followed the Zouaves as they marched along Pennsylvania Avenue with the Washington Battalion, the Marine Band, and the Baltimore Grays. The Grays and the Cadets left Washington at 5:30 that afternoon.

Finally, the end was in sight for the exhausted Zouave Cadets. They drilled in Pittsburgh, at the Fair Grounds as guests of the Duquesne Greys, the Independent Blues, the Lafayette Blues, Pittsburgh Zouaves, Turner Rifles, National Guards, and the Allegheny Rifles. Under the baking sun, in East Coast humidity, the Cadets marched, sharing the field with their brother units. After a short break, a hollow square was formed wherein Lieutenant R. Biddle Roberts of the Duquesne Greys presented Ellsworth with a valuable, historic sword bearing the inscription, "Presented to Col. E. E. Ellsworth, of the Chicago Cadets, by the Duquesne Greys, as an appreciation of their matchless drill." That evening, a train specially provided by Andrew Carnegie, the superintendent of the Pittsburgh Division of the Pennsylvania Railroad Company, took Ellsworth and his men to the depot, where they departed for Cincinnati. At last the Zouave Cadets turned toward home.[40]

They were to make two more stops, in Cincinnati and St. Louis. By now their woolen uniforms, after numerous marches and performances in the summer sun, were no longer pristine. The cheers, though still thrilling, were beginning to sound the same to those who heard them every day. The bouquets had long since wilted and been tossed away. The small pieces of paper containing names and addresses of "your best friend" were grubby and unreadable. The floors of the armories were getting harder, and the rich food was becoming tasteless. "The road" is never the ongoing celebration it initially seems. There is a point on every tour when everybody just wants to go home. The Cadets had reached that point.

On Wednesday, August 8, at 5:00 a.m., the train pulled into the Little Miami Depot in Cincinnati and was met by the Rover Guards, the Mentor's Band, and several hundred citizens who had braved the early hour to cheer for the Zouaves. They were escorted to the Melodion Hall, where they were to stay, and then whisked away to the Burnet House for breakfast. When the Cadets returned to the Hall, the usual speeches were made. There was not much difference in the text of the speeches—just a change in the place name. Ellsworth had his own set piece, tweaked for each host city, to be given in reply. His words on this occasion are printed in Charles Ingraham's *Elmer Ellsworth and the Zouaves of '61*:

On behalf of the Zouaves, I thank you for the sentiments you have expressed and assure you that we fully appreciate the spirit in which they were conceived. We thank you

---

40 George Thornton Fleming, *History of Pittsburgh and Environs* (New York and Chicago: The American Historical Society, Inc., 1922), 231; Ingraham, *Zouaves of '61*, 100; Ingraham, "Ellsworth," KCWM/LFAC.

especially for the manner in which you have alluded to our Eastern visit. We started east with great solicitude and many misgivings; we knew that . . . we should be obliged to combat prejudice in the minds of our Eastern brethren—the belief that nothing worthy of admiration in a military way could come from the West. . . . How far we have succeeded in upholding the military character of the Western people and in overthrowing these prejudices, it is not for us to say; we have done our best. We beg leave to thank the people of Cincinnati for the cordial reception they have given us. We feel more at home here than in any city we have visited; we are in a western city and among western men, and anticipate a great deal of gratification during our brief visit. Trusting that our own efforts may have contributed to the promotion of a true military spirit in the West, and that we may soon have throughout our great western states a military organization worthy of their proud and influential position in the Union, we return our sincere thanks to our friends for their generous reception.[41]

Reaching deeply into their tired hearts, the U.S. Zouave Cadets gave one of their most acclaimed exhibitions on Thursday, August 9. Under the heat of a late summer sun, the men performed at the Orphan Asylum Grounds before thousands, including the children of the asylum, who filled the windows of the buildings with cheers and flags. The drill piece "fire at will" again astonished the audience. Not only did the entire company undertake the nine required movements of the manual of arms, but they also added the firing of their rifles, all choreographed to end in a single shot. This was repeated three times—thirty movements, repeated perfectly. The Cadets gave another drill performance that evening, after which Ellsworth received a pair of epaulets worn by Captain Presley N. Enyart, who had served in the Mexican War and was the founder of the Independent Guthrie Grays. The exhausted men left for St. Louis by 4:00 the next morning.[42]

St. Louis passed in a blur. The Cadets arrived on Friday, August 10, at 7:30 p.m. They charmed the city with their elegance and military bearing, performed their exhibition at the Fair Grounds at 4:00 the next afternoon, rested on Sunday, and

41 *Cincinnati Daily Press*, August 10, 1860, online version: www.newspapers.com/ image/ 186746870/?terms=Chicago+Zouave+Cadets, accessed November 1, 2017; Ingraham, *Zouaves of '61*, 102; Ingraham, "Elsworth," KCWM/LFAC.

42 *Pittsburgh Daily Post*, August 8, 1860), online version: www.newspapers.com/ image/87566913/?terms=Chicago%2BZouave%2BCadets, accessed November 2, 2017; Ingraham, *Zouaves of '61*, 103; Ingraham, "Elsworth," KCWM/LFAC.

left early Monday morning, August 13.[43] The Zouaves had only one stop left on their tour: Springfield, Illinois, home of lawyer and Republican nominee for the presidency, Abraham Lincoln. Springfield was also home to Ellsworth's and Lincoln's mutual friend, Col. John Cook, who was now commanding Ellsworth's former unit, the Springfield Grays. Ellsworth had lived with John Cook's family during his last stay in Springfield, so the capital city of Illinois thought of Ellsworth as one of its own. The friends he had made in Springfield hoped that, after this tour was over, Ellsworth would move there to join the law practice of Herndon and Lincoln as clerk and law student.

The Springfield Grays, eager to see their former commander, met the road-weary Cadets at the train station. The Zouaves were escorted through the streets of the city by the joyful noise of a marching band and several thousand cheering locals who joined the impromptu parade. Later, on that hot afternoon of August 13, 1860, Abraham Lincoln and his sons stood under the shade of a cottonwood tree to watch Ellsworth and his Zouave Cadets perform on the Sixth Street parade ground.[44]

The sun glinted off the golden braid on the colorful, patriotic uniforms of the fifty young men, who executed their drill in flashes of bright red from their loose trousers, held tight to their legs by white canvas gaiters. Their collarless, deep blue jackets were encrusted with even more gold braid, and were worn over a soft shirt of light blue. They wore red kepis with gold braid designs and a black brim. The men performed in the hot sun for over two hours, smoothly and effortlessly forming stars, squares, and octagons. They lunged, withdrew, fell to the ground, and loaded their rifles from a prone position. They even built a human ladder and pulled the last man to the top, hand over hand, up a stack of rifles. Willie and Tad Lincoln watched the entire performance, but their father focused most of his attention on the small, elegant, boyish-looking man who skillfully led his team.

Lincoln had first met Ellsworth in Springfield in December 1859, when Ellsworth was drilling the Springfield Grays. Everything Lincoln saw that day supported his initial impression of the young colonel, especially his talent as a military commander. Lincoln often spoke highly about Ellsworth. "Ever since the beginning of our acquaintance, I have valued you highly as a personal friend, and at the same time (without much capacity for judging) have had a very high estimate of

---

43 *Pittsburgh Daily Post*, August 8, 1860, online version: www.newspapers.com/image/ 87566 913/?terms=Chicago%2BZouave%2BCadets, accessed November 2, 2017; Ingraham, *Zouaves of '61*, 104; Ingraham, "Ellsworth," KCWM/LFAC.

44 "Russell" to Elmer Ellsworth, August 14, 1860, KCWM/LFAC.

your military talent."[45] Lincoln later said of Colonel Ellsworth, "He is the greatest little man I ever met."[46]

On Tuesday, August 14, at 11:00 a.m., the Springfield performance ended. The Cadets finally turned toward Chicago—for *home*. When the train pulled into the Chicago depot at 10:00 that night, it seemed as if the whole city was waiting for them. The crowd that welcomed the returning Zouave Cadets back was, if possible, even more extensive than the one which had seen them off. Bonfires, illuminated buildings, brass bands, beautiful women, rockets and roman candles, Mayor "Long" John Wentworth, the Common Council, every military company in the city, groups of Wide-Awakes with their torches, the fire department, political clubs, social clubs, and unattached citizens—they all swarmed around the exhausted Zouaves, folding their "boys" back into their figurative arms. A "grand illumination" was presented.[47]

Later in the evening, the crowds escorted the tired young men to the Wigwam, which was still standing even though the Republican Convention was over. There, Mayor Wentworth delivered a congratulatory address, welcoming the Cadets home from their successful tour:

> We all claim you as our own. And, as our own, we have rallied to meet you tonight as Chicago people never rallied before. When you look around upon this vast concourse . . . you should remember that each and every one bears toward you a common affection. . . . Anxious, if not envious eyes have followed you from the day of your departure to that of your return, amid the enchantments of fashion, allurements of vice, and fatigues of body; but they have failed to find one single act inconsistent with the rigid moral discipline that has from the beginning been characteristic of your organization.[48]

45 Abraham Lincoln to Elmer Ellsworth, April 15, 1861, in Roy Prentice Basler, *Abraham Lincoln: His Speeches and Writings* (Boston: Da Capo Press, 2001), 592.

46 Henry Clay Whitney, *Life on the Circuit with Lincoln: With Sketches of Generals Grant, Sherman, and McClellan, Judge Davis, Leonard Swett, and Other Contemporaries* (Boston: Estes and Lauriat, Publishers, 1892), ebook edition, 548; "Elmer Ellsworth: Quick Facts," www.nps.gov/people/elmer-ellsworth.htm, accessed June 12, 2018.

47 Ingraham, *Zouaves of '61*, 107-108; Ingraham, "Elsworth," KCWM/LFAC. A list of the members of the Springfield Grays can be found at www.rootsweb.ancestry.com/ ~scprnyz/ ZouaveArchive/UnionZouaves/Illinois/Illinois_7thInfantryRegiment.html?cj=1&sid=j9j7w a7cro000bpr007mn&netid=cj&o_xid=0003952406&o_lid=0003952406&o_sch=Affiliate+E xternal.

48 *Sangamon Journal/Illinois State Journal*, August 9, 1860, online version: idnc.library. illinois. edu/cgi-bin/illinois?a=d&d=SJO18600809.1.3&srpos=16&e=—en-20-SJO-1—txt-txIN-Ch icago+Zouave+Cadets—, accessed November 1, 2017; Ingraham, *Zouaves of '61*, 109; Ingraham, "Elsworth," KCWM/LFAC.

A proud Colonel Ellsworth accepted the honors on behalf of his men, whereupon they went to the Briggs House at the corner of Randolph and Wells Streets for a banquet in their honor. They were toasted far into the night. Chicago politician James Hubert McVickers's salute seemed to sum it all up: "Well done, good and faithful soldiers."[49]

An analysis shows that the importance of the U.S. Chicago Zouave Cadets' northeastern tour cannot be overstated. It made Elmer Ellsworth and his Cadets the most famous men of their day. Platen after platen of ink was used to describe the thrilling visual spectacle of the Zouaves' performances, but no one could agree upon exactly what it was that left audiences breathless. Reporters created verbal snapshots of soldiers running in formation, turning somersaults, and doing handstands; the geometrical precision of the moving triangles, squares, crosses, and revolving circles; the flashes of bright color; and the combined movements of the bayonet thrust. It must have been a colorful, thrilling performance. For many people it was the commitment the men made to the "Golden Resolutions" of no alcohol and gentlemanly behavior at all times that rang so true: "That a company of our Chicago young men should travel the distance you have, amid so many exposures, without once partaking of the intoxicating cup, is a source of greater pleasure to us, your fellow citizens, than the unexampled honors you have received or your perfection in the military arts."[50]

Sometimes the Zouaves induced some gentle satire, such as in an article in one New York paper which exaggerated the prowess of the average Zouave soldier: ". . . if his commanders needed someone to reconnoiter the enemy's lines, a Zouave would climb into a skyrocket, blast a thousand feet into the air, and have a complete set of photographs and hand-drawn maps ready by the time he alighted on the ground."[51] Sometimes they induced poets to extol their virtues:

> Your Zouave corps, O haughty France!
> We looked on as a wild romance,
> And many a one was heard to scoff

49 *U.S. Zouave Cadets, Governor's Guard* (Chicago:1860), 29, online version: books. google.com/books?id=xhONR_s3B54C&pg=PA28&lpg=PA28&dq=return+of+Chicago+ Zouave+cadets+to+Chicago+1860&source=bl&ots=gA3GNXzfV8&sig=lgKc2u79c8pose uZmgmDYABlG-Y&hl=en&sa=X&ved=0ahUKEwikmuispKHXAhWH8oMKHZuABfw Q6AEIYDAO#v=onepage&q=return%20of%20Chicago%20Zouave%20cadets%20to%20 Chicago%201860&f=false, accessed August 3, 2015; Ingraham, *Zouaves of '61*, 110-111; Ingraham, "Ellsworth," KCWM/LFAC.

50 Dammann, "All Glory and No Gore."

51 Q. K. Philander "Doesticks," P. B. (Mortimer Thomson), "The Progress of My Zouave Practice," *The Saturday Evening Post*, Summer 1860.

At Algiers and at Malakoff;
Nor did we Yankees credit quite
Their evolutions in the fight.
But now we're very sure what they
Have done can here be done to-day,
When thus before our sight deploys
The gallant corps from Illinois,
American Zouaves![52]

There is no doubt that the tour was extremely effective in motivating thousands of meto join or create local military units. In an article for *The Atlantic Monthly* in July 1861, John Hay wrote that new Zouave corps, inspired by the Chicago Cadets' brilliant crimson and gold, "blazed up like phosphorescence in the wake of a passing ship."[53]

That men would be leaving hearth and home to march off to war within a year was not yet a reality, but it was anticipated by many. The United States Zouave Cadet Tour successfully raised national awareness of the importance of military preparedness, especially in a country that depended on volunteers to swell the ranks of the army during times of duress. Forty-nine out of the fifty Cadets who were on the tour served in the American Civil War, many becoming officers, and all using the skills they had developed as Cadets.

Elmer Ellsworth and his Zouaves were also an example of a unique nineteenth century infatuation. The average person of that time did not give a great deal of thought to fitness or physicality. Suddenly, here were young men—not circus performers, actors, or dancers, but clerks and shop assistants—who were actively involved in perfecting their bodies so that they could perform the demanding drill routines of the Zouave Cadets. They were not large men, but slightly undersized; they were gymnasts, not weightlifters; they were merely tanned and sober young men who became the darlings of the North for six weeks in 1860.

Looking back at the surviving *cartes de visite* and newspaper sketches, it is sometimes difficult to see the attraction, especially from the view of twenty-first century tastes. At five feet, six inches tall, Ellsworth was short, even by the standards of the mid-1800s. He wore his curly hair long, and sometimes it looked messy in his pictures. His clothes often overwhelmed him, especially in the photographs taken when he was in his late teens. Ellsworth's face seems young and

52 "Elmer Ellsworth and the Zouave Craze," anonymous poem, 1860; "Fifth New York Volunteer Infantry—Duryea's Zouaves," www.zouave.org/craze.html, accessed summer 2011.

53 John Hay, "Ellsworth," *The Atlantic Monthly*, Number 45, July 1861.

unformed, no different from any other teenager. In later photographs, he wears a mustache, described as "skimpy" by his friend John Hay, and in others he even has a small, "soul patch" goatee. Nevertheless, Hay wrote,

> His pictures sold like wildfire in every city of the land. Schoolgirls dreamed over the graceful wave of his curls, and shop-boys tried to reproduce the Grand Seigneur air of his attitude. Zouave corps, brilliant in crimson and gold, sprang up, phosphorescently, in his wake, making bright the track of his journey. The leading journals spoke editorially of him, and the comic papers caricatured his drill.[54]

Hay described another photograph, now lost, that showed only Ellsworth's arm. "The knotted coil of thews and sinews looks like the magnificent exaggerations of antique sculpture."[55] Adam Goodheart perhaps expresses it best when he points out that, with the output of the new art of photography available in almost every town, Ellsworth became the first male "pinup" in America's—maybe even the world's—history.[56]

How did this fame affect the doubting Spaffords of Rockford? Their letters no longer expressed any dissatisfaction with Ellsworth's military choice, nor was the word "lawyer" mentioned as often. The Spaffords had always liked Elmer as a person, and now they were extremely proud of his accomplishments. The U.S. Zouave Cadet tour had both raised awareness of the need for better military preparedness and had given the North some relief from political and social tensions. Everyone involved had counted the tour a success. When Ellsworth returned to Springfield, the Spaffords presented him with a handsome bible, inscribed with "much love."[57] Unfortunately, most of the letters written by Carrie to her fiancé during the tour are lost, but she must have been very proud of him as well.[58] After all, she was engaged to "the most talked-of man in the country."[59]

---

54 Michael Burlingame, ed., *At Lincoln's Side: John Hay's Civil War Correspondence and Selected Writings* (Carbondale, IL: Southern Illinois University Press, 2006), 147.

55 Hay, *Atlantic Monthly*, 122.

56 Goodheart, *1861*, 204.

57 Randall, *Colonel Elmer Ellsworth*, 191, 192.

58 Carrie's letters to Ellsworth are often referred to by their contents, but to this date a packet of her letters has never been found. After Elmer's death, Carrie wrote to John Nicolay and asked if he had any of her correspondence. Quite often Ellsworth asked Nicolay to hold his personal mail for him. This may have included letters written during the Zouave Cadets' tour. Whether Carrie asked Nicolay to destroy or return them is not known, but the fact of Carrie's later marriage makes their destruction more plausible.

59 Hay, *Atlantic Monthly*, 123.

CHAPTER 7

One of Lincoln's Men

"Lincoln & Liberty"

Hurrah for the choice of the nation
Our chieftain so brave and so true
We'll go for the great reformation
For Lincoln and liberty, too

Success to the old-fashioned doctrine
That men are created all free
And down with the power of the despot
Wherever his stronghold may be.

Then up with the banner so glorious
The star-spangled red, white and blue
We'll fight 'til our banner's victorious
For Lincoln and liberty, too.[1]

Jesse Hutchinson, Jr., 1860

THE political climate of the summer of 1860, in both geographic sections of the United States, was tense. Which way was the country headed? Smoky tendrils of war hung in the air, waiting for the presidential election in November to see if sparks could be fanned into flames. The South curried its horses, tightened saddle cinches, and dusted off its cavalier plumes in anticipation. The North uniformed its young men, taught them how to march, and

1 Irwin Silber and Jerry Silverman, *Songs America Voted By* (Harrisburg, PA: Stackpole Books, 1971), 98. This song can be heard in many versions online: www.youtube.com/watch?v= wxWwDgOj0oE (The Weavers) and www.youtube.com/watch?v= me597aIB6RQ (Matthew Sabatella and the Rambling String Band) are two examples.

waited for the signal to put weapons in their boys' hands. During the summer of 1860, the nation began to crumble. Every major city in the North held debates, and the South threatened that if Lincoln was elected president that fall, secession would surely follow.

It was into this atmosphere that Ellsworth stepped when he returned to Chicago. As soon as he recovered from the travel stress of the last few weeks, Ellsworth resigned his colonel's commission and formally disbanded the U.S. Zouave Cadets. He felt that the team should be dissolved after its national triumph, rather than deteriorate under a less vigorous schedule. Ellsworth turned his immediate efforts toward answering the massive number of letters and other correspondence generated by the triumphant tour. The Chicago firm of Edward Mendel's Lithographing Engraving offered to reprint Ellsworth's own *Manual of Arms* if he would provide them with colored illustrations and directions concerning the Zouave uniform. Ellsworth did so, adding a second version of the regular uniform, for "active service," as well as a dress uniform.[2]

He also organized a new militia regiment of Zouaves in northern Illinois, officered by the best men of the Cadets. The members of the original U.S. Zouave Cadets had fulfilled their obligations to their previous unit, and not all of them were able to continue their involvement. Nevertheless, many of the former Zouave Cadets stepped forward to teach the new recruits their basic drill. Ellsworth presented this unit to Governor John Wood for use as an inspiration for the rest of the state to attain a greater degree of military preparedness. This group of militia soldiers created the nucleus of the unit which, on June 17, 1861, was formally mustered into federal service as Companies A and K of the 19th Illinois Infantry, popularly known as "Colonel Scott's Zouave Regiment."[3] This was the first formation and transfer of trained and officered men, of any organized force other than the Regular Army, in anticipation of Civil War. Ellsworth was fully aware of the fear held by many that an armed struggle with the South was inevitable, and that, if shots were fired early on, volunteer units would need to know how to drill, shoot, and fight until the Regular Army was brought up to strength. These men, commanded by U.S. Zouave Cadet veterans, provided an important military

---

2 Elmer Ellsworth, "Designs for Uniforms," New York State Military Museum and Veterans Research Center, Saratoga Springs, New York (hereinafter cited as NYSMM).

3 James Henry Haynie, ed., *The Nineteenth Illinois; A Memoir of a Regiment of Volunteer Infantry Famous in the Civil War of Fifty Years Ago for its Drill, Bravery, and Distinguished Services* (Chicago: M. A. Donohue & Co., 1912), 6, online version: archive.org/details/nineteenthillino 01hayn, accessed November 13, 2017.

beginning for Illinois, one that became a model for encouraging and organizing military volunteerism in other states.[4]

Ellsworth had promised fiancée Carrie Spafford and himself "one week of unadulterated enjoyment" if the tour proved successful.[5] It was, and Ellsworth traveled to Rockford as quickly as he could, once his obligations in Chicago were fulfilled. He stayed with the Spaffords from August 25 to September 15, just before Carrie left for another year of schooling in Brooklyn. This time she would be under the tutelage of her uncle, Edward Warren, and living with his family.[6]

From Rockford, Ellsworth traveled to Springfield, making good on his verbal promise to Abraham Lincoln, John Cook, and Charles Spafford that he would join the Lincoln-Herndon law firm as a clerk and finish his legal studies. When Ellsworth arrived in Springfield, he was quickly reunited with his friends John Hay and John Nicolay, and together they plunged into the excitement of Lincoln's presidential campaign.

Much has been written about Abraham Lincoln's friendship with Elmer Ellsworth. Adam Goodheart specifically notes the "sudden, school-boyish crush" Lincoln appears to have on the younger man.[7] Seen through twenty-first century eyes, some common practices of one hundred sixty years ago seem strangely

---

4 Ibid., 45-53, including complete initial rosters of the 19th Illinois Volunteer Infantry. Haynie writes:

While Ellsworth's famous U.S. Zouave Cadets Company were still in existence, and soon after the Presidential campaign of 1860, a company of "Wide-Awakes"—semi-military bodies of young and old Republicans—wishing to continue its organization, took for its title Company B, Chicago Zouaves, with "Jim" Hayden for its Captain. He had been First Sergeant of the original Ellsworth Zouaves Company—the one that out-drilled every other military company in the United States, and of which our own gallant "Joe" Scott was First Lieutenant—and he was second only to the more famous Captain Ellsworth as drillmaster. The first call for volunteers found Hayden almost prepared for war. The ranks were soon filled, and, as Company A, Chicago Zouaves, the "boys" were ready to march wherever ordered. Meanwhile, the Chicago Light Infantry, Captain Harding commanding, had also filled its ranks; the same is true of Company B, Chicago Zouaves; and when marching orders came on that Sunday of the twenty-first of April, these three companies—with the artillery and the two other Infantry companies already mentioned—after listening to a short address from General Swift, proceeded to the main station of the Illinois Central Railroad, at the end of Lake Street. That march will never be forgotten by the survivors of those who participated in it. It seemed as though the whole of Chicago had assembled along Lake Street to see us off.

5 Ingraham, "Ellsworth," LCWM/LFAC; Randall, *Colonel Elmer Ellsworth*, 196.

6 Elmer Ellsworth to Carrie Spafford, October 28-29, 1860, LCWM/LFAC.

7 Goodheart, *1861*, 106.

Ellsworth campaigned vigorously for candidate Lincoln, usually in the company of John Hay.
Library of Congress

intimate. Men often shared beds and wrote prose to each other that sounds positively "loverish" to today's ears. Letters to other men were often signed "my dearest friend," "all my affection," "yours most lovingly," and other gender-bending valedictions. In several ways, Lincoln and Ellsworth were similar. Both were self-made men in the sense that anything either had accomplished had little to do with parental money or position, and they shared military experience, as Lincoln had served in a militia company during the Black Hawk War. Ellsworth seems to have viewed Lincoln as a father figure, while Lincoln may have noticed something of himself in the starving law clerk who suddenly became a national hero. Lincoln described their relationship as "intimate," but he was not a man who developed intimacies easily or quickly, so perhaps their differences were a point of attraction as well.[8] Although Lincoln referred to Ellsworth as "the worst law clerk that ever lived, and the best executive to handle young men that I ever saw," it was clear that Lincoln's affection for Ellsworth was personal.[9] Mary Todd Lincoln's secretary, William O. Stoddard, wrote that Lincoln "loved him [Ellsworth] like a younger brother."[10] Lincoln's longtime friend, Henry C. Whitney, made his own observation: "A relation like that

---

8 C. A. Tripp, in his controversial and much-maligned book *The Intimate World of Abraham Lincoln*, clarifies one undeniable fact about Ellsworth:

Ellsworth was definitely and explicitly heterosexual. As a rigorously disciplined character he had early and firmly fallen in love with Carrie; his every mention and thought of her reflects a head-over-heels enthrallment of a kind that is fully in tune with robust, ongoing heterosexual fantasies.

9 Goodheart, *1861*, 207.

10 Guy C. Fraker, *Lincoln's Ladder to the Presidency: The Eighth Judicial Circuit* (Carbondale, IL: Southern Illinois University Press, 2012), 254.

of knight and squire of the age of chivalry existed between the two."[11] It was probably during this period that Lincoln and Ellsworth discussed the platform of the Republican party, including slavery. No letter has been found, no diary entry exists, and no quote has been remembered to indicate how Elmer Ellsworth felt about slavery. He had seen both enslaved and free people of color his entire life. Prior to leaving home, he had watched the slaves driving the coaches and waiting on Southerners visiting Ballston Spa and Saratoga Springs. In New York City and Chicago, freed people lived and worked citywide. Still, Ellsworth offers no clue as to his opinions. There is no doubt, however, about his affection for Abraham Lincoln, and slavery was often on Lincoln's mind.

John Nicolay, Lincoln's private secretary, worked in the Lincoln-Herndon law office, which doubled as campaign headquarters. One of Nicolay's most demanding jobs was that of shielding Lincoln from the onslaught of men, and perhaps a few women, who thought that Lincoln's "open-door" policy entitled them to his time and attention, no matter what their issue, or the time of day. He also answered the now-voluminous correspondence Lincoln was receiving. As the editor of a small newspaper called the *Pike County Free Press*, Nicolay had known Lincoln for several years. He had been a "Lincoln Man" since hearing him speak on October 27, 1856, at a Free-Soil Rally. Lincoln supported Nicolay's journalistic efforts, and received several positive editorials from him, until Nicolay at last had to give up the newspaper business to begin studying law in Springfield, under orders similar to Ellsworth's from a future father-in-law. When Lincoln was nominated as the Republican presidential candidate, Nicolay hoped to be asked to write Lincoln's official campaign biography. To his disappointment, Ohio poet William Dean Howells got the job. Nicolay turned to a friend, Ozias Hatch, for some words of comfort. Hatch smiled, telling Nicolay, "Never mind. You are to be private secretary."[12]

Nicolay and Hay were already friends at the time, and each gladly renewed his relationship with Elmer Ellsworth when the latter returned to Springfield. Almost immediately, Ellsworth and Hay went out on the campaign trail. This aspect of Ellsworth's commitment to Lincoln's bid for the presidency has not been given much attention, but research indicates that Ellsworth was a very active Lincoln

---

11 Henry Whitney, *Life on the Circuit: My Time with Abraham Lincoln Before He was President* (Amazon Digital Services, Kindle edition, 2013), 2:87-88.

12 Burlingame, ed., *With Lincoln in the White House*, xvi.

Candidate Lincoln, beardless in 1860. *Library of Congress*

campaigner. In Hay's elegant "Obituary of Elmer Ellsworth," written on June 3, 1861, he remembered:

> It was not possible for Ellsworth to be neutral in anything, or idle while others were working. With the whole energy of his nature he entered into the struggle. He became one of the most popular speakers known to the school-houses and the barns of Central Illinois. The magnificent volume of his voice, which I never heard surpassed, the unfailing flow of

his hearty humor, and the deep earnestness of conviction that lived in his looks and tones, were the qualities that struck the fancy of the Western crowd. Besides, it was very novel and delightful to see a soldier who could talk.[13]

It is not known whose decision it was to use Ellsworth "on the stump" to rally votes for candidate Lincoln. Perhaps Lincoln, an unusually tall lawyer, was hoping that the popularity of Elmer Ellsworth, an unusually short military drillmaster, would rub off on his candidacy. The excitement of the campaign, with fireworks, flags, and parades, was certainly familiar territory to the soldier. Here Elmer was, a famous young man, well-known in Illinois, handsome and charismatic, thoroughly devoted to Lincoln ("I had the distinguished honor of quite a chat with Mr. Lincoln yesterday, he is as unconcerned and calm as if he had nothing at stake in the coming contest. He is a glorious good man."), willing to make campaign speeches, and good at it.[14] The idea was a brilliant one, no matter who made it.

In a letter to Carrie on October 20, Ellsworth wrote:

> Yesterday I launched my bark on the troubled sea of politics. That means, in plain English, that I made my maiden speech (on political topics I mean). I had no intention of engaging in this campaign as I thought it would require at least two months hard application to the study of political matters to fit myself for speaking. But . . . I sat down to work, studied very closely for eight days and made my debut yesterday. . . . I am to speak every day untill [sic] the election, in the county precincts. Hurrah for the next President.[15]

Ellsworth spoke primarily in central Illinois. The northern part of the state was relatively locked in for Lincoln, and the southern part was considered Stephen Douglas territory. The best place to influence votes was in places like Sangamon County, and this is where Ellsworth, often accompanied by John Hay, was sent. The *Springfield Illinois State Journal* lists a series of speaking engagements:

October 24: Chatham
October 25: Dawson
October 26: Wolf Creek, Constant's
October 27: Williamsville

---

13 Burlingame, ed. *Lincoln's Journalist*, 69.

14 Elmer Ellsworth to Carrie Spafford, October 8, 1860, KCWM/LFAC.

15 Ibid; October 20, 1860.

October 29: Breckinridge's Mill
October 30: Buckhart
October 31: Brennan's School House
November 1: Auburn
November 2: Mt. Pleasant
November 3: Laomi
November 5: Dawson

The only days of rest were Sundays, October 28 and November 4.[16]

An 1860s political rally was an exciting event. There were traditional activities such as the raising of a painted and decorated political pole, and music by marching bands. The atmosphere was festive, and participants looked forward to barbeques, picnics, and parades. According to one newspaper, the participants at a Lincoln pole raising in Jackson Township, Henry County, Iowa, included "many ladies" who "graced the occasion with their presence, good looks, and smiles of approval."[17]

Springfield's Illinois Daily State Journal described a rally at Dawson held on Monday evening, November 5. This was the last rally of Lincoln's campaign, and everyone—Republicans and Democrats alike—were "cordially invited to be present."

> The Wide-Awakes will all be on hand!
> The meeting will be addressed by Col. Ellsworth, and other able and eloquent speakers.
> LET OUR REPUBLICAN FRIENDS OF THAT REGION
> NOT FAIL TO DO JUSTICE TO THEMSELVES AND TO THE CAUSE.[18]

November 6, 1860 was election day. A sunrise cannon salvo thundered over Springfield, celebrating the end of six months of campaigning for the office of president of the United States. Lincoln himself had made very few appearances, as was the habit of the times, but his team had barnstormed the Illinois area for weeks, and his name had made headlines as the legend of "The Rail Splitter" fired

16 [Springfield] *Illinois Daily State Journal*, October 23, 1860.

17 O. A. Garretson, "A Lincoln Pole Raising," *The Palimpsest*, vol. VI, no. 4 (April 1925), online version: iagenweb.org/henry/History/lincolnpole.htm, accessed August 23, 2016. A political pole marked the speaking area for a candidate and his supporters at an outdoor rally.

18 *Illinois Daily State Journal*, October 31, 1860.

imaginations everywhere; everywhere except the South, that is. In that section, he was known as a "Black Republican," the "Original Gorilla," and a variety of other insulting terms. And now the agonizing ballot count began.[19]

By election day the American voters had four candidates from which to choose. The Democratic Party had broken into two factions—Northern and Southern—which also guaranteed to split their voting bloc. Northern Democrats felt that their best chance to beat the abolitionist Black Republicans was to nominate Stephen Douglas, whom Lincoln had debated several times in 1858 when Douglas defeated him in the Illinois senatorial election. Southern Democrats, upset about Douglas's support of "popular sovereignty," or the right of a state or territory to choose whether to allow slavery, nominated then-Vice President John Breckenridge in a separate convention. The Republicans met at the Wigwam in Chicago and nominated Abraham Lincoln on the third ballot. The moderate Constitutional Union Party, made up of older politicians and distinguished citizens who were satisfied with the status-quo and took no stand at all on the subjects dividing North and South, met in Baltimore and nominated John Bell, a Tennessee slaveholder.

Due to the sectional squabbles fissuring the Democrats, Lincoln had every reason to think he might win the election, but he was also completely aware of the effect his victory might have on the nation as a whole. None of the seriousness of these matters seemed to affect Springfield on November 6, however. Spirits were high in Lincoln's hometown. Determined to "get out the vote," local Republicans, Democrats, and Constitutional Unionists hired bands to parade through the city in wagons while playing patriotic music. They roped in anyone within the vicinity to wave flags and hand out broadsides exhorting the candidate of the moment. People stood on street corners hollering the virtues of "their man," and milled around the city's polling places attempting to subvert the vote by passing out already-marked ballots. Today's election polls have rules in place to prevent this sort of mayhem, but in 1860, anything was possible. Banners like the one that advertised, "A Home President for Springfield," were displayed all over the town, from windows, balconies, and street signs alike. Ellsworth's usually cheerful countenance was even more inclined to gaiety on this auspicious day.[20]

19 Ronald C. White, *A. Lincoln: A Biography* (New York: Random House, 2009), 3.

20 *New York Daily Tribune*, November 7 and 10, 1860; Octavia Roberts Corneau and Georgia L. Osborne, eds., "A Girl in the Sixties: Excerpts from the Journal of Anna Ridgely (Mrs. James L. Hudson)," *Journal of the Illinois State Historical Society*, 22 (October 1929), 418.

On November 6, Lincoln woke up in his own home in Springfield. Inside the plain, neat-looking two-story house, he donned his usual attire: a formal black suit with a frock coat worn over a stiff-collared shirt, a black vest, and a loosely knotted black tie. He ate his usual breakfast—an egg, toast, and coffee—said goodbye to his wife Mary and his sons, nine-year-old Willie and seven-year-old Tad, plucked the high, black stovepipe hat from its peg on the wooden rack in the front hall, and stepped outside. The Illinois state capitol building, where his law office and campaign headquarters were located, was about five blocks northwest of the Lincoln home. He walked to work every day and had decided that today would be no different. Maybe candidate Lincoln looked at the sky, studying the weather. Inclement weather would negatively affect the number of rural voters who would come to the polls, most of whom would be voting Republican. Although chilly early in the morning, the day was described in several Chicago papers as "a glorious fall day . . . a marvel." The entire geographic area was in a political uproar, and hurrahs and smiles augmented the banners and flags from town to town. It was time for candidate Abraham Lincoln to join his core group of supporters downtown.[21]

By the time Lincoln got to the state house, John Nicolay was already there, as were the midwestern journalists covering the local presidential candidate on election day. They described Lincoln as "disappearing into an armchair of liberal proportions," or "sitting in a tipped-back chair with his large feet on top of the heating stove," greeting people with a hearty "Come in, sir!" in an "easy, old fashioned, offhanded manner." All those who stopped by the law office on their way to vote were made welcome, and then left, "thoroughly satisfied in every manner."[22] Soon the indispensable duo of John Hay and Elmer Ellsworth arrived, adding to the boisterous congeniality of the office. "The boys"—Hay, Ellsworth, and Nicolay—spent the day in the office with Lincoln, his law partner William H. Herndon, long-time friend and fellow lawyer Ward Hill Lamon, Illinois Secretary of State Ozias Hatch, and whoever happened to drop by to offer support, or simply to talk and laugh. Lines of poetry were exchanged in literary duels. Laughter was the response to Lincoln's sharing of his opinion that "elections in this country were like 'big boils'—they caused a great deal of pain before they came to a head, but after

---

21 *Bloomington Illinois Daily Pantagraph*, November 7, 1860.

22 *Sacramento Daily Union*, August 15, 1860.

the trouble was over the body was in better health than before."[23] The local Wide-Awakes wore their slickers and oilskin hats one more time as they merrily hit the streets to get out the vote for their candidate.[24]

From morning until dusk voters, agitators, and interested onlookers milled around the two-story, oblong-shaped building that was the Sangamon County Courthouse, where voters cast their ballots. A voter had to pick up the preprinted ballot of his choice outside, and then go up two flights of stairs to the courtroom. Once there, he checked his candidate in the privacy of a partially enclosed "voting window." The voter then announced his name to a polling clerk, who had to observe him placing his ballot in a large, clear glass bowl. There was little that was secret about the effort, as the preprinted ballots were of different colors and highly decorated. This knowledge created some arguments and hard feelings, and often fights that had to be broken up. Initially, Lincoln was not going to vote. According to Herndon, Lincoln felt that a candidate for the office of President of the United States ought not to vote for his own election. When asked how he was going to vote, Lincoln laconically replied, "by ballot."[25]

At about 3:30 p.m., voter turnout began to thin on the streets of Springfield. As he looked out the window to the street below, Lincoln finally made up his mind to saunter the short distance to the courthouse and cast his ballot. Flanked on one side by Ward Hill Lamon and on the other by Elmer Ellsworth, then followed by Nicolay, Hatch, and Herndon, Lincoln walked leisurely down the street. John Hay and several others, having voted earlier in the day, stayed behind to keep watch over the office. The closer the group got to the courthouse, the larger the mass of followers became, with onlookers, even those known to be Douglas supporters, cheering Lincoln along the way. In the words of some who were in attendance:

> All party feelings seemed to be forgotten, and even the distributors of opposition tickets joined in the overwhelming demonstrations of greeting.

> Every Republican agent in the street of course fought for the privilege of handing Lincoln his ballot.

23 [St. Louis] *Daily Missouri Democrat*, November 7, 1860.

24 Ibid.

25 *New York Daily Tribune*, November 10, 1860.

A throng followed him inside, pursuing him in dense numbers along the hall and up the stairs into the court room, which was also crowded. From the time he entered the room until he cast his vote and again left it, there were wild huzzahs, the waving of hats, and all sorts of demonstrations of applause rendering all other noises insignificant and futile.[26]

Lincoln cast his vote a little differently than other men that night. He cut his own name and those of the electors pledged to him from the top of the preprinted ballot, and then put the rest of the ballot in the glass bowl, voting for other Republicans without voting for himself.

Lincoln, Lamon, Nicolay, Herndon, Hatch, and Ellsworth walked, with difficulty, back to the office. The crowd pushed against them, shouting and yelling encouragement. Ellsworth yelled back, using his voice to control the crowd. The group returned to Lincoln's "more quiet quarters" by 4:00, but the quiet was relative and did not last long. The excitement continued to build as a steady stream of supporters came by Lincoln's office. The people's decision was only hours away.

Lincoln left his friends around 5:00 p.m. to return home for dinner. He stayed there until almost 7:00, after which he returned to the office. During his absence, Hay, Nicolay, Ellsworth, and the rest had been gleefully reading telegraph dispatches in the governor's suite. The state house was filled with a continuous flow of well-wishers and the Republican faithful.[27] The first returns, from Decatur, showed a Republican lead. By 8:00, more good news came from Jacksonville. An hour later, Lincoln decided to go across the square to the Western Union telegraph office himself. Nicolay, Hatch, and Jesse K. Dubois went with him, leaving the rest, including Ellsworth, to take care of the crowds at the state house. According to Nicolay, Lincoln sat on a sofa, "comfortably near the instruments." The crowd in the room grew slowly, but remained quiet, with the only sounds coming from "the rapid clicking of the rival instruments, and the restless movements of the most anxious among the party of men who hovered around the clattering machines."[28] The results came slowly at first, then good news began arriving more and more rapidly. Wins for Douglas were much smaller than expected, while those for Lincoln were resounding. Lincoln won Chicago by 2,500 votes, and all of Cook County by 4,000. When Lincoln sent the results over to the state house, the cheering could be heard across the square. Indiana, Wisconsin, Iowa, and

26 Ibid.

27 Ibid.

28 Ibid.

Connecticut returned large majorities "for Honest Old Abe." By 10:00 p.m., the swing state of New York had not yet been heard from but results from the South had begun to arrive. Then two telegrams came almost simultaneously. Senator Simon Cameron of Pennsylvania announced "Penna Seventy Thousand for you. New York Safe. Glory Enough," and Simon Draper, the Republican chairman of New York wrote, "The City of New York will more than meet your expectations." The overwhelmingly Democratic metropolis had failed to produce enough votes to offset the Republican tallies from the rest of the state. More good news of victory in Massachusetts quickly followed.[29]

At midnight, Mr. and Mrs. Lincoln walked to William W. Watson & Son's ice cream parlor, across Capitol Square. A group of local Republican women had prepared refreshments for everyone, and the tables were set out with coffee, sandwiches, and homemade cake. Ellsworth and the rest of the crowd from the Lincoln-Herndon law office attended as well, cheering and toasting Lincoln as "Mr. President." Telegrams were brought continuously from the Western Union office and read aloud. When the official New York telegram arrived, giving Lincoln enough electoral votes to win the election, the crowd overwhelmed both of the Lincolns with congratulations. Nicolay wrote, "Men fell into each other's arms, shouting and crying, yelling like mad, jumping up and down. Bedlam let loose. Hats flew into the air, men danced who had never danced before, and huzzahs rolled out upon the night."[30] As the news spread through Springfield, the roar shook windows and woke men and women from sleep. Church bells pealed.

Lincoln finally slipped out of Watson's at about 12:30 a.m., and went back to the telegraph office, alone. The black sky, with its sprinkling of stars, remained cloudless. The autumn constellations of Leo and Virgo were nearing the horizon to disappear until the next night, and the noise of birds and insects had finally stilled.[31] Lincoln's boots crunched on the dirt and gravel as he crossed the road to the telegraph office. The last telegram from New York read, "We tender you our congratulations upon this magnificent victory." In frightening prophecy, however,

29 Samuel R. Weed, "Hearing the Returns with Mr. Lincoln: The Unpublished Story of a Reporter Who Spent Election Day of 1860 in Springfield with the Candidate," *New York Times*, February 14, 1932. Weed served as a visiting correspondent for the *St. Louis Daily Missouri Democrat* and filed two stories from the scene. He wrote his reminiscences in the 1880s.

30 *New York Times*, November 8, 1860.

31 Jim Kaler, *Measuring the Sky: A Quick Guide to the Celestial Sphere*, http://stars.astro.illinois.edu/celsph.html,, accessed October 10, 2013.

the final telegram of the night read, "God has honored you this day, in the sight of all the people. Will you honor Him in the White House?"[32]

Beginning the next day, Lincoln had to deal with the backlash of being elected. Southern states began talking of secession, and by December 20, 1860, South Carolina had left the Union. Other states threatened to follow.

*   *   *

Although Elmer Ellsworth celebrated with the Lincoln party, he still had his own set of problems. His parents had been crushed by the illness and death of son Charley Ellsworth in Chicago just before the U.S. Zouave Cadet tour, and they had not seen Elmer for any length of time since his last trip home in 1859. They wrote, begging him to come, but for now, his letters would have to suffice. He told them:

> My Mother if you knew how I long to meet you again, how bitterly I regret that circumstances over which I had no control, have prevented me from following the dictates of my affection, and left me . . . an exile from home. —and when I tell you that ambitious as I am and ever shall be . . . all other schemes and wishes sink into insignificance beside the dearest wish of my heart, to see you placed in the position you deserve to occupy—your old age rendered comfortable and happy by the possession of everything [a] heart can desire.[33]

Elmer wanted to help them, somehow, but he had neither unlimited funds nor viable ideas. Another problem involved his study of the law. He had been working at it for several years, but he had not yet taken the Illinois bar exam. The Spaffords, concerned about Carrie's eventual support, were still pressuring him, although less so since Ellsworth's return from the Zouave tour. His letters to Carrie during this time were angst-ridden and confused. He wrote a long, elaborate explanation to her on December 20, 1860, detailing his problems. "Events that will tinge and color *my* future are crowding thick and fast upon me. Let us look at them together, Kitty, and see if I am wrong in my views."[34] He continued, telling her his parents were now physically unable to carry on at home in Mechanicville (although there is no proof of this, other than his mother's palsy), and this concern, coupled with

32 Anonymous to Abraham Lincoln, telegram, November 6, 1860, ALPLC.

33 Ellsworth, "Memoranda," 19, KCWM/LFAC.

34 Elmer Ellsworth to Carrie Spafford, December 20, 1860, KCWM/LFAC.

Charley's death, forced Ellsworth to consider either going to Mechanicville to live with his parents, or bringing his parents to live with him. In either case, he was under the impression that he would soon become their sole support. His solution, as described to Carrie, was:

> A permanent location, an immediate income sufficient for my increased expenses must be secured as soon as possible. And, in brief, these are my plans—first to obtain the position of clerk in the War Department, for which I am a candidate. In the event of obtaining this I should be compelled to reside in Washington for four years, the salary being just sufficient to support a family in the most economical manner. At the expiration of the term I should go to New York City and commence the practice of law.[35]

He explained to her that this was not the life he had been hopeful of offering her, knowing she had been brought up in a world of privilege. "Could you expect happiness with me under such circumstances?" he asked. "And would *you* be able to *bear the change* and *become the woman with whom I could be contented and happy?*"[36] Elmer's agony was evident, and he was unsure of Carrie's feelings about these matters. He closed his letter with a repeat of his promise that "*notwithstanding this change, you will become the woman that I dare to marry and lavish upon a wealth of love—now held in check*," and asked that she take at least a day to think on all he wrote before she answered.[37]

At the same time, Ellsworth focused on passing the Illinois bar. He had a little over three months to prepare for the exam, and he did so diligently. In one of his January letters to Carrie he mentioned both the "Act for the Reorganization of the Militia of Illinois," which he was in the process of presenting to the Illinois Legislature, as well as his own professional future. At one point he seemed unsure of just which direction he should go: "You ask what I should do if I fail, I don't know."[38] The letter has a note written in the margin indicating that this particular "fail" referred to the bar exam. In an earlier missive, he was thinking about the same issues: "The result of this winter will decide whether I am to be a lawyer,

35 Ibid.

36 Ibid.

37 Ibid.

38 Ibid; January 18, 1861.

soldier, politician or a good-for-naught!"[39] The *Washington Chronicle* of May 26, 1861 stated that Ellsworth was admitted to the Illinois bar in February of that year. Confirming the details of this event was impossible until the spring of 2017, when the findings of the Joint Secretary of State & Supreme Court Restoration Project of Illinois Attorney Oaths were made public. This long-term restoration project combined the efforts of both the Supreme Court of Illinois and the Illinois Secretary of State's office in an effort to discover and preserve essential documents relating to the history of the Illinois Supreme Court. Signing an oath is the final step an attorney must take before practicing law in Illinois. The oath stipulates that the newly minted attorney will support the constitutions of the United States and of Illinois, and faithfully execute the duties of an attorney. Among the boxes, some damaged by mold and water, were the signatures of Clarence Darrow, President Barack Obama, two Supreme Court justices, twelve U.S. senators, twelve Illinois governors, five Chicago mayors . . . and Elmer Ellsworth. The receipt for the signature is dated February 14, 1861, and proves that Ellsworth not only completed his legal studies but had become a lawyer before he left Springfield.[40] As soon as the election was over, Ellsworth redoubled his studies, and passed the exam just days before the Lincolns began their trip to Washington for the inauguration.

Ellsworth felt confident concerning his future in the upcoming Lincoln administration. Lincoln had all but promised him a job in the War Department when everyone got to Washington. This promise was based on a great deal more than just Lincoln's fondness for him; Ellsworth had been working on a legal project to improve the efficiency and readiness of the state militias for months. One goal of the Zouave Cadet tour had been to publicize the need for a more active militia movement nationwide. On January 6, 1861, he wrote Carrie from Springfield: "The Legislature have been assembling this week and I have been preparing a law—have had to work night and day." The legislation, "An Act for the Reorganization of the Militia of Illinois," detailed his plan for militia reform.[41]

To read this plan makes Ellsworth's grasp of the scope of national issues profoundly evident, especially since he has never been given credit for his

---

39 Elmer Ellsworth to Carrie Spafford, October 28, 1860, KCWM/LFAC.

40 *Illinois Courts Connect*, "Joint Secretary of State & Supreme Court Restoration Project of Illinois Oaths Complete," April 19, 2017, online version: www.illinoiscourts.gov/ Media/ enews/2017/041917_Restoration_Project.asp, and www.cyberdriveillinois. news/2017/ march/170330d1.pdf, accessed November 13, 2017.

41 Elmer Ellsworth to Carrie Spafford, January 6, 1861, KCWM/LFAC. A copy of Ellsworth's proposed legislation can be found at the NYSMM.

far-reaching ideas. Elmer Ellsworth has been previously portrayed in most biographical sketches as a charismatic and capable military leader of a group of one thousand or so men, and a friend to Lincoln. His death was seen by many of his contemporaries as sad, but somehow inevitable, given his youth and enthusiasm. But he was much more.[42] When he presented his ideas concerning military preparedness to Abraham Lincoln, he immediately recognized what promise the plans held. Lincoln considered Ellsworth's military aptitude "the best natural talent, in that department, I ever knew," at least according to a letter from Ellsworth to Carrie dated January 18, 1861.[43] Lincoln was tremendously interested in what Ellsworth had to offer, especially at a time when the North would need all the military strength and talent it could muster. Though some continued to deny it, the nation was on the brink of civil war. The entire United States Army numbered less than 16,000 men, and these troops were spread out over 3,000 miles, many in the far western states and territories. If the South seceded and formed another nation, the potential existed that a significant part of the army's officer corps would resign and "go home." This loss would include some of the most experienced and capable officers currently in the army. Neither section of America, North or South, was prepared to carry any type of armed conflict to the other. Something had to be done at a local level, and Ellsworth's plan was an excellent beginning.

The first iteration of the "Act for the Reorganization of the Militia of Illinois" was introduced into the legislature on January 15, 1861. Ellsworth jumped into the deep end of the legislative pool, feet first. Three days later he wrote to Carrie, "I'm just now engaged in the highly interesting occupation of *lobbying*, trying to get a bill through for the legislature—for the Militia. I want to do them a favor before I *leave* the State *forever*." He explained that he was being forced to attend legislative hearings constantly, and was even composing his letter "near the Speaker's desk and [was] half-compelled to listen to a *large talk* about *Disunion* and its results."[44]

The bill itself was nineteen pages long. It provided for the division of the state military forces into three classes: the active militia, the reserve militia, and the

---

42 When Ellsworth was killed, the North was shocked and convulsed with mourning. There seems to have been little attempt to "blame the victim" for not securing the Marshall House before he entered it, or for ignoring the rights of James Jackson when he entered Jackson's establishment. Instead, newspaper accounts and personal letters refer to Ellsworth as an impetuous young man, and as such, his death was inevitable. Youth, inexperience, etc., are blamed rather than Ellsworth's strategic errors.

43 Elmer Ellsworth to Carrie Spafford, January 18, 1861, KCWM/LFAC.

44 Ibid.

exempt militia. Two of its stipulations, characteristic of Ellsworth's personal interests, deserve special mention. The first provided for the formation of a "State Elite Corps," made up of four men from each company in the state troops who had shown themselves to be the most gifted soldiers in their respective companies. This Elite Corps battalion was to be officered by the staff of the commander in chief and would serve in the capacity of the "Governor's Guard." These honors, together with the opportunity to earn others, would promote a high degree of efficiency in state military service. The other stipulation was as follows:

> No liquor shall be allowed in any armory, or within the limits of any drill, review, parade, or camp grounds (except a sufficient quantity for medical purposes, in the charge of surgeons), under penalty of forfeiture of commission of all officers concerned, and a fine of not less than five dollars, nor more than fifty dollars, for each member of the State Troops concerned.[45]

The bill was successful in the house but failed in the senate due to timing—the Civil War had, by May 1861, already begun. Nevertheless, the contents of the bill, combined with the uniqueness of the Zouave drill, potentially laid the groundwork for an early version of military "special forces."

That Elmer Ellsworth had become an intimate of the Lincoln circle was firmly established long before election night, but from then until February 11, 1861, when the Lincoln entourage left Springfield, everything in Elmer Ellsworth's life began to move at an ever-increasing rate of speed. He returned to work at the law office, meeting daily with Lincoln, Hay, and Nicolay. He was often seen entering "the little gate in front of the Lincoln home," for dinner and to spend time with the Lincoln family. Willie and Tad, the youngest of the Lincoln boys, were known for their pranks and good humor, if not for their manners and discipline. The household welcomed Elmer's youth and cheerful enthusiasm. Mary Lincoln, not yet known to be particularly "difficult," felt warm, motherly affection for the handsome bachelor, so close in age to Robert Lincoln, their oldest son. Elizabeth Todd Grimsley, Mary's cousin, claimed that by this time Ellsworth had become "a great pet of the family."[46]

---

45 Elmer Ellsworth, "An Act for the Reorganization of the Militia of Illinois," NYSMM.

46 Ruth Painter Randall, *Mary Lincoln: Biography of a Marriage* (New York: Little, Brown & Co., 1953), 184.

In January 1861, Ellsworth was on edge, and continually wrote Carrie that his plans were not firmed up. His best friends, Hay and Nicolay, were moving to the nation's capital, and he hoped for an invitation as well. Lincoln finally issued one in late January. Ellsworth joined his friends in the capacity of a military officer, in charge of maintaining crowd control at each of the stops between Springfield and Washington. He took this job of protecting the president-elect at the various whistle stops and longer, overnight stays very seriously. Ellsworth's offer to bring a small contingent of his former Zouave Cadets with him was turned down. Not only was there not enough room to accommodate extra men, but Abraham Lincoln did not, under any circumstances, want to project an image of fear or the need for a military presence. Threats had already been made against Lincoln's life. The seceding South was furious about the outcome of the election. In January, Lincoln had been hanged in effigy in Florida. Mrs. Lincoln had received an anonymous Christmas gift of a painting showing her husband tarred, feathered, chained, and with a rope around his neck. At first Lincoln had asked Mary and the boys not to make the trip with him, but Mrs. Lincoln had stoutly refused. She agreed to start a day later than he, but caught up quickly, meeting him on his birthday, February 12.

Lincoln placed his faith and his safety in the hands of his friends. At the urging of New York political boss Thurlow Weed, Senator William Seward, and Representative Erastus Corning, a former railroad official, William S. Wood, had been put in charge of the formal arrangements for the journey.[47] Wood chose a route that gave Lincoln opportunities for full exposure in the larger northern cities without delaying his timely arrival in the capital. The official list of the traveling party—the "Family and Suite"—was given to the press. It included the president-elect and Mrs. Lincoln, their three sons (Robert Lincoln had taken time from his studies at Harvard to make the trip), Mary's cousin Lockwood Todd, Lincoln family doctor William S. Wallace, John Hay and John Nicolay as Lincoln's private secretaries, Illinois politician Norman Judd, a Harvard friend of Robert Lincoln's named George C. Latham, Colonel James M. Burgess, Lincoln's friend and self-appointed bodyguard Ward Hill Lamon, Captains George W. Hazzard and John Pope, Major David Hunter, Colonel Edwin Vose "Bull" Sumner, and Lincoln's personal valet, William H. Johnson. Wood and his assistant, Burnett Forbes, would be making the trip as well.

---

47 Burlingame, ed., *At Lincoln's Side*, 190.

Finally, joining the uniformed-but-unarmed military contingent of this august list of personages was the celebrated young colonel of the U.S. Zouave Cadets and Lincoln family friend, Elmer Ephraim Ellsworth.[48]

48 Harold Holzer, *Lincoln, President-Elect: Abraham Lincoln and the Great Secession Winter, 1860-1861* (New York: Simon & Schuster Paperbacks, 2008), 280.

Chapter 8

The Inaugural Express

Col. E. E. Ellsworth of United States Zouave Cadets fame, is so well and favorably known in this city that a detailed personal notice would be superfluous. His many New York friends will doubtlessly welcome him back with pleasure. The Colonel excited general admiration on the way hither by the great skill with which he managed to protect the President-elect from the importunities of curious crowds. It may be considered certain that he will occupy a high position in the War Department, for which the four officers of the regular army attached to the suite pronounce him eminently qualified.[1]

From William S. Wood, to the Committee of Arrangements for the RECEPTION OF THE PRESIDENT-ELECT:

First: the President elect will under no circumstances attempt to pass through any crowd until such arrangements are made as will meet the approval of Col. Ellsworth, who is charged with the responsibility of all matters of this character, and to facilitate this, you will confer a favor by placing Col. Ellsworth in communication with the chief of your own escort, immediately upon the arrival of the train.[2]

ELMER Ellsworth was going to Washington on the Inaugural Express. Lincoln formally asked him to do so early in January 1861, and any other plans or concerns he may have had were immediately forgotten, or at least never mentioned to Carrie in a letter again. Ellsworth still had no idea what his future held beyond getting Lincoln to Washington City safely. He felt he could only count on himself, even though the president-elect had promised the young man that he would find a place for him in the military. Lincoln had been necessarily vague as to the

---

1 New York Daily Herald, February 20, 1861, www.newspapers.com/image/ 329306093, accessed August 1, 2018.

2 William S. Wood, *To the Committee of Arrangements for the RECEPTION OF THE PRESIDENT ELECT*, handbill, Box 2, National Poetry and Literature Center, Library of Congress (hereafter cited as NPLC/LOC).

particulars. Both men were novices at steering their way through the convoluted waters of statecraft at the executive level, but each was hopeful of a positive result.[3] In the meantime, Ellsworth was to be in charge of managing the crowds and the movement of the presidential party during the trip from Springfield. He had offered to bring along an entire regiment of his former U.S. Zouave Cadets, but William Wood, who had been chosen to plan and direct the undertaking of delivering the president-elect to Washington, assured him that such a show of force was not necessary.[4] Lincoln had already told the press that he would be traveling without a military escort, and besides, Wood was running out of room on the train.[5] As defined by Wood, Ellsworth's duties were to accompany Lincoln at every moment he was off the train and not inside a building. Every local stop was ordered to have someone in charge of security. This person was to contact Ellsworth as soon as the train arrived and present the local arrangements made for Lincoln to move from place to place. If the plans were not to Ellsworth's liking, he would revise them on the spot.[6]

The participants in the inaugural train trip received an official pass. The expensive paper was engraved with the words: "You are respectfully invited to participate in the courtesies extended to Hon. ABRAHAM LINCOLN, President-elect, by the several railway Companies, from Springfield to Washington."[7] William Wood's orders were precise. He assigned a specific carriage in the procession that moved the presidential

3 Ingraham, *Zouaves of '61*, 116; Elmer Ellsworth to Carrie Spafford, January 6, 1861, KCWM/LFAC.

4 This is the same William S. Wood who wormed his way into the confidence of Mary Lincoln during the journey to Washington. John Hay wrote that Wood was a "scoundrel" who was sent to Springfield by the eastern railroads to entice Lincoln to make the journey to the capital for the inauguration. Wood further ingratiated himself with Mrs. Lincoln by giving her a blooded team of carriage horses. Wood accompanied her to New York on the first of several unfortunate trips to purchase furnishings for the Executive Mansion. Wood continued to sully the name of the new president until the fall of 1861, when his various duplicities were uncovered, and he was replaced by an order of Congress. For more information, see Michael Burlingame's *At Lincoln's Side: John Hay's Civil War Correspondence and Selected Writings*, and *The Inner World of Abraham Lincoln*.

5 Holzer, *Lincoln, President-elect*, 280.

6 Wood, *To the Committee of Arrangements*.

7 *New York Times*, February 18, 1861, www.newspapers.com/image/20510331. In the engraving process, ink is applied to paper under intense pressure, which creates images with a unique look and feel. Type and graphics are raised because the metal plates are etched with a recessed image. One of these tickets is in the Rare Book and Special Collections Division, Alfred Whital Stern Collection, Library of Congress.

party from the station to whatever lodgings or entertainments had been provided.[8] Lincoln, of course, rode in the first carriage, along with his hosts in that particular city or town. Lincoln's political team, consisting of Norman Judd, David Davis, David Hunter, and "Bull" Sumner rode in the second.[9] The third carriage contained John Nicolay and Elmer Ellsworth, while Robert Lincoln and John Hay rode in the fourth. Mrs. Lincoln and the younger boys, along with her local hosts, were in additional carriages, and not part of the formal procession. This was no slight to Mrs. Lincoln; Victorian-era women typically did not take part in official parades.[10]

A series of light-hearted letters between Nicolay and Ellsworth shows how excited they were about the upcoming trip. Of the two, Ellsworth was much more the dandy in his dress, wearing attention-getting neckwear and bright colors. Nicolay was more conservative in his choices, and nowhere near as concerned with "image" as his friend. Ellsworth traveled to Chicago before the Inaugural Express was to leave Springfield to finish business with his militia bill and to do a little shopping. Ellsworth also planned to do some extra shopping for Nicolay, who needed a new suit for the trip and for his post as presidential secretary; he asked that Ellsworth order the suit in Chicago. Measurements exchanged hands and were duly given to the tailor. Ellsworth teasingly wrote:

> I am getting a pair of pants & vest from the same style of goods which I think for traveling and morning wear would suit you admirably. Understand me I have now ordered for you a business style of frock of black cloth and a dress vest of black velvet and pants of doeskin. Now, 'In Re.' Shirts, as we lawyers say—I find upon close inquiry among those who wear the article that a good quality of shirt costs $24 pr Doz—I will however extend my reshirtses—(dont let John see this) and may do better. I find that this matter of

8 This sort of intricate planning of a presidential event was a precursor of the work now overseen by the Secret Service, which was formally established after the assassination of President William McKinley in 1901.

9 Norman Judd was a delegate to the 1860 Republican National Convention and a member of Lincoln's nominating team. David Hunter was a career army officer serving at Fort Leavenworth, Kansas. He began a correspondence with Lincoln prior to the election of 1860 and was invited by Lincoln to accompany him on the inaugural train ride from Springfield to Washington. He served the Union as a sometimes-controversial brigadier general during the Civil War. Edwin Vose Sumner was also a lifelong military officer stationed at Fort Leavenworth. His early concern about Lincoln's safety earned him the assignment from Lieutenant General Winfield Scott as the senior officer accompanying the Lincolns on the Inaugural Express. He commanded the II Corps of the Army of the Potomac under George McClellan until his resignation in January 1863. He died two months later.

10 Wood, *To the Committee of Arrangements.*

accompanying the President Elect involves an expense which, if I were not a (prospective) million-air would make my pocket-book exceedingly easy of transportation.[11]

After these tasks were completed, all was in readiness. The Lincolns held a final reception on February 6 at their home in Springfield, where "hundreds of well-dressed ladies and gentlemen gathered at the Presidential mansion to spend this last evening with their honored hosts."[12] In this manner, Lincoln's life at Springfield came to an end. There had been threats and portents that harm might come to the future president, but his team had done everything possible to keep Abraham Lincoln safe. The only area of concern was Baltimore, a city not entirely within the Union fold.

*   *   *

It was miserably cold in Springfield on February 11, 1861.[13] Although it was not snowing, clouds and freezing drizzle greeted the Lincoln party as it left the Chenery House Hotel, where the Lincolns had been staying since the closure of their family home. During this time, their personal belongings were being freighted overland to Washington. By 7:30 a.m., everything necessary for the inaugural journey was packed on the exquisitely designed, private, three-car train waiting at Springfield's Great Western Depot. The engine was a modern marvel of gleam and steam, hissing in readiness with its smoke-retarding funnel stack towering over the vast crowd of well-wishers bundled up against the weather to see the president-elect off on the first leg of his journey to Washington. A baggage car followed the steam engine. The last part of the small train was a yellow passenger car, its wooden trim varnished to a high

---

Facing page: As people jockeyed for room in the passenger car, Lincoln went up the steps at the rear platform and looked out over the crowd to deliver a farewell address to his Springfield friends and neighbors. Unbeknownst to anyone, it would be his final farewell to his hometown. *Library of Congress*

11 Elmer Ellsworth to John Nicolay, undated (but possibly late January or early February 1861), BU/JHC.

12 *Weekly Gazette and Free Press* [Janesville, WI], February 15, 1861, www.newspapers. com/image/74052393/?terms=Abraham%2BLincoln, accessed March 3, 2015.

13 "The Lincolns in Springfield 1849-1861," National Park Service (last updated April 10, 2015), www.nps.gov/liho/learn/historyculture/springfield2.htm, accessed November 13, 2017; "History of Federal Weather Services in Central Illinois," online version: www.weather.gov/ilx/nwshistory, accessed November 13, 2017; *Harper's Weekly*, February 16, 1861, online version: www.sonofthesouth.net/leefoundation/civil-war/ civil-war-valentine-1861.htm, accessed November 13, 2013.

PRESIDENT LINCOLN'S
FAREWELL ADDRESS

TO HIS OLD NEIGHBORS,

SPRINGFIELD, FEBRUARY 12, 1861.

My Friends

No one not in my position can appreciate the sadness I feel at this parting. To this people I owe all that I am. Here I have lived more than a quarter of a century; here my children were born, and here one of them lies buried. I know not how soon I shall see you again. A duty devolves upon me which is, perhaps, greater than that which has devolved upon any other man since the days of Washington. He never would have succeeded except for the aid of Divine Providence, upon which he at all times relied. I feel that I cannot succeed without the same Divine aid which sustained him, and on the same Almighty Being I place my reliance for support, and I hope you, my friends, will all pray that I may receive that Divine assistance without which I cannot succeed, but with which success is certain. Again I bid you an affectionate farewell.

gloss, and its sides so brightly painted that it shimmered amid the steamy mist, festively draped with bunting and hung with flags.[14] Abraham Lincoln, Ward Lamon, John Nicolay, and Elmer Ellsworth approached the locomotive, not talking too much, each sad in his own way to be leaving a place where life had gone so well. Nicolay wrote that the "stormy morning" added "gloom and depression, subdued anxiety, almost of solemnity" to their departure.[15]

By 8:00, Lincoln had said goodbye to his wife, and young Willie and Tad. Robert Lincoln and his college friend George Latham, both taking a short break from Harvard for the trip, preceded Lincoln aboard the train. Mrs. Lincoln had forced a last-minute change of plans after an argument over her plea for "an office for one of her friends."[16] According to journalist Henry Villard, the Lincolns had arrived at the Great Western Depot at 7:00 a.m., but they were scheduled to be there earlier. Mary Lincoln had thrown herself on the floor of the Chenery House and refused to let her husband leave until he met her demands. "As was usually the case, Lincoln yielded and was then able to leave his family."[17] A placated Mary rejoined the party the next day, her husband's birthday.

Ellsworth had earlier expressed his hope to Nicolay that there would be no problems during the journey. After all, this was his area of responsibility, and Wood had made his lists and timetables with an eye to protocol more than safety.[18] "People here are in a huge sweat about secession matters," and "there is a belief among the better-informed that some attempt on Mr. L—'s life will surely be made."[19] Still, Lincoln had trusted Ellsworth enough to control any expected crowds in the cities they were to pass through on their way to the capital. If there were problems, the nation would know all about it, as writers from seven newspapers, including three from New

14 Holzer, *Lincoln, President-elect*, 296.

15 John Hay and John G. Nicolay, *Abraham Lincoln: A Life*, 10 vols. (New York: The Century Company, 1880), 3:290.

16 Harold G. Villard and Oswald Garrison Villard, *Lincoln on the Eve of '61: A Journalist's Story by Henry Villard* (New York: Alfred A. Knopf, 1941), 70-71.

17 Ibid.

18 Daniel Stashower, *The Hour of Peril: The Secret Plot to Murder Lincoln Before the Civil War* (New York, Minotaur Books, 2003), 111.

19 Elmer Ellsworth to John Nicolay, undated (but possibly late January or early February 1861), BU/JHC.

York, one from Chicago, one from *Frank Leslie's*, and several correspondents of the newly-created Associated Press were included in the group going to Washington.[20]

As the rest of the party jockeyed for room in the passenger car, Lincoln went up the steps at the rear platform and looked out over the crowd. He took off his signature black stovepipe hat and raised his hands for quiet. Then he made the last speech Springfield citizens would ever hear from him in person. Lincoln had not prepared any written remarks, and his voice trembled with emotion as he thanked his neighbors and constituents for their support, asked for their blessing upon his new endeavors, and expressed his profound sadness at leaving the place where "all my children were born; and . . . one of them lies buried."[21] He bid them "an affectionate farewell," then turned to go into the passenger car. The audience erupted into three mighty cheers. Lincoln turned back to the people and raised his right hand to them, in a waving salute. The ropes were pulled to ring the bells, the train whistle screeched, the steam billowed from the smokestack and, in John Hay's words, "The crowd stood silent as the train moved slowly from the depot."[22] Neither Elmer Ellsworth nor Abraham Lincoln would ever see Springfield again.

Ellsworth's first test at crowd control came at Decatur, Illinois, the first scheduled refueling stop on this leg of the twelve-day journey of the Inaugural Express. When they arrived, Lincoln got off the train to stretch his famously long legs. He walked through the cheering crowd with Ellsworth and Hay on either side, shaking hands with people, smiling, and making politically appropriate small talk. After the train refueled, the three men safely reboarded the passenger car, which sped along the track to Tolano, Illinois, the second planned stop. All along the route hundreds of Illinoisans waved hands and handkerchiefs, shouting encouragement to the president-elect. Tolano greeted him with the boom of a cannon and more cheering well-wishers. Lincoln stayed on the train this time but made a short speech of thanks from the rear platform of the passenger car, with Ellsworth standing firmly by his side.

At noon, the little train crossed the state line into Indiana, and the party had luncheon. The train cars were linked to a new engine that was compatible with the Toledo and Wabash track gauge, which was of a different size than the one over which they had previously traveled. Lincoln again spoke briefly to the people who had come

---

20 Tom Wheeler, *Mr. Lincoln's T-Mails: How Abraham Lincoln Used the Telegraph to Win the Civil War* (New York: HarperCollins, 2006), 94-95.

21 Roy Prentice Basler, ed., *Abraham Lincoln: His Speeches and Writings* (Boston: Da Capo Press, 2001), 568.

22 Burlingame, ed., *Lincoln's Journalist*, 24.

to see him. "I am happy to meet you on this occasion and enter again the state of my early life."[23] Lincoln continued to make versions of this whistle-stop speech at small towns and crossings, wherever people gathered to cheer him. Lincoln marveled at the speed of the train—up to thirty miles an hour—and by 5:00 p.m. they arrived at Indianapolis. In the state capital, the crowds gave Lincoln his most rousing welcome yet. The cheers were deafening. "Apparently," wrote Hay, "the entire population of Indianapolis and the surrounding territory" was in attendance, "and its enthusiasm at fever heat."[24] The governor of Indiana, Oliver Perry Morton, ordered a thirty-four-gun salute—one blast for each state of the Union, including Kansas, which had just been admitted to statehood on January 29, 1861. This was the first thirty-four-gun salute of the trip, but it would not be the last. Lincoln made his eighth speech of the day, to loud, prolonged cheering and applause. Then he left the train and rode, standing, in a landau drawn by four white horses, to the Bates House, where he would be staying the night. Bands, marching units of National Guardsmen, Zouave-themed militias, fire brigades, and spontaneous parade participants accompanied him.

The first problem of the trip surfaced when, after Lincoln's landau left, no more carriages were available. All William Wood's careful plans began to fall apart when the reality of the situation did not match his orders. The carriages hired to convey the Lincoln party to the Bates House did not appear. Lincoln's entourage had to walk to town, carrying their hand luggage.[25] Journalist Henry Villard wrote in his *Memoirs* that Lincoln, even riding in the landau, was almost "overwhelmed by merciless throngs" before he reached the hotel.[26] Nicolay, Hay, and Ellsworth walked together, worried, but laughing and glad to have the first day of travel finished.[27] Now they had to confront the Bates House.

The hotel was overcrowded, and Lincoln was extremely tired. Orville Browning, a fellow Republican from Illinois and a member of Lincoln's nomination team, wrote in his diary, "All the streets in front, and the halls and stairways of the house were so packed with an eager crowd that we could scarcely make our way through them." He further complained that not only did he have to share his room with Jesse Dubois,

23 Basler, *Speeches and Writings*, 572-573.

24 Burlingame, ed., *Lincoln's Journalist*, 29.

25 Holzer, *Lincoln, President-elect*, 308.

26 Villard and Villard, *Lincoln on the Eve of '61*, 78.

27 Ibid.

Ellsworth was one of a troika of young men Lincoln depended on. John C. Nicolay (left) and John Hay (right) were the other two. *Library of Congress.*

George Latham, and two other men, but that they slept "two to a bed."[28] According to running newspaper reports, Lincoln's earlier speech, given in the company of Governor John Wood, had been poorly constructed and poorly received. Lincoln was aware of and concerned about its deficiencies. Informal speeches, useful on the campaign trail, proved ineffective now that he was elected. Earlier, Lincoln had jotted some notes concerning remarks he wished to make on his inaugural journey and packed them, along with the copious and irreplaceable working copies of his inaugural address itself, already typeset, in a small, black valise that he had given to his son, Robert. When Lincoln asked where it was, Robert, tired, distracted, and rumored to be a little drunk, told his father that he no longer had it.[29] When questioned, he admitted to his father that he had handed it to a waiter and had no idea where it might have been placed. Lincoln's face paled. Nicolay was standing next to Lincoln and remembered the scene:

> A look of stupefaction passed over the countenance of Mr. Lincoln, and visions of that Inaugural in all the next morning's papers floated through his imagination. Without a word he opened the door to his room, forced his way through the crowded corridor down to the office, where, with a single stride of his long legs, he swung himself across the clerk's counter, behind which a small mountain of carpetbags of all colors had accumulated. Then drawing a little key out of his pocket he began delving for the black ones, and opened one

28 Theodore Calvin Pease and James G. Randall, eds., *The Diary of Orville H. Browning, 1850-1881* (Springfield, IL: Illinois State Historical Society, 1931), vol. 1, 454. Orville Browning was appointed to the United States Senate in 1861 to replace Stephen A. Douglas, who had died that June.

29 There is some uncertainty as to eighteen-year-old Robert Lincoln's state of intoxication, or lack thereof, during his trip on the Inaugural Express. In *Lincoln, President-elect*, Harold Holzer writes (p. 311), "But Robert, distracted and bedazzled by the attention locals were bestowing on 'The Prince of Rails'—and perhaps 'tight in the bargain,' as one journalist hinted—no longer had possession of it [the bag valise]." The journalist in question is end-noted as being a writer for the *Rochester Union*, and is also quoted in the *New York Illustrated News*, March 9, 1861. In *The Lincolns: Portrait of a Marriage*, Daniel Mark Epstein refers to "Bob" Lincoln as having imbibed a great deal of Catawba wine "with the Republican youths of Cincinnati" (p. 284). Daniel Stashower writes in *The Hour of Peril: The Secret Plot to Murder Lincoln Before the Civil War* (p. 152): "The bag had been entrusted to the care of Robert Lincoln, who, perhaps as a consequence of his close adherence to the refreshment car earlier in the day, had now lost track of it." Finally, Henry Villard mentions the sparkling Catawba wine on p. 81 of *Lincoln on the Eve of '61*, and may well be the journalist quoted above by Epstein. In my research I have turned up nothing that indicates Robert Lincoln had a "problem" with alcohol, He died at age eighty-two of a stroke complicated by heart disease, a typical death for the time. Nevertheless, it is not difficult to believe that an eighteen-year-old young man, first son of the future president of the United States, good looking and Harvard-bound, might not have done some celebrating that involved adult beverages during the two weeks he was on the journey from Springfield, Illinois to Washington City.

by one those that the key would unlock, to the great surprise and amusement of the clerk and bystanders, as their miscellaneous contents came to light.[30]

Eventually, Nicolay was relieved to report, "Fortune favored the President-elect, for, after the first half-dozen trials, he found his treasures."[31]

Later, Nicolay commiserated with Ellsworth and Hay about the near catastrophe: "It is a severe ordeal for us and increased about tenfold for him." The hotel arrangements had been so badly mangled that all three young men had to share the same room. After all the excitement of the evening, no one went to sleep before midnight.[32]

The next morning, February 12, was Lincoln's fifty-second birthday. Mary, Willie, and Tad joined the group at about 11:00 a.m., just in time to leave Indianapolis. After the near disaster of almost losing the inaugural address the evening before, Lincoln gave the black valise containing his speeches and notes to Orville Browning, who remained in Indianapolis for a few days, to read and comment upon Lincoln's speech. Ebenezer Peck and Jesse Dubois were two more Lincoln friends staying behind with Browning. Before the Lincolns left, Dubois, who knew Ward Hill Lamon better than he knew Elmer Ellsworth, took Lamon's arm and whispered this warning: "We entrust the sacred life of Mr. Lincoln to your keeping; and if you don't protect it, never return to Illinois, for we will murder you on sight."[33]

When the party arrived at the Indianapolis depot, a new engine was waiting. To the delight of Willie and Tad, it was a gleaming, impressive piece of machinery, draped with flags and bunting. Thirty-four white stars embossed the smokestack, and lithographic portraits of Lincoln's presidential predecessors lined its sides. The contingent left Indianapolis at about 11:00 a.m., bound for Cincinnati.[34] The journey continued, in John Hay's words, "on the crest of one continued wave of cheers."[35] Indiana sped by,

---

30 John G. Nicolay, "Some Incidents in Lincoln's Journey from Springfield to Washington," in Burlingame, ed., *An Oral History of Abraham Lincoln: John G. Nicolay's Interviews and Essays* (Carbondale, IL: Southern Illinois University Press, 1996), 107.

31 Ibid.

32 Ibid; John G. Nicolay to Therena Bates, February 11, 1861, NPLC/LOC.

33 Dorothy Lamon, ed., *Recollections of Abraham Lincoln, 1847-1861* (Chicago: McClurg, 1879), 33.

34 Brian Wolly, "Lincoln's Whistle-Stop Trip to Washington," *Smithsonian Magazine* (February 9, 2011), online version: www.smithsonianmag.com/history/lincolns-whistle-stop-trip-to-washington-161974/, accessed November 13, 2017.

35 Burlingame, ed., *Lincoln's Journalist*, 29.

and the train crossed into Ohio. By 3:00 p.m. the train pulled into Cincinnati, to the usual gratifying welcome. Lincoln addressed the crowd, then went, flanked by Ellsworth and Nicolay, to a rally organized by working men of Germanic heritage. This ethnic group had supported Lincoln overwhelmingly and his speech, supporting immigrant rights, did not disappoint. That evening, the party stayed at Cincinnati's plush Burnet House, where, thankfully, Wood reserved enough rooms to accommodate everyone. At the planned hotel reception, Ellsworth, this time with Col. Sumner and Maj. Hunter, had a busy evening, as it took all three men to guard Lincoln on this occasion. The crowds were tremendous and seemed never to end:

> The reception given by Mr. Lincoln, in the large dining-room of the Hotel, was a very unique and Democratic affair. The room is very large, very long, very wide. Its ceiling and several walls were very tastefully decorated with that favorite bunting, the American flag. . . About two thirds of the distance from the doors was placed a square platform, six inches high, on which were two chairs. On the platform stood Mr. Lincoln; on one chair stood Mayor Bishop; around the platform was a cordon of policemen, and behind the hero of the occasion stood Col. Ellsworth, Col. Sumner, and Major Hunter. "Let 'em come," roared out Ellsworth—the doors were flung open and in they rushed.[36]

One journalist described the throng as "all classes, all sorts, all conditions, all employments, all ages, both sexes, all styles, all nations, and apparently all creation."[37] Ellsworth's general plan to deal with the crowd was simple and effective: keep them moving. When a group or individual lingered in one place, one of the three military men would "accidentally" bump into them, moving them along.[38] Again, a safe day and night were had, with beds enough for all . . . except for one thing: Norman B. Judd had received an alarming letter from detective Allan Pinkerton, sent from Baltimore. Pinkerton and his agents were working undercover to make sure Lincoln arrived safely in Washington. Judd shared its disturbing contents with no one.[39]

By 9:00 the next morning, the trip was again underway. The weather was warming, with no rain, and the crowds lining the tracks along the way smiled and cheered as they waved their hats and flags. The now-familiar thirty-four-gun salute began as soon as the

---

36 *New York Times*, February 18, 1861, www.newspapers.com/image/20510331/? terms= Abraham%2BLincoln, accessed August 2, 2018.

37 Ibid.

38 Burlingame, ed., *Lincoln's Journalist*, 30.

39 Allan Pinkerton to Norman Judd, February 12, 1861, ALPLC.

train was sighted outside Columbus, about 2:00 p.m. This time the entire Lincoln family, along with Elmer Ellsworth, left the train to make a public appearance. At 4:30, the anxiously awaited telegram bringing important news from the Electoral College had been delivered to Lincoln personally. When Lincoln realized that his election was confirmed, he smiled, and then put the dispatch into the pocket of his black frock coat.[40] After lunch at the governor's mansion, Lincoln was given a "military" escort by Ellsworth, Sumner, and Hunter to the state capitol to make a speech, but again the papers reported that his effort was disappointing. The president-elect was extremely tired, and his words seemed erratic and contradictory. After the speech, the crowd pressed forward again, but Lincoln's fatigue was evident. Ellsworth, with the help of Ward Lamon, who was almost as tall as Lincoln and was described by Nicolay as "a man of extraordinary size and herculean strength," finally got him to a staircase in the vestibule of the capitol. With both Ellsworth and Lamon in front of him, Lincoln mounted a few steps and put himself physically out of the reach of the mass of well-wishers.[41] Nicolay described immense receptions such as this one as being "so large, it had become difficult to prevent his being killed with kindness."[42] Finally, by 9:00 p.m., it was over. The third day of the trip had passed without incident, and Lincoln, bone-weary even at this early stage of the journey, rested comfortably.

Another new engine, bedecked with flags, shining within its cocoon of steam, was waiting for the Lincoln party on Thursday morning, February 14, at the Columbus train depot. The Lincolns traveled through Ohio, waving at the people standing by the track, and slowing down at Cadiz Junction to receive a carefully wrapped, elegant dinner from the wife of the president of the Steubenville and Indiana Railroad.[43] The tracks hugged the shoreline of the Ohio River, headed north, then turned east toward Pennsylvania. The Inaugural Special was held up for some hours by a derailed freight train at Allegheny City (modern-day Northside), just outside Pittsburgh. The weather had again turned into pelting rain, but the Pittsburgh depot was filled with people waiting to see the president-elect. Once the train reached the depot, Lincoln and Ellsworth took a carriage to the Monongahela House, battling crowded streets all along the way. Lincoln made a brief speech on the hotel balcony, and then went to bed. The weather was

40 Michael Burlingame, ed., *An Oral History of Abraham Lincoln: John G. Nicolay's Interviews and Essays* (Carbondale, IL: Southern Illinois University Press, 2006), 109.

41 Ibid., 113.

42 Burlingame, ed., *With Lincoln in the White House*, 27.

43 *New York Times*, February 15, 1861, www.newspapers.com/image/20509977/? terms= Abraham%2BLincoln%2BCadiz%2BJunction, accessed March 5, 2015.

uncooperative, but the trip had progressed peacefully. Another day of rest would do Lincoln, and everyone else, a great deal of good.[44]

During the night the rain became worse. Still, the crowds were waiting for Lincoln at 8:30 the next morning, February 15. He gave the speech he had planned to deliver the night before, but in it, Lincoln avoided mentioning what the press was starting to call "the condition of the country."[45] This omission had become a recurring theme of criticism by those who felt Lincoln was ignoring issues created by the Southern states and their political representatives in Washington. At 4:30 p.m. the train reached Cleveland, where the spitting rain had turned into a snowstorm. Unfortunately, this time Lincoln's cold, tired supporters were so unruly that Ellsworth needed help from the police and military to get the president-elect safely into the Weddell House.[46] The newspapers again criticized Lincoln's evening balcony speech for claiming the crisis building between the North and the South was artificial.[47] Miserable weather, intractable crowds, and a cynical press notwithstanding, the inaugural party was safe and warm by bedtime. Ellsworth had done his job well yet again.[48]

As the train departed Cleveland the next morning at 10:00, February 16, Lincoln's voice was reduced to a whisper. Eccentric social reformer and erratic politico *New York Tribune* editor Horace Greeley, in his typical bombastic fashion, yellow coat flapping and red and black scarf wrapped around his whiskered neck, boarded the train at the town of Girard. He had attended the Republican Convention in Chicago and was intent on following Lincoln both in person and in his paper. Greeley was not always a supporter of Lincoln, but the *Tribune* carried great political influence.[49] He managed to snare a short private interview with the President-elect, claiming incredulously that he had gotten on the wrong train.

44 Ibid.

45 Henry Villard, *Memoirs of Henry Villard, Journalist and Financier* (Boston: Houghton Mifflin, 1904), 152.

46 Ibid.

47 John G. Nicolay to Therena Bates, February 17, 1861, NPLC/LOC.

48 Newspaper accounts of the Inaugural Express come from two sources: local reporters who attended the events in their towns, and the reporters Lincoln took with him on the journey, such as Henry Villard. Local reporters focused on their own townsfolk and politicians, and the national press focused on Lincoln and his policies, which were evolving as he travelled. There is little mention of those who were also part of the journey. Even Mrs. Lincoln and Ellsworth got little coverage, and Lamon, Hay, and Nicolay got no press at all.

49 Robert C. Williams, *Horace Greeley: Champion of American Freedom* (New York: NYU Press, 2006), introduction.

At this point in the journey, the members of the inaugural party began to look for something to break up the tedium and add a bit of levity; they found both in Poughkeepsie, New York. Having paused for a few moments at the Poughkeepsie Depot, a crowd of well-wishers had collected to view Lincoln's train. Lincoln spoke, and then the crowd saw Mary Lincoln in the car behind him. The *New York Times* reported:

> A pleasing incident occurred here. Mrs. Lincoln, who was recognized in the cars, was warmly welcomed by the crowd. In response she raised the window, and returned the salutations of the people. "Where are the children? Show us the Children," called a loud voice. Mrs. Lincoln immediately called her eldest son [Willie, in this case] to the window, and he was greeted by a hearty cheer. "Have you any more on board?" "Yes," replied Mrs. Lincoln, "here's another"—and she attempted to bring a tough, rugged little fellow [Tad], about eight years old, into sight. But the young representative of the House of Lincoln proved refractory, and the more his mother endeavored to pull him up before the window the more stubbornly he persisted in throwing himself down on the floor of the car, laughing at all the fun . . .[50]

A far more charming event occurred at the small New York village of Westfield. Apocryphal stories are always told about famous people, but the story about the young girl who wrote to then-candidate Lincoln and suggested he grow whiskers is true. When the train pulled into the Westfield depot, Lincoln was eager to speak to the crowd:

> I suppose you are here to see me, but I certainly think I have the best of the bargain. Some three months ago, I received a letter from a young lady here; it as a very pretty letter, and she advised me to let my whiskers grow, as it would improve my personal appearance; acting partly upon her suggestion, I have done so; and now, if she is here, I would like to see her.[51]

A boy in the crowd pointed out an eleven-year-old girl with black hair, holding a bouquet of roses, blushing and excited. Mr. Lincoln walked to the end of the rear platform and down a couple of steps, reached out to little Grace Bedell, took her hand,

50 *New York Times*, February 20, 1861, www.newspapers.com/image/20510411, accessed August 2, 2018.

51 "Lincoln's Beard," *Philadelphia Inquirer*, February 25 1968, www.newspapers.com/.

and kissed her cheek. She told the story for the rest of her life, admitting she was so excited that she forgot to give him the roses.[52]

The train continued to follow the shoreline of Lake Erie, greeted by the usual well-wishers lining the tracks, holding banners and waving flags. By 4:30 p.m., February 16, the train pulled into Buffalo. Ellsworth had written a short letter to Carrie, posted from Indianapolis and dated February 11. In it he tried to set up some time to see his fiancée, telling her that the Lincoln party was scheduled to arrive in New York City on Tuesday, February 19.

> As matters look now it will be absolutely impossible for me to leave the party for an hour. Can you not arrange with some proper escort to be at the Hotel [the Astor House] in the Ladies part when we arrive?[53]

Buffalo was the site where, for the first time, someone on the inaugural journey sustained a physical injury. Ellsworth, Major Hunter, Colonel Sumner, and the redoubtable John Nicolay considered it a disaster. The crowd was boisterous and unable to be restrained in the usual fashion by "keeping the moving." In the quelling of the near riot, Major Hunter's shoulder was at least dislocated, and perhaps broken. After being seen by a local doctor, Hunter was ordered to keep his arm in a sling for the remainder of the journey.[54] Losing Hunter in this way weakened Ellsworth's team, but they persevered.

The Lincoln party was finally able to make its way to the American Hotel, where it was to spend the night. Lincoln made his customary balcony speech. Later that evening, across from the hotel reception, the Young Men's Christian Association hung up a sign that Lincoln saw: "We will pray for you, the defender of the Constitution as it is." The sign was appropriate, as the next day was Sunday, and the Lincoln party rested.[55]

The group did not leave Buffalo until Monday, February 18. A rear sleeping car was added to the Inaugural Special for the Lincoln family. This car was patriotically

---

52 Grace Bedell Billings to John E. Boos, January 24, 1934, *The Forbes Collection of American Historical Documents, Part Six* (New York: Christie's catalogue, May 22, 2007), 63.

53 Elmer Ellsworth to Carrie Spafford, February 11, 1861, KCWM/LFAC.

54 *Buffalo Commercial*, February 18, 1861, www.newspapers.com/image/264399806/ ?terms= Major%2BHunter, accessed August 2, 2018.

55 *Buffalo Commercial*, February 19, 1861, www.newspapers.com/image/ 264399887/?terms= Abraham%2BLincoln%2BInaugural%2BTrain, accessed August 2, 2018.

decorated for the occasion, with a portrait of George Washington at one end, and one of Lincoln at the other. An American flag covered the car's ceiling. The train chugged out of Buffalo at about 5:00 a.m. under a sky that threatened storms. The tracks went east, along the path of the Erie Canal. After leaving the city, the engine sped through the countryside at speeds of sixty miles an hour. The citizens of Syracuse met the party with a live eagle, and Utica was in the middle of a snowstorm. The train pulled into Albany, the capital of New York, at 2:30 in the afternoon. John Hay described the journey in three words: "Crowds, cannon, and cheers."[56]

By 7:45 the next morning, February 19, still another new train chugged out of Albany. Because they were going to be arriving in New York City, the president-elect and his party were traveling aboard the most opulent, most gilded set of rail cars the Union had to offer. From the beginning of the journey, each railroad company had tried to outdo the one before it in the speed, comfort, and looks of its train. The one that took Lincoln to the "Empire City" was a fantastic compilation of every type of art that could be brought together to create a steam locomotive. The passenger car was shellacked with orange spar varnish, giving the oak a soft golden glow. Curling Victorian flourishes painted in black and brown ornamented the exterior of the vehicle. National flags, bunting, streamers, and ribbons decorated it as well. Two modern, powerful steam locomotives—the *Union* and the *Constitution*—pulled this magnificent traveling hotel. More than five hundred railroad employees worked all along the line to ensure that Lincoln arrived at the Hudson River railroad terminal without incident.[57]

Seven hours later, at 3:00 p.m., the train reached its destination. The weather in New York City had cleared, and the afternoon was "mild and beautiful." Lincoln, Ellsworth, Judge Davis, Col. Sumner, and Nicolay boarded the first of thirty-five carriages transporting the party, which had grown at each whistle stop along the way from Albany, to the Astor House. That evening, Mary Lincoln took Willie to see the sights at P. T. Barnum's showplace, leaving Lincoln to deal with politics. Vice president-elect Hannibal Hamlin met Lincoln in New York, had dinner with him at the Astor, and then went, together with various members of the Lincoln party, to the Academy of Music to see Verdi's new opera, *Un Ballo in Maschero.*[58] Unfortunately for

---

56 John Hay, diary, undated, BU/JHC.

57 *New York Herald,* February 20, 1861, www.newspapers.com/image/329306217/ ?terms=Abraham%2BLincoln, accessed March 2, 2015.

58 From the very beginning of his service in Congress, Hannibal Hamlin was a prominent opponent of the extension of slavery. He was a conspicuous supporter of the Wilmot Proviso, and spoke against the Compromise of 1850 and the Kansas-Nebraska Act. In 1856 he

Verdi fans, their arrival caused such a commotion that the performance was interrupted, the orchestra played an impromptu "Hail Columbia," an American flag was found somewhere and unfurled on stage, and the principal singers of the opera company sang "The Star-Spangled Banner." Lincoln, realizing that the cheering was not going to stop, suggested that they leave before the start of Act II.[59]

It is not known if Ellsworth accompanied Lincoln to the Academy of Music, where his Zouaves had performed less than a year earlier. What *is* known is that Ellsworth was able to successfully arrange to meet his fiancée, Carrie Spafford, and her uncle, Edward Warren, at the Astor House. Ellsworth's letter to Carrie asking her to try to meet him in New York City had borne results. He had suggested she might "arrange with some proper escort" a way to be available during the limited amount of time he could get away from his responsibilities.[60] She arrived at the Astor House escorted by her uncle. A letter to Carrie, written about two weeks later, refers to Warren's request for a government appointment: "Tell your Uncle I am making the strongest kind of effort for him."[61]

On February 20, the Inaugural Express reached Philadelphia. In its review of the trip so far, the *Philadelphia Inquirer* named several participants in the effort, saluting their contributions. It sympathetically mentioned Maj. Hunter's injured arm, singled out Capt. John Pope's "strongly expressed devotion to the Union," and lauded Col. Elmer Ellsworth for managing "to protect the President-elect from the importunities of curious crowds."[62] Not one of these men had any idea that their biggest

---

withdrew from the Democratic Party and joined the newly organized Republican Party, causing a national sensation. The Republicans nominated Hamlin for governor of Maine; he carried the election by a large majority and was inaugurated on January 8, 1857. In the latter part of February 1857, however, he resigned the governorship. He returned to the Senate, serving from 1857 to January 1861. Hamlin was nominated as the candidate for vice president in the 1860 election on the Lincoln ticket. Given that Lincoln was from Illinois, a vice presidential nominee from Maine made sense in terms of regional balance. As a former Democrat, Hamlin could also be expected to try to persuade other anti-slavery Democrats that joining the Republican Party was the only way to ensure slavery's demise. There are several biographies of Hamlin; see Charles Eugene Hamlin, *The Life and Times of Hannibal Hamlin by His Grandson Charles Eugene Hamlin* (Cambridge, MA: Riverside Press, 1899) and H. Draper Hunt, *Hannibal Hamlin of Maine: Lincoln's First Vice President* (Syracuse, NY: Syracuse University Press, 1969).

59 *New York Daily Herald*, February 21, 1861, www.newspapers.com/image/ 329306235/, accessed August 2, 2018.

60 Elmer Ellsworth to Carrie Spafford, February 11, 1861, KCWM/LFAC.

61 Ibid; March 7, 1861.

62 *Philadelphia Inquirer*, February 22, 1861, www.newspapers.com/image/ 167494182/ ?terms=Abraham%2BLincoln, accessed August 2, 2018.

challenge—protecting Abraham Lincoln from possible assassination—was lying directly ahead.

Supper was scheduled at about 7:00 p.m., and at 9:00 the same evening Philadelphia celebrated Lincoln's election with a glorious display of pyrotechnics. The grand finale of the fireworks show was a static display of grandiose proportions. Within a red, white, and blue wall of fire, silver letters forming the words, "Welcome, Abraham Lincoln. The Whole Union" were illuminated.[63] About an hour later, most people thought the fireworks were over, but in truth, they had just begun. Norman Judd urged Lincoln to attend a secret meeting after the fireworks had faded from the winter skies. Judd explained that he was in close contact with Allan Pinkerton, whose company, the Pinkerton Detective Agency, had been hired by the Philadelphia, Wilmington, and Baltimore Railroad to investigate a plot to do damage to its property during Lincoln's stop in Baltimore.[64] Not long into the investigation, the Pinkerton team had uncovered a far more sinister plot. The state of Maryland was seen as a possible candidate for secession, and there was much anger and discontent about Lincoln's election among the Southern sympathizers in its largest city, Baltimore. Upon sending undercover operatives into the city to investigate the railroad matter, Pinkerton instead had discovered rumors of a plan to assassinate Abraham Lincoln. Judd told Lincoln that Pinkerton had kept him informed him of all happenings since Cincinnati. As the stop in Baltimore approached, however, Judd could no longer sit idly by.[65]

At about 10:15, Pinkerton made his way to Lincoln's suite in the Continental House. Ellsworth, guarding the door that night, imposed himself between the detective and the room in which the president-elect was sleeping. After a brief argument, Pinkerton asked Ellsworth to come with him to talk to Norman Judd, who ordered Ellsworth to stand down.[66] Judd, Pinkerton, and Ellsworth made their way back to

---

63 Ibid.

64 Allan Pinkerton was a Scottish-born, self-taught detective. He founded the Pinkerton National Detective Agency in 1850 with partner Edward Ricker, a Chicago attorney. He solved several criminal robberies for the Illinois Central Railroad, bringing him to the attention of Abraham Lincoln, the lawyer for the railroad. Prior to the Civil War and for two years thereafter, Pinkerton also headed the Union Intelligence Service. It was during this time that Pinkerton's agents uncovered the plot to assassinate Lincoln as he passed through Baltimore on his way to Washington. For more information concerning this interesting man, see *Allan Pinkerton: The First Private Eye*, by James Mackay, or *Lincoln's Spymaster*, by Samantha Seiple.

65 Alan Hynd, *Arrival: 12:30: The Baltimore Plot Against Lincoln* (Camden, NJ: Thomas Nelson and Sons, 1967), 13-25.

66 Daniel Stashower, *The Hour of Peril: The Secret Plot to Murder Lincoln Before the Civil War* (New York: Minotaur Books, 2013), 234.

Gurney & Son   Photo. NY

On this and the facing page: While Nicolay and Hay served in the White House, Ellsworth served in the field. As this carte de visite, published after Ellsworth's death, explains, the uniformed Ellsworth conjured images of "the Goddess of Liberty." The inspiring figure Ellsworth cut demonstrates why, in life, Ellsworth proved so useful to Lincoln as a military figure. *Library of Congress.*

EXPLANATION.

MESSRS. GURNEY & SON.   *New York, Nov. 3d, 1863.*

GENTLEMEN,—It is two years and a half since the death of the first martyr to liberty, which, at the time, came like a thundershock, penetrating the heart of every loyal citizen. Ellsworth was a warm friend, and one whose loss I ever live to regret. He was with me in the van-guard of Volunteers. I visited the place where he fell and possessed myself of some of the blood-stained floor upon which he breathed his last.

In July, 1861, under very singular circumstances, I received the following letter, purporting to come from him, and a fac-simile of his hand-writing:

"DEAR FRIEND,—Go on to victory. I can accomplish more now than if I had survived my fate. I was impressed of my end before it came.   ELMER E. ELLSWORTH."

No doubt you will (as well as myself) think this strange. Last evening, on looking in a lady's album, the first likeness I saw was that of Ellsworth—one which I never saw before, although, as I am informed, it was published by you just after his death. I not only noticed the well-known face of Col. Ellsworth, but at the same instant, by his side, a beautiful classic head of the Goddess of Liberty,—evidently an accident,—yet it is a singular coincident, and the more so that it should remain unnoticed by thousands for years, until discovered by myself. I also discovered, in the destined to become strange and curious picture, many other faces, which are plainly visible to all who look for them. I am not superstitious: but that such an accident should occur on that peculiar picture of the lamented hero and my personal friend, and that I should first bring it to light, seems an indication of something more than human agency, and impresses me strongly that his blood was but the germ of an universal liberty which is to spring up throughout the world.

Allow me to ask you when that picture was first taken, and if accidental?   Yours Truly,   R. D. GOODWIN, *late Col. U. S. V.*

Gurney's Gallery, 707 Broadway,
New York, Nov. 6th, 1863.

DEAR SIR,—In reply to yours of the 3d inst., would state, that we, as well as every person connected with our establishment, have been perfectly ignorant of the very strange and beautiful coincident of other faces being on the photographic likeness of Col. Ellsworth.

This picture was retouched in India Ink (from a negative in our possession) immediately after the death of Col. Ellsworth, and we assure you that, until our attention was called to the remarkable face of the Goddess of Liberty by yourself, we had never noticed it, and, on our part, consider it purely accidental,—yet, for the discovery of which, please accept our thanks,—and beg to remain

Yours Respectfully,

COL R. D. GOODWIN   J. GURNEY & SON

THE MYSTERIOUS LIKENESS OF COL. ELLSWORTH, AND LETTERS, entered, according to Act of Congress, in the year 1863, by M. E. Goodwin, in the Clerk's Office of the District Court of the United States for the Southern District of New York.

Lincoln's room. Ellsworth again stationed himself outside the door. Inside, Pinkerton outlined the Baltimore assassination plot for Lincoln and his confidant, Ward Lamon. Pinkerton explained that Calvert Station in Baltimore had an odd configuration; to get from the inbound trains to the outbound trains, one had to pass through a narrow pedestrian tunnel. Lincoln would have to travel by carriage through the same tunnel to get to the Eutaw House, where he was to stay in Baltimore. Southern sympathizers had plotted to create an altercation down the tracks from Lincoln's train, which would draw the Baltimore police away from the tunnel. When Lincoln's party entered the tunnel, at least eight men were to be ready to either stab or shoot the president-elect.

In answer to Lincoln's shocked, disbelieving questions, Pinkerton suggested this plan: Lincoln would leave Philadelphia that night, go to the Philadelphia, Wilmington, and Baltimore station, and from there take the 11:00 p.m. train to Washington.[67] Lincoln thoughtfully considered Pinkerton's suggestion, then responded that he could not alter his plans in so significant a way. He was scheduled to speak at Independence Hall the next morning, and raise a flag that, for the first time, would include the new, thirty-fourth star celebrating the statehood of Kansas. Then he was to go to Harrisburg to address the Pennsylvania Legislature. After leaving Harrisburg on the afternoon of the 22nd, however, he would be amenable to changing his schedule.[68]

Early on the morning of February 22, Washington's Birthday and a public holiday, Lincoln made a rousing, highly emotional speech at Independence Hall, and raised the new version of the Star-Spangled Banner.[69] By 9:30, he had left Philadelphia and was on the train to Harrisburg. While Ellsworth and Nicolay sat outside the door of Lincoln's compartment, Norman Judd met with Lincoln in the private car, where he explained the plans for that evening.[70] Judd told Lincoln that a one-car train would be waiting in Harrisburg to take him back to Philadelphia, where he would board another

---

67 Ibid; Hynd, *Arrival: 12:30*, 51-60.

68 Ibid.

69 The text of the short speech made by Lincoln on February 22, 1861, includes the phrase, "But if this country cannot be saved without giving up that principle, I was about to say I would rather be assassinated on this spot than surrender it." At the end of his oration, Lincoln said, "I supposed it was merely to do something toward raising the flag. I may, therefore, have said something indiscreet." A close reading of this speech certainly indicates that Lincoln was aware of the Baltimore assassination plot, and that it was on his mind. The text of the speech can be found in Roy Basler's *Collected Works of Abraham Lincoln*, v. 4, 241, and an online version of it may be found at www.abrahamlincolnonline.org/lincoln/speeches/philadel.htm (text) and www.c-span.org/video/?298139-1/presidentelect-lincolns-inaugural-train-trip (a reenactment presented by the National Park Service), accessed November 10, 2017.

70 Stashower, *Hour of Peril*, 234.

train for Washington at 11:00 p.m. Then the president-elect asked a question: how was he to get out of the Jones House in Harrisburg and onto a train to Washington without being recognized? Judd explained that Pinkerton wanted him to wear a disguise and walk in a bent-over manner to make himself appear shorter than he really was. It was agreed that Lincoln, wearing a soft felt hat and a "man's shawl" of tartan plaid, stooping and appearing frail, would assume the part of the ailing brother of one of Pinkerton's female operatives, the fabulous Mrs. Kate Warne, America's first female detective and a valued employee of Pinkerton.[71]

As Judd and Lincoln leaned toward each other, their voices fell to whispers, and the plan began to take shape. From Pinkerton's initial idea, Lincoln and Judd made it their own, workable and believable. Nicolay knocked, nervously entered the car, and sat down beside the two men, his concern palpable. His friend, soon to be the commander-in-chief of the nation, was in grave danger. He addressed Judd: "Something is in the wind—something serious. Is it proper that I should know what it is?" Within minutes Nicolay's role was made clear. He and Ellsworth were to continue as they had been, giving their combined strength and confidence to Lincoln, and to the Lincoln family. If the public saw no change in the group of people surrounding the president-elect, then no suspicions would be raised that anything was amiss. Considering Mrs. Lincoln's reaction to the situation, this was a bigger chore than it might initially appear.[72]

During Abraham Lincoln's presidency, there were no crowds of men and women in dark suits and sunglasses clustered around the chief executive and his family. There was no Secret Service, and no Federal Bureau of Investigation to help the Secret Service ferret out an assassination attempt. There were only the friends and political associates who had taken upon themselves the responsibility of keeping the Lincoln family safe from any dangers, real or perceived. When it came time to let Nicolay and Ellsworth in on the plan, Norman Judd made it clear to them that the total size of the Lincoln party was a problem. Not all of them could be protected, so Lincoln would have to be separated from the rest and taken to Washington alone. It would be the responsibility of Nicolay and Ellsworth to get the rest of the group, including Mary, Robert, Willie, and Tad Lincoln, to Washington on the regularly scheduled train, and

71 Ibid., 264.

72 Hynd, *Arrival: 12:30*, 73-77; Daniel Mark Epstein, *The Lincolns: Portrait of a Marriage* (New York: Ballantine Books, 2009), 296-297; Alexander K. McClure, *Abraham Lincoln and Men of War-Times* (Philadelphia: Times Publishing Company, 1892), 52, online version: archive.org/details/abrahamlincolnme01mccl, accessed on July 12, 2006.

make everything look so normal that few would realize Lincoln was no longer with the party. "This secret is a secret of vital importance. And the fewer people who know about a secret of vital importance the better it is for everybody concerned," said Judd, quoting Pinkerton.[73]

Mary Lincoln and the rest would ride out of Harrisburg the next morning as if nothing had happened. It is not known how much of the plan Mrs. Lincoln knew, but she certainly understood that her husband would be going to Washington by a different route than had been planned initially. According to Pinkerton's account, "Mr. Lincoln had remarked that none should be acquainted with his secret but Mrs. Lincoln."[74] Mary Lincoln was visibly upset. She emphatically insisted that Ward Hill Lamon accompany her husband to Washington, knowing Lamon was fiercely loyal to Lincoln, and that he would defend her husband to the death.[75] Pinkerton's strategy for securing the president-elect was complete, and it protected Mrs. Lincoln and her children as well. This part of the plan is rarely mentioned, however. No one knew about it except a few men and one nervous woman who, for perhaps the first time in her married life, was powerless over decisions concerning her husband and family. With trusted friend Elmer Ellsworth firmly ensconced at her side, the train pulled out of Harrisburg at 9:00 a.m.

A telegram announcing the news of Lincoln's arrival in Washington had already been delivered to Baltimore by the time the Inaugural Express pulled into Calvert Station. The telegram had been assumed to be a ruse and the people of Baltimore were unruly and hostile.[76] According to the *Chicago Tribune*, "All the party were on the train, but few think we shall reach Washington without accidents. Colonel Ellsworth expects the train will be mobbed at Baltimore." Ellsworth was correct; "the very worst characters in Baltimore were there congregated, to restrain whom, under existing circumstances, would have been impossible. All things considered, there were chances and indications of real danger."[77]

73 Ibid.

74 Douglas L. Wilson and Rodney O. Davis, *Herndon's Informants: Letters, Interviews, and Statements about Abraham Lincoln* (Carbondale, IL: University of Illinois Press, 1997), 322; Epstein, *The Lincolns*, 296.

75 Ibid.; Epstein, *The Lincolns*, 296-297.

76 Wilson and Davis, *Herndon's Informants*, 324; Stashower, *Hour of Peril*, 243.

77 *Chicago Tribune*, February 26, 1861, www.newspapers.com/image/370732529, accessed March 7, 2015.

New York Times reporter Joseph Howard, who accompanied Mary's party on the train, wrote that Mrs. Lincoln became very upset when "some rude fellows entered the private compartment in which Mrs. Lincoln was sitting . . . but were promptly turned out by John Hay, who locked the door."[78] Baltimore police detectives, joining forces with "Colonel Sumner, Major Hunter, and Colonel Ellsworth . . . ran a gauntlet of abuse including an exhibition of rude vulgarity and disregard of personal comfort that I have rarely seen equaled. . . . We were compelled to stand still, and sustain, as well as we were able, the terrible rush of an excited, rude, and thoughtless populace."[79] After about thirty minutes of fighting their way through the obnoxious crowd, Mrs. Lincoln and her sons were quickly escorted to a carriage, in which she and her entourage, including Ellsworth, were delivered to the home of John S. Gittings, a prominent banker and former president of the Northern Central Railway.[80] After a luncheon with southern sympathizer Gittings and his wife, an invitation accepted to demonstrate that no feelings of ill-will or suspicion exited toward Gittings himself, Mrs. Lincoln's group rejoined the train to continue their journey.[81]

Luckily, during this trying and difficult period, Mary Lincoln was able to put her trust in family friend Elmer Ellsworth. She, her boys, and Ellsworth would stand at the end of the train, smiling and waving as if nothing unusual were happening at all. Nevertheless, even complacent John Hay had been anxious concerning Maryland. He had earlier written to a friend: "Tomorrow we enter slave territory. There may be trouble in Baltimore. If so, we will not go to Washington, unless in long, narrow boxes."[82] Luckily, any such trouble had been averted.

*   *   *

For many years, few believed there had been a "Baltimore plot." Lincoln was ridiculed for his seemingly "paranoid" arrival in Washington, hunched under a shawl

78 Joseph Howard, New York Times, February 25, 1861, www.newspapers. com/image/20510847/?terms=Mrs.%2BLincoln, accessed March 6, 2015.

79 Ibid.

80 "Gittings, John Sterett, 1798-1879," Archives of Maryland Historical & Biographical Series, msa.maryland.gov/megafile/msa/speccol/sc3500/sc3520/001500/001546/pdf/bio_gittings 1.pdf, accessed November 23, 2017.

81 Isaac Markers, "Why President Lincoln Spared Three Lives," *Confederate Veteran Magazine*, 40 vols. (Nashville, TN, 1893-1932), vol. XIX (1911), 382; Stashower, *Hour of Peril*, 292-293; Epstein, *The Lincolns*, 300-301.

82 John Hay to Annie E. Johnson, February 22, 1861, BU/JHC.

like a sick, old man. He ignored the jibes and cartoons, and the horror of the Civil War soon pushed the incident out of the minds of the press and people. Pinkerton's official report and its corroborating evidence, released by the Pinkerton National Detective Agency in 1867, revealed the truth. There *had* been a plot, it *had* been discovered and foiled by a combination of undercover detective work, the cooperation of the railroads and the telegraph, the ability of Lincoln's friends, including Elmer Ellsworth, to lovingly support and protect the Lincoln family, Judd's involvement, and the expert planning of detective Allan Pinkerton. Charles Gould, the railroad magnate under whose instructions Pinkerton had initially been hired, said later of the incident:

> . . . he is no longer Mr. Lincoln. We have elected him to the office of President; and on his life and his inauguration rests the question of government or revolution. We must not run a risk, for the car that carries him to Washington carries the welfare of a great nation.[83]

When Pinkerton telegraphed those on the train that,

PLUMS HAS NUTS
ARRIVED AT BARLEY
ALL RIGHT
the relief must have been palpable.[84]

*   *   *

Montgomery Blair, an abolitionist and future member of the Lincoln cabinet, offered the Lincolns the hospitality of his palatial home in Silver Spring, Maryland, just outside Washington. Lincoln had graciously refused, telling Blair that it might look preferential. "The truth is, I suppose I am now public property; and a public inn is the place where people can have access to me."[85] Lincoln chose Willard's Hotel as the place where his family would stay until President Buchanan and his niece, Harriet Lane, vacated the White House. Author Nathaniel Hawthorne described the famous hotel as

---

83 Henry C. Bowen to Abraham Lincoln, February 5, 1861, ALPLC; Charles Gould to Henry C. Bowen, February 5, 1861, ALPLC.

84 Douglas L. Wilson, Rodney O. Davis, Terry Wilson, William Henry Herndon, Jesse W. Welk, eds., *Herndon's Informants: Letters, Interviews, and Statements about Abraham Lincoln* (Carbondale, IL: University of Illinois Press, 1998), 291.

85 Lamon, *Recollections*, 34-35.

the true center of Washington and the Union, more so than the capitol building, the White House, or the State Department.[86] Willard's was where the men of power held late-night meetings, cut deals, and lobbied their various causes. It was replete with meeting rooms and two bars, perfect for seekers of power and position within the new Lincoln government.

The Lincolns stayed in Parlor Six, and the rest of his team was spread out over Willard's, often "doubling up," making it easier to maintain close contact with the center of power. Abraham Lincoln spent the next nine days reacquainting himself with Washington, having his official portrait taken by Alexander Gardner at Mathew Brady's studio, finishing his inaugural address, and making the incredibly difficult decisions necessary to build his cabinet, the famous "Team of Rivals" so accurately named by Doris Kearns Goodwin. [87]

Elmer Ellsworth had an agenda as well, although compared to the stress of the last two weeks it seemed simple. His February 25 letter to Carrie was postmarked from Washington. "I've only time to say that we arrived safely, and I received your letter yesterday. You must not expect a letter from me until after the Inauguration. . . . send love to mother in your next letter."[88] Carrie had managed to visit Ellsworth's parents earlier in the year, and the Ellsworths now thought of the young woman with great affection. She had, at Elmer's request, begun to write to them, relaying any news she had concerning his activities. Other than the letter of the 25th, there is nothing from Ellsworth's pen to indicate what he did in Washington during the remainder of the time between Lincoln's arrival and his inauguration as president of the United States on March 4, 1861.

Nevertheless, Ellsworth, Hay, and Nicolay were in the capital city of the United States, they were staying at the famous Willard's Hotel at the expense of the inauguration committee, and they were an intimate part of the new team of the most powerful man in Washington. The world was theirs. They must have had a grand time walking the streets of the city, getting to know the place they assumed would be their home for the next four years.

Monday, March 4, the day of the inauguration, was brilliantly sunny. Lincoln spoke to a vast crowd, estimated at 30,000, gathered in front of the east portico of the capitol and its half-finished dome. Security was tight as Lincoln mounted the platform to

---

86 Nathaniel Hawthorne, "Chiefly About War Matters," *The Atlantic Monthly*, Number 45 (July 1861), 59-60.

87 *Harper's Weekly*, April 27, 1861.

88 Elmer Ellsworth to Carrie Spafford, February 25, 1861, KCWM/LFAC.

speak. Sharpshooters were stationed on top of the capitol, and every soldier the city could spare was there, in uniform and armed. Police ringed the capitol grounds, eyes scanning the crowds for any sign of danger to the president.[89] Near the central platform, Ellsworth, Hay, and Nicolay sat to Lincoln's left, among the politicos and patronage men, listening to the "rail splitter" from Illinois for whom they had worked so wholeheartedly. Their dedication to both Abraham Lincoln and the Union must have felt justified by Lincoln's inaugural words, addressing the secession of several of the Southern states:

> We are not enemies, but friends. We must not be enemies. Though passion may have strained, it must not break our bonds of affection. The mystic chords of memory, stretching from every battlefield and patriot grave, to every living heart and hearthstone, all over this broad land, will yet swell the chorus of the Union, when again touched, as surely they will be, by the better angels of our nature.[90]

*   *   *

The next day, *The New York Times* wrote a society review of Lincoln's inaugural ball, held in a temporary plank structure constructed behind Washington's city hall. The "Palace of Aladdin" was hung with muslin and divided into areas for dancing and eating. City hall offices became dressing rooms for the evening.[91] The review describes the entrance into the brilliantly gas-lit, rainbow-colored dance of three young men who arrived together. One was tall, bearded, and wore a black tailcoat, a starched white cotton shirtfront, and a small black bow tie. One was shorter, with softly tousled light brown hair, wearing a cutaway and a poetically loose silk cravat over the soft, bleached linen of his shirt. And one was shorter still, with long black hair softly curling around the deep blue collar of the regimental frock coat and gold braid of the dress uniform worn by a colonel of the U.S. Zouave Cadets. John Nicolay, John Hay, and Elmer Ellsworth entered the inaugural dance, great friends, and Lincoln men to the marrow of their bones.

---

89 Winfield Scott to Abraham Lincoln, March 3, 1861, ALPLC.

90 "First Inaugural Speech," in Basler, ed., *Speeches and Writings*, 579-590.

91 *New York Times*, March 5, 1861; David S. Rothenstein, "Civil War Lost and Found: Lincoln's First Ballroom," *History Sidebar*, June 27, 2011, blog.historian4hire.net/2011/06/27/inaugural-ballroom/, accessed May 2, 2012.

Chapter 9

The Union Goes B'hoy Crazy

I want the New York firemen, for there are no more effective men in the country,
and none with whom I can do so much. Our friends at Washington are sleeping
on a volcano and I want men are ready at any moment to plunge into
the thickest of the fight.[1]

Elmer Ellsworth to "a friend," May 3, 1861

As the Lincoln family moved into the White House, Elmer Ellsworth settled in at Willard's at the Lincolns' expense. He no longer had to share a room with John Hay, but he was, after all the excitement of the last several months, alone in Washington City without employment or any means of support. Lincoln had made promises to Ellsworth, but once in the capital, they were not easily fulfilled. Before he left Springfield, Ellsworth had written to General Simon Bolivar Buckner, his friend from the Chicago militia days, requesting a letter of recommendation to the secretary of war. Ellsworth hoped for a position as a clerk in the war department, but in a response dated February 18, 1861, letter Buckner argued that he should strive higher:

I do not think it [the clerking position] would suit you. If you wish to be a soldier, I advise you to apply for an appointment as Lieutenant in the Army; such a place is in the gift of Mr. Lincoln, and he will doubtless give it to you. The policies which his administration appears disposed to adopt will in all probability occasion your rapid advancement. There are vacancies already existing; and if you obtain a Second Lieutenancy in a regiment in which

1 John Stevens Cabot Abbott, *The History of the Civil War in America: Comprising a Full and Impartial Account of the Origin and Progress of the Rebellion, of the Various Naval and Military Engagements, of the Heroic Deeds Performed by Armies and Individuals, and of Touching Scenes in the Field, the Camp, the Hospital, and the Cabin*, 2 vols. (New York: Henry Bill, 1863), 2:120; "Exercises Connected with the Unveiling of the Ellsworth Monument, at Mechanicville, May 27, 1874" (Mechanicville, NY: The Ellsworth Monument Association, 1874), 36; Randall, *Colonel Elmer Ellsworth*, 230; Ingraham, *Zouaves of '61*, 128.

there are many Southern men, you will probably advance rapidly in rank. This is better for you, and better suited to all your tastes and genius than clerking in the War Department. Avoid the latter and become a real soldier.[2]

Buckner was, at that time, commandant of the Kentucky State Guard at Louisville. He was in the unfortunate position, as were so many army officers, of looking ahead and seeing nothing but war. Despite a West Point education and service with the U.S. Army in the Mexican War, Buckner eventually joined other Southern officers and left the Union for a commission with the Confederates. He remained loyal, however, to his friend Elmer Ellsworth, and recommended him for a second lieutenancy in the Union army:

Headquarters Ky State Guard
Louisville, Feby. 18. 1861
Sir:

I take pleasure in recommending my young friend, Major Elmer Ellsworth, late commander of the Chicago [Zouave] Cadets, for appointment as 2d Lieutenant in the U.S. Army. He has much energy and industry, is intelligent, is a gentleman, and has qualifications which if rightly directed would make him an excellent officer for the U.S. Army. His connection for several years with Volunteer Companies, during which time I have known him well, has proved that he is admirably qualified to enter the military service of the Country.

Your obt. Svt. S. B. Buckner
Inspector Genl. & Major Gen. Comdg. Ky. St. Gd.[3]

Ellsworth did not submit Buckner's recommendation letter. Instead, he decided to go ahead with the petition for the war department clerkship. Others might have to wait in line to speak with the president-elect, but not Ellsworth. He had discussed at length his proposal for the reorganization of state militias with Lincoln. The plan, though complex, was designed so that a militia unit could enter the army with as little disruption as possible to overall army readiness. It was an expanded version of the plan Lincoln had earlier encouraged him to try to get passed into law in Illinois. Less than twenty-four hours after his inauguration,

2 Simon Buckner to Elmer Ellsworth, February 18, 1861, BU/JHC.

3 Ibid.

among the multitude of tasks before him, Lincoln wrote new Secretary of War Simon Cameron his own letter of support for Ellsworth. Lincoln's idea was to get Ellsworth into the army at some level, then create a Department of Militias and name Ellsworth to lead it.

Executive Chamber
March 5, 1861
Dear Sir:

If the public service admits of a change, without injury, in the office of chief clerk of the War Department, I shall be pleased of my friend E. Elmer Ellsworth, who presents you this, shall be appointed. Of course, if you see good reason to the contrary, this is not intended to be arbitrary. Yours truly.

A. Lincoln[4]

Lincoln wrote the note to Cameron in Ellsworth's presence. When Ellsworth told the story in a letter to Carries mother, Abigail Spafford, he added, "Lincoln swung around in his chair, and said in a peculiarly deliberate manner, 'I've been thinking on the way, and since we have been here, a long while in fact, that by and by, when things all get straightened out and I can see how the land lays, that I'd put you in the Army, somewhere . . .'"[5]

When Lincoln discovered that the clerkship had been promised to someone else, he again spoke to Ellsworth. On March 18, around 8:00 p.m., Ellsworth went to the president's office, this time with Maj. David Hunter and Capt. John Pope, who had accompanied Lincoln on the Inaugural Express. Simon Cameron was there as well. Ellsworth painstakingly presented his case to Cameron for the establishment of a "Bureau of Militias," of which he, Ellsworth, would be in charge. Hoping to help the cause, Maj. Hunter then added that if Ellsworth could first be appointed to the pay department, where there was already a vacancy, then an appointment to chief of the militia bureau would be easy. Lincoln added that his only hesitation was that such an appointment would not "tread on anybody's toes." He and Cameron agreed to arrange for Col. Ellsworth's idea to become a reality. Ellsworth decided to take a lesser army commission first, since the chief of a newly created military bureau could only be given to a ranking army officer. Even Mrs.

4 Abraham Lincoln to Simon Cameron, March 5, 1861, in Basler, *Speeches and Writings*, 273.

5 Elmer Ellsworth to Mrs. Spafford, March 1861, KCWM/LFAC.

Lincoln spoke to Cameron before he left that evening, making him promise at least a major's rank to her friend Ellsworth.[6] The official letter from Lincoln to Cameron read as follows:

Executive Mansion, March 18, 1861
To the Secretary of War:

Sir:

You will favor me by issuing an order detailing Lieut. Ephraim E. Ellsworth, of the First Dragoons,* for special duty as Adjutant and Inspector General of Militia for the United States, and in so far as existing laws will permit, charge him with the transaction, under your direction, of all business pertaining to the Militia, to be conducted as a separate bureau, of which Lieut. Ellsworth will be chief, with instructions to take measures for promoting a uniform system of drill for Light troops, adapted for self-instruction, for distribution to the Militia of the several States. You will please assign him suitable office rooms, furniture &c. and provide him with a clerk and messenger, access to public records, &c. as he may desire for the successful prosecution of his duties; and also provide in such manner as may be most convenient and proper, for a monthly payment for Lieut. Ellsworth, for this extra duty, sufficient to make his pay equal to that of a Major of Cavalry. Your Obt. Servt.

A. Lincoln[7]

*It is not known why Lincoln assigned the role of "Lieutenant of the First U.S. Dragoons" to Ellsworth in this letter. This is repeated in every copy of the letter, including Basler's authoritative compilation of Lincoln's writings, but Ellsworth never served with the Dragoons in any manner. In fact, from 1856 until they were redesignated as the 1st Cavalry Regiment in 1861, the First U.S. Dragoons served at Fort Tejon in California. Perhaps the title and designation were honorary and came from Ellsworth's association with Col. Edwin V. Sumner, who had been assigned by Gen. Scott as the senior officer to accompany Lincoln from Springfield to Washington in February 1861. It may also have come from Ellsworth's aforementioned "rank" of major in the Illinois State Militia. The commission, although with the salary of a higher rank, was that of a lieutenant. To give Ellsworth the grade of major would ruffle a lot of dark blue feathers belonging to Regular Army captains who were due for promotion. Being well aware of the issues that could arise if Ellsworth was to receive such a rank, especially any possibly negative comments directed toward Lincoln, a new president in an already-precarious position, Ellsworth told Cameron, "I would do nothing to cause ill feeling toward Mr. L [Lincoln] or himself [Cameron], and I would not therefore take the Majority."[8]

6   Ibid.

7   Abraham Lincoln to Simon Cameron, March 18, 1861, in Basler, *Speeches and Writings*, 177-178.

8   Elmer Ellsworth to Mrs. Spafford, March 1861, KCWM/LFAC.

In a letter to Mrs. Spafford, to be forwarded to Carrie, Ellsworth laughingly continued,

> that's the manner in which I kicked myself out of a three-thousand-dollar *life* position, into the Cold! The next best thing was to take a Lieutenancy—about $1,850 a year (Cameron has positively *promised* to make it up to $3000) and be ordered to duty at Washington and placed in charge of my Bureau.[9]

Nothing previously written about Ellsworth sheds much light on the issue of exactly why Lincoln could not create a place in the army for his young protégé. The problem had very little to do with Ellsworth himself, and everything to do with military protocol and a colonel named Charles Pomeroy Stone. Winfield Scott had personally selected Col. Stone to coordinate Washington's various militia groups in order to keep the mostly secessionist city safe for the arrival of the president-elect and his family.[10] As commanding general of the U.S. Army, Scott ordered Stone to organize the Washington Light Infantry, the National Rifles (even though it had many secession-minded members), and several regiments of Regular troops as guards and police to ensure safety along the inaugural route on March 4, 1861.[11]

Scott asked Stone to serve as inspector general of the District of Columbia, at the rank of colonel, as of January 1, 1861. This made Stone the first volunteer officer mustered into the Union Army.[12] Although he did not know Lincoln personally, Stone was a Washington resident and had his finger on the pulse of citizenry's loyalty, or lack thereof, to the new administration. He was a West Pointer with combat experience in Mexico, and had a reputation as an "able, creative administrator."[13] Scott's choice was excellent. Colonel Stone quickly utilized informants within the local militias to ferret out those who were choosing to use their militia connections to send guns and other equipment south, and to sway the loyalties of other members southward as well. Stone identified traitors to

---

9 Ibid.

10 John S. D. Eisenhower, *Agent of Destiny: The Life and Times of General Winfield Scott* (Norman, OK: University of Oklahoma Press, 1999), 352.

11 Ibid, 353-355.

12 David J. Eicher and John H. Eicher, *Civil War High Commands* (Stanford, CA: Stanford University Press, 2002), 513.

13 Blaine Lamb, *The Extraordinary Life of Charles Pomeroy Stone: Soldier, Surveyor, Pasha, Engineer* (Yardley, PA: Westholme Publishing Company, 2015), 85.

the Lincoln administration in the ranks of the National Volunteers and the National Rifles, returned the ordnance, and replaced with loyal officers those whose allegiance lay elsewhere. He armed and drilled the city's militia units and helped Gen. Scott prepare a safe inauguration for the new president.[14] Colonel Charles Stone is the person other historians refer to when they mention "someone else" to whom the loosely defined post of "militia commander" had been promised.

Stone and Scott kept the capital safe, secure, and on track for Lincoln's inauguration, and managed the massive influx of Union volunteers that followed his call for troops after the fall of Fort Sumter. Together, they skillfully merged state volunteers, Regulars, and random militia forces into what would eventually become the Union Army. Could Elmer Ellsworth have fulfilled the job so tentatively offered? He was certainly capable of understanding the situation and organizing a solution. But at this point in his career, he knew nothing about the ins and outs of Washington or the army, and he had no working relationship with Scott. It does credit to Ellsworth's character that he graciously accepted reality and remained mindful of his relationship with Lincoln.

Due to his position in the Lincoln household and his U.S. Zouave Cadet tour the previous summer, Ellsworth received some sharp criticism from the press. No one is a press darling forever, and he was no exception. The tour had given him and his Zouaves extremely high visibility, and newspaper comments, even when favorable, noted that "not a drop of blood had been shed" at any of the performances. Zouave mania was stronger than ever. *Godey's Ladies Book* touted Zouave jackets as extremely fashionable for women, and the most famous composers of the day had written music for Ellsworth and the Zouave Cadets. Rag-type dolls were made, dressed as Zouaves.[15] There were dance steps based on the Zouave drill, and Ellsworth's *carte de visite* was a best seller for every merchant who carried it.[16] By this time, many local and state militias had adopted a version of

---

14 Ibid., 88-89.

15 Even Tad and Willie Lincoln had a Zouave doll. His name was Jack, and he was a very poor soldier indeed! He was found to be "derelict of duty" regularly by Tad, then "court-martialed" and "executed." The groundskeepers usually found poor Jack hanging from a tree or buried in the gardens somewhere. At one point, after the war had started, Tad and Willie heard their father pardon soldiers whose families came to him, pleading for mercy. They decided to plead Jack's case before their father, who actually wrote an official pardon for "Jack the Doll." Perhaps Jack might even be considered one of the first "action figures."

16 Burlingame, ed., *Lincoln's Journalist*, 67-68.

the Zouave dress—baggy pants, collarless jackets, a lot of gold trim and buttons—as their preferred uniform. That the papers would now poke a little fun in Ellsworth's direction was not surprising.

Most of Washington knew that Ellsworth was a welcome, almost-daily visitor to the Lincoln Executive Mansion. Mrs. Lincoln's cousin, Elizabeth Grimsley, had come to live with the Lincolns, giving Mary some much-needed support as she adjusted to her new duties as first lady. Grimsley wrote of Ellsworth, "He had been a member of the family ever since we went to Washington . . . and was much beloved."[17] She further described him as "a magnetic, brilliant young fellow, overflowing with dash and spirit."[18] Ellsworth's two best friends, Hay and Nicolay, now lived at the Executive Mansion, sleeping in the small bedrooms down the hall from Lincoln's office. When Ellsworth stayed over, which was often, he slept in Robert Lincoln's bedroom. He played regularly with Willie and Tad, roughhousing around the living quarters, and Mrs. Lincoln grew especially fond of him. Unfortunately, all this attention had made Ellsworth some powerful enemies.

Exalted the summer before, now the press began to write sarcastically about Ellsworth's bid to get a powerful army rank over the heads of regular officers, who were confident in their own abilities to influence events. Among Ellsworth's possessions was an undated article clipped from the *Chicago Times*:

> Zouave, Oh! The Telegraph announces that Mr. Lincoln has requested Gen. Cameron to appoint Col. Ellsworth of Chicago Zouave notoriety, to the fat office of Chief Clerk of the War Department. Oh, my! Calico Colonels are in the ascendant. And who is it, pray, that Mr. Lincoln is so anxious to put into a twenty-two-hundred dollars a year office? A mere adventurer; formerly the pompous captain of the Chicago Zouave Cadets, who went into the show business and travelled on free passes all over the Union last Summer; a second edition of 'fuss and feathers.' . . . Vive la humbug! Won't he make a roaring chief clerk of the War Department?[19]

S. D. Beekman, a former reporter for the *New York World*, sent Ellsworth an article clipped from that paper. He was concerned that Ellsworth might think he

---

17 Elizabeth Todd Grimsley, "Six Months in the White House," *Journal of the Illinois State Historical Society*, vol. 19, no. 3/4 (October 1926-January 1927), 19.

18 Ibid.

19 *Chicago Times*, undated newspaper clipping, KCWM/LFAC.

had written it, and added a personal note assuring Ellsworth that the opinions were not his. The *World* article quotes a similar piece from the *Chicago Post*:

> In spite of Lincoln's unaccountable attachment for him, Ellsworth was finally choked off with a lieutenancy in the regular army where he may perhaps be useful, if not spoiled by being petted. He is not large in stature, but a most gigantic humbug.[20]

> The dress of the gallant 'Colonel' is at least unique. His boots are of the approved patent leather, his pants black, and lie out over the boot after the fashion of sailors; at the waist they have the appearance of being fastened with a strap and buckle—or perhaps he ties his suspenders round his middle instead of passing them over the shoulders; waistcoat short, with only three buttons; . . . over his chest hangs a huge bosom neck-tie, decked out with dazzling trumpery from some 'dollar jewelry store'; hair dark and long, poked behind his ears which are also long. . . . No visitor to Washington can fail to recognize the original. He will be regarded with amusement or mortification, as the spectator is the opponent or friend of President Lincoln, who seems to have adopted him, and is determined to make a great man of him.[21]

These were not the only unkind cuts Ellsworth received. John Hay, always a sympathetic friend, wrote that the weeks following their arrival in Washington:

> . . . were the least pleasant of Ellsworth's life. They were brightened only by the society of those he trusted most and by the unvarying friendship and confidence of the President and his family . . . he was placed in a false position. He never wished office for its honor or its profit, but you can never get office-seekers or office dispensers to believe any such story.[22]

In addition to feeling publicly humiliated by bad press, Ellsworth was not physically well. He initially thought he was developing a bad cold, but soon his general wretchedness and fever were more clearly explained. Two days after Tad and Willie Lincoln came down with the measles, so did Elmer Ellsworth. When he first saw the red spots, he immediately thought of his brother's death the year before, from what was initially considered to be smallpox. Sometimes Ellsworth overreacted to stresses in his life, and this was one of those times. He locked himself in his room at Willard's Hotel, convulsed in self-pity. The Lincolns were

---

20 S. D. Beekman to Elmer Ellsworth, March 28, 1861, BU/JHC.

21 Ibid.

22 Burlingame, ed., *Lincoln's Journalist*, 69.

concerned, and it did not take much to get John Hay and John Nicolay to pound on Ellsworth's door at Willard's, trying to reason with him. Reluctantly, Ellsworth let them in. Hay and Nicolay visited regularly during the weeks Elmer lay in bed, terribly ill and sometimes delirious from fever. In moments of lucidity, they tried to talk to him of current events. Hay wrote:

> While he lay there, the news from the South began to show that the rebels were determined upon war, and the rumors on the street said that a wholesome Northwesterly breeze was blowing from the Executive Mansion. These indications were more salutary to Ellsworth than any medicine. We were talking one night of coming probabilities, and I spoke of the doubt so widely existing as to the loyalty of the people. Here joined, earnestly,—"I can only speak for myself. You know I have great work to do, to which my life is pledged; I am the only earthly stay of my parents; there is a young woman whose happiness I regard as dearer than my own; yet I could ask no better death than to fall next week before Sumter. I am not better than other men. You will find that patriotism is not dead, even if it sleeps."[23]

As Ellsworth recovered, he wrote to Carrie on March 21 about his health scare:

> I have strength enough to write a letter for the first time since my illness. . . . I am so weak it is very difficult to write at all. I have been confined to my bed by the measles and inflammation of the chest. The crisis of the disease was reached today and the physician thinks I will recover rapidly and perhaps be about again sometime next week. I supposed I had the small pox, and of course I wrote to no one.[24]

As Ellsworth realized that he would recover, his focus changed to the problems that had beset him before he became ill. He wrote to the Spaffords, and Carrie, about his promise of a commission from Lincoln and Cameron, the hoped-for organization of a Bureau of Militias, and his problems with the jealousy of staff officers in the Regular Army and the established military bureaucracy. He also expressed his hurt at the sarcastic editorials about him in the newspapers: "Now a word about that [*Chicago*] *Times* and *Post* trash; I have received, read, and preserved it all; . . . Once these things would have almost killed me; now they wound only so far as they affect my chances of success . . ."[25]

---

23 Burlingame, ed., *At Lincoln's Side*, 149.

24 Elmer Ellsworth to Carrie Spafford, March 21, 1861, KCWM/LFAC.

25 Ibid.

There was one last convulsion of Ellsworth's self-pity. He wrote to Carrie again on March 24: "Why don't *you* write to *me*——? Here I've been sick unable to leave my bed for a long while every day longing for a letter, but none came. You mustn't stand on your dignity, little one, in these piping times."[26] Carrie's letters had been held up in the pre-war mail confusion, but they arrived very soon afterward.

*   *   *

As Ellsworth had told Hay, patriotism was asleep. It awakened with a jolt on April 12, the day after Ellsworth's twenty-fourth birthday. Fort Sumter, a federal garrison located in Charleston Harbor, South Carolina, refused to surrender to the Confederates. Sixty-eight soldiers under the command of Major Robert Anderson had been in the fort since December 26, and their supplies were dwindling. When Lincoln decided to resupply the garrison, the Confederacy considered his actions an assault on their sovereignty. In the middle of the night of April 11-12, Southern emissaries Colonel James Chestnut, Colonel James Chisholm, and Captain Stephen D. Lee brought Maj. Anderson an ultimatum: "Either surrender by 4 AM or the Confederate batteries will open fire."[27]

Anderson replied: "I shall await the first shot and, if you do not batter us to pieces, we shall be starved out in a few days."[28] At 4:30 a.m., General Pierre Gustave Toutant Beauregard gave the order to open fire, and Anderson surrendered on the afternoon of April 13. The American Civil War had begun.

By April 15, when Lincoln put out a national call for 75,000 troops, Elmer Ellsworth took action so quickly that it was obvious he had long prepared for this day. He resigned his hard-won second lieutenant's commission and went directly to the White House to speak with Lincoln. Once there, he laid out his plan to go to New York City and raise a regiment from among the city's firemen, and bring them back to Washington. Lincoln gave Ellsworth an open letter of introduction to take with him, again displaying his regard for the young man and establishing broad privileges for Ellsworth in the president's name. Abraham Lincoln showed this regard to very few people, but he trusted Elmer Ellsworth explicitly:

26 Ibid.; March 24, 1861.

27 William C. Davis, *Brother Against Brother: The War Begins* (Alexandria, VA: Time-Life Books, 1983), 139-143.

28 Ibid.

Recruiting for the New York Fire Zouaves began immediately. *Library of Congress*

To Elmer E. Ellsworth
Col. E. E. Ellsworth

Washington, April 15, 1861 My Dear Sir:

Ever since the beginning of our acquaintance, I have valued you highly as a personal friend, and at the same time (without much capacity of judging) have had a very high estimate of your military talent. Accordingly I have been, and still am anxious for you to have the best position in the military which can be given you, consistently with justice and proper courtesy towards the older officers in the army. I cannot incur the risk of doing them injustice, or a discourtesy; but I do say they would personally oblige me; if they could, and would place you in some position, or in some service, satisfactory to yourself. Your Obt. Servt.

A. Lincoln[29]

Ellsworth arrived in New York City on April 18. His first stop was the office of Horace Greeley, editor of the New York *Tribune*. As Ellsworth and Greeley had met during Lincoln's inaugural journey, he immediately reintroduced himself, showed Greeley the president's letter, and asked for help. Ellsworth declared:

I want the New York firemen, for there are no more effective men in the country, and none with whom I can do so much. They are sleeping on a volcano at Washington, and I want men who are ready at any moment to plunge into the thickest of the fight.[30]

Ellsworth's decision to recruit New York firefighters was based on several good reasons, coupled with personal experience. He had been instrumental in the

29 Elizabeth Grimsley to John Stuart, May 24, 1861, in Harry E. Pratt, *Concerning Mr. Lincoln: In Which Abraham Lincoln is Pictured as he Appeared to Letter Writers of His Time*, (Springfield, IL: The Abraham Lincoln Association, 1944), 81.

30 "Col. Elmer Ellsworth Became a Legend and Martyr Early in the Civil War," *About.com*, history1800s.about.com/od/civilwar/ss/Death-of-Elmer-Ellsworth_2.htm, accessed July 23, 2011.

choosing and training of three hundred men in Chicago for the Chicago Fire Brigade, and he knew that firefighters were trained to work together as a single unit, each doing his duty, and keeping an eye on the men around him. They could respond quickly, obey orders, organize, and execute upon command. They also could work alone, looking about for where help was needed and joining right in. Ellsworth believed men with these attributes would make good soldiers. With Greeley's help and encouragement, Ellsworth immediately placed ads in newspapers and blanketed the city with posters. Two days after arriving in New York, he awarded officer commissions to New York City Fire Company leaders and to former members of the U.S. Zouave Cadets, several of whom had agreed to help him in his endeavor. Then Ellsworth began recruiting in earnest.

Like those in other large cities, in 1861 New York's fire department was a volunteer organization staffed by "b'hoys" (an Irish version of the word "boys") from a variety of backgrounds who responded when their district's fire tower sounded an alarm and "ran with the masheen" to the site of the fire. The physical exertion required to run a huge fire engine through the streets and then pump water, climb ladders, and pull hoses meant that the volunteers had to be in good physical shape. The men had earned a mixed reputation, fighting each other almost as often as they fought fires. Although these rough b'hoys were of varying political viewpoints—mostly Democratic and influenced by Tammany Hall—and, like many New Yorkers, may have initially felt sympathetic toward the South, the attack on Fort Sumter caused New York to fall firmly in line on the side of the Union. Within three days of his arrival, Ellsworth had at least 1,200 men signed up for a tour of duty lasting ninety days. On April 27, 1861, the *New York Leader* chronicled Ellsworth's efforts in vivid detail:

> Colonel Ellsworth and his officers have been active in preparing this regiment for service. More work has been done in six days than seemed possible. The men have been mustered into service; the officers elected; the uniforms made, and on Sunday afternoon eleven hundred as efficient and hardy soldiers as ever handled a gun, will start for the scene of rebellion.

> Col. Ellsworth arrived in this city on Thursday of last week. On Friday he called together a number of the principal men of the department. On Saturday he selected his officers. On Sunday he mustered one thousand men. On Monday he drilled them. On Tuesday inspected them. On Wednesday commenced giving them clothes. On Thursday had them

in quarters, and yesterday, (Friday), he was ready and waiting for supplies. Today he will receive them, and to-morrow march through the city escorted by the whole Fire Department on board the steamer *Baltic* direct for the seat of war.[31]

Ellsworth was immediately elected regimental colonel, and the former Zouave Cadets who had served with him began drilling the volunteers. Over the next two days enlistments soared to about 2,300 volunteers, enough for two full regiments of men. The state of New York could neither arm nor provide uniforms for so many troops. Additionally, since many of the volunteers were also firefighters, New York City grew concerned that its fire-fighting preparedness would be severely compromised should thousands of firefighters leave the metropolis at once. By a combination of Ellsworth's hard drilling and complete physical examinations, the company's surgeon, Doctor Charles Carroll Gray, who had served in this capacity in the British army during the Crimean War, cut the total to 1,100 men, or one regiment. There were whispers that a few of the b'hoys had actually been "g'hals," but there is little evidence to document this rumor.

The patriotic citizens of New York City raised about $60,000 to purchase rifles for the troops. Ellsworth had requested Sharps rifles, but for the moment his men had to make do with an assortment of at least ten different kinds of firearms. They were gladly received, however, and served the immediate purpose.[32] Later the unit was issued Springfield rifles (Model 1855) from the U.S. Army, but Ellsworth's effort to equip the Fire Zouaves with Sharps rifles continued. Ellsworth had designed the uniforms worn by the volunteers, sewn in red, blue, and gray worsted wool. These were paid for by subscription and, as contract work, were put together quickly in New York garment factories. Later it was found that they were not made of worsted wool at all, but a substance made of cutting room floor scraps cut into bits and, with glue, felted together. This fabric, called "shoddy," began to fall apart quickly.[33] Ellsworth, Lieutenant Stephen W. Stryker, and Quartermaster Alexander M. C. Stetson were rightly appalled at this deception and worked hard to remedy

31 "11th Infantry Regiment, New York, Civil War Newspaper Clippings," NYSMM, online version: dmna.state.ny.us/historic/reghist/cicil/infantry/11thinfCWN.htm NYSMM, accessed August 6, 2011.

32 Ingraham, *Zouaves of '61*, 128; "11th Infantry Regiment," NYSMM, online version: dmna.ny.gov/historic/reghist/civil/infantry/11thInf/11thInfCWN.htm, accessed November 25, 2017.

33 Ingraham, *Zouaves of '61*, 128-129.

the condition.[34] These issues of corruption were army-wide, and were, in part, the reason for the creation of the Joint Committee on the Conduct of the War in December 1861.[35]

Several military units left New York City for Washington between April 19 and 29: the Sixth New York, the Fifth and Eighth Massachusetts, and even the famous Silk-Stocking Brigade—now designated the Seventh New York—those darlings of the wealthy. It is doubtful, however, if any regiment equaled the excitement created by Ellsworth's Fire Zouaves. They left New York City on April 29 amid colorful, emotional celebrations.[36]

Newspaper reporters flocked to "Zouave Quarters," at the Devlin Building on Canal Street, to report on their departure. From the *New York Evening Post*:

> The headquarters just previous to the departure at 2:45 PM presented a scene of extraordinary activity as the men were marched by companies into the basement of the building to receive their arms, which consisted of Sharps rifles and knives—a sort of bowie-knife about 16 inches long, sometimes called an "Arkansas toothpick," which fitted the rifles and could be used as a bayonet—and revolvers.[37]

Ned House, who wrote for both the *New York World* and the *New York Tribune* and who would accompany Ellsworth's men to Washington, wrote:

> Inside the building, everything wore a military business-like air; many soldiers were packing their knapsacks, fitting their belts and uniforms, while others were undergoing a preliminary drill, under the directions of their enterprising captains. The busiest man of the whole regiment, however, was Col. Ellsworth himself . . . his step was as brisk and his voice as deep and sonorous as when New Yorkers first beheld him at the head of his famous company of Chicago Zouaves. One moment . . . the little Colonel . . . was marching at the head of an enthusiastic company of butcher boys, the next he would be assisting a colored servant to carry a box of muskets across the room, or buckling the knapsack to the broad

34 "11th Infantry Regiment," NYSMM, online version: dmna.ny.gov/historic/ reghist/ civil/infantry/11thInf/11thInfCWN.htm, accessed November 25, 2017.

35 "Joint Committee on the Conduct of the War, Notable Senate Investigations, U.S. Senate Historical Office, Washington, D.C.," www.senate.gov/artandhistory/history/ common/ investigations/pdf/JCCW_Fullcitations.pdf, accessed December 3, 2017.

36 Ingraham, *Zouaves of '61*, 129-130; "11th Infantry Regiment," NYSMM, online version: dmna.ny.gov/historic/reghist/civil/infantry/11thInf/11thInfCWN.htm, accessed November 25, 2017.

37 *New York Evening Post*, April 29, 1861.

shoulders of some volunteer who "hadn't exactly gotten the hang of the infernal contrivance."[38]

Poets even composed odes:

'Tis thus the New York Firemen
When in their Country's cause,
Unite in common Brotherhood
For to sustain her laws.
And crush the serpent—Treason
By killing every knave
Who would insult the Stars and Stripes
Wherever they may wave.[39]

At 2:00 on the afternoon of the 29th, the farewells began. Earlier in the day, there had been a special farewell for Elmer Ellsworth. Phebe Ellsworth, Elmer's mother, had come to the Astor House to bid her son good-bye. Robert Sears, the family friend from Elmer's Mechanicville days, had brought Mr. and Mrs. Ellsworth down the Hudson to New York City. Although small and trembling from her slowly advancing Parkinson's disease, her dark eyes gladdened when he finally appeared. "I hope God will take care of you, Elmer," were her last tremulous words to him, and he answered, "He will take care of me, mother. He has led me to this work, and He will take care of me." Neither mother nor son realized that these would be the last words they would ever share.[40]

*   *   *

The final farewell ceremonies began when the New York Fire Zouaves, as the regiment was now known, lined up on Canal Street. Mr. W. H. Wickham, president of the New York City Fire Department, presented the men with a large, white silk flag, bordered with a tri-colored fringe of red, white, and blue. The center of the flag was painted with hooks, ladders, and other firemen's tools, and a fireman's ax

38 *New York Tribune*, April 29, 1861.

39 Ibid.

40 Randall, *Colonel Elmer Ellsworth*, 233.

Mr. W. H. Wickham, President of the NYC Fire Department, presented the men with a large, white silk flag, bordered with a tri-colored fringe of red, white, and blue. *New York State Military Museum.*

topped its staff. Wickham spoke: "When the fire bell rings in the night, the citizen rests securely, for he knows the New York firemen are omnipotent to arrest the progress of destruction. You are now . . . called to quench the flames of rebellion. Our hearts are with you, at all times and in every place."[41]

General John Adams Dix, the former United States treasury secretary, and Augusta Astor, the wife of wealthy New York businessman John Jacob Astor, III, presented the next flag, made of red silk, with Dix reading Mrs. Astor's letter of presentation:

Colonel Ellsworth—Sir:

I have the honor of presenting the accompanying colors to the First Regiment New York Zouaves. In delivering the ensign of our nation into the charge of the brave men under

41 Ingraham, *Zouaves of '61*, 131-132.

The final farewell ceremonies began when the New York Fire Zouaves, as the regiment was now known, lined up on Canal Street. As they marched out of town, the New York City Fire Department escorted them. *Frank Leslie's Illustrated Newspaper*

your command, I am happy in the confidence that I entrust it to men whose heads are moved by a generous patriotism to defend it, and whose hearts feel now more deeply than they have ever done that the honor of their country's flag is as sacred and precious to them as their own.

Accustomed as we are to think of them in the discharge of their ordinary duties with grateful sympathy and a well-founded pride, these feelings grow stronger the solemn moment when they are going from us to engage in a new and still more perillous[sic] service. I pray, sir, that Heaven's gracious protection may be over you and over these, to preserve and bring you back in safety to those whose hearts will follow you each day with prayer, and a hopeful expectation of being gladdened through your success. Believe me yours,

With much respect and true regard,

Augusta Astor[42]

42 Mrs. Augusta Astor to Colonel Ellsworth and the 11th New York Fire Zouaves, "11th Infantry Regiment," NYSMM, online version: dmna.ny.gov/historic/reghist/civil/ infantry/ 11thInf/11thInfCWN.htm, accessed May 14, 2011.

Actress Laura Keene presented the third flag. Ms. Keene addressed her letter to "Brother Soldiers."[43] Many more flags, flowers, and banners were presented until, loaded with laurels, the Zouaves and several bands began the march down Broadway to the pier where the steamship *Baltic* was waiting to take them to Annapolis, from which they would proceed to Washington by train.

A small setback occurred when a concern that the Zouaves had not complied with army regulations arose. A regiment was to consist of one thousand men, and Ellsworth was boarding one hundred more men than that number. General John E. Wool, commander of the Department of the East, had met Ellsworth in 1860 during the Zouave Cadet tour. He assumed responsibility for the embarkation of the Fire Zouaves, and they boarded the Baltic with no more delay. In the words of Arthur O'Neil Alcock, a volunteer Zouave and "special correspondent" for the *New York Atlas*:

Finally, the last good-bye having been uttered, the last hand shaken, the fasts were let go, and the noble Baltic glided from the pier out into the broad stream, amidst the deafening cheers of the multitude that had accompanied us . . . flags were run up to the peaks and mast-heads, bands played, the 'Star Spangled Banner' waved proudly in the breeze, the flag of the Fire department floated out in all its beauty . . . and we were away! Still, however, as the cannon boomed the parting salute, anxious eyes were kept on the docks lined with the red shirts and leather hats of our comrades left at home, and the tears might be seen in the eyes of brave and stalwart men.[44]

The Zouaves reached Washington on the evening of May 2. All concerned were both pleased and relieved. John Hay, who had referred to the Fire Zouaves as Ellsworth's "blood tubs," was glad that the trip from New York to Washington went without incident for his good friend. After meeting Ellsworth and his regiment at Union Station, and noting that the now-colonel was dressed like his men, and had even cut his hair, he wrote:

Tonight Ellsworth and his stalwart troop arrived. His face was thin from constant labor and excitement; his voice had assumed that tone of hoarse strength that I recognized at the

43 Ibid. Ms. Keene was playing the role of Florence Trenchard in *Our American Cousin* at Ford's Theatre the night Lincoln was assassinated.

44 Arthur O'Neil Alcock, *New York Atlas*, April 30, 1861, in Patrick Schroeder and Brian C. Pohanka, *With the 11th New York Fire Zouaves In Camp, Battle, and Prison: The Narrative of Private Arthur O'Neil Alcock in The New York Atlas and Leader* (Lynchburg, VA: Schroeder Publications, 2011), 22.

end of the triumphant tour last year. He seemed contented and at ease about his regiment. He indulged in a little mild blasphemy when he found that no suitable quarters had been provided but was mollified by the proffer of the 69th's rooms [at] the Capital.[45]

Much to the consternation of everyone except the New York Fire Zouaves, Ellsworth chose to quarter his regiment in the chamber where the House of Representatives usually met. Much has been written about the behavior of the Zouaves from May 2 until May 11, when they were moved to "Camp Lincoln," outside the city limits, but there is little agreement as to the facts. John Hay described the b'hoys as "the largest, sturdiest, and physically the most magnificent men I ever saw collected together," and he was awed by the animal energy they generated. They were accustomed to physical exertion in work, in play, and in settling a dispute. Suddenly they were in a strange city, under comparatively stringent rules, and they had little to do. At no time in history has the lethal combination of testosterone and circumstance ever worked out perfectly, and this time was no exception.

According to legend, the first question asked by one of the Zouaves when leaving the train in Washington was, "Can you tell us where Jeff Davis is? We're lookin' for him."[46] Things went downhill from that point. The *Philadelphia Press* gave a good summary of the most serious problems. They claimed that the "b'hoys" chased imaginary secessionists through the streets, terrifying old ladies. They went into restaurants, ordered meals, and told the owners to charge them to Jeff Davis or the Confederacy. Even John Hay called them "a jolly, gay set of blackguards in a pretty complete state of *don't care a damn*."[47] Several letters and newspaper accounts provide anecdotal evidence about the time the Zouaves spent quartered in the House of Representatives' chamber. It was all too much temptation for the high-spirited soldiers. Zouaves sat in the seats of the elected officials, abolished the sitting House, and set up a new one. They elected their own

---

45 John Hay, diary entry, April 30, 1861, in Michael Burlingame and John R. Ettinger, eds., *Inside Lincoln's White House: The Complete Civil War Diary of John Hay* (Carbondale, IL: Southern Illinois University Press, 1977).

46 *Chicago Tribune*, May 5, 1861.

47 John Hay, diary, May 2, 1861, 17, BU/JHC.

"speaker," then went "into session," dissolving the Union, then reconstructing it according to Zouave dictates.[48]

Ellsworth's correspondence from this period proves that most of the charges against the New Yorkers were true. Letters from restaurant owners, photography studios, property owners, and the chief engineer of the New York City Fire Department provide additional evidence. Rumors of the Fire Zouaves' antics had reached as far north as New York, and Fire Commander L. N. Hudson wanted the names of the offenders so they could be discharged from the department. Even Carrie Spafford needed reassurance about Ellsworth's regiment. He wrote to her a few days after May 7: "The reports that the men are bad and that 150 have been sent back is false. We have sent back but 6—and the men do well."[49]

According to the memoirs of Corporal Francis Brownell, Col. Ellsworth paid the bills for food, *cartes de visite*, and property damage out of his own pocket. Even with all the bad publicity, the Lincolns never commented on any of the misdeeds of Ellsworth's men. Eleven-year-old Willie Lincoln wrote a letter to a friend in Springfield on May 3, 1861. He eagerly described the excitement in the capital:

> I suppose that you did not learn that Colonel E. E. Ellsworth had gone to New York, and organized a regiment,—divided into companies, and brought them here, and to be sworn in—I don't know when. Some people call them the B'hoys, and others call them, the firemen.[50]

The date for the transfer of Ellsworth's "pet lambs" to the Regular Army was Tuesday, May 7. Initially, the regiment had volunteered for a ninety-day enlistment. Now the men were being asked to renew that enlistment for three years. There were complaints, and several objections, but by the end of the day, only twelve soldiers had refused to serve any longer than the original agreement.[51] On Tuesday afternoon, Col. Ellsworth formed his men in a hollow square on the east side of the capitol grounds. President Lincoln, accompanied by Willie and Tad, reviewed the troops from a coach. The crowd that gathered to hear General Irvin McDowell

48 "Late Headquarters of Colonel Ellsworth, of the N.Y. Fire Zouaves, at the Capitol, at Washington: The New York Fire Zouaves Quartered in the House of Representatives at Washington, D.C.," *Harpers Weekly*, May 25, 1861, www.history.house.gov/Collection/Detail/29429, accessed August 23, 2016.

49 Elmer Ellsworth to Carrie Spafford, May 7, 1861, KCWM/LFAC.

50 Randall, *Colonel Elmer Ellsworth*, 236-239.

51 Schroeder and Pohanka, *11th New York Fire Zouaves*, 52.

swear in Ellsworth's men was large and enthusiastic. John Hay was also thereto support his friend, and he recorded his observations about the ceremony:

> It was a great speech. . . . There was more common sense, dramatic power, tact, energy, and that eloquence that naturally flowers into deeds in le petit Colonel's fifteen-minute harangue than in all the spread-eagle speeches recently heard in Congress. . . . He spoke to them as men. Made them proud in their good name; spoke bitterly and witheringly of the disgrace of the enlistment of other regiments for "thirty days only" while the Fire Zouaves were enlisting "for the War." Ellsworth closed with wonderful tact and dramatic spirit by saying, "Now laddies, if anyone of you wants to go home, he better sneak around the back alleys, crawl over fences, and get out of sight before we see him." He must have run with this crowd sometime in his varied career—he knows and handles them so perfectly.[52]

In front of President Lincoln, the cheering crowds, Gen. McDowell, and the half-finished dome of the capitol, the Fire Zouaves swore to support the constitution and the government of the United States for the duration of the war. In so doing, they officially became the Eleventh New York Volunteer Infantry.

When Ellsworth and his regiment arrived in Washington, there were no completed plans for quartering any of the large numbers of troops converging on the city. Every state had a quota of volunteers to fill, and patriotic support ran high in the North. Southern states were seceding; the Confederacy had elected a president and was raising an army of its own. Perhaps when Lincoln asked for 75,000 troops, he did not think they would show up so fast, although initially, he despaired of any showing up at all. But they did show up, and land had not been leased, tents had not been delivered, food was unavailable, and weapons and uniforms were scarce. Very little had been done to take care of the new Union army now forming in the streets and neighborhoods of Washington. The Fire Zouaves were lucky to have arrived in the city when they did. The chambers of the House of Representatives may not have been very military, but they added to the excitement of the whole adventure.

By early May, however, things were beginning to shape up. Across the eastern branch of the Anacostia River, over the Navy Yard Bridge, was Uniontown. It was a bucolic setting, especially compared to other parts of Washington. Fields of tobacco and wheat encircled a few small cottages. On the seventeenth-century land grant known as St. Elizabeth's, behind a massive brick wall, rose the Government

---

52 Tyler Dennett, ed., *Lincoln and the Civil War in the Diaries and Letters of John Hay* (Boston: Da Capo Press, 1988), 20.

Hospital for the Insane, designed by Thomas Walter, the man responsible for many of the grand buildings in the city. The hospital grounds gave way to more fields, and finally to a dense forest. Abruptly, the road passed from the forest to a large clearing that overlooked Giesboro Point. The government leased this land for several army camps, including "Camp Lincoln," so named by Ellsworth. The supply situation improved daily, but the camp would not be ready for occupation until May 10.[53]

Of course, it was not just the troops Col. Elmer Ellsworth brought to the capital that were unruly. Of the more than 20,000 volunteers occupying Washington, there was the distinct probability that more than just Ellsworth's "b'hoys" were unable to live up to the promises of constant gentlemanly deportment. Ellsworth did what he could, finally narrowing the problems in his regiment down to just a few men.[54] He increased drilling, and more than doubled the number of guards around the House chamber.[55] Finally, help for the rehabilitation of his regiment's reputation arrived in a form ideally suited to New York firefighters—a fire!

At 2:00 a.m. on May 9, a small building near Willard's Hotel began to burn. Washington's Franklin Volunteer Fire Department quickly extinguished it, but not thoroughly. Two hours later, the building was again in flames, and this time the extent of the fire was much greater. Realizing that this blaze was significantly more dangerous than the previous one, Brigadier General Joseph K. Mansfield, commanding the troops in Washington, called for the services of Col. Ellsworth and his Fire Zouaves, still quartered in the capitol. Ellsworth quickly ordered ten men from each company to follow him down Pennsylvania Avenue, then across the street to Willard's. Not willing to be left behind, the rest of the regiment began pouring out the windows of the capitol building, yelling commands to each other as they had done in New York.[56] Grabbing the speaking trumpet from the Franklin Fire chief, Ellsworth took control of the situation When the chief objected,

53 John B. Leverich, "From our own Correspondent," May 17, 1861, NYSMM, online version: www.dmna.ny.gov/historic/reghist/civil/infantry/11thInf/11thInfCWN.htm, accessed November 16, 2017.

54 Robert E. Denney, *The Civil War Years: A Day-by-Day Chronicle* (New York: Grammercy Books, 1998), 40-41.

55 Ibid.

56 *New York Times*, "From the Fire Zouaves: How the B'hoys Put Out the Fire At Willard's," May 11, 1861, www.nytimes.com/1861/o5/11/news/from-the-fire-zouaves-how-the- boys-put-out-the-fire-at-willard-s-html, accessed fall 2012.

Ellsworth replied that he would only give it up if the chief was able to show that he had more men on the ground than did Ellsworth.[57]

The fire blazed hotly on all four floors of the building, which housed a tailor's shop. Patrons of Willard's abandoned their rooms and were lining the sidewalk, clutching robes and valises of government papers. If Willard's burned down, at least half of official Washington would be homeless, and the rest would lose their favorite place to meet and discuss official (and unofficial) business. A group of Zouaves, pulling a hose reel that belonged to the Franklin Fire Department, arrived quickly. As soon as the first engine was close enough, the hose was attached. Sixteen men moved into position. Ellsworth raised the fire trumpet to his lips, shouting the command to the pump men: "Unit A, commence!"

The Zouaves, falling back on their experience as veteran New York firefighters, fought the blaze for over an hour. They formed pyramids on one another's shoulders to climb to the lightning rods, where they suspended a man headfirst from the burning rooftop so he could reach a hose extended from below and aim it into the upper-story windows. When Unit A was exhausted, Ellsworth called for Unit B, and the pumping continued. A detachment of Zouaves guarded the furniture and luggage removed from Willard's, and frightened bystanders were calmed and comforted by the big men. The fire was extinguished and, other than fear and some smoke damage, Willard's Hotel was untouched. Ellsworth's gallant Fire Zouaves were congratulated all around and thanked by the Willard brothers for saving their hotel. The heroes ate breakfast in Willard's dining room, where Gen. Mansfield expressed the thanks of a grateful city. The Zouaves had redeemed themselves, repaired their somewhat-tattered reputation, and given the press a good story with, finally, something positive to say about Ellsworth's "pet lambs."[58]

On May 10, a Zouave work party under the command of Lieutenant Colonel Noah Farnham was dispatched to erect tents and set up the other conveniences of an encampment on the heights commanding the Navy Yard, near the insane asylum. The next day, Ellsworth and his regiment received orders to move into their now-prepared camp. The tents provided for them were the first Sibley-style tents issued by the war department. Looking vaguely like a combination of teepee and carnival pavilion, each Sibley was capable of affording decent accommodations for twenty men, although sixteen occupied each during the life of Camp Lincoln. Once in a formal encampment, the men were brought immediately under the eyes

57 Ibid.

58 Ibid.

On May 9, 1861, just a week after their arrival in Washington, the Fire Zouaves had the chance to put their fiery reputation to work dousing a blaze that threatened Willard's Hotel. *Library of Congress.*

of their officers, and discipline issues fell to a minimum.[59] As a result, the Zouaves regained their former popularity in the hearts of the citizens. Even Willie and Tad Lincoln organized some of their friends into a "soldier company" and named themselves "Mrs. Lincoln's Zouaves." Tad's uniform was modeled on Ellsworth's own, and Ellsworth, Hay, Nicolay, and the Lincolns reviewed the small military company. With appropriate presidential dignity, Abraham Lincoln presented them with a flag. Zouave dolls were on the market, and Ellsworth's *Manual of Arms* was becoming a best seller.[60]

As the regiment settled into life at Camp Lincoln, John Hay and John Nicolay rode out to visit. Hay remarked in his diary on May 12:

59 Ibid.

60 Randall, *Colonel Elmer Ellsworth*, 243.

We spent this afternoon at Camp Lincoln, the habitation of Ellsworth's "pet lambs." The men seem very comfortable and happy. Ellsworth was playing [base] ball with them as we approached. Looking fine and blousy in his red shirt. We went to his tent.[61]

Sunday seemed to be visiting day, as a week later, May 19, Ellsworth went into the city, going immediately to the White House. Finding the upstairs empty, he waited in the president's office. According to the memoirs of William Stoddard, the president's third secretary, he heard Ellsworth's footsteps and shouted up the stairs, "Hullo! Ellsworth? Are you here?"

Ellsworth answered cheerfully, "Yes, I'm all the President there is on hand this morning. I got away from camp to run over and see him [Lincoln] and the boys." Stoddard was happy to see Ellsworth and have his complete attention for a while. In April, Stoddard had enlisted for a three-month term in the National Rifles, a militia unit he described as "a company of select and eminent young gentlemen who regarded themselves as the pink of chivalry."[62] Stoddard, whose White House duties kept him from attending drill regularly, was hoping Ellsworth could give him some pointers, especially concerning the handling of a rifle. Conveniently, an Enfield rifle just happened to be lying around the presidential office, so Ellsworth picked it up. He was demonstrating the drill to Stoddard when both young men suddenly ducked for cover. "He [Ellsworth] was standing too near the south window, and the order which brought the butt of the gun against his shoulder sent the muzzle of it through the glass." The crash and tinkle of the broken window surprised them both. As is all too common for young men in their early twenties, they immediately began concocting excuses for the glass on the floor, but partway through a far-fetched story about an assassin, they both began to laugh. They realized the truth would be a better story.[63]

Later in the week, on the evening of Wednesday, May 22, Ellsworth returned to the mansion to visit with Nicolay and check his mail. Since his arrival in Washington, in February, Ellsworth's mail had been forwarded to the White House, then held for him by Nicolay or Hay. Mail delivery had become erratic, and he had not heard from Carrie in a few weeks. He hoped his letters had reached her, but he needed one of hers to reach him. Nicolay met him on the porch and handed

61 John Hay, diary, May 12, 1861, BU/JHC.

62 William O. Stoddard, *Inside the White House in War Times* (Lincoln, NE: Bison Books, 2000), xi.

63 Stoddard, *Inside the White House*, 20.

Ellsworth what all soldiers away from home hope for—a letter from his sweetheart.[64]

CHAPTER 10

The Fall of a Sparrow

*Whatever may happen cherish the consolation that I was engaged in the performance
of a sacred duty—and tonight thinking over the probabilities of the morrow and the
occurrences of the past I am perfectly content to accept whatever my fortune
may be,confident that He who noteth even the fall of a sparrow
will have some purpose even in the fate of one like me.*

Elmer Ellsworth to his parents, May 24, 1861

I**T** was a typical early summer night on the Potomac River, clear and mild. The full moon, its reddish sheen thoroughly illuminating the landscape, gave the misleading effect of tranquility to the hour, just after midnight on Friday, May 24, 1861. In the camps, the activity was constant but quiet, and locusts could still be heard in the grass and trees. The dewy air was perfumed by the profusion of wildflowers that surrounded the land next to the river, and a hundred or more bell-shaped Sibley tents, each lit from inside, appeared like enormous transparencies. The glistening flames of the few remaining campfires were reflected in the moonlit surface of the Potomac's smooth, silver expanse beyond the wharves.[1]

---

1 E. H. House, "From Washington: A Night with the Ellsworth Zouaves—Interesting Particulars of the Expedition to Alexandria—The Murder of Col. Ellsworth," dated "Washington, Friday, May 24," *New York World*, May 27, 1861. Ned House was a member of the small party that accompanied Ellsworth into Alexandria and the Marshall House Hotel. He was at that time a reporter for the *New York World*, and was embedded with the 11th New York Fire Zouaves for several days before and after Ellsworth's death on May 24, 1861. His first-hand account is used by both Randall and Ingraham and is considered definitive. House, wearing civilian clothing and an eye patch, can be seen directly behind Col. Ellsworth in Alonzo Chappel's painting *The Death of Ellsworth*. Other newspaper correspondents used House's information when they wrote their own accounts of the incident, and again when it was recounted during the journey of Ellsworth's remains from Washington to Mechanicville for burial.

Alexandria, 8 miles south of and across the river from Washington, had finally quieted down. All evening, the citizens of the Virginia town had celebrated their ratification of secession in grand style, with small gatherings joining up to create larger parties, bourbon and branch water at the ready, fireworks lighting the skies above the river, cannons booming, and streets lit with flambeaux and lanterns, giving light and hope to the fledgling Confederacy. The Virginia Senate had voted for secession on April 17, but it was necessary to have the citizens of the state ratify such an extreme measure. When the votes were counted (958 for secession, 106 against) and the ordinance of secession was finally ratified, Alexandria joined the celebration with the rest of northern Virginia.

Abraham Lincoln's concern about the old colonial city was great. Its proximity to Washington, the seat of Union government, was a danger in all respects. Alexandria was an important port and railroad center, potentially useful to the Confederate cause. Until Virginia was no longer part of the United States, a move could not be made against her soil or citizens. On May 23, 1861, however, the secession of the Old Dominion was an established fact by a public vote of three to one, and Lincoln could finally send troops to occupy the city. According to Gen. Winfield Scott's orders, two Union regiments were to converge on Alexandria and place the city under military occupation. Colonel Ellsworth's Fire Zouaves, now officially the Eleventh New York Volunteer Infantry, were chosen to share this honor with the First Michigan Infantry, under Colonel Orlando B. Wilcox. Together, these regiments were to complete the inaugural land-based mission of the war. Of the two commanders, only Col. Ellsworth had asked Gen. Joseph Mansfield if he and his Zouaves could be given the honor of being the first regiment to occupy the town.[2]

Lincoln and Scott detailed the plan for the initial occupation of Alexandria. The First Michigan would cross the Potomac on Andrew Carnegie's newly refurbished Long Bridge and come down from Arlington, while the First Michigan Cavalry would take the Chain Bridge across the river. The Zouaves were to arrive directly at the Alexandria wharf aboard three steamers. They were to march through Alexandria, securing the railroads and telegraph office, then deploy Union

---

2 Hayand Nicolay, *Abraham Lincoln*, 4:312; Elmer Ellsworth to Carrie Spafford, May 19, 1861, KCWM/LFAC. The battle of Sewell's Point was actually the first official combat mission of the war. On May 18-19, 1861, two union gunboats dueled the Confederate batteries at Sewell's Point in Norfolk, Virginia. They were attempting to enforce the Union blockade of Hampton Roads. Little harm was done to either side. Online version: www.nps.gov/ abpp/ battles/va001.htm, accessed December 2, 2017.

The Marshall House Hotel, complete with flag, could be seen from Lincoln's study with the use of a telescope. The flag irritated Lincoln whenever he thought of it. *Library of Congress*

soldiers within the confines of the city. The men were to look for pockets of Southern sympathizers who might resist the occupation.[3] A warning was sent to the city government listing the timeline for the Union troops' arrival, as Lincoln was determined that not a shot be fired unless wholly justified.[4] Technically, under a military cease-fire, the men had nothing to fear, and everything appeared to be under control on both sides of the political divide . . . except for that "huge damned flag."[5]

3 *The War of the Rebellion: A Compilation of the Official Records of the Union and Confederate Armies*, 128 vols. (Washington, DC, 1880-1901), Series 1, vol. 2, page 38. Hereafter cited as *OR*. All references are to Series 1 unless otherwise noted.

4 Hay and Nicolay, *Abraham Lincoln*, 4:309-310.

5 I have not found any accounts of Elmer Ellsworth's death or the occupation of Alexandria that did not mention Lincoln's knowledge of the flag atop the Marshall House. Yet, during my research time at the Kenosha Civil War Museum, curator Doug Dammonn questioned the truthfulness of this part of the Ellsworth story. He contends that it would have been impossible for Lincoln to see the flag from the White House due to the southward bend in the Potomac before it passes Alexandria. It is generally agreed upon that Lincoln had at least a hand-held

As soon as the Virginia Senate had voted for secession, a huge (fourteen-foot hoist by twenty-four-foot fly) Confederate flag appeared above the Marshall House, a boarding house in central Alexandria at the corner of King and South Pitt Streets.[6] James W. Jackson, who lived there with his family, managed this establishment. Jackson was well known in Alexandria as being an ardent supporter of states' rights and the Southern war effort. The flag in question was a version of the first national flag of the Confederacy, the "Stars and Bars." Alexandria sail-maker John W. Padgett talked his wife, Libby, and her sister into making the flag for Charles Taylor, another Alexandria dock worker. Taylor offered to pay thirty dollars for the heavy wool flag but did not have any place to display such a huge banner. James Jackson found out about the endeavor and suggested flying the flag from a tall pole atop the Marshall House, his hotel. The upper left quadrant of the flag, which was of the Confederate National Flag design, was a field of blue, with a circle of stars. Every time another state joined the Confederacy, Jackson paid Mrs. Padgett to add a large white star to the flag. Jackson flew the huge banner proudly. When news of Virginia's ratification reached Alexandria, Mrs. Padgett readied another star to sew on the flag, this time in the middle of the circle of seven stars.[7]

A story is often told concerning the Marshall House Flag and its relation to Abraham Lincoln: John Hay and John Nicolay, in their ten-volume biography of the president, wrote that he could see the flag from his office in the Executive Mansion, flaunting "defiance at the national capital."[8] The legend of Lincoln and the flag also includes other "evidence" that Ellsworth and Lincoln had discussed this flag many times since April 17, when it first appeared. The story mentions such details as "Lincoln had called it 'an insult,' and kept a brass telescope by the window so he could look at it." Randall's biography of Ellsworth claims that hehad been in the president's office many times since mid-April, and during most of these occasions, he had heard Lincoln complain about the "rebel flag." President Lincoln

---

"spyglass" in his office, perhaps a pair of binoculars, or a larger viewing apparatus of some variety, but I cannot swear on personal experience if this was enough to allow Lincoln to see Jackson's flag.

6 These Marshall House Flag measurements are based on a personal observation of the actual flag by the author during a visit to the New York State Military Museum and Veteran's Research Center in August 2012.

7 "Marshall House Flag Confederate National Flag, First National Pattern, 1861," NYSMM, dmna.ny.gov/historic/btlflags/other/CSA_MHF1995.3033.htm, accessed August 2, 2016.

8 Hay and Nicolay, *Abraham Lincoln*, 4:313-314.

considered it a physical nose-thumbing at his efforts to maintain the Union.[9] Allegedly, *everyone* in the White House knew how offended Lincoln was by its very presence. If one follows this line of thinking, then on the evening of May 24, the hated banner would be another star stronger and even more offensive.[10]

The northern side of the Potomac was busy that night. After evening drill, Col. Ellsworth called his regiment together. Addressing the men, he said, "All I can tell you is to prepare yourselves for a nice little sail, and, at the end of it, a skirmish."[11] He then explained that President Lincoln had informed Alexandria of the timetable of the mission and wanted it to be accomplished with as little bloodshed as possible. A message under a flag of truce would be sent ahead, giving the Confederate soldiers at least an hour to evacuate the town. Ellsworth warned his Zouaves that they, as a regiment, were under scrutiny. Alexandria citizens had expressed concern about being occupied by the Eleventh New York, which had a reputation for unruly behavior:

> Boys, no doubt you felt surprised on hearing my orders to be in readiness at a moment's notice, but I will explain all as far as I am allowed. Yesterday forenoon I understood that a movement was to be made against Alexandria. Of course, I was on the *qui vive*. I went to see General Mansfield, the commander at Washington and told him that I would consider it a personal affront if he would not allow us to have the right of the line, which is our due, as the first volunteer regiment sworn in for the war. . . . Go to your tents, lie down, and take your rest until two o'clock, when the boat will arrive, and we go forward to victory or death. When we reach the place of destination, act as men; do nothing to shame the regiment; show the enemy that you are men, as well as soldiers, and that you will treat them with kindness until they force you to use violence. I want to kill them with kindness. Go to your tents and do as I tell you.[12]

The soldiers were ecstatic. They had all read the newspaper accounts about their regiment: its colorful uniform, and its exaggerated lack of discipline. They had also read that much was expected of them. Now Ellsworth's Fire Zouaves would truly begin their service to the Union—a service for which they had pledged three

---

9 Randall, *Colonel Elmer Ellsworth*, 244.

10 Ibid.

11 Burlingame, ed., *At Lincoln's Side*, 150.

12 Frank Moore, ed., *The Rebellion Record: A Diary of American Events with Documents, Narratives, Illustrative Incidents, Poetry, etc.* (New York: G. P. Putnam, 1862), 57, online version: books.google.com/books?id=1el2AAAAMAAJ&pg=RA1-PA57&lpg=RA1-, accessed October 2, 2017.

years of their lives, not just ninety days. Cheers, laughter, and singing could be heard in the early evening around Camp Lincoln. One member of the 11th wrote:

> Men were ordered to be on the parade ground armed and equipped and ready to move at 2:00 a.m. The men received "a rifled musket, bayonet. 40 rounds, canteen, and 24 hours rations." Approximately 870 of the men set out on this expedition across the river to Alexandria.[13]

Another recalled Col. Ellsworth's speech:

> When we started, he drew us in line, and made a thrilling speech, every word went to our hearts. He told us we might meet with a warm reception, that some of us might fall. He warned us to be firm, that he would not lead us where he was afraid to go. He never knew such a word as fear.[14]

As the sun set, the seriousness of the next day's work made itself felt in a gradual silencing of the camp. Ellsworth spent the early part of the evening seeing to his men, visiting each tent, asking questions, encouraging them, making sure they packed their rations. He walked out to the bluff above the Potomac, looking for any signal or movement, then back to his men again. As the sun descended, he sat in front of his own tent, chatting easily with his staff. Edward H. "Ned" House, a reporter for the *New York World* who had followed Ellsworth all evening, described him as "full of humor and wit, in most excellent spirits." Someone asked, "Colonel, are we to be quartered in Alexandria tomorrow?"[15]

"No," Ellsworth answered quickly, flashing his charming smile. "*Quartered?* No." Then he pointed at the officer's fierce knife-style bayonet and said, "You wouldn't think of being *quartered*, I hope, while you had a thing like that at your command." The men laughed at the pun, feeling the relief a joke can give when there is tension in the air.[16]

---

13 "W. H. H.," letter, May 25, 1861, in R. L. Murray, *"They Fought Like Tigers": The 11th New York Fire Zouaves, 14th Brooklyn and the Irish 69th New York at First Bull Run* (Wolcott, NY: Benedum Books), 12; "Army of the Potomac Journal," www.nyincivilwar.com.

14 Wilber A. Apgar, letter, May 30, 1861, in Murray, *"They Fought Like Tigers,"* 12; "Army of the Potomac Journal."

15 E. H. House, *New York World*, May 27, 1861.

16 Ibid.

Ellsworth looked up at the full moon, breathed in the fresh air, glad to finally be away from the sewer stench of Washington, and then turned to go into his tent. He had taken care of everyone with whom he had come into contact, and now he must take care of those who were *not* in camp. Ellsworth went to his desk, a small, portable table issued to officers, sat down in his camp chair, and trimmed the candle's wick so it did not flicker. He had two letters to write before he could get ready for Alexandria. Elmer knew that if anything happened to him, his parents and Carrie would be deeply affected. In the life of a Civil War soldier, death was never far away, and neither was the anguish of the ones he may have left behind. The letters he wrote would be the only way to communicate with those he loved most if his voice were to be silenced. Ellsworth's carelessly elegant script flew across the pages, and when he was through, he put them carefully into the inside pocket of his frock coat. To his parents he wrote, on the back of a Brady *carte de visite*:

My dear Father and Mother,

The regiment is ordered to move across the river tonight. . . . I am inclined to the opinion that our entrance to the city of Alexandria will be hotly contested. . . . Should this happen my dear parents it may be my lot to be injured in some manner. Whatever may happen cherish the consolation that I was engaged in the performance of a sacred duty—and tonight thinking over the probabilities of the morrow and the occurrences of the past I am perfectly content to accept whatever my fortune may be, confident that He who noteth even the fall of a sparrow will have some purpose even in the fate of one like me.
My Darling and ever-loved parents, good bye. God bless, protect, and care for you.

Elmer[17]

. . . and to his Carrie:

My own darling Kitty,

My regiment is ordered to cross the river and move on Alexandria within six hours. We may meet with some warm reception and my darling among so many careless fellows one is somewhat likely to be hit.

If anything should happen—Darling just accept this assurance, the only thing I can leave you—the highest happiness I looked for on earth was a union with you. You have more than realized the hopes I formed regarding your advancement—and I believe I love you

17 Elmer Ellsworth to Ephraim and Phebe Ellsworth, May 23, 1861, KCWM/LFAC.

with all the ardor I am capable of. You know my darling any attempt of mine to convey an adequate expression of my feelings must be simply futile. God bless you as you deserve and grant you a happy and useful life and us a union hereafter.

Truly your own,

Elmer.

P.S.—Give my love to mother and father (such they truly were to me) and thank them again for all their kindness to me—I regret I can make no better return for it—Again Good bye. God bless you, my own darling.[18]

Elmer had never considered himself prescient, but he had always been able to picture himself making the next step in his future. As a child, he looked forward to being a young man. As that young man, he imagined being employed away from home. In New York, he considered living in Chicago, and in Chicago, he saw himself at the head of a contingent of soldiers. His vision kept him focused on the future. A self-made man always looked ahead, and Ellsworth was a self-made man in every regard. When he had written to Carrie so long ago about finding a mentor to "pat me on the head and adopt me as his own," little did Elmer realize that man would be the president of the United States. When he chose not to seek a West Point appointment, not willing to spend an additional four years before he could become a soldier, he never thought he would be commanding troops at the beginning of a civil war. Elmer Ellsworth's diary, his letters, old newspaper clippings, a few daguerreotypes and photographs, and the remembrances of those who loved him—as a son, a lover, a friend—these are all that remain of his short life to help reconstruct his story.

Colonel Ellsworth asked Captain John "Jack" Wildey, his aide-de-camp, to come to his tent after 1:00 a.m. to help him dress for this first mission as a commanding officer. Ellsworth had laid his uniform out on the camp bed: freshly laundered undergarments; gray trousers with a red stripe down the outside of each leg; a soft red shirt with a high collar; his blue-gray frock coat with its polished brass buttons; and his carefully shined boots, gleaming in the moonlight. Ellsworth stood

18 Elmer Ellsworth to Carrie Spafford, May 23, 1861, KCWM/LFAC.

quietly, thinking over his choices, and then said to Capt. Wildey, "I was thinking in what clothes I shall die."[19]

Wildey laughed and tried to change the subject with a few joking words, but Ellsworth just shook his head, saying nothing for a moment. Then, smiling, he went to his trunk and opened it. He withdrew an entirely new uniform, tagged and packaged from the tailor. "If I am to be shot tomorrow, and I have a presentiment that my blood is immediately required by the country—it is in this suit that I shall die." Wildey helped him put on the new uniform, and within moments Ellsworth was his usual confident self. Wildey wound the red silk officer's sash around Ellsworth's narrow waist. Ellsworth then made certain his Army Colt revolver and officer's sword, cleaned and polished just hours before, were in good order, and placed in holster and scabbard. His gloves, of the softest yellow leather, were folded and slipped under his belt. Ellsworth's kepi had been brushed until the burnished gold trim glowed against the deep red wool. It was as if he was preparing for the festivities of a wedding party instead of for a battle.[20]

The last two things Col. Ellsworth added to his coat were the badge presented to him by New York's Columbian Engine 14, of which he had been made an honorary member, and the circular medallion he had received from the Baltimore City Guard during his 1860 tour. This pin, placed over his heart, said, in Latin, *Non Solum Nobis, sed Pro Patria*, ("Not for ourselves alone, but for the country").[21] The inscription reveals exactly how Ellsworth viewed the military—as service, not for political advancement, not as merely a job, not as some exciting adventure, but genuine, heartfelt, and responsible.

Ready at last, Ellsworth patted his right side, where the letters lay, having been transferred to the inside pocket of his new frock coat. He thanked Capt. Wildey, smiled, and walked across the parade ground toward the bluff, where the three steamboats were waiting to take him and his men into harm's way. Just before 2:00 a.m., Ellsworth's Zouaves marched double quick down to the water's edge. The *James Gray*, the *Baltimore*, and the *Mount Vernon* were in the middle of the Potomac, and the Zouaves would have to be carried out to them in rowboats. Once aboard, the great paddles began to move the ships down the river. It had finally begun—Ellsworth's men were part of the riverine landing, while the Michigan

19 Francis Brownell, *Philadelphia North American*, circa May-June, 1861, quoted in Ingraham, *Zouaves of '61*, 148.

20 Ibid.

21 Randall, *Colonel Elmer Ellsworth*, 263.

infantry, under Col. Wilcox, marched across the bridges at Washington and Georgetown. The muffled hooves of cavalry horses quietly made their way across the Chain Bridge.[22]

No one knew what awaited them at Alexandria. Each man was prepared for the worst. The surgeons and nurses of the military hospital at Georgetown had made their grim preparations as well, laying out surgical supplies and readying beds in anticipation of casualties. Ned House described the early morning arrival of the steamboats "just as the dawn began to shine over the hills and through the trees."[23]

About 5:00 a.m., as the Zouaves disembarked, the few remaining Confederate sentinels fired their guns in the air. Ellsworth's men briefly returned fire, thinking these were the opening shots of the battle, but it was not so. The Union sloop-of-war *Pawnee* had already sent communications under a flag of truce to the Confederate authorities at Alexandria, telling them "the time had come," and as the Union army entered the city, the last of the Confederate army left it. The Zouaves then formed up on Union Street facing the river.[24]

As a train whistle blew in the morning stillness, signaling the evacuation of the last of the Rebels from Alexandria, Ellsworth detailed Company E to destroy the railroad track leading south to Richmond. He then chose a small group of men to accompany him to the center of town to cut the telegraph wires, leaving the rest of the Zouaves under the command of Lieutenant Colonel Noah Farnham. The men Ellsworth chose were an odd combination for the chore ahead: Capt. John Wildey, regimental military secretary Lieutenant H. J. Winser, Chaplain E. W. Dodge, and *Tribune* journalist Ned House. Thinking more soldiers and less superfluous civilians might be needed, Winser suggested adding, as guards, Private Francis Brownell, three other corporals, and a single squad of men under Sergeant Richard Marshall from the First Company.[25]

The group turned away from Union Street and began to head up Cameron, where they rounded the corner and jogged the additional block left along Pitt to King Street, Alexandria's largest thoroughfare. Ellsworth stopped. The facade of the three-story Marshall House was just to their right, and looming atop the building was James Jackson's huge Confederate flag, complete with a new star sewn

22 House, *New York World*, May 27, 1861.

23 Ibid.

24 Ibid.

25 Ibid.

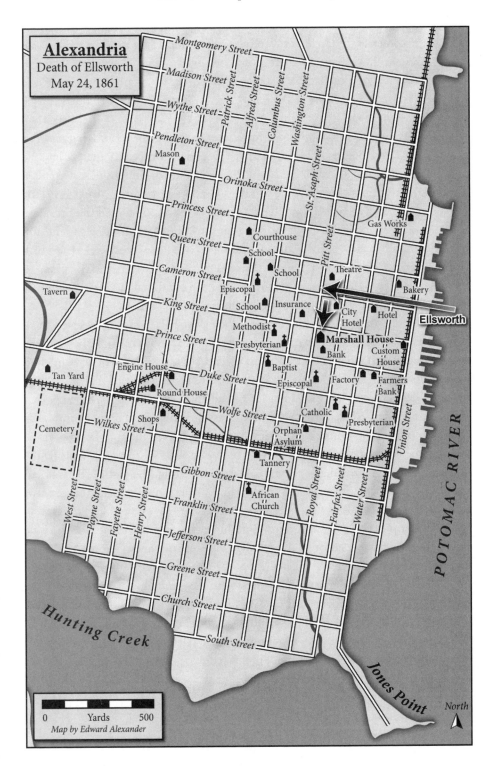

Alexandria
Death of Ellsworth
May 24, 1861

Montgomery Street
Madison Street
Wythe Street
Pendleton Street
Mason
Orinoka Street
Princess Street
Queen Street
Courthouse
School
Cameron Street
School
Episcopal
Tavern
King Street
School
Insurance
Methodist
Prince Street
Presbyterian
Engine House
Tan Yard
Duke Street
Round House
Baptist
Episcopal
Shops
Wolfe Street
Catholic
Cemetery
Wilkes Street
Orphan
Asylum
Presbyterian
Tannery
Gibbon Street
African
Franklin Street
Church
West Street
Payne Street
Fayette Street
Henry Street
Jefferson Street
Greene Street
Church Street

Patrick Street
Alfred Street
Columbus Street
Washington Street
St. Asaph Street
Pitt Street
Gas Works
Theatre
Bakery
City
Hotel
Hotel
Marshall House
Bank
Custom
House
Factory
Farmers
Bank
Union Street
Royal Street
Fairfax Street
Water Street

Ellsworth

POTOMAC RIVER

Hunting Creek

South Street

Jones Point

0   Yards   500
Map by Edward Alexander

North

right in the center of the circle of seven other stars. According to House, Ellsworth said, "Boys, we must have that flag down before we return," then ordered Sgt. Marshall to return to Col. Farnham and have him order Company A to come to the Marshall House and take care of the flag.[26] The sergeant saluted, then hurried back down Cameron Street.

Ellsworth and his small group turned away from the corner of King and Pitt Streets and again began to jog toward the telegraph office. At that point, the memories of Lincoln's complaints about the flag, and what an insult it was, must have returned to Ellsworth in a flash. Yes, a Union flag was now flying from the town flagpole, but the enormous Rebel banner that had so taunted the president for weeks also waved in the damp morning air. On impulse, or due to his friendship for Lincoln, or because of his youthful pride—no one knew precisely—Ellsworth stopped again, turning to look back at the red brick hotel. No! He was not going to have that flag removed by his orders, but by his own hand, and he would personally present it to the president. He owed Lincoln at least that much.

Elmer Ellsworth returned and entered the Marshall House with seven men: Winser, Dodge, House, Brownell, and three enlisted Zouaves. Just beyond the door, a sleepy, half-dressed man came to meet the group. Ellsworth demanded to know who had put the flag on the roof of the hotel. The disheveled man just shook his head, claiming he was only a boarder and had no idea. The colonel then posted one of his soldiers to guard the front door. As the group started the climb to the roof of the boarding house, he posted another soldier on the first floor, and the third at the foot of the stairs. The rest of the group—House, Lt. Winser, the chaplain, and Pvt. Brownell—accompanied Ellsworth up the rest of the stairs to the top floor, which contained two small bedrooms. It is not known if these rooms were occupied.

At the top of the stairs, Ellsworth and his men approached the ladder to the trap door, which opened onto the roof. Army Colt in hand, Colonel Ellsworth climbed the short ladder and pushed it open. Lieutenant Winser was right behind him. The flag, hanging on its tall flagpole, was to their right, toward the front of the building. The men approached it quickly. Ellsworth handed Winser his revolver and borrowed Winser's large Bowie knife to cut the ropes that held the flag aloft. As soon as the halyards parted, the flag was hauled down and fell into Ellsworth's arms. Ellsworth started back through the trap door, pulling the enormous banner

---

26 Ibid; map of "Old Alexandria," www.nps.gov/gwmp/learn/historyculture/ alexandria. htm, accessed August 5, 2016.

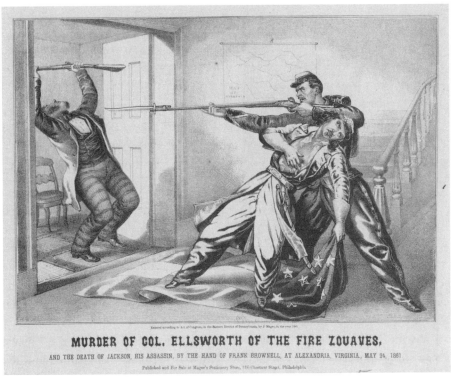

MURDER OF COL. ELLSWORTH OF THE FIRE ZOUAVES,

AND THE DEATH OF JACKSON, HIS ASSASSIN, BY THE HAND OF FRANK BROWNELL, AT ALEXANDRIA, VIRGINIA, MAY 24, 1861

Published and For Sale at Magee's Stationery Store, 316 Chestnut Street, Philadelphia.

This image shows a simplified, romanticized version of Ellsworth's death, but it's typical of the lithographs quickly produced to commemorate the event. *Library of Congress*

---

behind him. Winser grabbed it and tried to stuff it down the hatch in front of him as he left the roof after Ellsworth.

The little group started back down the stairs, dragging the flag with them. They descended in this order: Pvt. Brownell, rifle in hand; Col. Ellsworth, eyes on the unwieldy flag he was trying to fold into some semblance of order; Ned House, following Ellsworth, steadying the colonel with one hand on his shoulder; and Lt. Winser, clumsily trying to roll the flag up over his arm.[27]

After descending twelve steps, Brownell turned the corner at the landing between the third and second stories. A man wearing pants and a nightshirt stepped from the shadows. Ignoring Brownell, he leveled a double-barrel shotgun directly at Col. Ellsworth, who stood just above Brownell, on the steps. Private Brownell tried to turn the shotgun with his bayonet, but the shooter held a steady

27 Ibid.

An early sketch by artist Arthur Lumley for the June 1, 1861, issue of *Frank Leslie's Illustrated Newspaper,* based on an account of Ellsworth's death provided by eyewitness Dr. Charles Grey. Grey stands next to the staircase; Ellsworth on the landing, reels back from a gunshot (left) while Brownell, next to him, takes a shot at Jackson, at the foot of the stairs. *Becker Collection, Boston College*

aim and discharged one barrel straight into Ellsworth's chest. Ellsworth pitched forward instantly, pulling the flag fabric taut as he fell. Ned House wrote, "I think my arm was resting on poor Ellsworth's shoulder at the moment; at any rate, he seemed to fall almost from my grasp. He was on the second or third step from the landing, and he dropped forward with that heavy, horrible, headlong weight which always comes of sudden death . . ."[28]

As the man pivoted to unload the other barrel into Brownell, the Zouave successfully knocked the gun aside. The shot was harmlessly discharged into the paneling above the landing. House's description of events continued:

Simultaneously with this second shot and sounding like an echo of the first, Brownell's rifle was heard, and the assassin staggered backward. He was hit exactly in the middle of the face and the wound, as I afterward saw it, was the most frightful I ever witnessed. Brownell did not know how fatal his shot had been, and so before the man dropped, he thrust his saber bayonet through and through the body, the force of the blow sending the dead man violently down the upper section of the second flight of stairs, at the foot of which he lay with his face on the floor.[29]

In the precious seconds of silence before the terrible reality of what had happened overwhelmed everyone, James Jackson and Col. Elmer Ellsworth lay dead. Their mingled blood—South and North—soaked into the floorboards and stained the crumpled flag with gore. The gold medallion Ellsworth wore over his

28 Ibid.

29 Ibid.

heart was driven so deeply into his breast by the shotgun blast that the words *Non Nobis, Sed Pro Patria* were forever inscribed there in bruises and in blood.[30]

Ellsworth memorials of all kinds became popular ways to commemorate the martyr's death. This one features photos of Ellsworth, Brownell, and the Marshall Hotel. *Library of Congress*

30 Ingraham, "Elsworth," KCWM/LFAC. Ingraham's notes contain both an unidentified newspaper clipping and several pages of notes concerning Ellsworth's autopsy at the Navy Yard by Dr. Charles Gray, regimental surgeon.

CHAPTER 11

Memento Mori

. . . Americans came to fight the Civil War in the midst of a wider cultural world that sent them messages about death that made it easier to kill and be killed. They understood that death awaited all who were born and prized the ability to face death with a spirit of calm resignation. They believed that a heavenly eternity of transcendent beauty awaited them beyond the grave. They knew that their heroic achievements would be cherished forever by posterity. They grasped that death itself might be seen as artistically fascinating and even beautiful. They saw how notions of full citizenship were predicated on the willingness of men to lay down their lives. And they produced works of art that captured the moment of death in highly idealistic ways.

from *Awaiting the Heavenly Country* by Mark S. Shantz[1]

THE death of Elmer Ellsworth immediately plummeted the North into a state of shared mourning. Flags flew at half-staff, and church bells tolled their sorrow.[2] What exactly happened at the Marshall House has been disputed, but the words of journalist Ned House were the words of a man who not only wrote news but was a direct observer of the events. There were very few eyewitnesses, but there were two distinctly different points of view about what happened—that of the Union, and that of the Confederacy. The one detail upon which both sides could agree was that there two dead men were lying in pools of blood on the floor of the Marshall House on the morning of May 24, 1861. Ned House's description of the actions after both guns were fired is the same in almost every detail as the one given by Lt. Henry J. Winser and Pvt. Francis Brownell in later accounts.

1 Mark S. Schantz, *Awaiting the Heavenly Country: The Civil War and America's Culture of Death* (Ithaca, NY, and London: Cornell University Press, 2008), 2.

2 Unidentified newspaper clipping, probably E. H. House, KCWM/LFAC.

Ellsworth's officer's frock coat, with the hole over the left side of the chest. The pin he wore was driven into his body so deeply it was not recovered. *New York State Military Museum*

Those who lived at the hotel peeked out their doors, but no one stepped forward to attempt to help Jackson. The distressed men who had accompanied Ellsworth turned toward their colonel. Ellsworth had fallen on his face, and the blood from his chest wound was copious. Reverend George W. Dodge turned him over gently, and Ned House called his name. There was some confusion in later accounts as to whether Ellsworth answered, but House eventually decided that the colonel had not uttered a thing since the shotgun blast had struck him. House acknowledged that, in his initial report, he had claimed Ellsworth had spoken the words, "My God!" but he changed this to suggest that it may have been Brownell or Dodge instead, as both men were physically close to him. House and Lt. Winser carried Ellsworth's limp body to a nearby vacant bedroom, bringing with them the flag Ellsworth had died to cut down. They placed the dead colonel on the bed. Using the flag, both men attempted to clean the blood from Ellsworth's face, then they laid it at his feet, "purified by this contact from the baseness of its former meaning . . ."[3] They crossed Ellsworth's hands over his chest in the classic death pose and gazed sadly upon his young face. House wrote that "his expression in death was beautifully natural. The Colonel was a singularly handsome man, and, excepting the pallor, there was nothing different in his countenance now from what his friends had so lately been accustomed to recognize gladly."[4]

3 E. H. House, *New York World*, May 27, 1861.

4 Ibid.

At that moment, the detachment of Zouaves that Ellsworth had ordered up when he first passed the Marshall House could be heard arriving. None of the soldiers had heard the shotgun blast, or Brownell's return shot, so they were not aware of the terrible scene inside the old boarding house. Ellsworth's friend from the Chicago Zouave days, Lieutenant Edward Knox, was put in charge of the unit while their captain went inside to see what had happened. The captain returned quickly. In a low voice, he spoke to Knox, telling him the awful news. Knowing that Ellsworth and Knox had been friends, the captain suggested that he go inside:

> I ascended the stairs. Stepping over the body of Jackson, who still lay where he had fallen, I entered the room where all that was mortal of my beloved friend and commander lay silent in death. I will not attempt to describe my emotions while gazing upon that sad scene. I could scarcely credit my own senses. There lay one whom I had seen only a few minutes before full of life and the vigor of early manhood, cut down without a moment's warning by the hand of the assassin. His face wore a very natural expression, and, excepting its pallor, his countenance looked the same as in life.[5]

Knox returned to his unit, ashen-faced and shaken. He asked another Zouave to find and bring the regimental surgeon, Dr. Charles Gray, presumed to still be at the wharf with Lt. Col. Noah Farnham.

Knowing that Ellsworth had wanted to destroy the Western Union cable between Alexandria and the Confederate forces, Ned House went with two Zouaves a bit further up King Street to the wire service's office. Finding several persons inside the small office, House and the Zouave soldiers made enough noise on the short staircase leading to the office door to convince the Confederate telegraph operators to vacate the premises quickly. By the time House opened the door the place was utterly deserted, and he left the soldiers to their work.[6]

When House returned to the Marshall House, Mrs. Jackson was kneeling next to her husband's body, crying with heart-rending agony. She did not appear to notice the Union men in the hallway, but flung her arms in the air and seemed abandoned to her grief. Lieutenant Winser finally helped her understand that neither she nor her daughters were in any danger and that they would be left alone. Then a few of the b'hoys returned to the bedroom and wrapped Ellsworth in one of their famous, red

---

5 Ronald S. Coddington, "Lt. Knox Carries on His Friend's Legacy," *New York Times*, "Opinionator," May 24, 2011; Edward B. Knox military service record, National Archives.

6 James L. Huffman, *A Yankee in Meiji Japan: The Crusading Journalist Edward H. House* (Lanham, MD: Rowman & Littlefield, Publishers, 2003), 28.

Zouave Cadet bedrolls. They opened the door and improvised a stretcher from their rifles. Carrying the body of their colonel tenderly, the men bore him out of the Marshall House, back down King Street, and to the wharf. Doctor Gray and Lt. Winser endeavored to keep Ellsworth's death from the ears of the Fire Zouaves. These rough men had always evidenced great affection for "their colonel." After the news of his death spread, many were devastated and vowed to avenge his murder.[7] As Ellsworth's body lay waiting to be put aboard a steamer to return to Washington,

> Strong men came and looked upon the pallid features of him whom they had seen a moment before full of health and vigor, and as they gazed a convulsive sob and unbidden tear told how sincerely the gallant spirit that had so lately tenanted that mortal frame was mourned.[8]

Doctor Gray made preparations for the removal of Ellsworth's body to the capital. It was neatly wrapped in blankets and then transported to the boat on a litter carried by four of his men. A stunned Col. Farnham directed them to place their burden on board the steamer *James Guy*, and eight Zouaves, blinking back tears, stood guard next to their leader's remains, four on each side. From this moment on, Lieutenant S. W. Stryker, Lieutenant E. F. Coates, Pvt. Francis Brownell, Corporal John A. Smith, and Privates Joseph More, Michael Brennan, William H. Brennan, and Hiram Smith did not leave Ellsworth's body, except for the briefest of moments, until they were able to shovel the last spadeful of soil over their commander and comrade in the Hudson View Cemetery in Mechanicville.[9]

Ellsworth's body was taken first to the Navy Yard on the *James Guy*, whose flag was flying at half-mast.[10] In the hour it took the boat to arrive in Washington, word of the tragedy spread. The shocked men who received the body placed it in the engine house and began to drape the area in mourning. The news of Ellsworth's death spread from person to person, soon reaching the city itself, where church bells started to toll, and

---

7 "The Death of Col. Ellsworth; Full Particulars of the Assassination by an Eye Witness—The Zouaves Swear that they will be Revenged—Singular Coincidences," *New York Times*, May 26, 1861, online version: www.nytimes.com/1861/05/26/news/death-col-ellsworth-full-particulars-assassination-eye-witness-zouaves-swear.html?pagewanted=all, accessed June 24, 2012.

8 Ibid.

9 Ingraham, *Colonel Elmer Ellsworth*, 156.

10 E. H. House, *New York World*, May 27, 1861.

flags were lowered to half-staff. Western Union telegraphed the sad event across the North.

Sometime during the evening of May 23, before the 11th New York left the Washington side of the Potomac, two Zouaves, Private Arthur O'Neil Alcock and Lt. Stephen W. Stryker, approached Ellsworth with a request: to be permitted the honor of bearing the first dispatch concerning the capture of Alexandria to their commanding general, Winfield Scott. Ellsworth gave them permission, but the two men had no idea that they would be announcing the death of their colonel to the old general. Alcock and Stryker went to Lt. Col. Noah Farnham, who permitted them to carry out their last duty to their deceased leader. They accompanied Ellsworth's remains to the Navy Yard and then went directly to the war department. Scott gave them a somber yet warm reception. Alcock, reporting for the *New York Atlas*, wrote:

> The reception we met from General Scott—the hero of a hundred fights—was worthy of the gallant old chief. He shook us warmly by the hand, and while lamenting the untimely death of our Colonel, said, "You have done well, boys; you have captured the town of Alexandria, shot down the murderer of your brave Colonel, taken the rebel flag, many horses and men prisoners, a quantity of equipment, arms, and baggage. You have done well, boys." It was a most gratifying moment . . . and one we shall never forget.[11]

Three families were devastated by this news. On the morning of May 24, in upstate New York, Ephraim Ellsworth had walked through the streets of Mechanicville to the post/telegraph office. He guessed his son might be involved in the movement into Alexandria expected of the army; so he sat, waiting. The telegraph clicked throughout the early morning, then one of the operators suddenly gasped and burst into tears. In this unfortunate way, Mr. Ellsworth learned of the loss of his remaining son to a Southern shotgun blast. He walked home slowly and broke the sad news to his wife. Much of the happiness of their lives was extinguished at that moment. They would not mourn alone, however. The entire North would support them in their sorrow.[12]

In Rockford, Illinois, Ellsworth's fiancée, Carrie Spafford, had arrived home from school for the summer. The day before, she had severely turned her ankle in a riding accident, so perhaps she was still in bed when the awful news arrived. She was so

---

11 Alcock, *With the 11th New York*, 100.

12 Randall, *Colonel Elmer Ellsworth*, 261. There is no indication that this account of how Mr. Ellsworth learned of his son's death is apocryphal. No person has declared that they brought the news to the Ellsworth's at home, or that any other method of notification was used. Mechanicville was a village at the time, and according to Phebe Ellsworth's "Memoranda," the family was well known at the post office where the original message was received.

stricken by grief that she was unable to leave the house for several weeks, and then only clad in widow's black. All of Rockford mourned the loss of Ellsworth.[13]

The third family devastated by Elmer's death was the one that lived in the Executive Mansion. On the morning of May 24, naval Captain Gustavus Fox was detailed to bring the tragic news to Lincoln personally. He spoke with the president in the second-floor library, telling what he knew of the sad details. Abraham Lincoln, who loved Ellsworth as part of his presidential family, as a son, and as a special friend to his wife and children, burst into tears. No one had ever seen Lincoln cry publicly, but he cried for Elmer Ellsworth. Just as Capt. Fox left the White House, Senator Henry Wilson of Massachusetts and an unnamed reporter from the *New York Herald*, entered the library. They were there on "a pressing matter of public business," and John Nicolay did not yet know of Ellsworth's death, so he gave them access to the president. As the two men entered the office, Lincoln was standing with his back to the door, looking out a window toward the Potomac River. He did not move until the men were quite close to him. Then he turned to them, his eyes filled with tears and his whole countenance one of profound grief. He extended his hand, saying, "Excuse me, but I cannot talk." The men thought a cold had roughened his voice, but then Lincoln pulled a large handkerchief out of his pocket and again burst into tears.[14]

The reporter who had accompanied Senator Wilson recorded his impressions:

> He [Lincoln] walked up and down the room for some moments, and we stepped aside in silence, not a little moved at such an unusual spectacle in such a man and in such a place. After composing himself somewhat, Mr. Lincoln sat down and invited us to him. 'I will make no apology, gentlemen,' said he, 'for my weakness; but I knew poor Ellsworth well, and held him in great regard. Just as you entered the room, Captain Fox left me, after giving me the painful details of his unfortunate death. The event was so unexpected, and the recital so touching, that it quite unmanned me.[15]

Lincoln continued, concerned by the facts of Ellsworth's death. Wilson's news, that the loyal citizens of Alexandria were glad to be, again, under the Stars and Stripes, made little impression.[16]

---

13 Ibid.

14 Ingraham, "Elsworth," notes, *New York Herald* article, copied and undated, KCWM/LFAC.

15 Ibid.; [Portland] *Maine Temperance Journal*, "On Ellsworth's Death," June 22, 1861, online version: archive.org/details/civilwarofficerslinc_30, accessed August 8, 2016.

16 Ibid.

Mary Lincoln, grief-stricken that the "pet of the family" was gone, was the first to arrive at the Navy Yard to pay her respects to Ellsworth's body. She brought flowers with her, and spoke with Pvt. Brownell for some time, learning all the details she could. She was unable to view the remains, as Washington embalmer Dr. Thomas Holmes and his assistants were at work. Elmer Ellsworth was the first Union soldier to be embalmed. Mrs. Lincoln herself had requested the services of Dr. Holmes, who offered to do the work for free.[17] Holmes, considered the "father of American embalming," used a technique he had personally devised—arterial embalming. Ellsworth's right carotid artery, along with his right internal jugular vein, was used. About an hour later, Mrs. Lincoln returned with the president, and they sat quietly with Ellsworth. According to John Hay, they "gazed long and tearfully on the still face which had so often brought sunshine with it, into the Executive Mansion."[18] Lincoln was heard to say, "My boy! My boy! Was it necessary this sacrifice should be made?"[19] President Lincoln specifically requested that a guard of honor transport the remains from the Navy Yard to the East Room of the Executive Mansion, where the funeral would be held.

John Hay and John Nicolay reacted to Elmer Ellsworth's death both individually and together. Hay wrote, "All classes seem to regard his death as a personal affliction, yet there is a smaller circle who mourn him in tears as the truest, tenderest, most loyal-hearted man that ever died."[20]

Nicolay wrote his fiancée, Therena Bates:

I had supposed myself to have grown quite indifferent, and callous, and hard-hearted, until I heard of the sad fate of Colonel Ellsworth. I have been quite unable to keep the tears out of my eyes whenever I thought, or heard, or read, about it, until I have almost concluded that I am quite a weak and womanish sort of creature. I know the whole nation will mourn for him, yet I am grieved also to feel that they do not half appreciate his worth or their loss...[21]

---

17 *New York Times*, May 17, 1861; "Embalming and the Civil War," National Museum of Civil War Medicine, February 20, 2016, online version: www.civilwarmed.org/embalming1/, accessed spring 2016.

18 Burlingame, ed., *Lincoln's Journalist*, 70.

19 Ibid.

20 Ibid.

21 John George Nicolay to Therena Bates, May 25, 1861, in Burlingame, ed., *With Lincoln In the White House*, 43.

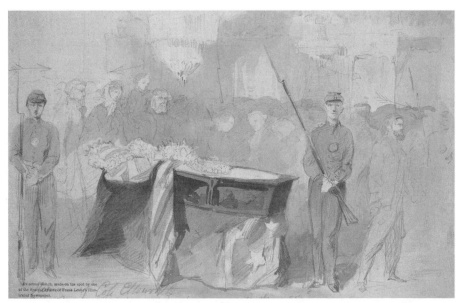

Ellsworth's body lay in state in the White House's East Room. *Frank Leslie's Illustrated Newspaper*

From their co-authored opus, *Abraham Lincoln: A History*:

Upon President Lincoln his [Ellsworth's] untimely death fell with the force of a personal bereavement. He had brought him to Washington as Aide and seen his magnetic influence to control crowds, along the route from Springfield, Ill., to Washington. Echoes of his cheery and manly voice seemed to linger in the corridors and rooms of the Executive Mansion, from which so recently he had looked on the flag of treason, now stained with his blood. When his comrades came with his body, Lincoln ordered it placed in the East Room, where Cabinet officers, diplomats, and military and naval dignitaries attended his funeral . . .[22]

Colonel Ellsworth was laid out in an iron "window" coffin. It was painted to look like rosewood, and the upper half of the coffin's lid contained an oval glass window to view the top part of the remains. He was dressed in his formal Zouave uniform and his jaunty red cap, formal sword, and kidskin gloves were placed on top of the casket. The captured Confederate flag, stained with Ellsworth's blood, was folded across the foot of the coffin, as it would be in subsequent services.[23]

22 Hay and Nicolay, *Abraham Lincoln*, 4:314.

23 "New York and the Civil War," (Albany, NY: New York Civil War Centennial Commission, June 1962), unpaginated pamphlet.

Ellsworth's was the first large public funeral of the Civil War. No one could have predicted at the time just how much blood would be shed, or how many casualties would come later. *Library of Congress*

The White House funeral was immense. The Lincoln family attended, as did many Washington dignitaries from society, the military, and politics. Abraham Lincoln had asked the Reverend Dr. Smith Pyne of Saint John's Episcopal Church to give the funeral oration. Near the head of the casket stood Pvt. Francis Brownell, the Springfield rifle with which he had "avenged" Ellsworth's death on his shoulder. After several hours of viewing, a full military cortege, complete with muffled drums, furled flags, and Ellsworth's riderless black horse, escorted the colonel's remains to Union Station. There, with an eight-member guard of New York Fire Zouaves, his body was put on a special funeral train for New York City.[24]

The train was met the next morning by Ellsworth's parents, and his coffin was taken to the "Governor's Room" in city hall to lie in state, with Brownell again sitting watch. Over ten thousand mourners filed past to pay their respects to this fallen leader of a famed New York regiment. Later in the day, a private service was held for him at

24 *Washington Evening Star*, May 27, 1861; *New York Tribune*, May 25-27, 1861; *Baltimore Republican*, May 27, 1861.

the Astor House, where his devastated parents took custody of his body. That evening, the steamer *Francis Skiddy*, draped in mourning, took the Ellsworth's, their son, and his honor guard up the Hudson River to Albany.[25]

When they arrived early on the morning of May 27, church bells tolled, and cannon saluted as the steamer docked at the state capital. The Albany Zouaves, a local militia unit organized just after Ellsworth's 1860 Zouave tour had performed in their city, met the coffin and escorted it to the capitol building, where they placed it on a large catafalque prepared in the State Assembly's chamber. Thousands of mourners streamed past, remembering that bright "Zouave" summer less than a year ago, and thinking of the sons, brothers, and husbands they had sent to Washington in response to Lincoln's first call for troops. Brownell left the coffin only once, to speak to Governor Morgan and tell him, firsthand, the story of what had happened in Alexandria. The *Francis Skiddy* then carried Ellsworth's body to Troy, New York, where a procession of his friends from earlier times accompanied the coffin to the railroad depot. At Mechanicville, the sad journey was completed. The distance from the depot to the hilltop burial ground was a little over a mile. In the funeral procession were Ellsworth's parents, the Black-Plumed Riflemen of Stillwater—at least those who had not joined the army—most of the local townspeople, and Ellsworth's Zouave honor guard, still marching together in sad cadence. A late May afternoon thunderstorm erupted in the middle of the procession, referred to as "tears from God himself."[26] It finally cleared up, and mourners filed past the casket for three hours.

Private Brownell sat on the wooden platform, holding the flag that had started it all. The crowd asked to see the flag, so he stood and unrolled it, to groans at the sight of Ellsworth's bloodstains. Brownell then dropped the flag to the wooden floor and stomped on it with his booted foot. At 5:00 p.m., ropes finally lowered the coffin into the ground. The Zouave honor guard fired three volleys in salute, then put down their rifles and picked up shovels. Those eight men buried their little colonel, each saying a final, private goodbye.[27]

Due to the war and the subsequent dispersal of the original 11th New York members, it took several years to get a marker for Ellsworth's grave, but in 1873, the

25 *Scientific American: An Illustrated Journal of Art, Science, & Mechanics*, (New York: Munn & Company, June 8, 1861), vol. IV, no. 23, 354, online version: www.scientificamerican.com/magazine/sa/1861/06-08/, accessed September 25, 2012.

26 Janice Gray Armstrong and Martha V. Pike, *A Time to Mourn: Expressions of Grief in Nineteenth Century America* (New York: The Museums at Stony Brook, 1980), 7-8.

27 Ibid.

The Marshall House Flag was "souveniered" almost beyond repair until it came to the New York State Military Museum. Work continues to restore and curate this outstanding relic. *New York State Military Museum*

New York State Legislature erected a tall, imposing granite obelisk in Mechanicville. Subscriptions and a donation from the First Regiment Zouaves helped cover the cost of the marker, which is now topped by a black iron eagle. The money from the First Regiment came from the five hundred dollars given to Ellsworth by the Willard brothers in gratitude for the heroism the First New York Fire Zouaves displayed in dousing the fire at Willard's Hotel in April 1861.[28]

*   *   *

The nineteenth-century world in which Col. Elmer Ellsworth lived and died viewed death very differently than the twenty-first-century world does. Before Ellsworth was killed, he had already experienced the death of his brother from typhoid. He lived in a time when infant mortality was so high that parents knew to prepare themselves for early loss. What seems unnatural to a person today—that a parent might bury a child—was seen as the natural order of things in antebellum America. This idea was especially significant to parents of a young man heading off to war. Ellsworth

28 Dr. Paul Loatman, Jr., "Elmer Ellsworth—Citizen Soldier," remarks given in Mechanicville, New York, May 21, 2000, online version: www.mechanicville. com/history/ ellsworth/citizensoldier.htm, accessed January 23, 2012.

himself was highly aware of this. Before he went to Alexandria, where he met his death, he wrote letters to his parents and fiancée Carrie Spafford. Although soldiers did not necessarily court death, it was always present in their lives. Elmer Ellsworth wanted his loved ones to know he was ready to make this final sacrifice, as this would help them mourn, if necessary.

"The Good Death," a concept concerning the understanding of mortality, presented an ideal death experience for both the dying and the living. Drew Gilpin Faust, in her book *This Republic of Suffering: Death and the American Civil War*, defines a "good death" as a set of rituals for dying based on Victorian beliefs. In mostly Christian America and Britain, how one died epitomized the life just ended, and predicted the quality of life everlasting.[29] The battlefield deaths of Civil War soldiers, dying unattended by family and unable to atone for improper actions, was going to be exceedingly difficult for Americans both North and South to accept, but that terrifying reality was still about two months away. Elmer Ellsworth was the last public figure of the time to be given the honor of a Good Death, and the northern half of the United States followed as many of the prescribed rituals as possible. For a historical moment, Col. Ellsworth became the Union's brother, son, and loved one.

*   *   *

Music, poetry, and art were ways in which Americans celebrated the life and death of the deceased, as these things kept the image of the fallen hero always visible. The North was quick to capitalize on the patriotic spirit created by everything Ellsworth had ever done. The nationalistic music industry was invigorated, with compositions written to honor Col. Ellsworth providing a large part of the energy. Of all the people who have ever lived in Chicago, more music was written about Ellsworth than anyone else in history.[30] An earlier piece of music, the "Zouave Cadets' Quickstep," was composed by A. J. Vaas, conductor of the Light Guard Band that had accompanied the U. S. Zouave Cadets on their Chicago tour. This piece was not a dirge or memorial piece—the Cadets had used it in their tour performances. Root and Cady, a Chicago publishing firm, produced a piano version of the piece, which sold well. "Messrs. Root

29 Drew Gilpin Faust, *This Republic of Suffering: Death and the American Civil War* (New York, Alfred A. Knopf, 2008), 9.

30 David M. Guion, "Musical Tributes to a Civil War Martyr: Elmer Ellsworth," May 24, 2011, online version: music.allpurposeguru.com/2011/05/musical-tributes-to-a-civil-war-martyr-elmer-ellsworth/, accessed February 2, 1012.

3

Washington D.C.
May 25. 1861

To the Father and Mother of Col. Elmer E.
Ellsworth:

My Dear Sir and Madam,

In the untimely loss
of your noble son, our affliction here is scarcely
less than your own. So much of promised
usefulness to one's country, and of bright
hopes for one's self and friends, have rarely
been so suddenly dashed as in his fall.
In size, in years, and in youthful appearance a boy only, his power to command
men was surpassingly great. This
power combined with a fine intellect,
an indomitable energy, and a taste
altogether military, constituted in him,
as seemed to me the best natural talent,
in that department, I ever knew.

And yet he was singularly modest
and deferential in social intercourse. My
acquaintance with him began less than two years
ago; yet through the latter half of the

This and facing page: On May 25, 1861, President Lincoln wrote to Ellsworth's parents to express his sympathy for their son's death. "On the untimely loss of your noble son, our affliction here is scarcely less than your own," Lincoln admitted. *Library of Congress*

intervening period, it was as intimate as the disparity of our ages, and my engrossing engagements would permit. To me, he appeared to have no indulgences or pastimes; and I never heard him utter a profane or an intemperate word. What was conclusion of his good heart, he never forgot his parents. The honors he labored for so laudably, and in the end so gallantly gave his life, he meant for them, no less than for himself.

In the hope that it may be no intrusion upon the sacredness of your sorrow, I have ventured to address you this tribute to the memory of my young friend, and your brave and early-fallen child.

May God give you that consolation which is beyond all earthly power.

Sincerely your friend
in a common affliction
A. Lincoln

and Cady . . . are daily receiving orders by the hundred, from all the principal cities of the Union."[31] When Ellsworth died, the steady stream of patriotic music became a flood. At least nine different musical tributes can be found in various library collections

31 *ChicagoTribune*, August 20, 1860.

nationally, and these are completely written and inscribed. Funeral marches, dirges, and ballads bear witness to the national outpouring of grief and mourning that took place for Col. Ellsworth.[32] Major Ralph W. Newton, commander of the 2nd Battalion, Boston Light Infantry, suggested to his unit's famous glee club that Ellsworth's name be substituted for that of John Brown when they sang, "John Brown's Body," now more popularly known as "The Battle Hymn of the Republic."[33] As late as 2011, composers were still writing music honoring Ellsworth; that year, Dave Burrell honored him with a separate piece in his suite, *Portraits of Civil War Heroes*.[34]

Death poetry as part of the outpouring of grief in the rituals of the Good Death had long been a staple in antebellum America, but the Civil War brought a new permutation—the "Dying Soldier Poem." It was a stylized type of verse that sought to give heroic significance to individual war deaths, which in reality may have occurred *en masse*, or from disease rather than in battle. This poetry brought the reader directly to the point at which the death occurs, where the soldier fearlessly confronts the inevitable while keeping his thoughts on the heavenly rewards which were surely his due. In a "Dying Soldier Poem," every death was beautiful and heroic. Today such works might be considered painfully formulaic and maudlin, but they served a specific purpose: to help the living remember their soldier and to realize that no war death was in vain, no matter what the actual circumstances of that death.[35] So many memorial poems appeared after Ellsworth's death that it is almost impossible to catalog them. One appeared in *Harper's Weekly* on June 8, 1861:

ELLSWORTH: A BATTLE HYMN FOR ELLSWORTH'S ZOUAVES

Who is this ye say is slain?

Whose voice answers not again?
Ellsworth, shall we call in vain
On thy name to–day?
No! from every vale and hill
One response all hearts shall thrill:

---

32 Ibid.

33 Christian McWhirter, *Battle Hymns: The Power and Popularity of Music in the Civil War* (Chapel Hill, NC: University of North Carolina Press, 2012), 48, online version: www.newmarketnhhistoricalsociety.org/profiles/edgerly-charles-and-john-brown-s-body/, accessed August 6, 2016.

34 Dave Burrell, *Portraits of Civil War Heroes*, musical piece presented January 19-22, 2011 at The Rosenbach Museum, Philadelphia.

35 Schantz, *Awaiting the Heavenly Country*, 98-99.

"Ellsworth's fame is with us still,
 Ne'er to pass away'."
Bring that rebel banner low,
Hoisted by a treacherous foe:
'Twas for that they dealt the blow,
 Laid him in the dust.
Raise aloft, that all may see,
His loved flag of liberty.
Forward, then, to victory,
 Or perish if we must!

Hark to what Columbia saith:
"Mourn not for his early death;
With each patriot's dying breath
 Strength renewed is given
To the cause of truth and right,
To the land for which they fight.
After darkness cometh light,
 Such the law of Heaven."

So we name him not in vain,
Though he comes not back again
For his country he was slain;
 Ellsworth's blood shall rise
To our gracious Savior–King
'Tis a holy gift we bring;
 Such a sacred offering
 God will not despise.[36]

Because Elmer Ellsworth was the first Union "hero" to fall in a time when the war was more an idea than a reality, he became a cult-like figure in the eyes of the Union. Poems, songs, sermons, and memorial envelopes lamented his loss, thousands of parents named their babies after him, and streets and towns still bear his name. Memorial images of Ellsworth's death appeared in every northern city's news publications. The best of these is the painting by Alonzo Chappel, a very well-known painter of famous men and military events, who also painted Lincoln and other prominent American historical figures. Copies of the painting were made in the years

---

36 Anon., "Ellsworth—A Battle Hymn for Ellsworth's Zouaves," *Harper's Weekly*, June 8, 1861, online version: www.sonofthesouth.net/leefoundation/civil-war/1861/june/ ellsworths-death.htm, accessed February 3, 2012.

"Remember Ellsworth" became a common rallying cry to support the war effort, especially in the war's earliest years. As time wore on, the North's first martyr would be lost in a sea of national mourning as hundreds of thousands of other young men fell. *Leon Reed*

following Ellsworth's death.[37] The print firm of Currier and Ives rushed to their presses a stylized version of the event, which included Francis Brownell and James Jackson. Although this print is less historically accurate than Chappel's painting, it was the most widely distributed of all the images created. Many are still in existence today, although they are much more expensive than the pennies they originally cost.[38]

Both *Harper's Weekly* and *Frank Leslie's* were lavishly illustrated papers, and their artists returned to the topic of Ellsworth many times after his murder. Newspapers created drawings of Ellsworth's *carte de visite* images as well as other images made by photographers of the day. Both Brownell's image, as well as that of Stephen W. Stryker, was copied from his portrait sitting, after Ellsworth's death, at the Mathew Brady Studio in Washington, as well as a photograph of him taken in Albany during the

37 "Alonzo Chappel: The Complete Works," www.alonzochappel.org/, accessed February 1, 2012.

38 "Currier and Ives: The History of the Firm," www.currierandives.com/, accessed February 2, 2012.

funeral procession.[39] All these images were widely distributed throughout the North and helped to fuel the feelings of national mourning that engulfed the region.

Elmer Ellsworth did not die at home, his hand held lovingly by Phebe or Carrie. He was killed in a Virginia hotel, bleeding out on worn wooden floorboards. He was the first of many denied a Good Death by a war that would quickly become known as "cruel" by all concerned. Reconstructing the Good Death when a loved one had died far away from home was one of the greatest challenges of the Civil War. The best solution, North or South, was a letter of condolence, a "letter home," from a comrade or a commander. All soldiers struggled within themselves to make sense of the slaughter, but even more so, they struggled to communicate this to those eager to know the fate of the men so dearly loved and missed.

Knowing the deceased might never be found and moved to a home cemetery, the letter of condolence assumed an importance it had never enjoyed before. Homage given to the dead was not only offered out of respect; it was a way of reclaiming a sense of selfhood in a situation where individuality barely existed. The sanctity and integrity of human life, so obviously absent from a pile of severed limbs or corpses, could be reaffirmed in a personal letter. Most soldiers hoped that, if they were killed, someone would do the same for them, recognizing and honoring their existence.[40] Receiving a condolence letter from Abraham Lincoln himself honored Ellsworth's family. Lincoln was famous for his elegant words in speeches and writings, and his letter of condolence to Elmer Ellsworth's parents is one of his most famous pieces of personal correspondence. It was written the day after Ellsworth's funeral in the East Room. According to David Homer Bates, who had given the telegram announcing Ellsworth's death to Gustavus Fox, Lincoln laid the telegram on his desk, where it remained for several days.[41] With deep compassion, Lincoln praised his friend Ellsworth to his grieving parents. It is easy to picture the still-distraught president sitting at his desk, the telegram to his left:

39 "The Death of Colonel Ellsworth," *Harper's Weekly*, June 8, 1861, online version: www.sonofthesouth.net/leefoundation/civil-war/1861/june/ellsworths-death.htm, accessed August 2013.

40 Faust, *This Republic of Suffering*, 79.

41 David Homer Bates, *Lincoln in the Telegraph Office: Recollections of the United States Military Telegraph Corps During the Civil War* (New York: The Century Company, 1907), 29.

Washington, D. C.
May 25, 1861
To the Father And Mother of Col. Elmer E. Ellsworth:

My dear Sir or Madam, In the untimely loss of your noble son, our affliction here, is scarcely less than your own. So much of promised usefulness to one's country, and of bright hopes for one's self and friends, have rarely been so suddenly dashed, as in his fall. In size, in years, and in youthful appearance, a boy only, his power to command men, was surpassingly great. This power, combined with a fine intellect, an indomitable energy, and a taste so altogether military, constituted in him, as it seemed to me, the best natural talent, in that department, I ever knew. And yet he was singularly modest and deferential in social intercourse. My acquaintance with him began less than two years ago; yet through the latter half of the intervening period, it was as intimate as the disparity of our ages, and my engrossing engagements, would permit. To me, he appeared to have no indulgences or pastimes; and I never heard him utter a profane, or intemperate word. What was conclusive of his good heart, he never forgot his parents. The honors he labored for so laudably, and, in the sad end, so gallantly gave his life, he meant for them, no less than for himself.

In the hope that it may be no intrusion upon the sacredness of your sorrow, I have ventured to address you this tribute to the memory of my young friend, and your brave and early fallen child.

May God give you that consolation which is beyond all earthly power.

Sincerely your friend in common affliction,

Lincoln [42]

Lincoln's letter was not the only tribute to Ellsworth. John Hay, who supplemented his secretary's salary by writing for a variety of newspapers, penned one as well, and it was published in *The Atlantic Monthly*. Hay's obituary for Ellsworth could not help but be colored by his deep friendship with the young soldier:

His loss at this time cannot be too deeply deplored. He had every requisite for great military success; he had a wonderful memory and command of details—immense industry and capability of enormous mental and bodily labor, great coolness of mind, an original and inventive brain, and most of all, the power of grappling to his heart with hooks of steel the affections of every man with whom he came in contact. Then there is a smaller circle who mourn him in tears as the truest, tenderest, most loyal-hearted man that ever died.

42 Abraham Lincoln to Ephraim D. and Phebe Ellsworth, May 25, 1861, The Huntington Library, Art Collections and Botanical Gardens, Abraham Lincoln Special Collection.

This is the bead-roll of his virtues. I do not remember but two faults that he had, and they were magnificent ones. He was too generous and too brave. The one subjected him to the most cruel slanders from sordid men, and the other caused the disaster which has plunged a people into mourning.[43]

Why did the Union embrace the death of Elmer Ellsworth so completely? Did Lincoln's grief set the tone, or was there some indescribable something, realized only in the atoms of Union bone marrow, that whispered the promise of a long, sad war? Politicians and the military on both sides had predicted a short war, and an end to the "unpleasantness" before it was fairly begun; but then, Colonel William Tecumseh Sherman knew better: "[Y]ou might as well attempt to put out the flames of a burning house with a squirt gun. I . . . think it is to be a long war—very long—much longer than any politician thinks."[44]

In a nation used to adhering to rigid customs regarding the body of the deceased and its burial, and mourning, the Civil War would create many changes in form, although not in underlying attitudes. Colonel Elmer Ellsworth's elaborate multi-state funeral was the last of its kind, until that other terrible death in April 1865. In between, two nations sought ways to ease the grief of broken bodies and broken hearts. Resting in peace was impossible while the war still ripped the country apart. Many Union families were quickly exhausted by their personal experiences with loss, which could not be appropriately honored or remembered in the old ways. The memory of one soldier's grand funeral would have to suffice. It must have given comfort to forlorn families, as many of them simply never saw their loved ones again. The last paragraph of John Hay's eulogy for his friend Elmer Ellsworth became a national letter of condolence for every Union soldier:

One last word. May he rest forever in peace, under the Northern violets and the Northern snows. May his example sink into the hearts of Northern youth, and blossom into deeds of valor and honor. His dauntless and stainless life has renewed the brightest possibilities of the antique chivalry, and in his death we may give him unblamed the grand cognizance of which the world has long been unworthy—*Le chevalier sans peur et sans reproche*.[45]

43 John Hay, "Ellsworth," *The Atlantic Monthly*, vol. 8, issue 45 (July 1861), 119-126, online version: ebooks.library.cornell.edu/cgi/t/text/text-idx?c=atla;g=moagrp;xc=1;q1=elmer%20ellsworth;view=toc;cc=atla;idno=atla0008-1;node=atla0008-1%3A14, accessed June 14, 2012.

44 Samuel M. Bowman and Richard B. Irwin, *Sherman and His Campaigns; A Military Biography*, (New York: Charles B. Richardson, 1865; GQ Books reprint edition, 2010), 25.

45 Burlingame, ed., *Lincoln's Journalist*, 71.

The martyred Ellsworth was memorialized in song with marches and requiems.
Library of Congress

"Never," said the *New York Times* "has a man of Ellsworth's age commanded such national respect and regard in so short a space."[46]

46 Randall, *Colonel Elmer Ellsworth*, 266; *New York Times*, May 27, 1861, www. newspapers.com/image/20456553, accessed July 29, 2018.

Epilogue: April 20, 1865, 3:00 a.m.

O Captain! my Captain! our fearful trip is done,
The ship has weather'd every rack, the prize we sought is won,
The port is near, the bells I hear, the people all exulting,
While follow eyes the steady keel, the vessel grim and daring;
But O heart! heart! heart!
O the bleeding drops of red,
Where on the deck my Captain lies,
Fallen cold and dead.

O Captain! my Captain! rise up and hear the bells;
Rise up—for you the flag is flung—for you the bugle trills,
For you bouquets and ribbon'd wreaths—for you the shores a-crowding,
For you they call, the swaying mass, their eager faces turning;
Here Captain! dear father!
This arm beneath your head!
It is some dream that on the deck,
You've fallen cold and dead.

My Captain does not answer, his lips are pale and still,
My father does not feel my arm, he has no pulse nor will,
The ship is anchor'd safe and sound, its voyage closed and done,
From fearful trip the victor ship comes in with object won;
Exult O shores, and ring O bells!
But I with mournful tread,
Walk the deck my Captain lies,
Fallen cold and dead.[1]

Walt Whitman, 1865

---

1 Walt Whitman, "O Captain! My Captain!", www.poetryfoundation.org/poems/45474/
o-captain-my-captain, accessed September 23, 2018.

I T was a still night if the weather was the only thing that counted. President Lincoln's untimely death created an aura of busyness in Washington. The Executive Mansion, draped inside and out with mourning, was surrounded by military guards, and by citizens who ranged from morbidly curious to brokenhearted. Even at such an hour, people milled around the grounds of the residence, perhaps hoping for a glimpse of Mary Lincoln, who had not left her bedroom since last viewing her dying husband six days earlier, or of young Tad, who had stayed with his mother.[2]

The afternoon before, April 19, Lincoln's remains were moved from the East Room, where his embalmed body had lain in state for three days, to the capitol rotunda for a last round of public viewing. The great black coach, pulled by six white horses, had borne the casket forward, flags muffled and tied with black ribbons, silent but for the tramp of marching soldiers and the occasional strangled cry of grief. Ward Hill Lamon, marshal of Washington City and Lincoln's close friend, carefully choreographed the procession, and gave strict orders that anyone making an outcry in support of the Confederacy's now-lost cause be dealt with immediately and firmly.[3] The cavernous East Room itself stood empty, while outside the army protected the mansion and its brokenhearted inhabitants from prying eyes, and prying fingers.

On December 8, 1861, the East Room had finally been opened to the public in newly refurbished splendor. Mary and Abraham Lincoln held their first levee, an afternoon reception, which opened the winter social season. The company was spangled, hooped, and feathered, and there was a large contingent of shoulder straps and swords. General McClellan was the evening's guest of honor, accompanied by his staff officers and, almost as an afterthought, his small, hazel-eyed wife, Ellen.[4]

Gone were the shabby ornaments of Buchanan's time. All the old furniture was reupholstered in heavily figured satin of deep crimson, tucked and folded in the latest decorating fashion. The wood had been cleaned and freshly varnished. The crystal drops and garlands of the gas chandeliers were removed and polished, then rehung to glitter like winter stars above the heads of the crowd at the Lincolns' reception. The walls of the East Room were newly covered in heavy Parisian velvet

2 James L. Swanson, *Bloody Crimes: The Chase for Jefferson Davis and the Death Pageant for Lincoln's Corpse* (New York: William Morrow/Harper Collins, 2010), 188.

3 Ibid.

4 Margaret Leech, *Reveille in Washington: 1860-1865* (New York: Carroll and Graf, 1941), 121.

paper. Its complex floral pattern was picked out in colors of crimson, garnet, and gold, and had cost over eight hundred dollars. A new Scottish woolen carpet from the mills of Glasgow covered the old floor. It was made all in one piece, with designs of fruit and flowers in vases, wreaths, and bouquets. Buchanan's tattered velvet draperies had been replaced with new ones in crimson French brocatelle. They were trimmed with heavy gold fringe and tassels and hung from newly gilded cornices. Beneath the luxurious drapes hung inner curtains of white, needlepoint Swiss lace.[5] Several large ornamental shields were scattered along the walls, honoring those under arms in the service of the Union. The refurbishments were referred to as "flub dubs" by the president, but Mary Todd Lincoln was an extravagant woman.[6]

By 1864, the open-door policy of the White House had ruined the first lady's efforts. The public pulled the velvet paper from the walls and cut it into strips and squares for souvenirs. Large pieces of brocade and damask drapery material were sliced from the curtains. Small pieces of the elegant French upholstery were cut from every piece of furniture. Memento seekers stole the gold cords and tassels that held back the floor-to-ceiling crimson drapes, as well as a few of the white lace under-curtains. The remaining curtains hung in rags from the depredations of sightseers who clipped the flower designs out of the lace for who-knew-what purposes. The red, blue, and gold ornamental shields had been stolen. General McClellan was gone as well.

For the last few days however, none of the damage could be seen. It all lay under yards and yards of black crepe. Earlier in the week, carpenters were called to build a fifteen-foot-high catafalque, an elevated platform resting on a stair-stepped dais, which would hold Lincoln's coffin. The black-swathed canopy over the bier was so tall that the center chandelier of the East Room was removed to accommodate its height. Other carpenters had built risers around three of the walls, so that as many people as possible could be seated for the funeral on the evening of April 19.

Although the casket had been taken to the capitol building by 3:00 on the afternoon of April 18, the seating was still there, covered in black. A few chairs were scattered over the carpet. Under the risers and along the East Room walls were strewn the remains of black ribbon badges with printed pictures of Lincoln glued to them, small American flags, black-edged mourning ribbons, and a handful

5 Ibid., 293-294.

6 Ibid.

of crumpled tickets to the funeral, also bordered in black—the abandoned detritus, broken underfoot, of the almost-seven hundred people invited to the official religious service.[7]

Assistant Secretary of the Treasury George A. Harrington planned Lincoln's state funeral in just sixty-eight hours.[8] Among those helping him were chief of staff Major General Henry Halleck, and Major General C. C. Augur, commander of the Military District of Washington. Even with help, the job seemed overwhelming. "What shadows we are and what shadows we pursue . . . the whole charge of the funeral fixed for Wednesday has been put on me," Harrington wrote in a letter to his friend, former treasury secretary William Fessenden.[9] Still, it all got done.

The East Room had only been used one other time for a presidential funeral, after Zachary Taylor died in office on July 9, 1850. A religious service in the presence of Taylor's coffin was conducted in the East Room.[10] Now the great public chamber was changed from a reception area for America to a *chapelle ardente*, a candlelit "vault of gloom," and in this dark hour, even the candles were extinguished. The towering catafalque still stood in the middle of the room, surrounded by bits of flowers and greenery. The domed canopy, made of black crepe lined in fluted white satin, still hung over the empty bier. Its four pillars were festooned in translucent black silk. No window was open this night to admit the soft, early spring breezes that might have set the black draperies into gentle motion. The fragrance of the lilies from the cross that had stood at the head of Lincoln's silver-starred casket mixed with the scent from the anchor of roses that had been at its foot. No door stood ajar to let the funereal sweetness escape.

The two remaining chandeliers, one at each end of the large room, were also swathed in mourning. The frames of the huge side mirrors were similarly darkened, and white crepe was hung over the reflecting glass. Black draperies were rigged to completely cover the ruined crimson curtains, and no light entered the room at all, even if there had been much of a moon to reflect a sepulchral whisper from the veiled mirrors. Having risen only an hour ago, the pale moon hung like a fingernail paring in the black sky.

7 Swanson, 187.

8 Edward Steers, *The Lincoln Assassination Encyclopedia* (New York: Harper Perennial, 2010), 345.

9 Swanson, 151.

10 "Presidential Funerals," Tapophilia.com, www.taph.com/presidential-burials/presidential-funerals-2.html, accessed June 2015.

On the previous Saturday, April 15, Lincoln's body had been brought from the Peterson House, a residential boarding house across the street from Ford's Theatre, to the Executive Mansion. The remains had been carried in a temporary casket by six young men from the quartermaster's department and placed in a carriage. An escort of light cavalry, under the command of Captain James B. Jameson, accompanied the casket. Behind the cavalry came General Augur, with General Rucker, depot quartermaster; Colonel Pelouze of the war department; Captain Finley Anderson, assistant adjutant general, Hancock's Corps; Captain D. G. Thomas, clothing depot; Captain J. H. Crowell; and Captain C. Baker; all of the officers were walking bareheaded.[11] The coffin was taken to the second-floor guest room, where army pathologist Doctor J. Janvier Woodward and his assistant, Edward Curtis, performed the autopsy.

After the embalming, on Monday evening, April 17, Lincoln's body was brought to the East Room, which John Alexander, decorator and assistant to George Harrington, had already prepared. The public viewing was held the next day, from 9:30 in the morning until 5:30 that afternoon. Tens of thousands of grief-stricken mourners, after waiting in line all night, filed past the single reliquary, mounting the steps to look upon Lincoln's face one last time. Black and white, male and female, old and young, they had stood in line for hours for a chance to say goodbye to the man who led the nation back to unity. The silence and the grief were profound.[12]

Later that evening, two hours were set aside for the official funeral, attended by Lincoln's cabinet, invited guests, and the military commanders, including Generals Meade and Grant, who had gathered in Washington to celebrate the end of the war, but stayed for the sad business of burial. They had all seen death many, many times, but never one that shook the entire country to its foundations as this one had.

The Reverend Mr. Hall, Bishop Matthew Simpson, and the Lincolns' minister, Reverend Dr. Phineas Gurley, spoke for two hours, attempting to make sense of the nonsensical.[13] Outside in the cool of the late evening, over fifty thousand people lined Pennsylvania Avenue, waiting for the procession to the capitol. Another fifty-thousand marchers and riders were lined up to escort the funeral

11 William T. Coggeshall, Lincoln Memorial: The Journeys of Abraham Lincoln From Springfield to Washington, *1861, As President-Elect; and From Washington to Springfield, 1865, As President-Martyred* (Columbus, OH: Ohio State Journal, 1865), 109.

12 Swanson, 183.

13 Ibid., 189-90.

cortege, assembled in the line of march assigned to them by the war department's printed order.[14]

The mourning would not end in Washington. Abraham Lincoln's grief-stricken friend, Ward Hill Lamon, planned the trip back to Springfield. Lincoln's body, along with that of his son Willie, who had died three years earlier, would have a funeral train of their own. Much grander than Ellsworth's funeral train, the coffins—one impressive and majestic, one plain wood—made Lincoln's now-famous Inaugural Express journey of 1861 in reverse, stopping at many of the cities on the original route for viewing and cannonades. From Washington to Springfield, Americans stood beside the train tracks, often in abysmal weather, to pay their respects to "Father Abraham." As the train progressed, it was met with bonfires and illuminations of all kinds. After the train passed, darkness fell behind it.[15]

From the time the body had been made ready for burial until the last service in the East Room, it was watched night and day by a guard of honor, the members of which were one major general, one brigadier general, two field officers, four line officers of the army and four from the navy. The coffin, the mourners, the military honor guard, the flowers—everything except the black crepe and the furniture—all were gone now. The cavernous room was empty of all the spirit and excitement it had ever held.

Ten days before Abraham Lincoln was assassinated, he told Ward Lamon about a dream he'd had:

> About ten days ago, I retired very late. I had been up waiting for important dispatches from the front. I could not have been long in bed when I fell into a slumber, for I was weary. I soon began to dream. There seemed to be a death-like stillness about me. Then I heard subdued sobs, as if a number of people were weeping. I thought I left my bed and wandered downstairs. There the silence was broken by the same pitiful sobbing, but the mourners were invisible. I went from room to room; no living person was in sight, but the same mournful sounds of distress met me as I passed along. I saw light in all the rooms; every object was familiar to me; but where were all the people who were grieving as if their hearts would break? I was puzzled and alarmed. What could be the meaning of all this? Determined to find the cause of a state of things so mysterious and so shocking, I kept on until I arrived at the East Room, which I entered. There I met with a sickening surprise.

14 Ibid.

15 Swanson, passim.

Before me was a catafalque, on which rested a corpse wrapped in funeral vestments. Around it were stationed soldiers who were acting as guards; and there was a throng of people, gazing mournfully upon the corpse, whose face was covered, others weeping pitifully. 'Who is dead in the White House?' I demanded of one of the soldiers, 'The President,' was his answer; 'he was killed by an assassin.' Then came a loud burst of grief from the crowd, which woke me from my dream. I slept no more that night; and although it was only a dream, I have been strangely annoyed by it ever since.[16]

The American Civil War began with the death of Elmer Ellsworth. His funeral, appropriate for the first fallen, was held in the East Room of the White House. Noah Brooks, a journalist and Lincoln biographer, wrote that Ellsworth "was among the very first martyrs of the War, as he had been one of its first volunteers."[17]

President Lincoln had been overwhelmed with sorrow by Col.Ellsworth's death. He sat alone, in grief-stricken meditation in the East Room, at the bier of his friend. Now, once again, the East Room had been a place of national sorrow. The Civil War opened with a funeral, had seen an uncountable number of funerals across five American spring times, and now it would close with a funeral. John Langdon Kaine, an original member of the New York Fire Zouaves, with whom he served as a drummer boy, summed it up when he wrote, "Colonel Ellsworth was the war's first conspicuous victim; Lincoln himself, the last."[18]

These two, dead, as well as over 750,000 more.
And now, in the silence of the great East Room,
only the ghosts remained.

16 Lamon, *Recollections*, 116-117.

17 Swanson, 166.

18 Rufus Rockwell Wilson, ed., *Lincoln Among His Friends: A Sheaf of Intimate Memories*, *CenturyMagazine*, February 1913, 95, www.mrlincolnandfriends.org/inside.asp?pageID= 93&subjectID=9, accessed June 2012.

OBITUARY:
Col. Elmer E. Ellsworth

New York *Times*
May 25, 1861
By John Hay

We are again called upon to record the death of the commanding officer of a New-York Regiment. The flags which, half masted, expressed to all beholders the sympathy extended by our citizens to the family of Col. VOSBURGH had but just flung forth from staff top their Stars and Stripes, when again they were lowered in token of bereavement.

Without a doubt, the name of Col. ELLSWORTH is more familiar to the ears of New-Yorkers than that of any other officer who has left this City during the present emergency. He was not a resident here, but the peculiar introduction afforded him by the exhibitions of his Chicago Zouave corps, his subsequent participation in the Presidential tour from Springfield to Washington, and finally the deep interest felt in the Fire Brigade by all ranks and conditions of citizens, have combined to render him popularly famous and deserving of more than ordinary notice. To these is added a last but unanswerable argument in support of his fame—for we learn by reliable dispatches from Washington, that while on Virginia soil, in performance of an honorable duty, he was shot and infamously murdered.

Of his earliest years, nothing of peculiar interest presents itself for consideration. He was born at Mechanicsville, [sic] in this State, where he received an ordinary Common School education, and not exhibiting any marked degree of interest in any individual study, while he at all times read with avidity and evident pleasure any work concerning campaigns, wars, and even ordinary manuals of tactics. While in later boyhood he was noted for his supremacy in all games requiring quickness of eye or limb, was an ardent champion for those weaker than himself, and courageous to a degree. His family was not affluent, and early in life he commenced to attend to his own wants. For awhile he followed the printer craft, and set up types in Boston, and subsequently in the West. With this he was not satisfied; he desired to enter the army, that he might the better develop his military tastes, and possibly attain distinction. Without powerful friends, in time of peace, he found it no easy task to obtain a position in the service, and, after fruitless trials, he gave up the project with regret. He then proposed the study of law, and in order to prepare himself for its rudimentary studies, he undertook a course of reading laid down for him by a distinguished lawyer of Chicago, with whom he for a short time remained.

It was at this time, that while connected with a local military company, he conceived the idea of organizing a company of Zouaves, based somewhat on the principles of the original Algerian Zouaves, and to a certain extent modeled after them. Having, after severe and laborious study, perfected himself in Zouave tactics, he raised a company and devoted time, energy and brain to their perfection in drill, discipline and effectiveness. This accomplished, he enlarged his company, and finally presented to the people of his city that body of men who are now so famous throughout the land. They traversed the country, giving exhibition drills at all principal points, and eliciting everywhere the highest commendation from most competent authorities. A new era dawned upon our military men, and simultaneously several of our favorite regiments started a Zouave corps and did not hesitate to acknowledge their indebtedness to Col. ELLSWORTH for the idea, and the evidence of its practicability and efficiency. Not only was this the case in this City, but at Philadelphia, Boston, Baltimore, Buffalo, Albany, and other interior places we know of Zouave companies formed after consultations and correspondence with ELLSWORTH. And since then, and particularly now, we hear not only of companies but of whole regiments that are uniformed, equipped, and drilled in pursuance of his plan and in consonance with his published directions.

After his tour, he redevoted himself to the study of law, and entered the office of President LINCOLN, at that time a lawyer in the comparatively unknown city of Springfield, Ill. There he continued until after the Presidential election, and up to the time of his legal examination and subsequent admittance to practice, was noted as a careful, intelligent and appreciative, student. His spare hours were devoted to the condensing and writing out of a theory concerning a Militia Organization for the entire country, which should bring the various State troops under a Federal head and supervision more immediately than is now the case. He had hoped to complete this and bring it before the War Department, with the ultimate probability of receiving some Bureau appointment in connection with it.

His intimate relations with Mr. LINCOLN, and the exceeding interest which the President-elect at all times manifested in his success, induced ELLSWORTH for the time to abandon his pet project and to apply for the position of First Clerk in the War Department. Of this we are personally confident, and also of the fact that not only he, but friends high in place, were exceedingly disappointed when it was ascertained that an early pledge of the present Secretary of War interfered with his desired appointment. During the Presidential trip from Springfield he was the life of the party, at all times happy, cheerful and courteous, ever ready to serve a friend and ever watchful of the desires or necessities of the party with whom he was traveling.

When he ascertained that it would be impossible for him to obtain the Clerkship, he applied for and received a commission as Second Lieutenant in the Army, in which capacity he was soon to be detailed for special service in connection with his long-cherished plan of reorganizing the State Militia. At this time the war news became threatening—volunteers were called for, and among the first who offered was ELMER E. ELLSWORTH, who resigned his commission in the army and came at once to this City, with the matured intention of raising a regiment from the firemen. His social qualities and his unvarying courtesy to members of the Press at times when he could be of service to them, rendered him an unusual favorite with them, so that, aside from the interest which they would naturally feel in a project so original and patriotic, they were also glad to reciprocate in a professional manner his kindness.

The regiment—a noble one—was raised, uniformed, equipped, drilled, transported and reported for service at the War Department in an extraordinarily short time, and had the honor of being the first to swear in FOR THE WAR, as they are now the first to attack and occupy a secession city. But little remains to be said. ELLSWORTH has filled, in a creditable manner, a very difficult position. At the head of 1,200 independent, daring, restless men he has maintained order, quiet, discipline and peace. His men are reputed to be as well drilled as any volunteer corps at Washington; they have been instrumental, with their Colonel at their head, in saving a vast amount of property from destruction at the Capital; they have been, though hitherto disappointed at finding little to do, perfectly under control, and in every way a credit to the City which sent them forth, and now they are recognized by one and all as the leaders in the advance movement against the foes of their country. We could with ease fill columns of our journal with interesting incidents connected with the camp life of Col. ELLSWORTH—of his self-denial, his courage, his devotion to the cause of his men—of his unflinching, yet kind discipline—of his uniform courtesy of demeanor and unvarying propriety of deportment,—but of what avail?

He has been assassinated! His murder was fearfully and speedily revenged. He has lived a brief but an eventful, a public and an honorable life. His memory will be revered, his name respected, and long after the rebellion shall have become a matter of history, his death will be regarded as a martyrdom, and his name will be enrolled upon the list of our country's patriots.

Another Point of View

THE MARSHALL HOUSE stood upon this site and within the building on the early
morning of May 24, 1861 JAMES W. JACKSON was killed by Federal soldiers
while defending his property and personal rights, as stated in the verdict of
the coroner's jury. He was the first martyr to the cause of Southern
independence. The justice of history does not permit his name to
beforgotten. Not in the excitement of battle, but cooly, [sic], and
for a great principle, he laid down his life, an example to all,
in defense of his home and the sacred soil of
his native state VIRGINIA[1]

text of the plaque formerly located at the Alexandrian Hotel

COLONEL Elmer Ellsworth's death immediately affected the
entire North, and the national mourning for his loss
rapidly increased the number of men who joined the army, as well as the amount
and varieties of industries necessary to support those recruits. Indeed, in a few
short months, more than 200,000 men joined the Union ranks. Rifles had to be
made, as well as cannon. Uniforms had to be cut and sewn, both at home and in
factories. Accoutrements by the thousands—canteens, knapsacks, belts,
drawers—were created in response to both government orders and private
purchases. The scene of his death itself created a vigorous "Elmer Ellsworth"
industry, specializing in souvenirs and artifacts. Journeying to
Washington following their enlistments and prior to being sent off into battle,
thousands of soldiers felt compelled to make pilgrimages to the scene of the
colonel's final moments. Dirges, marches, and ceremonial music were composed,
memorial poetry exhibiting a range of both pathos and talent was written, artists

---

1 Text of the Marshall House plaque, placed by the Sons of Confederate Veterans in 1929. It
was removed in 2017.

James W. Jackson, ardent secessionist and proprietor of the Marshall House Hotel in Alexandria, Virginia.
Fort Ward, Alexandria, VA and the United Daughters of the Confederacy, Alexandria, VA

created pictures of the "incident" at the Marshall House, and earlier images of Ellsworth were reprinted and sold by the thousands. Even parts of the carpet, flagpole, wallpaper, and staircase railing from the Marshall House were cut into bits and sold by enterprising Alexandrians (and Union soldiers) to those who would buy anything to memorialize the Northern martyr. In the Confederacy, however, there was another point of view.

James Jackson, the man who shot Col. Ellsworth at point-blank range through the heart, then lost his own life when Pvt. Francis Brownell returned fire and bayoneted him down the stairs, was considered by the Confederacy to be the true martyr of the event. Newspapers all over the South celebrated his "fearless defense" of the Confederate flag. Just as Ellsworth has been neglected in many histories, James Jackson has suffered the same fate. Very few historians can identify him by name. There is only one known biography of him: *Life of James W. Jackson, the Alexandria Hero and the Slayer of Ellsworth, and the First Martyr in the Cause of Southern Independence.* A man who claimed friendship with his subject but refused to put his name on the title page wrote this slim volume, which was published in 1862 "for the benefit of his [Jackson's] family."[2]

Prior to May 24, 1861, Jackson was merely one of many ardent secessionists populating the South. He had no national reputation equal to Ellsworth's, and if he is not to be completely lost to history as little other than "the man who killed

---

2 Anon., *Life of James W. Jackson, the Alexandria Hero and the Slayer of Ellsworth, and the First Martyr in the Cause of Southern Independence* (Richmond, VA: West & Johnson, 1862), 11, online version: archive.org/stream/lifeofjameswjack00rich/lifeofjameswjack00rich_djvu.txt, accessed September 25, 2012. Many possibilities have been put forward as to the identity of the author of this small booklet, but a short letter in the preface of the copy of the book in the holdings of Johns Hopkins University is fairly convincing of its accuracy:

Ellsworth," more should be known about his personal life. James was the seventh child of Richard Jackson of Fairfax, Virginia, and his wife, Jane Donaldson of Baltimore. The family home in Fairfax, "Prospect Hill," was described as a "fine old country house."[3] His father died when James was six months old, and he was raised by his mother. Jackson was not a particularly attentive student, although he was accepted at the Catholic College of St. Louis, in Kentucky. He attended the college briefly, staying with a brother, John, but soon returned to Fairfax. His unnamed biographer explains James's situation:

> Had his talents been diligently improved he would have been distinguished in some respect, for he had a fine judgment united with great shrewdness. He was fond of the open air and the hardiest sports that manhood indulges in. Indulging freely the rude bent of his inclination, he became involved in numerous hardy adventures . . . so that his name, when the writer of this first heard it, was, in his neighborhood, a synonym of athletic daring.[4]

The early part of his life was spent alternately with his mother in Fairfax and brother John in Kentucky. It was during one of his visits with John that he met Susan Maria Adams, the youngest daughter of a family that lived in Lebanon, Virginia. They married in 1847. In 1858, after living on a farm in Fairfax County for several years, Jackson moved his growing family to the town of Fairfax, where he leased the Union Hotel, and established himself as its proprietor. During his time in Fairfax, the hotel flourished. Jackson was known for being attentive to guests and having a well-supplied table. He even opened a small space in the hotel where he organized dances called "hops," and invited the public to join in the festivities. When he heard of a good musician in the area, Jackson offered him the opportunity to provide evening entertainment for hotel guests.

Besides music, the hotel offered some interesting historical artifacts. In the fall of 1859, abolitionist John Brown staged his raid on Harpers Ferry. This action had an electrifying effect on the state of Virginia. James Jackson had been one of the first to rush to Harpers Ferry, rifle over his shoulder and mounted on his own horse. He reached the small arsenal just as Brown and his men were overpowered. When Jackson returned to the Union Hotel, he carried with him one of the pikes used in the raid, and a piece of flesh he claimed belonged to the ear of John Brown, Jr. These "trophies" were put on exhibit in the hotel lobby, and Jackson entertained

3 Ibid., 13

4 Ibid., 14.

his clientele with the story of how they were obtained; no one had the audacity to question the truthfulness of his words.[5] To liven things up a bit, Jackson was often heard to threaten the sign outside his hotel. Although the establishment was named the Union Hotel, "Union" was not Jackson's favorite word. Whether anything was done to the sign by Jackson's hand or not, in April 1861, the board in front of the hotel disappeared. The wires that had held it fluttered from the post, but the sign that had pointed travelers to a place of rest was gone, and the post was snapped in two.

By the end of 1860, Jackson no longer leased the Union Hotel. He moved his family to Alexandria, the small port town across the Potomac River and 8 miles south of Washington City. There he leased another hotel, the Marshall House, on the southeast corner of King and Pitt Streets. It was a small, three-story brick hotel named for legendary Chief Justice John Marshall of the Supreme Court. When first built in the 1830s, it had been considerably more elegant, but by the time Jackson took over its management, it had seen better days.

Secession supporter Jackson was well known in Alexandria, and was listed as foremost among the custodians of the honor and rights of the state of Virginia, and of the South. He was extolled as "the glorious and high-spirited type of Southern gallantry, prompt to avenge insulted honor and ready to die rather than to submit to the insolence of wanton and lawless invasion."[6] The business cards Jackson had printed when he took over management of the Marshall House in early 1861 clearly showed this dedication to the Cause:

MARSHALL HOUSE
James W. Jackson, Proprietor
Corner of Pitt and King sts.
Alexandria, Virginia

Virginia is determined and will conquer under the command of Jeff. Davis[7]

As one of the most ardent citizens of Alexandria to espouse the ideas of secession and the Confederacy, Jackson boldly proclaimed his political stance by

5 Ibid., 18-22.

6 Ibid., 9.

7 Charles P. Poland, Jr., *The Glories of War: Small Battles and Early Heroes of 1861* (Bloomington, IN: AuthorHouse, 2006),15.

flying a flag from a thirty-foot pole placed through a trap door on the Marshall House's roof for support. It extended from the rooftop several feet down into the attic. The flagpole itself had an interesting history. Tall flagpoles were common in towns such as Fairfax and Alexandria, and this particular pole, flying the "Stars and Stripes," once had been used to denote the location of a Republican rally in Occoquan, Virginia. Even as Lincolnites "rallied round the flag," secessionists rallied to steal the flagpole. The story is told that Jackson, in front of a roaring, boisterous crowd and in imitation of the Republican "rail splitter" himself, took an ax and felled the flagpole. He proudly brought it with him when he moved to Alexandria.[8]

The Padgett's, a family whose sole support came from patriarch John Padgett's work as a sail maker, were residents of the Marshall House. At Jackson's request, Padgett's wife, Libby, made the enormous version of the Confederate "Stars and Bars," and her husband sold it to Jackson. Alexandria saw the flag raised for the first time on the afternoon of April 17, 1861, to loud cheers of approval and the firing of a celebratory cannon. Every time another state seceded, the flag was hauled down and Libby added another white star to the circle in the upper left-hand field of blue.[9] According to Alexandria diarist Judith W. McGuire, wife of local Episcopal clergyman John P. McGuire, the flag was a center of attention in the city from the moment it went up. It was one of the things she hated to see, because it reminded her, along with the change in the traffic on the Potomac, the military parades, and the Northern newspaper headlines, that both parts of a once-unified nation were "brothers gleefully preparing to draw their brother's blood."[10]

The Virginia State Convention initially met to decide the secession question on February 13, 1861. After Lincoln's inauguration on March 4, angry Southern fire-eaters wanted the state to join the Confederacy immediately. In spite of intense public pressure, however, Virginia maintained her slow, deliberate march toward disunion; after weeks of intense debate, the Convention finally voted to secede on April 17, four days after Fort Sumter fell. Virginia's statewide public referendum on secession took place on May 23, and it was only then that Virginia, the most populous slave state in the South, officially severed its ties with the Union it had been so historically instrumental in founding.

8 Jerome J. Harvey, *Occupied City: Portrait of Civil War Alexandria, Virginia* (Alexandria, VA: Alexandria Convention and Visitors Association, 2003), 12.

9 Ibid., 15-17.

10 Ibid., 15-16.

James Jackson and his pro-secession friends were ecstatic that Virginia had ratified the referendum. On the night of May 23, the city of Alexandria was the scene of happy celebration. Jackson, along with other Alexandria citizens, marched through the streets, serenading local members of the State Convention. The impromptu parade ended up at the Marshall House. There the partying continued until about 11:00 p.m., when the company finally broke up. James Jackson went to bed, satisfied with the day's political events.[11]

With Virginia no longer part of the Union, Lincoln, acting on Winfield Scott's concerns about the safety of the capital city, gave the order to occupy Alexandria late on May 23.[12] The occupation began at sunrise the following morning. In her diary, Mrs. McGuire recorded her impressions:

Fairfax Courthouse, May 25—

The day of suspense is at an end. Alexandria and its environs, including, I greatly fear, our home are in the hands of the enemy. Yesterday morning, at an early hour, as I was in my pantry, putting up refreshments for the barracks . . . the door was suddenly thrown open by a servant looking wild with excitement, exclaiming, "Alexandria is filled with Yankees!"

"Are you sure, Henry?" said I, trembling in every limb.

"Sure, Madam! I saw them myself . . . I went out and saw our men going to the [rail] cars . . . .and some marched out. I went to King Street, and saw such crowds of Yankees coming in! They came down the turnpike, and some came down the river; and presently I heard such noise and confusion, and they said they were fighting, so I came home as fast as I could."[13]

Newspapers in both the North and the South had their own interpretations of the events at the Marshall House, and each side also reported a great deal of erroneous information. They agreed, however, that it was common for citizens of Alexandria to kid James Jackson, saying, "On such and such a day, Master Abe was going to send someone down to lower this banner."[14]

---

11 Poland, *Glories of War*, 17.

12 *OR*, 2, part 9, 40-41.

13 Judith Brockenbrough McGuire, *Diary of a Southern Refugee During the War* (Lexington, KY: University Press of Kentucky, 2013), 17.

14 Ibid., 28.

Jackson was sure to give his standard reply with a smile. "There will be two dead men about when that flag comes down." Little did Jackson realize how prophetic his words were. Jackson's unknown biographer wrote:

> The main body of the force of six thousand, which achieved the glorious exploit of putting to flight four hundred men and capturing the town of Alexandria, came by land. The Zouaves, however, who had been encamped for some time in Prince George's County, Maryland, nearly opposite Alexandria, had embarked in steamboats and were landed on the Virginia side, some just above the town, some (comprising nearly all the regiment) at the wharves, with a large force of marines from the Navy Yard and the Pawnee. The landing took place just about, or a little after, daybreak. Jackson was asleep at the time. The Marshall House was not in the direct line of march of either force, and the neighborhood was, consequently, not alarmed until the Zouaves had arrived there.[15]

The story told above did not vary much from reports published in the Northern press, and also agreed with military reports, except for the thinly veiled sarcasm. Only when Colonel Ellsworth and his small group of soldiers and reporters—referred to as "admiring minions" by the southern press—arrived at the hotel, does the narrative begin to diverge from Union accounts. To return again to Jackson's biographer:

> On came the Zouaves up King Street. Arriving at the Telegraph office, Ellsworth first captured it and placed it under guard. As he came out the door, his eye fell on the flag of Jackson, flying from its pole on the other side of the street. 'Boys, that flag must come down!' he cried, and dashes up the street. We are not exactly familiar with Zouave discipline, nor do we understand by what orders he effected the halting of his men below, and the detailing of the two or three to go with and assist him in capturing the prize, as he considered it, but it was done. He walked or ran into the house and boldly demanded to be shown the way to the roof. The servants had shrunk away and the clerk and a few gentlemen in the office not answering him, they proceeded themselves to find it. Mounting the roof, he assisted in hauling down the flag while his admiring minions below gazed up with rapture at the scene.[16]

Jackson, according to this account, was asleep when Ellsworth and his men arrived. He was suddenly awakened to find his hotel overrun with "insolent

15 Ibid., 32.

16 Ibid., 32-33.

trespassers." Realizing what was happening, Jackson got partially dressed and grabbed the loaded shotgun he kept conveniently at hand. The biographer continued:

> He rushes by the nearest way to the main stair. He reaches the second story landing. Just as he does so, Ellsworth and his friends are descending the steps to the landing. Brownell in front. Ellsworth has commenced to wrap the flag around him, and remarks, as he receives it from one of the men, "I'll take the prize."

> "Yes, and here is another for you!" rings the determined voice of Jackson, and his stalwart form confronts the despoilers. He presents his gun at Brownell, the foremost one, when suddenly his eye catches sight of the flag around Ellsworth, and with terrible energy he changes his aim to him. In vain does Brownell attempt to strike up the gun. Quick as lightning, Jackson brings it down, the fear-strung nerves of the Zouave not availing against his desperate resolve, and in another instant Ellsworth's heart receives the contents of one barrel. Then he turns with fiercer fury on Brownell, but the Zouave has already aimed his piece, and as Jackson is pulling the second trigger he receives the dreadful Minie ball through his head . . . all was over in a few seconds, and while the Zouaves below are looking for the appearance of their colonel and his trophy, the surgeon of the regiment rushes out and informs them that their leader had just been "brutally assassinated."[17]

The South's main criticism—and it is legitimate—of Ellsworth's actions was that the Marshall House flag did not receive the treatment and respect which, as an enemy's banner, was its due. Additionally, there is still some question as to the legality of Ellsworth's actions. Technically, he should have summoned the manager of the hotel and, in correct and legal form, demanded the removal of the flag, as the city of Alexandria was currently under martial law. No battle was in progress, and as yet, no one had offered armed resistance. Ellsworth also could have chosen to honor his previous order for a group of his soldiers to go to the roof and remove the flag. Unfortunately, the colonel decided to get the flag *himself*, trespassing on private property and putting the civilians staying at the Marshall House in harm's way.

The press universally criticized the rashness of this act, even in the excitement of the moment. The prevailing sentimental opinion in the North, however, was that Ellsworth was a martyr and a hero who had removed the offensive flag to show his respect for President Lincoln. Jackson was cast in the same roles in the South.

17 Ibid., 33.

In the north, Jackson's death at the hands of Brownell was depicted almost as often as Ellsworth's death. *Leon Reed*

Legally, he was a citizen defending his rights and property. By the next day, the information regarding Jackson's actions was being spread throughout the Confederacy. Judith McGuire wrote:

> Poor Jackson had always said that the Confederate flag which floated from the top of his house [the Marshall House] should never be taken down but over his dead body. It was known that he was a devoted patriot, but his friends had amused themselves at this rash speech.[18]

Witnesses of the event said Jackson's body was still lying "where he had been killed" in the Marshall House at 2:00 p.m.[19] His wife, alarmed by the shots, confusion, and noise, had rushed out to the landing, only to find her husband dead. The company of Zouaves who had arrived a few moments after the shooting returned her to her room. Guards were placed at every door of the hotel to prevent a recurrence of violence, and to protect the property of the Marshall House from early souvenir hunters. Later in the day, Jackson's body was moved to a nearby

18 McGuire, *Diary*, 17-18.

19 Poland, *Glories of War*, 23.

room, cleaned up, and dressed in the uniform he had worn as a volunteer militia captain of artillery for burial.[20] Several weeks later, Justice James A. English held an inquest concerning Jackson's death and, after hearing the evidence in the case, the jury found that, "Jackson came to his death at the hands of the troops of the United States, whilst in defence [sic] of his private property, in his own house."[21]

Compared to Ellsworth's elaborate funeral journey, Jackson's obsequies were much simpler. Political circumstances prevented anything much larger, as the town of Alexandria was under Union military control. Witnesses recalled that, on May 25, 1861, when the hearse carrying Jackson's coffin approached Fairfax, the courthouse bell tolled, calling citizens and soldiers to meet the cortege and follow it about a mile to the family cemetery at the old Jackson home, Prospect Hill, on the Georgetown and Leesburg Turnpike.[22] Jackson's widow, Susan, and three young daughters, were naturally distraught. The eldest daughter, Amelia, about twelve at the time, began to cry hysterically, and she begged that the coffin be opened. When she again saw her father, she held his ruined head and wept so copiously that she had to be forcibly removed. The funeral service was performed by a neighborhood church elder who, when finished, gazed into the grave and was heard to say to the lowered coffin, "Would to God it were my son."[23]

Political circumstances did not stop many loyal Confederates from crossing the lines into the city to pay their respects at the Marshall House. The business of Ellsworth/Jackson *memento mori* that suddenly bloomed in the North has been severely criticized for its opportunism, but the same thing happened in Alexandria. One elderly man, a guest at the Marshall House, was seen cutting off locks of Jackson's hair to sell as souvenirs of "the first man who shed his blood in the cause of Southern independence." Another local entrepreneur, Richard L. Carnes, dipped his handkerchief in the pool of blood still on the landing. There is no telling how many times he dipped it, or from where the subsequent blood came, as he did a brisk and long-standing business selling "a relic of the first blood to be shed in defense of the Confederate Flag."[24]

---

20 Ibid., 38.

21 *Alexandria Gazette*, May 25, 1861, online version: www.newspapers.com/image/ 347334921 /?terms=%22James%2BJackson%22, accessed March 17, 2017.

22 Poland, *Glories of War*, 38-39, 44.

23 W. Burns Jones, Jr., "The Marshall House Incident," quoting from the *New York Tribune*, May 26, 1861, *Northern Virginia Heritage* (February 1988), 7.

24 Ibid., 39.

The anonymous author of the *Life of Jackson* wrote several paragraphs speculating upon the fate of both Jackson's corpse and that of his mother, who died after the Civil War. He was concerned about the possibility of the Yankees vandalizing both the Jackson home and family graveyard. What else could be expected of "such dastardly cowards who would as soon 'patch a hole to expel winter's flaw' with the bones of Mr. Jackson as they would use the bones as playthings 'to play at loggats with' for Yankee children?"[25] Nothing of the kind happened, however. The old house is still standing at 1157 Swinks Mill Road (Route 685) outside of present-day McLean. Jackson lay undisturbed until the death of Susan, his widow, in the late 1800s; he was disinterred and reburied next to Susan in Section I, Lot 43, of the Fairfax City Cemetery. At the time of this writing, a new wooden fence surrounds the Jackson family cemetery, which is beautifully maintained by the current property owner, a Jackson descendant. This respectful relative has erected two memorial obelisks across the graveyard from the marked burials.[26]

Jackson's mother was never mistreated or held captive, despite what Confederate diarist Mary Chestnut alludes to in her famous Civil War journal. Chesnut claimed that "they marched Jackson's mother, a poor old body, over eighty years old, to Washington," after which she was imprisoned in Rose Greenhow's home. There is absolutely no indication in Federal records that anything whatsoever happened to Mrs. Jackson.[27] Instead, there is much information showingthat subscriptions were raised throughout the South for the relief of Jackson's family, from $6.25 donated by the children of a school in Charleston, South Carolina, to $948.00 pledged from Memphis, Tennessee. Unfortunately, the money was "invested in Confederate State bonds for the benefit of the family."[28] Like so many other Southerners, James Jackson's widow and orphan daughters were left in debt, with little to sustain them, after the war ended.

As Ellsworth's death achieved symbolic status throughout the North, so did Jackson's death became a symbol throughout the South. Both were eulogized in poetry, which helped spread their fame and establish their positions as heroes and

25 Ibid., 40.

26 Jackson Family Cemetery, Find A Grave, www.findagrave.com/ cgi-bin/fg.cgi?page=cr& CRid=2350507, accessed May 5, 2012.

27 Mary Chestnut, *Mary Chestnut's Civil War* (New Haven and London: Yale University Press, 1981), 241.

28 Poland, *Glories of War*, 24-25.

martyrs. In the twenty-first century, James Jackson's is not a name one hears when Confederate heroes are listed, nor does he have much of a place in "Lost Cause" mythology. He seems mostly forgotten.*

Historically, the cause for which James Jackson died did not triumph. The admiration and respect in which he was held, however, was an inspiration to those who honored the Confederacy. The Richmond *Daily Dispatch* wrote:

> Glorious death! There exists not a mortal man in Virginia who does not envy his fate, who will not emulate his example, and who would not rather die than live to breathe an atmosphere polluted by such moral and social lepers as the degraded and murderous wretches whose hands are bathed in his heroic blood.[29]

For four horrifying years rhetoric such as this would be heard on both sides, and the result of this vitriol would be untold bloodshed and death. Within weeks, casualties from the battle of First Bull Run supplanted Jackson's name. Now, when asked, most people think the only "Jackson" the South ever had was called "Stonewall." Few people remember the events of May 24, 1861.

The Marshall House Flag was not the Confederate "Southern Cross," the battle flag the Confederacy adopted after confusion on the field at First Bull Run. It was the flag now known as the "Stars and Bars." This was the first national flag of

---

*Even the Marshall House no longer stands in modern Alexandria. At this writing, it has been replaced by "The Alexandrian" after being "The Hotel Monaco" for many years. The original Marshall House was torn down in the 1950s, and local archeologists have preserved artifacts uncovered during the construction process; these may be seen in the Alexandria Archeology Museum, housed in the Old Torpedo Factory, three blocks away on King Street. The Hotel Monaco once bore a plaque, placed there by the Sons and Daughters of Confederate Soldiers, but now removed and given to a local chapter of the United Daughters of the Confederacy with no explanation. Its text only mentioned Jackson's death, and not Ellsworth's.

---

29 Robert K. Nelson, "Of Monsters, Men—And Topic Modeling," *New York Times*, May 29, 2011, opinionator.blogs.nytimes.com/2011/05/29/of-monsters-men-and-topic-modeling/ #more-94157, accessed March 24, 2012.

The plaque in the Marshall House made no mention of Col. Ellsworth whatsoever. It is hoped that its removal will make way for a fuller and more nuanced interpretation of the incidents of May 24, 1861. *Albert Herring for Wikipedia Commons*

the Confederacy, with three wide stripes and a canton of blue with seven stars.[30] There is no information to indicate that Jackson was familiar with Alexander Stephens's pro-slavery "Cornerstone Speech," given two months earlier, although Jackson had a reputation as an impassioned secessionist. In the early days of the Civil War, most people on both sides did not necessarily have the same ideas about disunion and emancipation that they had by the time it ended. Even Abraham Lincoln's political position concerning slavery evolved and solidified as the war ground on.Elmer Ellsworth's main concern after Lincoln's election was the army, not politics.No letters or comments by Ellsworth that even mention slavery have been found among his effects.

These two men—Elmer Ellsworth and James W. Jackson—one a confidant of Abraham Lincoln, the other a staunch secessionist, are forever linked by their deadly encounter in an Alexandria, Virginia, hotel on May 24, 1861. This fatal meeting left both enshrined as the first fallen heroes in a long and ugly war.

---

30 "Flags of the Confederacy: Confederate Stars and Bars," http://www.usflag.org/confederate.stars.and.bars.html, accessed July 31, 2018.

The Gallant New York Firemen at First Bull Run

On the 21st of July, beneath a burning sun,
McDowell met the Southern troops in battle at Bull Run.
Above the Union vanguard, was proudly dancing seen
Beside the starry banner, 'twas old Erin's flag of green.

Col. Corcoran led the 69th on that eventful day,
I wish the Prince of Wales were there to see him in the fray.
His charge upon the batteries was a most glorious scene,
With the gallant New York firemen and the boys that wore the green.

In the hottest of the fire, there rode along the line
A captain of the Zouave band, crying, "Now, boys, is your time."
Ah, who is he so proudly rides with the bold and dauntless men?
'Tis Thomas Francis Meagher of Old Erin's isle of green.

Now the colors of the 69th, I say it without shame,
Were taken in the struggle to swell the victor's fame;
But Farnham's dashing Zouaves, that run with the machine,
Retook them in a moment, with the boys that wore the green.

Being overpowered by numbers, our troops were forced to flee.
The Southern Black Horse Cavalry on them charged furiously,
But in that hour of peril, the flying mass to screen,
Stood the gallant New York firemen with the boys that wore the green.

Farewell, my gallant countrymen who fell that fatal day.
Farewell, ye noble firemen, now mouldering in the clay.
Whilst blooms the leafy shamrock, whilst runs the old machine
Your deeds will live, bold Red Shirts! and boys that wore the green.

"The Boys Who Wore the Green," unknown writer
Recorded by David Kincaid in 1998

THE 11th New York Fire Zouaves were Elmer Ellsworth's most immediate legacy. Because the regiment was a favorite topic of the press, supporters and detractors alike watched carefully for any indication that the regiment would collapse without its colonel. Faced with serious issues such as fragmented unit cohesion and confusion about mission focus, the Fire Zouaves waited, along with the rest of the Union army, for what would come next. Without question, Ellsworth's men faced daunting challenges. There was no such thing as grief counseling for the stunned men of the 11th. They had no immediate leadership, training was irregular at best, and other than garrison Alexandria, there were no plans for the firemen to do what they had hoped, indeed had signed up, to do—put down the Southern rebellion and restore the Union. "Remember Ellsworth!" was their only unifying imperative.

Additionally, their reputation would be severely tarnished during the hearings of the United States Joint Committee on the Conduct of the War, when Congress was looking for a scapegoat to explain the Union defeat at Bull Run, among other things. Eventually the findings of the Joint Committee blamed the loss of the battle on Major General Robert Patterson's failure to keep Brigadier General Joseph E. Johnston's Confederates boxed in at Winchester, thereby allowing them to reinforce General P. G. T. Beauregard's army at Manassas, but for a while it seemed like the blame might fall on the 11th New York.[1] Damning testimony by Regular officers concerning the bravery of "Ellsworth's Zouaves" led to some disagreement as to their overall performance.[2] There was considerable prejudice by those officers against the volunteers under their command, and their hindsight often colored outcomes. The 11th New York fell victim to this, and the accusations of cowardice continue to this day. Nevertheless, the opinions of the Zouaves themselves, as well as the men with whom they fought, tell a much different story.

*   *   *

On May 24, while waiting for orders back at the wharf in Alexandria, the remaining Fire Zouaves milled around anxiously. Rumors had begun within an hour of Col. Ellsworth and his group leaving to enter Alexandria. Something bad

1 Bruce Tap, *Over Lincoln's Shoulder: The Committee on the Conduct of the War* (Lawrence, KS: University Press of Kansas, 1998), 41.

2 *Report of the Joint Committee on the Conduct of the War* (Washington, DC: Government Printing Office, 1865), vol. 2, 142-149, 168-177, 242-246. Hereafter cited as *JCCW*.

Lt. Col. Noah L. Farnham took over the 11th New York in the immediate aftermath of Ellsworth's death. He called it an "unwelcome opportunity." *Library of Congress*

had happened. Within two hours, Lt. Col. Noah Farnham and Maj. John Cregier returned from downtown Alexandria, and they did not appear to be bringing good news. As yet, no announcement of Ellsworth's death had been made. No one wanted to tell his men the truth; there was fear that the Zouaves would take revenge into their own hands.[3] The 11th was escorted back to the steamer *Baltimore* and taken to the middle of the Potomac in an attempt to preserve the safety of Alexandria. When informed of the death of their gallant colonel, the news plunged the Zouaves into bitter grief. Tears ran down the faces of the stalwart men. "Oh God bless him, God bless him! We'll never have a friend like him," mourned one soldier, whose face was wet with tears.[4] John Hay wrote that it was the flood of tears from the men of the New York Fire Zouaves that was Ellsworth's greatest consecration: "As I stood by his corpse at the Navy Yard, a Fire Zouave, whose ugly face had been washed almost clean with brine, said to me, 'Did you know him?'"

"Yes."

"Then," he replied, in a voice broken by sobs, "you knowed the bulliest little cuss that ever stood around in a pair of boots."[5]

The grief and anger of the 11th New York was intense, and men who were reputed to laugh at danger and take hardship as a gallant challenge "mourned the loss of their beloved colonel who had borne with their pranks and had championed

---

3 *Philadelphia Inquirer*, May 25, 1861, online version: www.newspapers.com/image/167236573/?terms=!!th%2BNew%2BYork%2BEllsworth%27s%2BZouaves, accessed December 21, 2017.

4 Randall, *Colonel Elmer Ellsworth*, 260-261.

5 Burlingame, ed., *At Lincoln's Side*, 123.

them in the presence of their traducers."[6] According to "Harry Lorrequer," a *nom de plume* for Arthur O'Neil Alcock, a Zouave who wrote for the *New York Leader*:

> The indignation of the men who were aware of the murder was extreme, and but for the wiser counsels and firmness of Lieutenant Colonel Farnham prevailed, there would not have been one stone of Alexandria left upon another at this time.[7]

When Ellsworth was alive, the regard and love that the men had for their commander were about all that held the wild New Yorkers in check, and when he fell, the morale of the 11th New York began to deteriorate. The hope of honor that the regiment may have won fairly for itself, under Ellsworth's leadership, now seemed ephemeral. The famous *esprit de corps*, which distinguished Ellsworth's Zouaves and gave their regiment a unique identity and a reputation for fearlessness, began to plummet. Under Ellsworth's leadership, the 11th might have earned a reputation second to none; without him, their future seemed bleak. Lieutenant Colonel Noah L. Farnham was the next in line to take command. Farnham, nicknamed "Pony" due to his short stature, was initially reluctant to take the job, calling it an "unwelcome responsibility." His appointment was temporary, and he was never commissioned as the regiment's official colonel, choosing instead to remain at his present rank while in command.[8] Farnham was personally popular with the enlisted men and the other officers in the 11th New York, and Ellsworth had trusted him as well.[9] One enlisted Zouave wrote in a letter home:

> We have great faith in Colonel Farnham, having known him long and intimately as one deserving the confidence and esteem of his associates, and fully deserving of the position that he now occupies.[10]

---

6 Ingraham, *Zouaves of '61*, 154.

7 "Letter from the Fire Zouaves, Shooter's Hill, near Alexandria, May 29, 1861," dmna.ny. gov/historic/reghist/civil/infantry/11thInf/11thInfCWN.htm, accessed June 12, 2012.

8 Murray, *"They Fought Like Tigers,"* 59; Frederick Phisterer, *Distant Drums: Herkimer County, New York and the War of the Rebellion, 1861 to 1865* (Albany, NY: J. B. Lyon Company, 1912); *New York Leader*, May 31, 1861.

9 *New York Times*, "The Successor of Col. Ellsworth," May 26, 1861, www.nytimes. com/ 1861/05/26/news/the-successor-of-col-ellsworth.html, accessed January 21, 2018.

10 "11th Infantry Regiment," NYSMM, online version: dmna.ny.gov/historic/ reghist/civil/ infantry/11thInf/11thInfCWN.htm, accessed January 21, 2018.

Alfred Waud did detail sketches of Ellsworth's Zouaves, including a sketch of Ellsworth himself (center). *Library of Congress*

Others recruited by Ellsworth, however, did not approve of Farnham, and caused a small controversy with their letters home:

Since the death of our lamented Colonel everything seems to go wrong, and I tell you we miss him as a child does his mother. I do not know what we are going to do for pants, as these nasty things are nearly worn out, and there is no prospect of getting others. Before the Colonel's death, he told us we had clothes making in New York and that he would hurry them on as soon as possible.[11]

And:

The delay in paying the Regiment has also been a source of very great inconvenience. Every other regiment . . . has been paid; and yet we are now going on three months in the service, and have received "nary red" yet. This is not on the square. . . . The want of this money is felt doubly by those who have left families at home who, for aught they know, may be suffering, especially now that their allowances have been stopped. . . . Let this be thought of and acted upon.[12]

On May 27, the regiment was moved to a camp about a mile and a half southwest of Alexandria, at a place called Shooter's (or Schuyter's) Hill, popularly called Fort Ellsworth.[13] It overlooked the Potomac from a bluff and was considered an attractive location. Private Arthur Alcock, formerly Ellsworth's

11 Murray, *"They Fought Like Tigers,"* 15; "W. S. letter," May 31, 1861, Benedum Books archives.

12 Arthur O'Neil Alcock (as "Harry Lorrequer"), "Letter from the Zouave camp," July 7, 1861, *New York Leader*, online version: dmna.ny.gov/historic/reghist/civil /infantry/11thInf/ 11thInfCWN.htm, accessed February 12, 2017.

13 Ibid., 102.

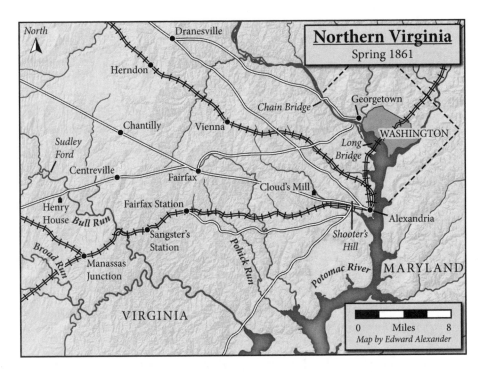

assistant military secretary, composed dispatches in the form of friendly letters sent back to the *New York Leader*, among other newspapers.[14] He wrote:

> Our men are drilled every day, and have had practice with ball cartridges, when their accuracy of aim surprised us. Colonel Farnham is, by an unremitting attention, making vast progress in the drilling of the men, and in making soldiers of them in every sense of the word. . . . A marked change for the better has come over our men, who, while they think he is a strict disciplinarian, believe him to be a valuable and efficient officer.[15]

Initially, Alcock spoke highly of the lieutenant colonel in his dispatches, but after Farnham denied him a promotion to sergeant and returned him to the ranks of Company A rather than allow him to continue as assistant military secretary, he had less

14 Ellsworth's senior military secretary was Lt. Henry J. Winser, who had worked for the *New York Times*. Both he and Edward "Ned" House, writer for the *New York World*, had accompanied Ellsworth to the Marshall House on May 24, 1861.

15 Ibid., 104.

to say about his commander. Then, in early July, Farnham became extremely ill with typhoid, and was hospitalized with a high fever for over two weeks.[16]

Farnham attempted to get his men back to their usual routines and continued to monitor the delivery of replacement uniforms, as the original ones were made of inferior material and were quickly wearing out. Wearing the Zouave uniform was part of the identity of the regiment, and it assumed more significance than that usually attached to military clothing. Additional grumbling arose over their promised weapons. The 11th was supposed to receive Sharps rifles, but had only gotten the Regular Army issue, .58 caliber Springfield Model 1855 percussion rifles, with "old fashioned" bayonets. Three weeks after Ellsworth's death, some soldiers were more hopeful about receiving new arms:

> We are improving every day in our Zouave drill (which had been temporarily abandoned), but not as well as we should if the lamented Ellsworth had lived. As I am writing a company is learning to load and fire laying flat on the ground, and they do it exceedingly well., and when we meet the enemy in earnest, the Fire Boys will make it too it for Old Jeff and his southern chivalry, as they call them.[17]

Arthur Alcock described life at "Fort Ellsworth," as their encampment was named, for his readers in New York. The personalities of the regiment come alive in Alcock's writing—the gentlemanly and experienced Dr. Gray, flirtatious young Capt. Wildey (formerly Ellsworth's aide-de-camp), and hapless Lt. Loeser's futile efforts to grow a mustache, aided by the application of some sortof patent medicine supplied by Quartermaster Stetson—all are described in friendly detail. A newspaper account also indicates that not all was sad and bitter with the Zouaves:

> The other day some of Col. Ellsworth's Zouaves, on taking a stroll through the country, some distance from their camp . . . came across a farmer who was busily engaged in planting corn, and as he expressed some concern that he should not be able to get the crop into the ground in season, they determined to help him out; so, pulling off their jackets,

---

16 Joseph K. Barnes, *The Medical and Surgical History of the War of the Rebellion (1861-1865),* (Washington, D. C.: Government Printing Office, 1870), pt. 1, vol. 2, 109-110, civilwardc.org/texts/cases/med.d1e7142.xml, accessed June 14, 2016.

17 Murray, *"They Fought Like Tigers,"* 15; Wilber A. Apgar, letter, June 11, 1861, Benedum Books archives.

they pitched in with hearty good will, and did the job in good order. They then marched back to camp, as tickled as a cat with two tails.[18]

Nothing is perfect, however, and discussions of problems were called "growling." The arrival of the new uniforms issued by the government created an intense growling session:

> The new uniform . . . is not received with favor by a large majority of the regiment, the loose Zouave dress being more in accordance with the ideas of firemen. It is our sincere hope that no trouble may come of it; but we cannot help saying that a close buttoned up uniform of any kind is not the thing for men who have been used to run to fires in a red shirt and pants. Meantime we would recommend our fellows to take what they can get. . . . It is war time, and we cannot get too much.[19]

According to Alcock's dispatches, camp life continued with some attempts at drill, a court-martial, hospital reports (which were low compared to other regiments—thanks, perhaps, to Dr. Gray's watchful eye), an occasional parade, and a flag raising. Various companies were detailed to occupy Alexandria or to guard Cloud's Mill, a small flour mill next to a sluggish stream. The 11th seemed to be the only regiment in the entire Union army that was glad to receive the cotton or linen havelocks produced in the thousands by civilian donors. These were either cloth rectangles, which fastened to the side buttons on a soldier's cap, or full kepi coverings, designed to protect a soldier's neck from the sun. Named for General Henry Havelock, whose British troops popularized their use in India, most letters home and unit histories disparage them unmercifully. The Fire Zouaves had nothing but gratitude for them, according to correspondence and reports.[20] In several drawings and paintings depicting the 11th New York at Bull Run, many men are shown wearing them.

Besides unit cohesion, another issue eating away at the Fire Zouaves was that of mission focus. Just as today this topic is of paramount importance to the success

---

18 *Buffalo Morning Express and Illustrated Buffalo Express*, May 28, 1861. These articles credit the *Washington Star*. Online version: www.newspapers.com/image/344175018, accessed December 12, 2017.

19 Ibid., 109.

20 Ibid., 120-121.

Ellsworth's Zouaves and the 1st Michigan put their backs into it digging fortifications around Alexandria. *Library of Congress*

or failure of any given military undertaking, so it was in the 1860s.[21] Ellsworth had always carefully explained things to his men, and copies of his orders are clear and concise.[22] Now the chain of command seemed broken, and no one was telling the distraught soldiers what to expect in the future. After Alexandria and Arlington Heights had been secured, picket lines were established. "Their [sic] is hardly a night passes but that some of our guards are fired at," wrote one member of the 11th.[23] Often the alleged attack was an intoxicated soldier trying to sneak back into camp, a cow bellowing, or a dog that failed to give the password. Nevertheless, the anxiety and drudgery of this kind of duty wore on men who had enlisted to fight for the Union, not spend every night in anticipation of a mythical attack. This issue continued to erode the unit cohesion of the 11th, which was unaware how soon it was going to be sent into battle.

The Fire Zouaves had not moved from Fort Ellsworth on Shooter's Hill since they had arrived in late May. On July 12, Alcock reported that regiments from Maine, Michigan, Minnesota, New York, and Vermont had joined them. The firemen had received no pay since leaving New York, and their rations were getting worse. These issues, added to the stress of the false alarms and the failure of the army to move, were a catalyst for discipline problems, but these mostly occurred in camp.[24] On July 14, the Fire Zouaves finally advanced, to a small, makeshift bivouac called Campbell's Run, about 3 miles from Alexandria. There they joined

---

21 "U.S. Policy for Individual and Collective Military Training," www.mod. gov.ba/files/file/dokumenti/defense/trainingpolicy.pdf.

22 www.angelfire.com/ny5/ellsworth/. The text of an order from Ellsworth reads in part:

"Have struck a lead. Am doing a good thing for the boys. Shall have to remain here until tomorrow 10 O'clock. Have the men pack knapsacks & fall in & commence drilling at precisely 9 O'clock. Drill by companies. Double the guard. Allow no man to leave the ground. Have the quartermaster meet me at Willards at precisely 8 0'clock /

Keep things going until I return."

23 Murray, *"They Fought Like Tigers,"* 15; Dunreath letter, July 4, 1861, Benedum Books archives.

24 Schroeder and Pohanka, *11th New York Fire Zouaves,* 121-122.

Maj. Gen. Irvin McDowell's main army, leaving their tents and belongings behind, to be brought up later by rail. At daylight on July 17, the Zouaves were ordered to march with the left part of the Third Division, under Major General Samuel Heintzelman, along Old Fairfax Road to Pohick Run.[25] Colonel Orlando B. Willcox's brigade of Heintzelman's division, in which the 11th New York served, continued from Pohick Run to Sangster's Station, arriving about 5:00 p.m.[26] This march was the first actual, sustained march in which the regiment participated, and it left many exhausted. Alcock wrote: "It was on this march that our Regiment first knew the hardships of military life in the field."[27]

Irvin McDowell's plan of attack called for the divisions under Heintzelman (Third) and Colonel Erastus Tyler (First) to converge at Fairfax Station by 8:00 a.m. and take Confederate General Milledge Luke Bonham's brigade by surprise. When this did not happen, there was plenty of blame to go around. McDowell finally assigned it to the men themselves, rather than admit to his inexperienced judgment. The march along the Orange and Alexandria Railroad might have worked if made by experienced, trained soldiers; but at this point, the Union volunteers were anything but experienced or trained. The divisions failed to keep to McDowell's schedule due to the constant falling out of the unseasoned volunteers. Blackberries were in season, and plentiful. The men were thirsty and left their units in droves to "go a berrying" to assuage their thirst, and, no doubt, also because vine-ripened blackberries simply could not be denied to young, eager volunteer troops who had never seen combat. The temperature in the area was recorded as 80 degrees by 2:00 that afternoon, but this did not include a humidity reading, which likely made it feel hotter.[28]There were sore feet as well, which begged for rest. All of these things hampered the steady march upon which McDowell had counted. According to correspondence from "J. A. S.," written to the editors of New York City's *Sunday Mercury* on July 25:

25 "Union Regimental Histories: New York, 11th Regiment Infantry, '1st New York Fire Zouaves'/'Ellsworth's Zouaves,'" *Civil War Archive*, www.civilwararchive.com/ Unreghst/ unnyinf1.htm, accessed January 21, 2018.

26 Bradley M. Gottfried, *The Maps of First Bull Run: An Atlas of the First Bull Run (Manassas) Campaign, including the Battle of Ball's Bluff, (June-October 1861)*, (El Dorado, CA: Savas Beatie, 2009), 10-11.

27 Ibid., 180-181.

28 Robert K. Krick, *Civil War Weather in Virginia* (Tuscaloosa, AL: University of Alabama Press, 2007), 30.

The men were given three days' provisions in their haversacks, consisting solely of six pilot biscuits, a piece of salt pork, one small cup of ground coffee, and a cup of sugar. Then, leaving our encampment at about 10 o'clock in the morning, we took the road for Fairfax Station. . . . [O]ur brigade, consisting of the Michigan First, Scott Life Guard, and our own regiment, took a circuitous route through the woods to outflank the enemy at Fairfax Station. . .[29]

During the march, a grand total of eleven Confederate soldiers were captured along with their colors as they attempted to retreat. When a small group of Fire Zouaves launched an attack on an entrenched group of Tennessee soldiers, Private John Johnson, who had served with Lady Washington Engine Co. 40, got credit for capturing their colors. They moved on, to and beyond Fairfax, where they encountered the 39th New York Infantry Regiment, known as the Garibaldi Guards. The Garibaldis, clad in the distinctive Bersaglieri-inspired uniform of a dark blue pants,red tunic, and broad-brimmed black hats, were mistaken for the enemy by the Fire Zouaves, who fired several shots at them before confirming their identity. The Zouaves, along with the other Union troops, then returned to Fairfax, and remained there until the afternoon of Saturday, July 20.[30] Late the next morning, they raised a United States flag, and left at 3:00 p.m. to march to Centerville:

Orders were immediately given to proceed as rapidly as possible, and at the same time we heard the most extravagant rumors that the New York Second and Twelfth Volunteers and the Sixty-ninth, had engaged some batteries near Bull's Run, and were badly cut up, so as to need our immediate assistance. The men made the most super-human exertions until we arrived in Centerville, when we were told that our services were not required.[31]

The misdirection indicated in this correspondence, from "J. A. S.," was widespread during the entire time preceding, including, and following the battle of Bull Run. There was well-documented confusion between similarly appearing flags and uniforms. Additionally, the nearness of the two armies meant that the soldiers often heard random musket fire. There was concern about the proximity of the firing, as evidenced by a local Confederate soldier who was guiding Brigadier

29 "J. A. S. to the Editors of the Sunday *Mercury*, July 25, 1861," in William B. Styple, ed., *Writing and Fighting the Civil War. Soldier Correspondence to the New York Sunday Mercury*, www.amazon.com/Writing-Fighting-Civil-War-Correspondence/dp.18839261300, 32-34.

30 Brian Pohanka, Marc A. Hermann, and Shaun C. Grenan, "Tiger! Zouave!," www.myrtle-avenue.com/firezou/, accessed June 2013.

31 Ibid.

General Thomas Jackson's men: "I could hear the click of musket locks being cocked all along the line, and I was mortally afraid they would fire on us." General Heintzelman commented: "This morning there was firing for hours so that it was really dangerous to be about. With these long-range muskets and raw vols. [sic] it is really dangerous to be near them."[32]

Lieutenant Edwin B. Knox was a former member of the Chicago Zouave Cadets. When Elmer Ellsworth came to New York City to recruit the firefighters, he asked Knox to join him and gave him the rank of lieutenant. His statement concerning the actions of the 11th New York Zouaves at Bull Run begins:

> The regiment was encamped about a mile this side of Centerville. At 2 o'clock AM on Sunday morning (July 21) the men were aroused and remained under arms until 7 o'clock AM, at which time they started forward. There were 950 men, all told, with "Pony" Farnham at their head. With cheers they moved briskly forward through the woods, singing and laughing and eager for the fight. They had marched about fourteen miles and were within three miles of the battlefield, when they heard the guns and saw the smoke from an eminence. This excited the men wonderfully, and at a double-quick step they pressed on, with the intention of joining Col. Wilcox, who, with the Michigan regiment, was a short way ahead. Halting at a pool of dirty water, they refreshed themselves, and went on until they came to a church three quarters of a mile this side of the battlefield, where they left their overcoats and haversacks, and having formed by companies, again went on at double-quick step.[33]

Finally, their brigade was ordered to move along the Warrenton Turnpike toward Manassas Junction, before branching off to the right and swinging north in the direction of Sudley Ford. The troops began to move at a double-quick, in a way that reminded many of them of the "random manner" in which firemen race down the street to a fire. A member of Company E recalled:

> . . . 'double quick,' if properly performed, is a very pretty movement, and one not excessively tiresome to the soldier. . . . But with our regiment, it was another matter, and performed in a manner not set down in our tactics. Anyone who has seen a closely

---

32 Samuel Peter Heintzelman Papers, Library of Congress, www.loc.gov/ loc.mss.ms010067, accessed February 26, 2018.

33 Edwin B. Knox, "Ellsworth's Zouaves at Bull Run," *The Weekly* [Madison] *Wisconsin Patriot*, August 3, 1861, online version: bullrunnings.wordpress.com/2011/07/20/letter-from-the-fire-zouaves/, accessed August 23, 2016.

contested race between two fire engine companies down Grand Street can form a good idea of what double quick was with us.[34]

Colonel Farnham, although still ill from typhoid fever, was determined to be at the head of his regiment in their first fight. True to his wishes (though against those of his doctors), he had rejoined the regiment that morning, riding up to the advancing column amid the cheers of the entire brigade. Private Lewis Metcalf wrote:

> Our colonel had been suffering from fever for several days and was not considered able to do any duty. To our great surprise, as we gained the top of the hill above our late camp, he came riding by us toward the head of the column, cheered again and again by our regiment and others who lined the roadside in order to see us pass.[35]

After moving at the double-quick for a distance of about 14 miles, the regiment came to a halt. Lieutenant Colonel Cregier ordered everyone who had not previously done so to take off their coats, drop blanket rolls, haversacks, and canteens. Private Metcalf continued:[36]

> Cheer after cheer rang out for our regiment at the prospect of at last finding the foe, and yet many among us were suffering from the intense heat and want of water, for nearly all the canteens were empty by this time.[37]

Ellsworth's Fire Zouaves were finally on the field of battle, but not everyone was glad to see the red-shirted volunteers. It was almost 1:30 p.m., and at this point, McDowell seemed to have the battle going his way. Matthews Hill had been under Federal control since noon, but McDowell realized that it would take more than an artillery duel to clear the field at the Henry House. He would need to move his artillery closer, and support it with infantry. He ordered his chief of artillery, Major William Barry, to direct Captain Charles Griffin and Captain James B. Ricketts to move their eleven guns across Young's Branch Valley and up to the Henry House Hill field. Both men, fearful of insufficient support, immediately protested. Captain

---

34 Pohanka, Hermann, and Grenan, "Tiger! Zouave!," accessed June 2013.

35 Lewis Herbert Metcalfe, "So Eager Were We All," *American Heritage Magazine* (June 1965), vol. 16, Issue 4, 1865, www.americanheritage.com/content/%E2%80%9C so-eager-were-we-all-%E2%80%A6%E2%80%9D, accessed August 23, 2017.

36 Pohanka, Hermann, and Grenan, "Tiger! Zouave!," accessed June 2013.

37 Metcalfe, "So Eager Were We All."

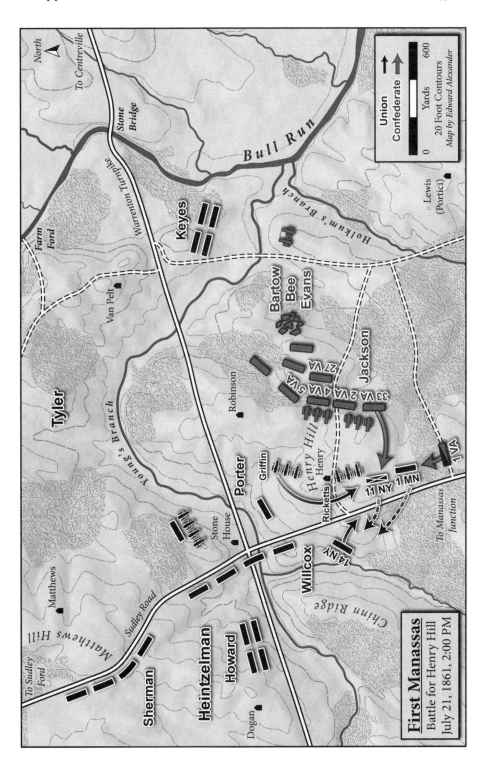

First Manassas
Battle for Henry Hill
July 21, 1861, 2:00 PM

Griffin suggested to Major William J. Barry that the foot soldiers go ahead, get into position on the hill, and then have the guns come up behind them. At that point, the infantry would fall back. Barry assured both captains that orders had already been given for the 11th New York to follow them to the field. Griffin, a Regular Army veteran, had little confidence in the ability of the flashy volunteer Zouaves to perform under fire. Barry, who had no intention of changing his commander's orders, replied, "Yes, they will. At any rate, it is General McDowell's order to go there."[38]

Griffin was not impressed. "I will go, but mark my words, they will not support us."[39]McDowell's orders, however, were firm. Griffin's three 10-pounder Parrott guns and two 12-pound howitzers were moved south along Sudley Road, while Ricketts turned his guns off the road and onto the field at Henry House Hill.

In spite of numerous delays and widespread confusion, McDowell still assumed that the battle was nearly won. All that was left was to clear out the nest of Rebel sharpshooters ensconced in the Henry House and then clear the surrounding hill. At about 2:00, just as Ricketts placed his six 10-pounder Parrotts south of the Henry House, the sharpshooters inside began to fire on the gun crews. Ricketts immediately turned the guns around and shelled the house.[40] When the sharpshooters realized what Ricketts had in mind, they fled back to the safety of their lines. Unfortunately, the elderly owner of the house, Judith Carter Henry, her two adult children, and a hired black servant remained behind. The fighting had been too intense earlier in the day to remove Mrs. Henry, who was an invalid. When Ricketts's ordnance began to pummel the house, not all the occupants were able to find shelter. Mrs. Henry was bedridden, and a shell crashed throughthe wall of her room, shattering her bed, wounding her in the neck and side, and blowing off one foot. She was thrown to the floor and died later in the afternoon, lying in a pool of blood. She was the only civilian casualty of the battle of First Bull Run.[41]

As Ricketts was clearing out Confederate sharpshooters, Griffin brought his five guns on the field, placing them north of the Henry House, and to Ricketts's

---

38 *JCCW*, 168-169.

39 Ibid.

40 Gottfried, *Maps*, 44.

41 "Resource #10: Untimely Death of Judith Carter Henry," from "Some Events Connected with the Life of Judith Carter Henry," unpublished manuscript in the files of Manassas National Battlefield Park, www.cr.nps.gov/nr/twhp/wwwlps/lessons/12manassas/ 12facts3. htm, accessed July 14, 2012.

left. His movement gave the Federals a total of 11 guns to face the Confederacy's 13. Major Barry rode to the Fire Zouaves' line to personally lead them to their position, to the right of the guns now being unlimbered about 300 yards from the enemy. Companies A and H were detached to act as a reserve. Private Metcalf wrote:

> Behind us in the valley, the 14th Brooklyn were drawn up in line and were resting. Oh, if we could but get some rest, just five minutes, to catch one good long breath,—one moment to get a sip of water. . . . No, not for us. Up rode an officer sword in hand ere we had hardly halted. "Colonel," he shouted. "The General [Heintzelman] has decided to put you right into it. Let the colors advance ten paces. Detail two of your companies as a reserve. Dress on your colors." 'Twas done. "Come on boys and show them what New York can do!" And with that the pet lambs were led to the slaughter.[42]

When Heintzelman caught a glimpse of the Southerners, he made the mistake of assuming they were Federals by their uniforms. The Rebels primarily wore civilian clothing, and they were just as confused as the Union troops. It was not until Heintzelman rode out between the lines that the confusion was cleared up—he was quickly fired upon, although not injured. Heintzelman ordered the Zouaves to charge, but before they could respond, the first volley from the muskets of the 33rd Virginia Infantry mowed down most of the 11th New York's front line. Upon reaching the summit of the hill, troops concealed in the wood line ahead also opened fire. "Down, every one of you!" shouted Farnham, and the regiment hugged the ground just as the Virginians unleashed another volley.[43]Some of the Zouaves began to rise and fire shots at the hidden enemy, yelling "Remember Ellsworth," as they worked. Others attempted to crawl closer to the wood line to deliver more accurate fire and escape their exposed position. Captain Jack Wildey remembered the peculiar "whizz" of the bullets, and that he experienced a sensation similar to the one he felt when entering an old-time fireman's brawl.[44]

The remaining soldiers, including some from the nearby 1st Minnesota, hit the ground and began to return fire from a defensive position. The artillery duel began, shaking the rolling, open terrain in front of the Henry House. Brigadier General

---

42 Ibid.

43 Metcalfe, "So Eager Were We All."

44 Augustine E. Costello, *Our Firemen: History of the New York Fire Departments, Volunteer and Paid* (New York: A. E. Costello, 1887), 726, archive.org/details/ourfiremenhistor00cost/ page/ 726/mode/2up, accessed February 2, 2021.

Thomas Jackson, who would earn the famous sobriquet of "Stonewall" on this day, calmly rode along the Rebel lines, reassuring his men. Captains Ricketts and Griffin, however, were less than calm. When the artillery duel had been long range, the Union held the upper hand due to their rifled guns, which had a much greater range than Jackson's smoothbores. Now, with the Confederates only 300 yards away, much of the Federal ordnance sailed harmlessly over the heads of the men in the Rebel lines. The reverse of this was that the Confederate artillery was now within range, and the combined firepower of the Southern infantry and artillery began to take a severe toll on the horses and men of the Union batteries.

As the 1st Minnesota and the 11th New York advanced to the top of the western slope of Henry House Hill, the 33rd Virginia, the leftmost regiment of Jackson's line of battle, under the command of Colonel Arthur Cummings, had them in their sights. Remnants of Confederate Colonel Francis Bartow's units, still on the field after losing Matthews Hill, had joined the 33rd Virginia. A Confederate soldier recalled the Federal advance:

> What a beautiful sight they were, as with well-preserved line they moved across the undulating field! I knew they were Yankees and my heart sank as I saw them move along in such a beautiful line.[45]

The Fire Zouaves rose and advanced, to the cry of "Ellsworth! Remember Ellsworth!"Some shouted the cheer of their old fire companies. With his sleeves rolled up and sword in hand, Lieutenant Daniel Divver led Company G's veterans of Eagle Engine Co. 13 with the shout of "Get down, Old Hague!"[46]

Colonel Orlando Willcox later wrote:

> The enemy opened a heavy . . . fire, the Zouaves returned the fire, but immediately fell back, bewildered and broken. The weight of metal against us was as of ten shots to one, of every class of projectiles . . . the whole regiment was swept back as by a tornado.[47]

---

45 John N. Opie, *A Rebel Cavalryman with Lee, Stuart, and Jackson* (Chicago: W. B. Conkey Company, 1899, The Classics.us reprint, 2013), 31.

46 Costello, *History of the New York Fire Department*, accessed June 2016.

47 Robert Garth Scott, ed., *Forgotten Valor: The Memoirs, Journals, & Civil War Letters of Orlando B. Wilcox* (Kent, OH: Kent State University Press, 1999), 291-292; John O. Casler, *Four Years in the Stonewall Brigade* (Charleston, SC: Arcadia Press, 2017), 27.

Ricketts had lost both gunners and horses to the deadly fire of the Virginians, and ran among the retreating soldiers crying, "For God's sake, boys, save my battery!" The Zouaves who were within earshot and a scattering of men from the 1st Minnesota returned to the guns, charging forward once more to defend the exposed cannon.[48] The Zouaves were nearly surrounded but continued to fight. The United States and the large, white fire department flag, gifted to them when they left New York, were the only colors the 11th New York carried that day. The Zouaves took fire from the front, but also were exposed to friendly fire from the rear in their attempt to recover the flags after they were briefly captured. When the flags were again with the 11th, the men tore both banners from their staffs and folded them up, hiding them under their shirts for safekeeping.[49]

In one letter, a young, unknown soldier from Company K, 2nd Vermont Infantry, which fought next to the 11th New York, wrote:

> We know something of the little scenes exacted just around us in battle—the truth is no one sees a battle—we hear the roar and see the smoke and know when the death struggle is going on. The Generals get a little wider view, but they depend mostly on the reports of their aides and couriers. 'Tis true no one sees except Him who sees all things. It must have been the direct agency of Providence to save so many of us from that fiery tempest that rained over us. As we came up among the whistling balls I took one long look at the sky and the smoking hills, then fixed my eyes on the enemy's lines, looked at my gun, and rushed in.[50]

He spoke for so many soldiers, in all wars, when he wrote that one man has but a limited view. The views were limited for civilian observers as well. Edward S. Barrett, who accompanied the 5th Massachusetts at Manassas, shared his view of the action on Henry House Hill:

> General McDowell now ordered a battery forward to take a position near a house on our right; the Fire Zouaves were ordered to support it. The position appeared to me, from my lookout, like a strong one, as it was on a hill on a level with the rebel batteries. Our battery started, the horses running at the top of their speed, and shortly began to ascend the

---

48 Gottfried, *Maps*, 44.

49 Pohanka, Hermann, and Grenan, "Tiger! Zouave!," accessed June 2015.

50 "Letter from the 2nd Regiment—The Late Battle," *The* [St. Johnsbury, VT] *Daily Caledonian*, August 9, 1861, online version: bullrunnings.files.wordpress.com/2014/02/ 1861-8-9-the-caledonian-2nd-vt-first-manassas.pdf, accessed November 14, 2017.

eminence, the Zouaves following closely; but scarcely had the battery halted and fired, before the enemy opened fire upon them from new masked batteries, and a terrific fire of musketry from the woods, and our artillery was driven back, many of the men and horses being killed. The Zouaves stood their ground manfully, firing in lines and then falling on their faces to load. Their ranks were becoming dreadfully thinned, yet they would not yield an inch . . .[51]

On the grounds of the Henry House, nearer the woods, the rest of the Minnesota troops gave ground, heading to the west. Within moments, they were joined by more New Yorkers and Minnesotans, some running to the woods, but most to Sudley Road. Colonel Farnham tried to keep his frightened and confused men in check, but the U.S. Marines, seeing the retreating Zouaves, immediately broke and fled back down Henry House Hill. When the first ranks of the 11th New York reached Sudley Road, they turned, trying desperately to reorganize under Farnham. Not a hundred yards south, however, was the 1st Virginia "Black Horse" Cavalry, 150 mounted Confederates under the command of James Ewell Brown "Jeb" Stuart. Stuart almost committed the "wrong uniform" error—he saw the uniforms of the nearby infantry were those of Zouaves, and since Zouave soldiers were popular on both sides during the battle, he shouted to the retreating men, "Don't run, boys! We are here." An errant breeze, noticeably absent from the battle all day, unfurled enough of the Stars and Stripes for Stuart to see his mistake, and he quickly followed his former words with the order to "Charge!" Private Samuel S. Hershey, Jr., of Company K, 4th Maine Infantry, wrote to a friend, telling him what he had seen:

A body of cavalry, charged on the Ellsworth Zouaves. The Zouaves opened their ranks and "took 'em in." Some went out alive. There cannot be anything imagined half so full of fight as a Zouave. They charged again and again and piled up the rebels in heaps.[52]

Civilian observer Edward S. Burnett added what he saw, and thought, as well:

---

51 Edward S. Barrett, "Scenes of the Battle Field—Personal Adventures at the Battle of Bull Run," *Boston Traveller*, August 1, 1861, online version: bullrunnings.wordpress.com/ 2014/09/ 15/edward-s-barrett-civilian-on-the-battle-1-2, accessed August 4, 2017.

52 Samuel S. Hershey, Jr., "On the Battle Field,"[Belfast, ME] *Republican Journal*, August 9, 1861, online version: bullrunnings.files.wordpress.com/2018/01/1861-8-9-belfast-me-republican-jpurnal=4th-me-two-letters4952.pdf, accessed January 17, 2018.

. . . suddenly out dashed the Black Horse Cavalry,* and charged furiously, with uplifted sabres upon them.—The Zouaves gallantly resisted this furious onset without flinching, and after firing their muskets—too sorely pressed to load—would fight furiously with the bayonet or any weapons they could seize, and in some instances drag the riders from their saddles, stabbing them with their knives. . . . Never, since the famous charge of the Light Brigade, was a cavalry corps more cut to pieces. There is a bitter animosity existing between the Black Horse cavalry and Ellsworth's Zouaves. A great many of the cavalry are citizens of Alexandria and Fairfax county and they resolved to kill every Zouave they could lay their hands upon to avenge the death of Jackson, and the Zouaves were equally determined to avenge the murder of Ellsworth; so no quarter was expected.[53]

Farnham was able to rally what he could of his men and establish a firing line along Sudley Road. Lieutenant Edward Knox described it: "They formed hastily in line, kneeling, semi-kneeling, and standing, that they might receive their enemies with successive volleys."[54] Their initial volley sent a "sheet of flame" into Stuart's troopers, shaking them badly. The cavalry regrouped and charged the fragile Federal line again. "For which," Knox continued:

. . . the Black Horse Cavalry paid most dearly. They were completely shattered, broken up and swept away. Not more than a hundred of them rode off, and as they went their rebellious ears were saluted with "One, two, three, four, five, six, seven, eight, Tiger, Zouave," and such a "tiger repeat" as one can only appreciate when he has heard it. What happened after that, it is hard to detail.[55]

After only a few minutes of fighting, the New Yorkers and the Minnesotans fled to the woods west of the Sudley Road. In less than 20 minutes, the 11th New

53 Barrett, "Scenes of the Battle," 1.

*Sometimes referred to as the "Black Horse Troop," the Black Horse Cavalry was actually just one company of Confederate horsemen, which eventually became Company H of the 4th Virginia Cavalry. It was initially formed as a militia unit by the young scions of Fauquier County's most prominent families. They were part of the escort that transported John Brown to the gallows in 1859. By the time of First Bull Run, the Northern press had written about them so often (along with "masked batteries" and the "Louisiana Tigers") that the name "Black Horse Cavalry" had become the moniker by which all Rebel cavalry was commonly, if incorrectly, known. At First Bull Run, Company H was attached to Lieutenant Colonel T. T. Munford's squadron of the 30th Virginia Cavalry. Even Confederate Brigadier General Edward Porter Alexander mentioned this great "bugbear" created by the press about these horsemen in his famous memoirs.

54 Knox, "Ellsworth's Zouaves at Bull Run."

55 Ibid.

Two of the most popular units to take the field at First Bull Run, the Union's Fire Zouaves and the Confederate Black Horse Cavalry, from the *New York Illustrated News*. *New York State Library*

York Fire Zouaves lost 38 men. By the end of the day, the Zouaves had suffered the fourth-largest number of casualties of any other Federal regiment engaged at First Bull Run, and 51% of the total losses of the Second Brigade.[56]

On Henry House Hill, the Federals were losing the battle for possession of the high ground. Captain Griffin decided to move his two howitzers over to aid Ricketts, where several companies of the 11th New York and the 1st Minnesota had returned to reinforce the guns. After firing two rounds, Griffin saw a large group of men in blue uniforms approaching from the woods to his right. He was preparing to fire when Maj. Barry rode up, shouting, "Captain, don't fire there; those are your battery support." Griffin argued briefly, but Barry held firm. Griffin's men held their fire. Unfortunately, these men were, in fact, Confederate General "Extra Billy" Smith's battalion, along with the 33rd Virginia. Marching to within 70 yards of Griffin's position, they opened fire with devastating effect. The remaining troops of the 11th New York were driven back down Henry House Hill to Sudley Road. Farnham rallied some of the Fire Zouaves, and at the behest of

56 Gottfried, *Maps*, 44.

Capt. Ricketts, who implored them for help, they charged forward once more. Seeing a troop of cavalry forming for an assault, the Zouaves turned and charged ahead at them, pursuing the horsemen back to the Confederate lines. Once there, they were nearly surrounded by Rebels and had to fight their way out.[57] Later, in his testimony before the Joint Committee on the Conduct of the War, Griffin stated, "That was the last of us. We were all cut down."[58]

Both sides had possession of the guns in the subsequent hand-to-hand fighting, but because the horses that had pulled them lay dead in their traces, it was impossible for anyone to remove the captured pieces from the field. Finally, by 3:15 p.m., after just over an hour of combat, the Confederates took final possession of the Union guns. When Gen. Jackson saw that the battle could be his, he rallied his soldiers with the shout, "We'll charge them now, and drive them to Washington!"[59] The Southern troops rose as one man, and for the first time, the Union army heard the eerie, quavering "Rebel Yell" as Jackson sent his massed forces to route the remaining Yankees running toward Sudley Road, cementing control of Henry House Hill for the Confederates. During this last part of the action, Capt. "Jack" Wildey was instrumental in recapturing the flag of the 69th New York. It was at this time also that Col. Farnham was hit in the head by a musket ball, which knocked him off his horse. Stunned, he remounted and continued to command his men on their retreat to Washington. After arriving in the capital, he was dragged from his mount and sent to the Washington Infirmary. The wound proved mortal; his earlier illness had so weakened him that it was impossible for surgeons to save his life.[60] Colonel Noah Farnham died in the hospital on August 14.[61]

By 4:00 p.m., with the major fighting done for the day, Irvin McDowell was resigned to defeat. The battle for Henry House Hill had ended, but the flood of soldiers and civilians retreating to Washington City had just begun. Elmer Ellsworth's proud, popular Fire Zouaves were nearly destroyed. Although accounts differ, most sources list 177 members of the 11th New York lost at Bull

---

57 Pohanka, Hermann, and Grenan, "Tiger! Zouave!," accessed June 2016.

58 *JCCW*, "Testimony of Captain Charles Griffin," 168-177.

59 Ibid.

60 *New York Times*, "The Late Colonel Farnham," August 16, 1861, www.nytimes.com/1861/08/16/news/the-late-col-farnham.html, accessed June 20, 2012.

61 Barnes, *Medical and Surgical History*, 109-110, ia802709.us.archive.org/2/items/medical surgical32barnrich/medicalsurgical32barnrich.pdf, accessed July 3, 2016.

Run, with over 40 killed, 74 wounded, and another 68 missing. Private Franklin Gates of the 12th New York Infantry wrote to his parents:

> Ellsworth's Zouaves suffered more than any other regiment, and about half their number was killed. No body of men ever fought more nobly and bravely than they did. They did not leave the field until they had laid one thousand of the rebels dead before them. Their brave Colonel [Farnham] fell from his horse at the first fire.[62]

They had performed many acts of personal courage, but the toll taken on the New Yorkers was enormous. Colonel Farnham was mortally wounded. Lieutenant Colonel John A. Cregier, 45 at the time of the battle, resigned in anger and disgust at the way "his" men had been managed. Charles M. Leoser became lieutenant colonel after Cregier's resignation and went with the remainder of the regiment to Hampton Roads. Surgeon Gray, hospital steward Perrin, and Pvt. Alcock, who had volunteered to do field medical duty, were captured at a makeshift hospital at the Stone House. All the men there who were attached to Union regiments were ordered by Confederate officers to leave the wounded and dying, despite their pleading and the fact that they were working on men from both sides. Sixty-eight men from the 11th New York were taken prisoner that day, and held for 10 months, initially in Harwood's Tobacco Factory in Richmond. In September they were transferred to Castle Pinkney in Charleston, South Carolina, where they remained until paroled the following May.[63] The regiment was then sent back to New York, where it was mustered out of service on June 2, 1862.[64]

*   *   *

There wasn't much of a breeze on that hot July day, and smoke from the rifles and cannon did not lift from the field for hours. If anyone ran during the battle, it would have been difficult to identify him. Accusations of cowardice and poor leadership were leveled at the Fire Zouaves, with some commanders going so far as to say the 11th fled after firing just a single volley. One fact is certain, however: Losses among the Fire Zouaves were statistically more substantial than those

62 Franklin E. Gates, "A Canastota Volunteer's Experience in Battle," *Utica* [NY] *Morning Herald and Daily Gazette*, unknown date; Gates to "Parents," July 23, 1861, dmna.ny. gov /historic.reghist/civil/infantry/12thInf/12thInfC.

63 Schroeder and Pohanka, *With the 11th New York*, 205.

64 Ibid., 186-189.

among most other Union regiments, and most of their casualties were sustained in the first half hour of the fighting. These numbers would not have occurred if the troops mentioned had been in full retreat. It is true that some men started running. Like many other Northern regiments, the Fire Zouaves lost all organizational cohesion but, as firefighters, they had been trained to help injured comrades and to go where they were needed most. Men who were individually brave enough to scale burning buildings had not yet mastered the art of troop movement. Other regiments, especially the 69th New York and 1st Wisconsin, wrote afterward of the numerous acts of courage and kindness they witnessed, including Capt. Wildey's group of Zouaves charging the Rebels and recapturing the bright green banner of the 69th.

The truth about the particulars of this part of First Bull Run may always remain incomplete. Soldiers in battle rarely see the overall battle plan; instead, they see the ground in front of them. The smoke, confusion, and death surrounding each individual make an accurate recollection difficult, especially when one's mind is trying to block out the carnage and human destruction of battle. Although numerous reports and recollections survive, few of them agree. Still, the flank of the Union army, held in part by the 11th New York, was turned, and there were many casualties. The North had lost this critical first battle to the South, and would have to retreat and rethink its entire war effort.

The battle of First Bull Run, July 21, 1861, referred to as First Manassas by the Confederacy, was the first real battle of the American Civil War. Compared to later fights like Shiloh, Antietam, and Gettysburg, it was small in terms of numbers of troops and casualties, but because it was the first, it was the template for all subsequent engagements. It consisted of about half a dozen smaller actions, many happening at the same time in different parts of a widely separated battlefield, stretching for miles in every direction. Woods, hills, undulating stream cuts, and houses blocked visibility and separated units from each other, and generals from their commands. The nature of the country, dotted with scattered farms and outbuildings, insured that houses and fences would become impediments or landmarks, depending on one's point of view. The homes of several unfortunate families—the Van Pelts, the Matthews, the McLeans, the Lewises, and the Henrys—would give their names to history. So would the 11th New York Fire Zouaves, fighting collectively, fighting individually, but always fighting to honor their slain colonel.

Would Ellsworth's plan for the incorporation of the volunteer militia companies into the Regular Army have worked? Would it have made a difference? Would Robert E. Lee's words, upon hearing of Colonel Elmer Ellsworth's death, have been proven prophetic? When he learned about the Marshall House incident, Lee is said to have remarked that, had Ellsworth lived, he would have become the commanding general of the Union army.[65] All this is guesswork. History is made of facts.

It is a fact that Abraham Lincoln had great confidence in and love for Ellsworth, and was willing to give him great responsibility in the military. It is a fact that John Hay and John Nicolay, Ellsworth's best friends, had great regret for the military mind lost to the nation. It is a fact that enlistments increased after Ellsworth died. Sadly, it is also a fact that Ellsworth has been mostly forgotten by an America now over 160 years removed from the Civil War. Colonel Elmer Ellsworth's death was the first nationally acknowledged Union fatality of the American Civil War. President Abraham Lincoln's death was the last.

---

65 Adam Q. Stauffer, "'The Fall of a Sparrow": The (Un)timely Death of Elmer Ellsworth and the Coming of the Civil War," *The Gettysburg College Journal of the Civil War Era*, vol. 1, article 6 (2010), 52, cupola.gettysburg.edu/gcjcwe/vol1/iss1/6, accessed August 2012.

After Ellsworth's Death

His dauntless and stainless life has renewed the bright possibilities of the antique chivalry,
and in his death we may give him unblamed the grand cognizance of which the
world has long been unworthy—*"Le chevalier sans peur et sans reproche."*

from John Hay, "Obituary," *Washington Chronicle*, May 26, 1861

COLONEL Elmer Ellsworth's death in an Alexandria boarding house set the Union on fire. Mourners from Virginia northward pledged lives and money to support the northern war effort in heretofore unseen amounts. "Remember Ellsworth" was a rallying cry for the entire North. On a personal level, however, his friends and family suffered even more than the country. When Ellsworth died, those who knew him well were left behind to carry on his memory. Carrie Spafford, his fiancée, was terribly young to have to confront such a tragedy on a national scale. Phebe and Ephraim Ellsworth, his parents, had now lost both of their sons to seemingly cruel twists of fate. Finally, Pvt. Francis Brownell found his life and the Marshall House flag intertwined for the rest of his years. Each made peace with the reality of a future without Elmer Ellsworth.

* * *

Carrie Spafford was 15 when she met Elmer Ellsworth in the summer of 1858. He was young also; he had turned 22 that May. Women commonly married at a younger age in the middle of the nineteenth century, an era in which a young man consulted a young woman's parents before any agreement to an engagement. In Carrie's case, the engagement was *not* agreed to until her suitor could offer a way to make a living.[1] Drilling militia units may have appeared glamorous, but it paid

---

1 Elmer Ellsworth to Carrie Spafford, November 6, 1858, CHS EE/AL Letters.

poorly. Additionally, the Spafford family was relatively forward in believing that their daughters be as well educated as possible. When Carrie and Elmer met, she was a student at the Rockford Female Seminary, the leading girls' school in her hometown. It is now known as Rockford University; Jane Addams, social reformer and founder of Hull House, graduated from Rockford in 1881.[2]

Their long courtship-by-mail began when Ellsworth left Rockford in the fall of 1858 to drill a school-based militia group in Madison, Wisconsin. Every letter exchange makes more evident what each expected of the other. Ellsworth took pains to hide his previous involvement, however slight, with another woman, and continuously reassured Carrie of his affection. He wrote: "I might spend half my time in the society of the ladies here, without lessening my friendship for you, dear Carrie, you can never suffer by comparison with any of them."[3] He wrote to her mother and father as well, putting himself in the best possible light and defending his actions when some unfortunate gossip surfaced.[4] He tried to explain himself in a letter to Mrs. Spafford, ending with an apology for causing any concern on the part of the parents of Miss Carrie:

> I cannot sufficiently express my regret that this circumstance should have given you a moment's pain, and I blame myself as the cause of it, though I beg you to believe that I had no thought of that letter being seen by you.[5]

By late 1858, Ellsworth had finished his contract in Madison and returned to Chicago. After attending a parade of the Illinois Governor's Guard on December 26 and continuing to make contacts with powerful Chicagoans, he traveled to see Carrie in Rockford.[6] It was during the next few weeks that Elmer proposed to her and began the long, arduous job of winning her father over to the idea of himself as a son-in-law. In Ellsworth's Chicago effects is a draft of a letter, dated January 20, 1859, addressed simply to "Sir." It begins an inquiry as to the possibility of being accepted as a student of law with a currently practicing lawyer, as was the custom at

2 "Our History," official website of Rockford University, www.rockford.edu/about/history/, accessed December, 2017.

3 Elmer Ellsworth to Carrie Spafford, November 15, 1858, CHS EE/AL Letters.

4 Elmer Ellsworth to "Friend Parks," KCWM/LFAC; Elmer Ellsworth to Mrs. Spafford, November 23, 1858, CHS EE/AL Letters.

5 Elmer Ellsworth to Mrs. Spafford, November 23, 1858, CHS EE/AL Letters.

6 Randall, *Colonel Elmer Ellsworth*, 77.

the time. Little else is known, but Mr. Spafford had evidently been influential in convincing young Ellsworth to pursue a career that would provide for his daughter in a more substantial (and dependable) way than being a sometimes-drillmaster.

The Spaffords were not quite ready for their daughter to be married, no matter what a suitor had to offer. During Ellsworth's visit to Rockford, Carrie's parents made clear to both young people that she would be leaving Illinois to study at the Tilden Seminary in New Hampshire for at least a year.[7] In April 1859, Carrie started east, stopping for a few hours in Chicago to say goodbye to her fiancé. To commemorate their parting, Ellsworth presented her with an "Album of Love," a commercially produced scrapbook he had filled with drawings and poems, all in an attempt to make sure she would not forget him. One of the ornate pages is inscribed:

> When you look upon these lines, dear Carrie, may they remind you of the fond hearts, filled with high hopes and bright anticipations of your future, whose prayers "that you may realize the glorious promise of your youth," nightly ascend to the Heaven.[8]

Carrie Spafford and Elmer Ellsworth did not see each other again until August 25, 1860. Elmer hoped that Carrie would be able to meet him in Buffalo during the Chicago Zouave Cadets tour, but her travel arrangements from New Hampshire to Rockville did not coincide with his schedule. His letters indicate that later he was able to spend about three weeks in Rockford visiting the Spaffords and renewing his love vows, but by the end of September, he was in Springfield, ready to study law with Abraham Lincoln.[9] By that time, Carrie had not returned to New Hampshire, but to Brooklyn, New York, to begin a two-year course of study at the academy of her uncle, Edward Warren. Evidently, she roomed with the Warrens, as Elmer's letters from this time continuously remind her to be respectful to her uncle, who would "guide and direct you in all things."[10] He mentioned his campaigning for Lincoln, making speeches and traveling between speaking engagements. "I take good care when going into a yard to hold an argument with a

7   Ibid., 84-85.

8   Elmer Ellsworth, "Album of Love," April 4, 1859, CHS EE/AL Letters.

9   Elmer Ellsworth to Carrie Spafford, September 23, 1860, KCWM/LFAC.

10 Ibid.; October 28-29, 1860, KCWM/LFAC.

strange mastif [sic] to leave the gate open behind me."[11] Elmer and Carrie were able to meet at the Astor House Hotel during Lincoln's Inaugural Express trip to Washington, with her uncle acting as chaperone. Neither knew at the time that the evening of February 9, 1861, was the last time they would ever see each other.

They continued to write to each other regularly, with Carrie's letters often being posted to the Executive Mansion, care of John Nicolay.[12] They discussed a plan to meet in Albany, but by April 12, the country was at war. The end of Carrie's school term saw her just returned to Rockford when the news of Ellsworth's death came over the telegraph. One may imagine the now eighteen-year-old woman filled with grief, which was deepened by the knowledge that she would not be able to attend any of the funeral services held to honor "her" colonel. A day or so earlier, Carrie had fallen from a horse and severely sprained (and perhaps broke) her ankle; she was bed-ridden.[13] The news of Ellsworth's death hit all of Rockford hard, and the city joined Carrie in her devastation. The next day there was a special memorial service held to honor the fallen soldier at the Second Congregational Church, with Dr. H. M. Goodwin giving the eulogy. Carrie, dressed in mourning, attended the service braced by the arms of her parents.[14]

Other than a short visit to Ellsworth's parents in August 1861, Carrie remained at her family's home, grief-stricken and not knowing quite what to do.[15] John Hay wrote in his eulogy for Ellsworth:

11 Ibid.

12 Burlingame, ed., *With Lincoln in the White House*, 44.

13 Randall, *Colonel Elmer Ellsworth*, 270.

14 *New York Herald*, May 27, 1861, online version: www.newspapers.com/ image/ 329329346/?terms=Colonel+Elmer+Ellsworth, accessed December 28, 2017; [Springfield] *Illinois State Journal*, May 25, 1861, online version: www.genealogybank. com/doc/ newspapers/image/v2%3A13D09C142C972071%40GB3N EWS-13D78FC5803 659E0% 402400921-13D3E871C8EFF920%401-13D3E871C8EFF920%40?h=3&fname=Colonel%2 0Elmer&lname=Ellsworth&fullname=Colonel%20%20Ellsworth&exsrch=1&kwinc=&kwe xc=&rgfromDate=May%2C%201861&rgtoDate=May%201861&formDate=&formDateFle x=exact&dateType=range&processingtime=, accessed December 28, 2017; newspaper clipping, *Cleveland Star*, September 25, 1907.

15 Carrie Spafford to John George Nicolay, August 13, 1861, Lincoln Financial Foundation Collection, Allen County Public Library (Fort Wayne, IN), www.lincolncollection.org/ search/results/item/?q=elmer+ellsworth&page=1&item=105948, accessed August, 2013.

... no man could have died more deeply lamented than the young hero ... the few who knew him well are mourning in the utter abandon of irremediable anguish, as if all the earth had for them of bright or beautiful or brave, went out with his last breath.[16]

Carrie wrote several letters to Ephraim and Phebe Ellsworth, indicating that at least a written relationship existed between the Spaffords and the Ellsworths. In one letter, dated January 20, 1862, she wrote that she was glad Mr. Ellsworth was able to purchase Elmer's horse: "[I]s [it] not a fine horse? What do you intend doing with it?"[17] Her sadness came through clearly, even several months later, when she added:

By way of proving to you my devotion to Elmers memory I will tell you of something that has lately happened-but remember I dont tell of it boasting by. More than three years ago I recd a gentleman here from Chicago-the son of one of the wealthiest men in the City-during the time I have seen him quite often he was a friend of Elmers he came to Rockford not long since-and offered me heart, hand and fortune but I decidedly refused all. Although I think a great deal of him as a friend, I could never think of his following the place I so long kept for another. It does not seem possible that I can ever love another consequently I do not think it would be right for me to marry. And I never intended to until forced to for want of a home.[18]

Carrie collected the newspaper clippings and sprigs of flowers sent to her by mail in a scrapbook and tried to look after what effects remained of her fiancé's life. The items he had left in Springfield were sent to his parents in Mechanicville. John Nicolay returned Ellsworth's trove of Carrie's letters to her, as well as some small, unnamed items.[19]

Gradually Carrie's name began to reappear in the Rockford newspapers. She was mentioned as being one of the hostesses for a reception given by her church, and as attending a literary or historical society tea. She began to rebuild her life,

---

16 Burlingame, ed., *Lincoln's Journalist*, 71.

17 Carrie Spafford to Mr. and Mrs. Ellsworth, January 20, 1862),"Today in the Civil War: January 20, 2012, Dispatches from The Rosenbach Collection," civilwar. rosenbach.org/ ?p=3957, accessed August, 2015.

18 Ibid.

19 Charles H. Spafford to John G. Nicolay, (May 27, 1861), Today in the Civil War: Dispatches from the Rosenbach Collection, www.lincolncollection.org/search/results/ item/?q=elmer+ ellsworth&page=1&item=105875, accessed August 2015.

although she would never again be simply "Carrie Spafford." She was spoken of as "Col. Ellsworth's Affianced Bride" in newspaper articles whenever something about Ellsworth was published.[20] By 1866 however, Carrie had found love once again. She married Frederick E. Brett at a ceremony in her family home on March 7 of that year. The Bretts spent the first years of their married life in Boston, and then in Chicago, where the 1880 census lists Mr. Brett as operating a dry goods store.[21] Carrie's obituary states that they traveled quite extensively as a couple, living in California and Florida for several months at a time.[22] In 1870 they had a son, Charles S. Brett, but by 1891-92, fate was, again, unkind to Carrie. Within six months she lost both her husband and her son, who died from typhoid fever weeks after graduating from Beloit College.[23] She moved back to her childhood home to care for her aging mother and father, who died in 1901 and 1902, respectively.[24] Carrie spent the rest of her life serving her community, taking a particular interest in the Young Women's Christian Association and women's issues and devoting herself to making the lives of women better. Carrie's sister, Eugenia (the baby named by Ellsworth), would eventually give the Spafford mansion on Madison Street to the YWCA.[25]

According to a newspaper clipping, Carrie died without warning at her childhood home "in the arms of her sister."[26] She was 68 years old, and although she had been married to Frederick Brett, Carrie was referred to as the "fiancée of

20 *Appleton* [WI] *Motor*, June 6, 1861, online version: www.newspapers.com/image/ 233975439, accessed December 2, 2017.

21 1880 United States Federal Census, online version: www.ancestry.com/ interactive/6742/ 4240470-00214?pid=46526111&backurl= search.ancestry.com/cgi-bin/sse.dll?indiv%3D1% 26dbid%3D6742%26h%3D46526111%26tid%3D%26pid%3D%26usePUB%3Dtrue%26_p hsrc%3DvMF41%26_phstart%3DsuccessSource&treeid=&personid=&hintid=&usePUB=t rue&_phsrc=vMF41&_phstart=successSource&usePUBJs=true9, accessed December 30, 2017.

22 Newspaper clipping, *Cleveland Star*, September 25, 1927.

23 Ibid.

24 1900 U.S. Federal Census, online version: www.ancestry.com/interactive/ 7602/4113814_ 00366/12957490?backurl=www.ancestry.com/family-tree/person/tree/9517814/person/34 0065425393/facts, accessed December 30, 2017.

25 Kathi Kresol, "Voices from the Grave: Carrie Spafford, a life of sorrow—the tragedy of one of Rockford's founding families," *Rock River* [Rockford, IL] *Times*, October 8, 2014, online version: history.rockfordpubliclibrary.org/localhistory/?p=10135&, accessed August 14, 2015.

26 *Rockford* [IL] *Daily Register-Gazette*, October 9, 1911, online version: history.rockford publiclibrary.org/localhistory/?p=6359, accessed December 4, 2015.

Col. Ellsworth" in her newspaper obituaries, which were reprinted all over the Northeast and West.[27] One modern writer, looking for a link to the sesquicentennial commemoration of Ellsworth's death, went so far as to say that Carrie haunts Cedar Bluff Cemetery in Rockford, where she is buried. Allegedly, she wears black, but ghost sightings are always dubious. Carrie was, however, sadly mentioned in a brief newspaper article in the *San Bernardino Daily Sun*. It is in a "Notice to Creditors," and asks that "all persons having claims against the said deceased, to exhibit them, with the necessary vouchers, within four months."[28] There were no known claimants. Carrie willed her effects to a variety of relatives, and several of her letters and scrapbooks reside at the Kenosha Civil War Museum in Wisconsin. Within one of those scrapbooks is a brief note from Kate Chase, daughter of Secretary of the Treasury Salmon Chase. Though the letter does not contain much about the death of Elmer Ellsworth, Ms. Chase expressed her condolences:

He spoke of you often, and with great affection. Although our acquaintance was brief, I can tell you sincerely that I believe his love for his country was outshone only by his love for you.[29]

* * *

Deeply affected by their son's death, Ephraim and Phebe Ellsworth had now lost both of their sons within a year of each other. They learned of Elmer's passing fairly quickly via telegraph, and were able to attend his funeral at New York City's Astor House thanks to the kind services of Robert Sears, the neighbor of long ago whose children had been playmates of both Ellsworth boys.[30] Newspapers described the solemn ceremonies in Washington, New York City, Albany, and

27 Ibid.; *Belvidere* [IL] *Daily Republican*, October 10, 1911, online version: www. newspapers. com/image69558255, accessed August 27, 2017.

28 *San Bernardino* [CA] *Daily Sun*, March 26, 1912, online version1: www.newspapers. com/ image47148492, accessed August 4, 2015.

29 Scrapbook of Carrie Spafford Brett, KCWM/LFAC.

30 *New York Daily Herald*, May 27, 1861, online version: www.newspapers. com/ image/329329346/?terms=Col.%2Belmer%2Bellsworth, accessed December 4, 2017; *Buffalo Commercial*, May 27, 1861, online version: www.newspapers.com/ image/264442721/ ?terms=Col.%2Belmer%2Bellsworth, accessed December 4, 2017; The *McArthur* [OH] *Democrat*, May 30, 1861, online version: www.newspapers. com/image/80054681/ ?terms=Francis%2BBrownell, accessed January 1, 2018.

finally Mechanicville, where Ellsworth's remains were laid to rest in the large Ellsworth family plot in Hudson View Cemetery.[31] At first there was no stone or marker, but a large flagstaff had been placed near the grave, and according to a brief article written for *The Advocate*, a "religious weekly devoted to the family circle" published in Buffalo, apparently an unknown benefactor raised the flag every morning and lowered it each evening.[32] Due to the war and issues concerning the funding from the 11th New York, the tall granite monument marking Ellsworth's tomb was not erected until 1874.[33]

Just after hearing of Ellsworth's death, President Lincoln wrote one of the most beautiful letters of condolence ever penned. Mr. Ellsworth did not answer Lincoln until June 19, 1861:

Mechanicville June 19th 1861
Mr. Lincoln
Dear Sir

Pardon us the long delay in answering your kind and sympathizing letter. It has not occurred through want of inclination to write, but from the many calls made upon our time. The fact that Elmer succeeded in gaining the love & esteem of those with whom he was associated is to us one of great joy, and the reception of a letter, expressing such sentiments, from one whom we all so much respect is highly gratifying.

It would be useless for us to attempt to describe our feelings upon the receipt of the sad news of Elmers death. Although the blow was severe, how severe God only knows, yet through his goodness & mercy we are enabled to say "thy will not ours be done" The sympathy of all true Christians, and lovers of that country in whose defence he perished has done much to assuage the intensity of our grief We sincerely believe that God has removed him from a life of strife to one of eternal peace.

He was indeed toward us all you represented him, kind loving & dutiful Our present comfort and future happiness always seemed uppermost in his mind. But he is gone and

---

31 *New York Daily Herald*, May 27, 1861; *Buffalo Commercial*, May 27, 1861; *McArthur Democrat*, May 30, 1861.

32 *The* [Buffalo] *Advocate*, October 1, 1861, online version: www.newspapers. com/image/ 254527696/?terms=Col.%2Belmer%2Bellsworth, accessed December 5, 2017.

33 "Hudson View Cemetery, Mechanicville," *Saratoga NY GenWeb Project*, www. saratoga nygenweb.com/HudVuA.htm, accessed February 14, 2012.

the recollections of his goodness alone is left us. We trust he did not die in vain, but that his death will advance the cause in which he was engaged.

With these few words accept our most grateful thanks for your kindness to and interest you have shown in our beloved son May it never repent you,

We would always be pleased to hear from you
We are with respect
Yours &c,
E. D. Ellsworth[34]

For the next few months, the Ellsworths worked at getting their son's effects sent to them from Springfield and Washington. They wrote to Carrie, to John Nicolay, and a variety of government officials. Ephraim traveled to Washington to purchase Elmer's horse and refused to let anyone have his son's official army sword, although there were presentation swords enough to share. When anyone came to see them, Phebe and Ephraim shared memories of their son along with cups of coffee, and this gracious behavior on the part of Ellsworth's parents continued throughout their lives.[35] As 1861 drew to a close, however, they began to worry about money. Their son's small, irregularly-sent checks had helped with expenses. Mr. Ellsworth went to the paymaster-general's office in Troy, New York, and picked up a money order for $123.43, Elmer's last paycheck for seventeen days of service.[36] On November 25, Mr. Ellsworth wrote a short letter to John Hay:

Mechanicville Nov 25,1861
Mr. John Hay
Dear Sir

Your kind letter is here & you must except our sincere thanks for your kindness on our behalf. Mrs. Ellsworth Sends her Love to you & the President & his Lady

Privat

34 Ephraim D. Ellsworth to Abraham Lincoln, June 19, 1861, Abraham Lincoln Papers, LOC, memory.loc.gov/cgi-bin/query/P?mal:2:/temp/~ammem_ArKA:, accessed January 18, 2013.

35 *The Advocate*, October 1, 1861.

36 *Buffalo Commercial*, September 18, 1861, online version: www.newspapers.com/ image/ 2644429639, accessed January 1, 2018.

Mr. Shephard informed me thare was a vacancy in the quarter master department & he thought that would suite me as I had worked at the Tailoring Business for twenty years. Mr. Shephard said that department was mostly Clothing. I thought I should be better qualified for that position but they have asined[sic] me to the ordnance department So I have Excepted that in hopes of getting the one I wanted. You must excuse this writing for I Can not write as Elmer could.

yours Truly, E.D. Ellsworth[37]

Elmer Ellsworth's constant worry about his parents' health and living circumstances—warranted or not—had been heard so many times by his friends that even President Lincoln was concerned about how the Ellsworths were going to support themselves.[38] Lincoln made sure that Mr. Ellsworth was employed, although finding the perfect place for him proved difficult.[39] Ephraim accepted an initial appointment, with the rank of captain, on November 25, 1861[40] In April 1862, Lincoln asked General James W. Ripley to consider a change in that employment: "I shall be very much obliged, if Mr. Ellsworth can be assigned to duty where the work will be lighter. A. LINCOLN."[41] This request was made in a letter addressed to Ripley from 1st Lieutenant Thomas G. Baylor, requesting that Ephraim D. Ellsworth, assigned to the Fort Monroe Arsenal as a military storekeeper, be relieved because of health.[42] The request resulted in a change of placement, as Mr. Ellsworth was sent to an available position at the Champlain Arsenal in Vergennes, Vermont. He remained there for nine years and received a

37 Ephraim D. Ellsworth to John Hay, November 25, 1861, Lincoln Papers, LOC, memory.loc.gov/cgi-bin/query/P?mal:1:./temp/~ammem_ArKA:, accessed January 18, 2013.

38 Albert A. Nofi, *A Civil War Treasury* (Boston: Da Capo Press, 1995) 381-383.

39 Letter to Thomas A. Scott requesting placement for Ephraim D. Ellsworth, undated, online version: www.fold3.com/image/299626453?terms=Ephraim%20D.%20Ellsworth, accessed January 2, 2018.

40 *Army Registers, 1798-1969*, Ordnance Department, 107, online version: www.fold3. com/image/312148895?terms=Ephraim%20D.%20Ellsworth, accessed January 2, 2018)].

41 Abraham Lincoln to James W. Ripley, April 16, 1862, in Basler, ed., *Collected Works of Abraham Lincoln*, Volume 5, online version: quod.lib.umich.edu/l/lincoln/lincoln5/1:429.1?rgn=div2;singlegenre=All;sort=occur;subview=detail;type=simple;view=fulltext;q1=Ellsworth, accessed December 14, 2017.

42 Ibid.

government pension upon his retirement on June 30, 1882.[43] After he left public service, he and his wife moved back to their home in Mechanicville, where they lived with Chester Denton, Elmer's childhood friend and cousin, until Phebe's death on March 20, 1889, at the age of 79.[44] Eight months later, on November 6, 1890, Ephraim followed his wife in death after fifty-three years of marriage.[45] His simple obituary mentions that he was the father of "Col. Ellsworth, who was killed at Alexandria, Va., in 1861, while taking a rebel flag from the Marshall House."[46]

The Ellsworth family burial plot, surrounded by a black ironwork fence, is located in the southeastern corner of the Hudson View Cemetery. Interred beside Col. Ellsworth are his parents, brother Charley, uncle John C. Denton, John's wife Abbie Skidmore, and Elmer's great-grandfather, George Ellsworth. The monument is 25 feet tall, 5 feet square at the base, and well proportioned. The western face has a bronze medallion depicting the likeness of the late colonel with a shield emblem above and the name of Ellsworth in bas-relief engraved below. On the south face is an inscription acknowledging the New York State Legislature as contributors, while the north face bears an engraving of pertinent biographical details. The east face contains a slab of white marble depicting a coat of arms designed by Ellsworth and an excerpt from his last letter to his parents. A large bronze eagle is perched atop the shaft. The monument, no mere piece of granite and bronze, has become a symbol adorning commemorative plates, banners, postcards, and other mementos. At any given time, the surrounding fence and gate may also be decorated with wreaths and flowers.

Ephraim and Phebe are buried together. Their headstone is engraved with:

There is no Death,

what seems so is transition;

This life of mortal breath

43 Francis B. Heitman, *Historical Register and Dictionary of the United States Army* (Washington, DC: Government Printing Office, 1903), 225, online version: www.fold3.com/ image/ 306348472?terms=Ephraim%20D.%20Ellsworth, accessed January 2, 2018.

44 Death certificate for Ephraim D. Ellsworth, www.ancestry.com/search/ categories/34/ ?name=Phebe_Ellsworth&child=Elmer+E._Ellsworth&gender=f&location=2&name_x=1 _1&priority=usa&spouse=Ephraim+D._Ellsworth, accessed January 3, 2018.

45 Death certificate for Phebe Ellsworth, www.ancestry.com/search/categories/ 34/?name=Phebe_Ellsworth&child=Elmer+E._Ellsworth&gender=f&location=2&name_x =1_1&priority=usa&spouse=Ephraim+D._Ellsworth, accessed January 2, 2018.

46 *Brooklyn Daily Eagle*, November 14, 1889, online version: www.newspapers.com/ image/50408585, accessed August 1, 2018.

is but a suburb of the life elysian
whose portal we call Death.⁴⁷

*   *   *

"Ellsworth's Avenger," Pvt. Francis E. Brownell, was just 20 years old at the
time, but by all accounts, he showed the calm maturity of a seasoned veteran as he
stood on the Marshall House's third-floor landing, looking at the man he had just
killed lying close to his slain colonel. Francis Edwin Brownell was born in Troy,
New York and, according to one newspaper story, "gave up a lucrative situation"
to join the 11th New York Fire Zouaves.⁴⁸ No biography of Brownell has as yet
been written; most of the details of his life are based on official records, newspaper
articles, and interviews with him after the war. These articles describe Brownell
much as James Franklin Fitts did in his article, "Ellsworth and His Avenger,"
printed in Noblesville, Indiana's *Hamilton County Democrat* on December 2, 1887:

> I met him at a G. A. R. camp-fire about five years ago, and heard him give a deeply
> interesting account of this young hero [Elmer Ellsworth], one of the earliest martyrs of the
> war. Lieutenant Brownell, when I met him, was a serious, intelligent man, grave in manner
> and address. He spoke very earnestly of his dead friend and commander, as he knew him in
> the days just preceding the war.⁴⁹

Brownell was twenty years old when he enlisted in the Fire Zouaves, advertised
on enlistment posters as the "Eleventh New York Volunteer Infantry First Fire
Zouaves." According to newspaper accounts, his father, "Mr. Charles Brownell, a
very worthy citizen and Acting Superintendent of the Poor" in Troy, was pleased
that his son enlisted, although this meant that Frank would be giving up his job as a
firefighter in the Washington Volunteer Fire Company of Troy, Engine Company

---

47 Photograph taken during a visit to Hudson View Cemetery, August 12, 2011, author's
collection.

48 *The Belmont Chronicle* [St. Clairsville, OH], June 6, 1861, online version: www.
newspapers.com/image/145487638/?terms=Francis%2BBrownell, accessed January 10,
2018. This article appeared in several newspapers around this time and does not appear to be
challenged for its voracity.

49 James Franklin Fitts, "Ellsworth and His Avenger," *Hamilton County* [IN] *Democrat*,
December 2, 1887, online version: www.newspapers.com/image/353876949/ ?terms=
Francis%2BBrownell, accessed January 10, 2018.

Number 1.[50] His time with the 11th New York was exemplary. Adjutant's reports do not mention Brownell causing any trouble in camp. The fact that he was chosen by Ellsworth to accompany the small group of men to the telegraph office in Alexandria speaks well for his reputation within the regiment. The 11th New York was designated to be in the vanguard of the body of troops that crossed the Potomac on the night of May 23-24, 1861, in order to put Alexandria under military control. Once the Union army arrived, Col. Ellsworth detailed a small group of men to accompany him to disrupt the telegraph sending information to Richmond. They were to walk to the telegraph office. As they passed the Marshall House Hotel at the corner of King and Pitt Streets, Col. Ellsworth spotted the large Confederate flag flying above the structure. There was some discussion concerning the disposition of the flag, but the small contingent of men continued a few more feet down King. Then they stopped and turned back toward the Marshall House, entered the hotel, climbed to the roof, and quickly cut down the flag. As Ellsworth carried it down the stairs, he and the rest of the men, led by Brownell, encountered the proprietor, James Jackson, an ardent secessionist. Jackson shot Colonel Ellsworth through the heart with one barrel of his double-barreled shotgun. In response, Pvt. Brownell shot Jackson just as the second barrel of the shotgun discharged. At this point, most sources usually mention that Brownell then bayonetted Jackson as he lay on the wooden floor of the landing. One of Brownell's brothers spoke about this in an interview printed in the *St. Louis Post-Dispatch* on March 15, 1894, the day Brownell died:

> Mr. B. H. [Benjamin Harmon] Brownell states that it is not generally known, but is a fact, nevertheless, that. . . his brother's act of transfixing Jackson upon his bayonet, at the moment of shooting him saved his own life, for that act inclined Brownell's head and body forward and at the same time elevated the muzzle of Jackson's gun over Brownell's head. Jackson discharged his second barrel just as he received his own death wound, and the bayonetting saved Brownell's life.[51]*

---

50 *Belmont Chronicle*, June 6, 1861.

51 *St. Louis Post-Dispatch*, March 15, 1894, online version: https://www.newspapers.com/image/137671334, accessed January 3, 2018.

*There is some disagreement as to whether Jackson was actually bayonetted by Brownell. Historian Brian Pohanka claimed that the autopsy of Jackson's body made no mention of a bayonet wound. He offers the suggestion that Brownell followed his shot with a bayonet thrust that may have merely pierced Jackson's clothing. This is confirmed in the writings of Arthur O'Neil Alcock.

CDV of Francis "Frank" Brownell, Medal of Honor winner, from a photograph taken in the Washington Brady studio. These were widely sold and collected for a variety of fundraisers. *Library of Congress*

Frank telegraphed his father "immediately after" Ellsworth's death, telling him, "FATHER—Col. Ellsworth was shot dead this morning. I killed his murderer. FRANK."[52]

Brownell kept Jackson's Confederate flag in his possession from the time it left Alexandria until Ellsworth's funeral in Mechanicville. At that point, however, Brownell's exact whereabouts become a bit uncertain. His service record indicates that he was rewarded for his efforts on Ellsworth's behalf by the offer of a commission in the Regular Army. He accepted the rank of 2nd lieutenant on July 4, 1861, and served as an officer in the 11th U.S. Infantry for the next two years, retiring with the rank of first lieutenant in November 1863.[53] Oddly enough, he is referred to as "Corporal" Brownell in many accounts of the Marshall House incident and as "Sergeant" Brownell in a few, but his military record does not indicate that he ever held either of those ranks. His service record does include the following army receipt: "Sergt. Brownell served as Corporal in this company from Apl 20 1861, to May 26/61; from May 26/61, he served as Sergt."[54] According to his service record, Brownell entered the Fire Zouaves as a private, and officially maintained this rank until he became a 2nd lieutenant in the 11th U.S. Infantry. He became a 1st lieutenant on October 24, 1861, and left the service about a year and a

52 *Belmont Chronicle,* June 6, 1861.

53 Muster Roll Abstracts: Francis E. Brownell (alias Frank Brownell), New York State Archives/Civil War, online version: www.fold3.com/search/#query=francis+E.+ Brownell &preview=1&cat=249 accessed March 11, 2015.

54 Ibid.

half later.[55] Brownell, his wife Cornelia, and daughter Cora then moved to Washington, where he worked as a clerk in the pension office until his death on March 15, 1894, of tuberculosis, at age 54.[56]

There is much more to Francis E. Brownell's story, however. He was accorded the status of a hero wherever he went, and a movement was begun to award Brownell the Congressional Medal of Honor. He made two attempts to obtain the medal on his own, but it took the influence of his congressman to finally make it happen.[57] Brownell was awarded the Medal of Honor, inscribed with his name and regimental designation, in 1877. A request to have his action described on the medal meant it had to be returned to the war department. A second medal was issued with this inscription:

> The Congress to Sergt Frank E. Brownell,
> 11th N.Y. Vol Inf'y
> for gallantry in shooting the murderer of Col. Ellsworth
> at Alexandria, VA, May 24, 1861.[58]

Although the rank of sergeant is incorrect, the date of the incident for which Brownell received it made his the first Medal of Honor awarded in the American Civil War, although it was presented sixteen years later.

---

55 Heitman, *Historical Register and Dictionary*, online version: www.fold3.com /search/#query= francis+E.+Brownell&preview=1&offset=22&cat=249, accessed July 13, 2015.

56 Burial Permit, Health Department, District of Columbia, Frank E. Brownell, 1894, online version: www.ancestry.com/ mediaui-viewer/tree/20244812/ person/ 20315809 689/ media/06de7a5a-a1d9-4d68-b334-d990a94df7f8?_phsrc=vMF89&_phstart=successSource, accessed January 11, 2018.

57 The information concerning the identity of Brownell's congressman is unclear. Brownell and his family lived in Washington, but the representative for the District of Columbia was a non-voting position, and therefore not a position with much influence. Troy is in New York's Congressional District 20, and was represented during the appropriate time period by a series of men, including Ambrose Clark and Addison Laflin. New York's senators at that time were Roscoe Conkling and Ira Harris. Conkling was a powerful force in politics and was in office for years, but the list of representatives is much weaker—lesser-known men with short tenures. As yet I have no proof that Conkling was the one who got Brownell his Medal of Honor, but the quest continues as of this writing.

58 Congressional Medal of Honor Society, www.cmohs.org/recipient-detail/ 174/brownell-francis-e.php, accessed January 3, 2018; "First Blood," Civil War@Smithsonian, Smithsonian Institution, www.civilwar.si.edu/firstblood_brownell_medal.html, acces sed January 3, 2018.

Brownell's obituary indicates that he was active in both the Grand Army of the Republic, a fraternal organization for Union veterans, and the Military Order of the Loyal Legion of the United States, a hereditary patriotic order still in existence. Additionally, Brownell spent, "a great deal of labor during the war ferreting out the mysteries of the Knights of the Golden Circle," and "his mind during his last illness was full of these old experiences," although there is some question about this.[59] Four brothers, his wife, and his daughter survived Francis Edwin Brownell, "Ellsworth's Avenger." He is buried in Bellefontaine Cemetery in St. Louis, Missouri.[60] His obituaries, published in newspapers nationwide, agree:

> From that day [May 24, 1861] Brownell was a person of national interest and importance. Everywhere he was confronted with honors as a hero and as a soldier. His conduct during the remainder of the great struggle was creditable in the extreme and he retired with a record enjoyed by few.[61]

*   *   *

And what about that vast flag that flew in defiance above the Marshall House Hotel in Alexandria? Tracing its provenance is both exciting and frustrating. There are many stories concerning the journey from its halyards in Virginia to its current honored place of rest, the New York Military Museum in Saratoga. Julia Taft Bayne tells one of these tales in her book *Tad Lincoln's Father*:

> The Confederate flag which Ellsworth was pulling down at Alexandria when he was shot, and which was stained with his blood, was given to Mrs. Lincoln, but it was so tragic a reminder of the death of the gallant young soldier that she could not bear to have it around

---

59 *St. Louis Post-Dispatch*, March 15, 1894, online version: www.newspapers. com/image /137671334, accessed January 3, 2018. The Knights of the Golden Circle (KGC) was a mid-19th century secret society whose original objective was to annex a "golden circle" of territories in Mexico, Central America, the Caribbean, and the Confederacy as slave states, to be led by Maximilian I. Its goal was to increase the power of elite Southern slaveholders to such a degree that it could never be dislodged. During the Civil War, some Southern sympathizers in the Union were accused of belonging to the Knights, and were imprisoned. Several accounts of this interesting side story have been written; I suggest David Keehn's *Knights of the Golden Circle: Secret Empire, Southern Secession, Civil War* (LSU Press, 2013).

60 Bellefontaine Cemetery, http://bellefontainecemetery.org; old.findagrave.com/ cgi-bin/ fg.cgi?page=gr&GRid=18508; www.findagrave.com/memorial/18508/ francis-brownell.

61 *Logansport* [IN] *Pharos-Tribune*, May 16, 1894, online version: www.newspapers. com/image 9626, accessed January 8, 2018.

and put it away in a bureau drawer. There Tad presently found it, and on more than one occasion proudly displayed it in the White House grounds to the horrified amazement of loyal citizens.[62]

Bayne writes that Tad, a small boy, sometimes took the 14' x 24' flag out of the bureau and ran through cabinet meetings with it, much to the chagrin of his father.[63] The visual appearance of the flag from the top of the Marshall House quickly contradicts the truthfulness of Bayne's account. The restored flag takes up most of an entire wall at the New York State Military Museum—quite a handful for a little fellow like Tad Lincoln.

Until May 24, 1861 everyone, allegedly even President Lincoln, knew where the Marshall House flag was; it was flying atop the Marshall House. Journalist Ned House, Lt. Henry J. Winser, and Pvt. Francis Brownell all provided eyewitness accounts that support each other, and according to them, both Ellsworth and Jackson bled on the flag. Colonel Ellsworth was almost immediately removed from the landing to a small, vacant bedroom off to the side. Both Winser and House brought the flag into the room with them and attempted to wipe the blood away from the colonel's face, looking for some sign of life.[64] Then Winser and House crossed Ellsworth's arms over his chest and folded the flag, placing it over his legs.[65] House then took a detachment of men and went to cut the telegraph from Alexandria to Richmond while Brownell waited outside the bedroom door for the arrival of Dr. Charles Gray, regimental surgeon of the 11th New York. Gray examined Ellsworth and declared him dead.[66] Several of the remaining Zouaves made a litter from their rifles and their signature red blankets to carry their fallen

62 Julia Taft Bayne, *Tad Lincoln's Father* (Lincoln, NE, 2001), 15-16.

63 Marc Leepson, *Flag: An American Biography* (New York: Thomas Dunne Books, 2005), 110-111.

64 House, *New York World*, May 27, 1861; Francis Brownell, "Our Special Correspondent," *The Troy* [NY] *Times*, May 28, 1861.

65 Ibid.; "The Death of Col. Ellsworth.; Full Particulars of the Assassination by an Eye Witness—The Zouaves Swear that they will be Revenged—Singular Coincidences," *New York Times*, May 26, 1861, http://www.nytimes.com/1861/05/26/news/death-col-ellsworth-full-particulars-assassination-eye-witness-zouaves-swear.html?pagewanted=all, accessed June 24, 2012.

66 House, *New York World*, May 27, 1861; "Our Special Correspondent," *Troy Times*, May 28, 1861; "Death of Col. Ellsworth," *New York Times*, May 26, 1861.

colonel back to the wharf.[67] None of these accounts specifically mention the flag, but it apparently accompanied the body when it was loaded onto the steamer *James Guy* and brought back across the Potomac. The ship's flag flew at half-mast as it sailed to the Washington Navy Yard.[68]

As previously mentioned, Mary Lincoln went to the Navy Yard to see Ellsworth's body, but was not allowed to do so while it was being embalmed.[69] She spent some time talking to Francis Brownell, giving him a small bouquet from the White House gardens. It may have been at this time that, if she received it at all, Mrs. Lincoln got the flag, or it could have been when she and the president returned later in the day to pay their respects and order the remains transported to the East Room. It is reasonable to imagine the Lincolns relieving Brownell of his bloody burden, promising to return it when the body arrived at the Executive Mansion.[70] In any case, the flag is distinctly visible in Alfred Waud's drawing of Ellsworth's funeral, draped over his casket.[71]

One argument against Mary Lincoln taking the flag from the Navy Yard is the photographic evidence that Brownell had it in his possession when he had his likeness made at Mathew Brady's studio. The iconic photograph is often used to represent all Civil War soldiers in such places as the National Archives, and Ken Burns's landmark documentary *The Civil War*.[72] Brady's image shows a young man wearing his 11th New York uniform, complete with Zouave jacket and red fireman's shirt. His left arm has a piece of black ribbon tied around it, a token of mourning for his fallen colonel. His rifle has a bayonet attached to it, and another bayonet is hooked to his belt. On the floor, lying in a pile under Brownell's left foot, is the bloodied flag. Perhaps Brownell took it with him from the Navy Yard to Brady's studio at 627 Pennsylvania Avenue for the photograph. What is definite is

67 *Buffalo Commercial*, May 25, 1861, online version: www.newspapers.com/image/ 264442702, accessed January 3, 2018.

68 *Philadelphia Inquirer*, May 24, 1861, accessed January 4, 2018.

69 Jerrold M. Packard, *The Lincolns in the White House: Four Years that Shattered a Family* (New York: St. Martin's Griffin, 2005), 49; C. Percy Powell, *Lincoln Day by Day: A Chronology 1809-1865* (Dayton, OH: Morningside Press, 1991), 43.

70 Packard, *The Lincolns in the White House*, 49; Powell, *Lincoln Day by Day*, 43.

71 Alfred R. Waud, "Funeral service over Col. Ellsworth at the White House East Room," sketch, 1861, LOC, www.loc.gov/item/2004660356/, accessed January 5, 2018.

72 "Military Records-Civil War," NARS, www.archives.gov/research/military/civil-war, accessed January 3, 2018.

that the flag was in Washington at that time. It arrived with Ellsworth's body and is seen clearly in a contemporary photograph and sketch.

After the funeral ended, the cortege bore Ellsworth's remains to Union Station. Newspapers noted that "[t]he hearse was followed by the Zouaves, among whom was the avenger of Ellsworth. Brownell carried the identical secession flag torn down by the deceased."[73] The flag was held aloft on the bayonet of Brownell's rifle:

. . . and on the point of his formidable sword-bayonet—which had been made red in the heart's blood of the assassin—he carried the conquered secession flag which has made the name of Ellsworth deathless in his country's history.[74]

Brownell, his group of Zouaves, and the Marshall House flag accompanied Ellsworth's casket to New York. The city's papers identified the flag as being present at the lavish Astor House funeral:

At the head of the corpse sat two stout Zouaves, armed with their rifles and sword bayonets. At their back stood Brownell, the avenger of Ellsworth, the observed of all observers. At the feet of these Zouaves was the secession flag, pierced by a bayonet, and drenched with the blood of the brave Ellsworth. The spectacle altogether was a sad and impressive one.[75]

The Zouaves and the flag accompanied Ellsworth's remains up the Hudson River on the *Francis Skiddy*, to Hudson View Cemetery in Mechanicville.[76] After Elmer's burial, the whereabouts of the Marshall House flag become a little more challenging to trace. All along the way, from Alexandria to Mechanicville, people cut out pieces of the flag as relics of the gallant Zouave officer. The banner is visible in a photograph taken at New York's Great Metropolitan Sanitary Fair, held in March 1864. It was part of a display that included Ellsworth's frock coat, complete with blood and a large hole over the heart area, and both guns used in the Marshall

---

73 *The Jeffersonian Democrat* [Chardon, OH], May 31, 1861, online version: www. newspapers.com/image/72204470, accessed June 14, 2016.

74 *New York Daily Herald*, May 27, 1861, online version: www.newspapers.com/ image/ 329329346, accessed January 3, 2018.

75 Ibid.

76 *Brooklyn Evening Star*, May 27, 1861, online version: www.newspapers.com/image/ 118186527/?terms=francis%2Bbrownell, accessed January 4, 2018.

House incident.[77] From what we can see—three stripes folded over a table of some sort—the flag looks as if it had been little damaged, but Cowan's Historical Auctions has produced some other treasures that compound the mystery. For example, one lot offered for auction included a letter, undated but signed by Captain Patrick R. Hall, three swatches of fabric, and a postcard depicting the Marshall House. The letter identifies the fabric fragments as follows:

> Portions of the secession flag captured by Col. Elmer E. Ellsworth and in his possession when assassinated at the Marshall House, Alexandria, VA by James W. Jackson May 24 '61. This is no "humbro" as we had the whole flag in office. It was hung up in the hall of the Fire Dept in New York City. Wm C. Wickham an act of our president of the fire dept and he had the flag. Capt P. Hall. Officer of Howland D. Aspinnall.[78]

It is apparent that the flag was in New York City, relatively intact, for a while, but a lack of specific dates hinders the investigation. The auctioned artifact is, however, very typical of the bits and pieces of the flag (and the stairs, stair railing, wallpaper, and the bloodstained floor) that showed up in many letters sent home by soldiers stationed in the Washington-Alexandria area. A look at the flag itself, now held in the New York State Military Museum in Saratoga Springs, makes it evident that pieces of it have been cut out, and several stars removed. The NYSMM's flag conservators jokingly refer to the pattern of cuts as being the after effect of "square bullets," which they have seen in many flags. A flag is an important symbol, and the Marshall House flag represented not only the martyrdom of Union Col. Elmer Ellsworth, but also the actions of Confederate supporter James Jackson as he defended his property. Such a flag would be heavily "souvenired," and photographs of it from the NYSMM clearly reflect this.[79]

Enough scattered pieces of the flag remain, tacked to pieces of paper signed by either Frank Brownell or his wife, to make it arguable that the flag was cut up at

---

77 This stereopticon image bears the label "E. & T. Anthony" on the reverse. It was auctioned by Cowan's Auctions on March 17, 2014, and was from the estate of Kenneth Erwin, of Portland, Michigan. Online version: www.cowanauctions.com/lot/stereoviews-civil-war-anthony-view-of-elmer-ellsworth-exhibit-at-the-great-metropolitan-sanitary-fair-136507, accessed April 23, 2016.

78 Cowan's Auctions, auctions.bidsquare.com/view-auctions/catalog/id/1497/lot/ 522172/ cowans-auctions-colonel-elmer-e-ellsworth-presentation-sword-and-archive, accessed January 4, 2018.

79 New York State Battle Flag Collection, NYSMM, dmna.ny.gov/historic/btlflags/ other/ CSA_MHF1995.3033.htm;www.youtube.com/watch?v=ylbPIKItur4, accessed June 2011.

regular intervals. An internet search using general keywords such as "Marshall House flag pieces" will turn up many images of these souvenirs. Some have traveled as far as California, while others have stayed as close as Fort Ward, near Alexandria.[80] The Smithsonian pieces of the flag and the Marshall House's floor, as well as both Brownell's rifle and Jackson's shotgun. The National Portrait Gallery displayed these artifacts in their Civil War Sesquicentennial exhibit, "The Death of Ellsworth."[81] The PBS series "History Detectives" even did an investigation on a piece of flag found in a set of Civil War letters that claimed the bit of fabric belonged to the Marshall House banner.[82] The "History Detectives" website features images of letters from Ira Wilson, a member of the 11th New York, written to his parents while a prisoner of war:

> I send you a piece of the secession Rag that the Colonel took down from the Marshall House but I forgot to tell you of it in my last [letter]. Keep it for me as a relic of the war for it was the first prize of the Zouaves. I have sent you a piece of cloth with a friend of mine with the Colonel's blood on it. Please keep it, Pop, for I would loose it here.[83]

Wilson's letter is in two parts and is dated August 31, 1861. This may indicate that the dissection of the flag began, at least in part, as early as the day Ellsworth died, which would be consistent with the idea that the flag never left Brownell's custody until he returned to the army on or about July 4, 1861. At that time, he may have given it to his family for safekeeping, along with Jackson's shotgun and his own rifle and bayonet.

Francis Brownell left the army in November 1863, and returned to Washington to work as a clerk. He died in 1894, and it was after his passing that pieces of the Marshall House flag began to turn up more frequently. Cornelia Brownell, his widow, sold these relics to supplement the small pension she

80 Joe Blackstock, "Just how did a piece of an early Confederate flag get to the Inland Empire?," *Inland Valley* [Ontario, CA] *Daily Bulletin*, www.dailybulletin.com/2016/ 10/31/ just-how-did-a-piece-of-an-early-confederate-flag-get-to-the-inland-empire/; www.alexandria va.gov/historic/fortward/default.aspx?id=39606, accessed June 4, 2011.

81 "150th Commemoration of the Civil War: The Death of Ellsworth, Smithsonian/National Portrait Gallery exhibit, April 29, 2011 to March 18, 2012, npg.si.edu/exhibition/ 150th-commemoration-civil-war-death-ellsworth, accessed June, 2011.

82 "Marshall House Flag," *History Detectives: Special Investigations*, www.pbs.org/opb/ history detectives/investigation/marshall-house-flag/, accessed April 2012.

83 "Letters Home from Ira Wilson," *History Detectives: Special Investigations*, www.pbs. org/opb/ historydetectives/investigation/marshall-house-flag/, accessed January 5, 2018.

Ellsworth's
Avenger.

Brownell, shown here after he turned in his Zouave uniform for lieutenant's stripes, became known as "Ellsworth's Avenger."

Library of Congress

received.[84] At some point, the Brownell family gave the guns to the Smithsonian. Ellsworth's uniform coat, with the large hole in the chest from Jackson's bullet, and the remains of the Marshall House flag were given to the New York State Military Museum. There it lay until the expert NYSMM flag curators prepared the large banner for an exhibit. It was carefully restored and finally shown to the public from July 2011 to June 2012 in an exhibition entitled "1861: Banners for Glory."[85] Due to its massive size and delicate condition, the flag rarely travels, but can be seen by special appointment at the NYSMM.

In the decades after the Civil War, over 20,000 families named their children "Elmer," "Ellsworth," or even "Elmer Ellsworth."[86] According to a search of the 1850 census and grouped by birth year, 822 babies named some combination of Elmer, Ellsworth, or Elmer Ellsworth were born from 1841 to 1850; this number increased to 2,814 born between 1851 and 1860. Then, 23,980 babies with these

---

84 General Index to Civil War and Later Pension Files, ca. 1949 - ca. 1949; NAI Number: 563268; Record Group Title: Records of the Department of Veterans Affairs, 1773-2007; Record Group Number: 15; Series Title: U.S., Civil War Pension Index: General Index to Pension Files, 1861-1934; Series Number: T288; Roll: 58, online version: search.ancestry.com/cgi-bin/sse.dll?indiv=1&dbid=4654&h=10527699&usePUB=true&_p hsrc=vMF77&_phstart=successSource, accessed March, 2017.

85 "1861: Banners for Glory," exhibit, NYSMM, dmna.ny.gov/historic/btlflags/ exhibits/BannersForGlory.htm, accessed January 3, 2018.

86 www.familysearch.org; www.nancy.cc/2011/04/12/civil-war-baby-names-lincoln- grant-elmer/. 20,000 is probably an underestimate. Nineteenth century censuses were not as accurate as those we have today, and researchers should probably err on the side of undercounting. More such names might have been lost in transcription, or were identified only by their initials, a common practice at the time. Additionally, it does not account for the approximately 18 percent infant mortality rate.

name combinations were born from 1860 to 1870. The trend spiked at that point, although the period of 1871-80 still listed almost 18,000 such births.[87] When Col. Elmer Ellsworth died, it seemed as if the entire North was affected. The 11th New York Fire Zouaves, still reeling from the events in Alexandria, went into battle on July 21, 1861 with the words "Remember Ellsworth," being screamed into the still, muggy air near a small stream named Bull Run.

Colonel Ellsworth's grave in the family plot at Hudson View Cemetery, New York. *Kevin Pawlak*

87 Ibid.

Abbreviations Used for Public Sources and Manuscript Collections

ALPLC: Abraham Lincoln Presidential Library Collection
BU/JHL: Brown University / John Hay Letters
HLAC/ALSC: Huntington Library Art Collection / Abraham Lincoln Special Collections
JCCW: Report of the Joint Committee on the Conduct of the War, U.S. Senate Historical Office, Washington, DC
KCWM/LFAC: Kenosha Civil War Museum / Lake Forest Academy Collection
LOC: Library of Congress
NARS: National Archives and Records Service
NPLC/LOC: Nicolay Personal Letters Collection / Library of Congress
NPS: National Park Service
NYSMM: New York State Military Museum
NYSPLS: New York State Public Library System
OR: *The War of the Rebellion: Official Records of the Union and Confederate Armies.*

Selected Bibliography

Published Primary Sources

Abbott, John Stevens Cabot. *The History of the Civil War in America: Comprising a Full and Impartial Account of the Origin and Progress of the Rebellion, of the Various Naval and Military Engagements, of the Heroic Deeds Performed by Armies and Individuals, and of Touching Scenes in the Field, the Camp, the Hospital, and the Cabin.* New York: Henry Bill, 1863.

Barnes, Joseph K. *The Medical and Surgical History of the War of the Rebellion (1861-1865).* 6 Vols. Washington, DC: Government Printing Office, 1870.

Basler, Roy Prentice. *Abraham Lincoln: His Speeches and Writings.* Boston: Da Capo Press, 2001.

Bates, David Homer. *Lincoln in the Telegraph Office: Recollections of the United States Military Telegraph Corps During the Civil War.* New York: The Century Company, 1907.

Bayne, Julia Taft. *Tad Lincoln's Father.* Lincoln, NE: University of Nebraska Press, 2001 (reprint).

Burlingame, Michael, ed. *An Oral History of Abraham Lincoln: John G. Nicolay's Interviews and Essays.* Carbondale, IL: Southern Illinois University Press, 1996.

Burlingame, Michael and Turner, John R. Ettlinger, eds. *Inside Lincoln's White House: The Complete Civil War Diary of John Hay.* Carbondale, IL: Southern Illinois University Press, 1997.

Burlingame, Michael, ed. *Lincoln's Journalist: John Hay's Anonymous Writings for the Press.* Carbondale, IL: Southern Illinois University Press, 1999.

Burlingame, Michael, ed. *At Lincoln's Side: John Hay's Civil War Correspondence and Selected Writings.* Carbondale, IL: Southern Illinois University Press, 2000.

Burlingame, Michael, ed. *With Lincoln in the White House: Letters, Memoranda, and Other Writings of John G. Nicolay, 1860-1865.* Carbondale, IL: Southern Illinois University Press, 2000.

Casler, John O. *Four Years in the Stonewall Brigade.* Charleston, SC: Arcadia Press, 2017 (reprint).

Dennett, Tyler, ed., *Lincoln and the Civil War in the Diaries and Letters of John Hay.* Boston: Da Capo Press, 1988.

Ellsworth, Elmer Ephraim. *Manual of Arms for Light Infantry: Adapted to the Rifled Musket, With or Without the Priming Attachment.* Charleston, SC: Nabu Press, 2011 (reprint).

Ellsworth, Elmer Ephraim. *Complete Instructions for the Recruit In the Light Infantry Drill.* Accessed on *The Authentic Campaigner: A Web Site For the Authentic Civil War Living Historian,* www.authentic-campaigner.com/forum/showthread.php?2614-Zouave Drill.

French, John Homer. *Gazetteer of the State of New York: Embracing a comprehensive View of the Geography, Geology, and the General History of the State, and a Complete History and Description of Every County, City, Town, Village and Locality: With Full Table of Statistics.* London: Forgotten Books, 2016, books.google.com/books?id=R_zHwh4xBy QC&printsec=frontcover&dq=gazetteer+new+york#v=onepage&q=saratoga%20county&f=false.

Gillis, J. M. *Meteorological Observations Made at the United States Naval Observatory During the Year 1861.* Washington: Government Printing Office, 1873.

Halstead, Murat. *Caucuses of 1860: A History of the National Political Conventions of the Current Presidential Campaign.* Reprint by Inman Press, 2008.

Hardee, William J. *Rifle and Light Infantry Tactics: for the Exercise and Manœuvres of Troops when acting as Light Infantry or Riflemen.* Philadelphia: Lippincott, Grambo & Co., 1855, babel.hathitrust.org/cgi/pt?id=hvd.hn6fre;view=1up; seq= 1.

Hay, John and Nicolay, John G. *Abraham Lincoln: A Life.* 10 Vols. New York: The Century Company, 1880.

Haynie, James Henry, ed. T*he Nineteenth Illinois; a memoir of a regiment of volunteer infantry famous in the Civil War of fifty years ago for its drill, bravery, and distinguished services.* Chicago: M. A. Donohue & Co., 1912, archive.org/ details/nineteenthillino01hayn.

Krick, Robert K. *Civil War Weather in Virginia.* Tuscaloosa, AL: The University of Alabama Press, 2007.

Lamon, Dorothy, ed. *Ward Hill Lamon: Recollections of Abraham Lincoln, 1847-1861.* Chicago: McClurg, 1879.

McGuire, Judith Brockenbrough. *Diary of a Southern Refugee During the War.* Lexington, KY: University Press of Kentucky, 2013.

Moore, Frank, ed. *The Rebellion Record: A Diary of American Events with Documents, Narratives, Illustrative Incidents, Poetry, etc.* New York: G. P. Putnam, 1862.

Randall, Samuel S. *A Digest of the Common School System of the State of New York.* Albany, NY: C. Van Benthuysen & Co., 1844.

Report of the Joint Committee on the Conduct of the War. 5 Vols. Washington, DC: U.S. Senate Historical Office, 1863-65.

Russell, William Howard. *My Diary North and South.* Boston: T. O. H. P. Burnham, 1863.

Schroeder, Patrick and Pohanka, Brian C. *With the 11th New York Fire Zouaves In Camp, Battle, and Prison: The Narrative of Private Arthur O'Neil Alcock in The New York Atlas and Leader.* Lynchburg, VA: Schroeder Publications, 2011.

Scott, Robert Garth, ed. *Forgotten Valor: The Memoirs, Journals, & Civil War Letters of Orlando B. Wilcox.* Kent, OH: Kent State University Press, 1999.

Stoddard, William O. *Inside the White House in War Times.* Lincoln, NE: Bison Books, 2000.

Styple, William B., ed. *Writing and Fighting the Civil War: Soldier Correspondence to the New York Sunday Mercury.* Kearny, NJ: Belle Grove Publishing Company, 2000, www.amazon.com/Writing-Fighting-Civil-War-Correspondence/dp.18839261300.

The War of the Rebellion: Official Records of the Union and Confederate Armies. 128 Vols. Washington, DC: Government Printing Office, 1881-1901.

Unknown. *Life of James W. Jackson, the Alexandria Hero and the Slayer of Ellsworth, and the First Martyr in the Cause of Southern Independence.* Richmond, VA: West & Johnson, 1862.

Villard, Henry. *Memoirs of Henry Villard, Journalist and Financier.* Boston: Houghton Mifflin, 1904.

Villard, Harold G. and Villard, Oswald Garrison. *Lincoln on the Eve of '61: A Journalist's Story by Henry Villard*. New York: Alfred A. Knopf, 1941.

Whitney, Henry Clay. *Life on the Circuit: My Time with Abraham Lincoln Before He was President*. Amazon Digital Services (Kindle edition), 2013.

Whitney, Henry Clay. *Life on the Circuit with Lincoln: With Sketches of Generals Grant, Sherman, and McClellan, Judge Davis, Leonard Swett, and Other Contemporaries*. Boston: Estes and Lauriat, Publishers, 1892, eBook edition.

Woodward, C. Vann, ed. *Mary Chestnut's Civil War*. New Haven and London: Yale University Press, 1981.

Published Secondary Sources

Ackerman, Kenneth D. *Abraham Lincoln's Convention: Chicago, 1860—The First Reports*. Falls Church, VA: Viral History Press, LLC, 2012.

Andreas, Alfred Theodore. *History of Chicago: From the Earliest Period to the Present Time*. 3. Vols. Chicago: The A. T. Andreas Company, Publishers, 1885, play.google.com/books/reader?id=iKE4AQAAMAAJ&printsec=frontcover&pg=GBS.PP.

Armstrong, Janice Gray and Pike, Martha V. *A Time to Mourn: Expressions of Grief in Nineteenth Century America*. New York: The Museums at Stony Brook, 1980.

Barton, William Eleazar. *The Life of Clara Barton, Founder of the American Red Cross*. 3 Vols. Boston: Houghton Mifflin Company, 1922.

Bernstein, Peter L. *Wedding of the Waters: The Erie Canal and the Making of a Great Nation*. New York and London: W. W. Norton & Company, 2005.

Blumenthal, Sidney. *All the Powers of Earth: The Political Life of Abraham Lincoln, 1856-1860*. New York: Simon & Schuster, 2019.

Bowman, Samuel M. and Irwin, Richard B. *Sherman and His Campaigns*. New York: Charles B. Richardson, 1865, 2010 (reprint).

Brands, H. W. *Andrew Jackson: His Life and Times*. New York: Doubleday, 2005.

Burlingame, Michael. *Abraham Lincoln: A Life*. 2 Vols. Baltimore: Johns Hopkins University Press, 2013.

Burns, Jeremiah. *The Patriot's Offering; or, the Life, Services, and Military Career of the Noble Trio, Ellsworth, Lyon, and Baker*. New York: Baker & Godwin, 1862.

Byrock, Ashley M. *"Embalming in Memory: Mourning, Narrativity, and Historiography in the Nineteenth-century United States."* Ph.D. dissertation, Northwest University, 2008.

Chudacoff, Howard P. *The Age of the Bachelor: Creating an American Subculture*. Princeton, NJ: Princeton University Press, 1999.

Coggeshall, William T. *Lincoln Memorial: The Journeys of Abraham Lincoln From Springfield to Washington, 1861, As President Elect; and From Washington to Springfield, 1865, As President Martyred.* Columbus, OH: Ohio State Journal, 1865.

Costello, A. E. *Birth of the Bravest: A History of the New York Fire Department from 1609 to 1887.* New York: Tom Doherty Associates, 2002 (reprint).

Cozzens, Peter and Gerardi, Robert I., eds. *The New Annals of the Civil War.* Chicago: Stackpole Books, 2004.

Davis, William C. *Brother Against Brother: The War Begins.* Alexandria, VA: Time-Life Books, 1983.

Davis, William C., Pohanka, Brian C., and Troiani, Don, eds. *Civil War Journal: The Legacies.* Nashville, TN: Thomas Nelson, Inc., 1998, books.google.com/books?id=rO2utXnI41oC&pg=PT212&sig=4f31en4hB7SwKuo2-RRXBpsYMX4&hl=en#v=onepage&q&f=false.

Denney, Robert E. *The Civil War Years: A Day-by-Day Chronicle.* New York: Grammercy Books, 1998.

Eicher, David J. and Eicher, John H. *Civil War High Commands.* Stanford, CA: Stanford University Press, 2002.

Eisenhower, John S. D. *Agent of Destiny: The Life and Times of General Winfield Scott.* Norman: OK: University of Oklahoma Press, 1999.

Epstein, Daniel Mark. *The Lincolns: Portrait of a Marriage.* New York: Ballantine Books, 2009.

Faust, Drew Gilpin. *This Republic of Suffering: Death and the American Civil War,* New York: Alfred A. Knopf, 2008.

Fraker, Guy C. *Lincoln's Ladder to the Presidency: The Eighth Judicial Circuit.* Carbondale, IL: Southern Illinois University Press, 2012.

Fleming, George Thornton. *History of Pittsburgh and Environs.* New York and Chicago: The American Historical Society, Inc., 1922.

Freeman, Joanne D. *The Field of Blood: Violence in Congress and the Road to the Civil War.* New York: Farrar, Straus, and Giroux, 2018.

Gallagher, Gary W. *The Union War.* Cambridge and London: Harvard University Press, 2011.

Goodheart, Adam. *1861: The Civil War Awakening.* New York: Alfred A. Knopf, 2011.

Gottfried, Bradley M. *The Maps of First Bull Run: An Atlas of the First Bull Run (Manassas) Campaign, including the Battle of Ball's Bluff, June-October 1861.* El Dorado, CA: Savas Beatie, 2009.

Green, Michael S. *Lincoln and the Election of 1860.* Carbondale, IL: Southern Illinois University Press, 2011.

Holzer, Harold. *Lincoln, President-Elect: Abraham Lincoln and the Great Secession Winter, 1860-1861*. New York: Simon & Schuster Paperbacks, 2008.

Huffman, James L. *A Yankee in Meiji Japan: The Crusading Journalist Edward H. House*. Lanham, MD: Rowman & Littlefield, Publishers, 2003.

Hynd, Alan. *Arrival: 12:30: The Baltimore Plot Against Lincoln*. Camden, NJ: Thomas Nelson and Sons, 1967.

Ingraham, Charles A. *Elmer E. Ellsworth and the Zouaves of '61*. Chicago, IL: The University of Chicago Press, 1925.

Ingraham, Charles A. *Colonel Elmer E. Ellsworth, First Hero of the Civil War*. Charleston, SC: Nabu Press, 2014, reproduced by the War College Series, Carlisle, PA, 2015.

Kimmel, Michael. *Manhood in America: A Cultural History*. New York and London: The Free Press, 1996.

Kushner, Howard I. and Sherill, Anne Hummel. *John Milton Hay: The Union of Poetry and Politics*. Boston: Twayne Publishers, 1977.

Lamb, Blaine. *The Extraordinary Life of Charles Pomeroy Stone: Soldier, Surveyor, Pasha, Engineer*. Yardley, PA: Westholme Publishing Company, 2015.

Leech, Margaret. *Reveille in Washington: 1861-1865*. New York: Carroll and Graf Publishers, Inc., 1949.

Longacre, Edward G. "Elmer Ephraim Ellsworth," in Carnes, Mark C. and Garrity, John A, eds., *American National Biography*. Vol 7. New York: Oxford University Press, 1999.

Mayer, Harold M. and Wade, Richard C. *Chicago: Growth of a Metropolis*. Chicago: University of Chicago Press, 1969.

Mason, Edward Gay. *Fergus' Historical Series*. Chicago: Fergus Printing Company, 1882, books.google.com/books?id=jdcNAQAAMAAJ&pg=PA75&lpg=PA75&dq=G eorge+Harris+Fergus+Elmer+Ellsworth&source=bl&ots=T0mUpX4-tp&sig=-bsJIcpJw4oGCm7v8s10SgFhaVk&hl=en&ei=LdXdTbj0M4eisQOpwfSXBw&sa =X&oi=book_result&ct=result&resnum=1&ved=0CBsQ6AEwAA#v=onepage &q=George%20Harris%20Fergus%20Elmer%20Ellsworth&f=false.

McClure, Alexander K. *Abraham Lincoln and Men of War-Times*. Philadelphia: Times Publishing Company, 1892, archive.org/details/abrahamlincolnme01mccl.

McWhirter, Christian. *Battle Hymns: The Power and Popularity of Music in the Civil War*. Chapel Hill, NC: University of North Carolina Press, 2012.

Miller, Nathan. *The Enterprise of a Free People*. New York: Cornell University Press, 1962.

Murray, R. K. "They Fought Like Tigers": *The 11th New York Fire Zouaves, 14th Brooklyn and the Irish 69th New York at First Bull Run*. Wolcott, NY: Benedum Books, 2005.

Opie, John N. *A Rebel Cavalryman with Lee, Stuart, and Jackson*. Chicago: 1899, reprinted by the classics.us, 2013.

Pease, Theodore Calvin and Randall, James G., eds. *The Diary of Orville H. Browning, 1850-1881*. Springfield, IL: Illinois State Historical Society, 1931.

Phisterer, Frederick. *Distant Drums: Herkimer County, New York and the War of the Rebellion, 1861 to 1865*. Albany, NY: J. B. Lyon Company, 1912.

Poland, Jr., Charles P. *The Glories of War: Small Battles and Early Heroes of 1861*, Bloomington, Indiana: AuthorHouse, 2004.

Pratt, Harry E., ed. *Concerning Mr. Lincoln: In Which Abraham Lincoln is Pictured as he Appeared to Letter Writers of his Time*. Springfield, IL: The Abraham Lincoln Association, 1944.

Randall, Ruth Painter. *Colonel Elmer Ellsworth: A Biography of Lincoln's Friend and the First Hero of the Civil War*. Boston: Little, Brown Publishing, 1960.

Randall, Ruth Painter. *Mary Lincoln: Biography of a Marriage*. New York: Little, Brown & Co., 1953.

Sandburg, Carl. *Chicago Poems*. New York: Henry Holt and Company, 1916.

Segal, Charles M., ed. *Conversations with Lincoln*. New Brunswick and London: Transaction Publishers, 2013.

Schantz, Mark S. *Awaiting the Heavenly Country: The Civil War and America's Culture of Death*. Ithaca and London: Cornell University Press, 2008.

Silber, Irwin and Silverman, Jerry. *Songs America Voted By*. Harrisburg, PA: Stackpole Books, 1971.

Stashower, Daniel. *The Hour of Peril: The Secret Plot to Murder Lincoln Before the Civil War*. New York: Minotaur Books, 2013.

Steers, Edward. *The Lincoln Assassination Encyclopedia*. New York: Harper Perennial, 2010.

Swanson, James L. *Bloody Crimes: The Chase for Jefferson Davis and the Death Pageant for Lincoln's Corpse*. New York: William Morrow/Harper Collins, Publishers, 2010.

Taliaferro, John. *All the Great Prizes: The Life of John Hay, from Lincoln to Roosevelt*. New York: Simon & Schuster, 2013.

Tap, Bruce. *Over Lincoln's Shoulder: The Committee on the Conduct of the War*. Lawrence, KS: University Press of Kansas, 1998.

Tripp, C. A. *The Intimate World of Abraham Lincoln*. New York: Free Press, 2005.

Villard, Oswald Garrison. *John Brown 1800-1859: A Biography Fifty Years After*. Gloucester, MA: 1910, Peter Smith, 1965 (reprint).

Warner, Ezra J. *Generals in Blue: Lives of the Union Commanders*. Baton Rouge, LA: Louisiana University Press, 1964.

Wheeler, Tom. *Mr. Lincoln's T-Mails: How Abraham Lincoln Used the Telegraph to Win the Civil War*. New York: HarperCollins, 2006.

White, Ronald C. *A. Lincoln: A Biography*. New York: Random House, 2009.

Williams, Robert C. *Horace Greeley: Champion of American Freedom*, New York: New York University Press, 2006.

Wilson, Douglas L. and Davis, Rodney O. *Herndon's Informants: Letters, Interviews, and Statements about Abraham Lincoln*. Carbondale, IL: University of Illinois Press, 1997.

Magazines and Journals

Corneau, Octavia Roberts and Osborne, Georgia L., eds. "A Girl in the Sixties: Excerpts from the Journal of Anna Ridgely (Mrs. James L. Hudson)," *Journal of the Illinois State Historical Society*, October 22, 1929.

Dammann, Doug. "All Glory and No Gore: Elmer Ellsworth's 1860 militia tour helped prepare the North for War," *Civil War Times*, December 2010, www.historynet.com/civil-war-timeselmerellsworthand his zouaves, accessed fall 2011.

Doesticks, P. B., Q. K. Philander (Mortimer Thomson). "The Progress of My Zouave Practice," *The Saturday Evening Post*, Spring 1859.

Edwards, Owen. "The Death of Colonel Ellsworth," *Smithsonian Magazine*, April 2011, www.smithsonianmag.com/history-archaeology/The-Death-of-Colonel-Ellsworth.html, accessed July 5, 2012.

Garretson, O. A. "A Lincoln Pole Raising," *The Palimpsest* (April 1925),Vol. VI, No. 4, iagenweb.org/henry/History/lincolnpole.htm.

Grimsley, Elizabeth Todd. "Six Months in the White House," *Journal of the Illinois State Historical Society*, (October 1926-January 1927),Vol. 19.

Hawthorne, Nathaniel. "Chiefly About War Matters," *The Atlantic Monthly*, July 10, 1861.

Hay, John. "A Young Hero: Personal Reminiscences of Colonel E. E. Ellsworth," *McClure's Magazine*, (1896), Vol. 6, accessed August 10, 2013.

Hay, John. "Ellsworth," *The Atlantic Monthly* (July 1861), Vol. 8, No. XLV, play.google.com/store/books/details?id=OFkCAAAAIAAJ&rdid=book-OFkCAAAAIAAJ&rdot=1, accessed June 2012.

Hay, John. "Ellsworth," *McClure's Magazine*, July 1861.

Jones, W. Burns, Jr. "The Marshall House Incident," *Northern Virginia Heritage*, February 1988.

Kaine, John Langdon. "Lincoln Among His Friends: A Sheaf of Intimate Memories," *Century Magazine*, February 1913.

Leibling, Robert. "America's Zouaves," *AramcoWorld*, March/April 2017, www.aramcoworld.com/ko-KR/Articles/March-2017/America-s-Zouaves, accessed November 1, 2017.

Lupton, John A. "Forsaking the Law to Save the Nation: Elmer Ephraim Ellsworth, Attorney," For the People: A Newsletter of the Abraham Lincoln Association, Vol. 39, No. 1.

Markers, Isaac. "Why President Lincoln Spared Three Lives," *Confederate Veteran Magazine*, 1911, Vol. III.

Metcalfe, Lewis Herbert. "So Eager Were We All," *American Heritage Magazine*, reprinted in Vol. 16, Issue 4, 1865, www.americanheritage.com/content/%E2%80%9Cso-eager-were-we-all-%E2%80%A6%E2%80%9D, accessed August 23, 2017.

"On Ellsworth's Death," *Maine Temperance Journal*, June 22, 1861, archive.org/details/civilwarofficerslinc_30.

Stauffer, Adam Q. "'The Fall of a Sparrow': The (Un)timely Death of Elmer Ellsworth and the Coming of the Civil War," *The Gettysburg College Journal of the Civil War Era*, Vol. 1, Issue 1/6, 52, cupola.gettysburg.edu/gcjcwe/vol1/iss1/6, accessed August 2012.

"Who Began the War?," *Scientific American: An Illustrated Journal of Art, Science, & Mechanics*, June 8, 1861, Vol. IV, No. 23, scientificamerican.com/magazine/sa/1861/06-08/.

Wolly, Brian. "Lincoln's Whistle-Stop Trip to Washington," *Smithsonian Magazine*, February 9, 2011, smithsonianmag.com/history/lincolns-whistle-stop-trip-to-washington-161974/.

Newspapers

Albany [NY] *Evening Journal*
Alexandria [VA] *Gazette*
Baltimore [MD] *Sun*
Boston [MA] *Post*
Buffalo [NY] *Commercial*
Buffalo [NY] *Morning Express and Illustrated Buffalo Express*
Chicago [IL] *Press & Tribune*
Chicago [IL] *Tribune*
Cincinnati [OH] *Daily Press*
Cleveland [OH] *Morning Leader*
Harper's Weekly
Janesville [WI] *Gazette and Free Press*
Los Angeles [CA] *Herald*
New York [NY] *Atlas*

New York [NY] *Daily Tribune*
New York [NY] *Daily Union*
New York [NY] *Evening Post*
New York [NY] *Times*
New York [NY] *World*
Olathe [KS] *Mirror*
Philadelphia [PA] *Inquirer*
Pittsburgh [PA] *Daily Post*
Richmond [VA] *Daily Dispatch*
Richmond [VA] *Enquirer*
Rockford [IL] *Daily Register-Gazette*
Sacramento [CA] *Daily Union,*
Sangamo [IL] *Journal/Illinois State Journal*
Springfield Illinois State Journal
St. Louis [MO] *Daily Missouri Democrat*
The [Nashville] *Tennessean*
White Cloud Kansas Chief

Public Documents

Birth certificate, Elmer Ellsworth, search.ancestry.com/search/category.aspx?cat= 123, accessed June 9, 2016.

Clay, Henry. "The American System," speech made on Senate floor, February 2-3, and 6, 1832, in *The Senate 1789-1989: Classic Speeches, 1830-1993*, Washington, DC: U.S. Government Printing Office, Vol. 3, Bicentennial Edition, www.senate.gov/ artandhistory/history/resources/pdf/AmericanSystem.pdf.

"11th Infantry Regiment, New York, Civil War Newspaper Clippings," NYSMM.

Ellsworth, Elmer."An Act for the Reorganization of the Militia of Illinois," New York State Military Museum and Veterans Research Center, Saratoga Springs (NYSMM).

Ellsworth, Elmer. "Designs for Uniforms," NYSMM.

"Exercises Connected with the Unveiling of the Ellsworth Monument, at Mechanicville, May 27, 1874." Mechanicville, NY: The Ellsworth Monument Association, 1874.

Illinois State Census Collection, 1825-1865, Federal Census Records, www.census finder.com/illinois.htm, accessed October 17, 2017.

"Joint Committee on the Conduct of the War, Notable Senate Investigations, U.S. Senate Historical Office, Washington, D.C.," www.senate.gov/artandhistory/ history/common/investigations/pdf/JCCW_Fullcitations.pdf.

"Joint Secretary of State & Supreme Court Restoration Project of Illinois Oaths Complete," *Illinois Courts Connect*, April 19, 2017, www.illinoiscourts.gov/ Media/ enews/2017/041917_Restoration_Project.asp and www.cyberdriveillinois. com/ news/2017/march/170330d1.pdf.

Map of "Old Alexandria," www.nps.gov/gwmp/learn/historyculture/alexandria.htm.

Marshall House plaque, placed by the Sons of Confederate Veterans, 1929, Alexandria, VA.

Military service records, Edward B. Knox, National Archives and Records Service.

"New York and the Civil War." Albany, NY: New York Civil War Centennial Commission, June 1962, unpaginated pamphlet.

"New York State Battle Flags," NYSMM, dmna.ny.gov/historic/btlflags/other/ CSA_MHF1995.3033.htm, accessed August 2, 2016.

Pension File, Charles Ellsworth, number W19226, NARA—"Revolutionary War Pension and Bounty-Land Warrant Applications Based on Revolutionary War Service, compiled ca. 1800-1912, documenting the period ca. 1775-1900," M804, 300022, New York State, accessed June 2011, www.fold3.com/image/ 17125638? terms=George%20Ellsworth.

Reagan, Ronald. Speech, Veterans Day National Ceremony, Arlington National Cemetery, VA, November 11, 1985, www.va.gov/opa/vetsday/ speakers/1985 remarks.asp.

Revolutionary War pension, Peter Ellsworth, in Saffell, William Thomas Roberts, *Records of the Revolutionary War*. Phoenix, AZ: Heritage Books Reprints, 2007, www. fold3.com/image/1/17125534, accessed June 20, 2012.

"Rural Education in New York State: One-Room Schools of the 1840s," New York Historical Association, 2009, www.fenimoreartmuseum.org/files/education_ pdfs/RuralEducation-Teacher.pdf, accessed August 30, 2017.

"The Patowmack Canal," Great Falls Park, VA, www.nps.gov/grfa/planyourvisit/ upload/patow-pg2-Converted.pdf, accessed June 10, 2016.

United States Census, 1850, Malta, New York, search.findmypast.com/ record?id=usc%2f1850%2f004203145%2f00077&parentid=usc%2f1850%2f0042 03145%2f00077%2f023&highlights=%22%22, accessed September 3, 2017.

United States Census, 1850, Town of Half-Moon, Saratoga, NY, uscensus.gov, accessed June 8, 2016.

Websites, Blogs, Social Networks, and Discussion Groups

About.com, "Col. Elmer Ellsworth Became a Legend and Martyr Early in the Civil War," history1800s.about.com/od/civilwar/ss/Death-of-Elmer-Ellsworth_2.htm accessed July 23, 2011.

Abraham Lincoln Online, "St. John's Episcopal Church," showcase.netins.net/web/creative/lincoln/sites/stjohn.htm, accessed June 1, 2011.

Alonzo Chappel, The Complete Works, www.alonzochappel.org, accessed January 18, 2012.

Blau, Max and Valencia,Nick,"Charlotte Police Shooting: What Happens Next?," September 26, 2016, www.cnn.com/2016/09/26/us/charlotte-police-shooting-what-happens-next/index.html, accessed July 31, 2018.

C & O Canal Trust, "Canal History: George Washington and the Patowmack Company," www.canaltrust.org/about-us/about-the-co-canal/history/canal-history-george-washington-the-patowmack-company/, accessed June 8, 2016.

Civil War Archive, "Union Regimental Histories: New York, 11th Regiment Infantry, "1st New York Fire Zouaves" "Ellsworth's Zouaves,"" www.civilwararchive.com/Unreghst/unnyinf1.htm, accessed January 21, 2018.

"Currier and Ives—The History of the Firm," www.currierandives.com accessed August 23, 2015.

Dreyfus, Benjamin. *The City Transformed: Railroads and Their Influence on the Growth of Chicago in the 1850s*, file:////The%20City%20Transformed.webarchive, accessed July 2012.

Durstewitz, Jeff."We Wave the Bloody Shirt—But Whose??," Free Republic, May 28, 2011, www.freerepublic.com/focus/f-bloggers/2726508/posts, accessed July 2011.

Egan, Patrick J, ed. "Rochester's Militia: 54th Infantry Regiment NY National Guard," www.scribd.com/document/16449496/Rochester-NY-54th-Regiment, accessed October 20, 2017.

Ellsworth, Ephraim to "Friend Jackson," January 26, 1862, from "Portraits of Civil War Heroes," The Rosenbach Museum and Library, Philadelphia, https://rosenbach.org, accessed July 27, 2011.

Geni.com. "Ephraim Daniel Ellsworth Family Tree," March 23, 2009, www.geni.com/people/Ephraim-Ellsworth/6000000003288068328#/tab/media, accessed September 5, 2017.

Gordon, Lesley J. "'Evanescent Courage': The Fire Zouaves Go to War," *Reflections on War & Society*, February 4, 2016, dalecentersouthernmiss.wordpress. com/

2016/02/04/evanescent-courage-the-fire-zouaves-go-to-war/, accessed Feb ruary 15, 2017.

Guion, David M. "Musical Tributes to a Civil War Martyr: Elmer Ellsworth," music.allpurposeguru.com/2011/05/musical-tributes-to-a-civil-war-martyr-elmer -ellsworth/, accessed May 24, 2011.

Kaler, Jim. *Measuring the Sky: A Quick Guide to the Celestial Sphere*, stars. astro.illinois.edu/celsph.html, accessed May 25, 2013.

Knox, Edwin B. "Ellsworth's Zouaves at Bull Run," *Wisconsin Weekly Patriot*, August 3, 1861, bullrunnings.wordpress.com/2011/07/20/letter-from-the-fire-zouaves/, accessed August 23, 2016.

Kresol, Kathi. "Voices from the Grave: Carrie Spafford, a life of sorrow—the tragedy of one of Rockford's founding families," *The Rock River Times*, rockriver times.com/2014/10/08/voices-from-the-grave-carrie-spafford-a-life-of-sorrow-t he-tragedy-of-one-of-rockfords-founding-families/, accessed October 8, 2014.

The Lehrman Institute. "Andrew Jackson," www.gilderlehrman.org, accessed June 4, 2016.

Levin, Kevin. "Who Are the Virginia Flaggers?," *Civil War Memory*, August 31, 2013, cwmemory.com/2013/08/31/who-are-the-virginia-flaggers/ 9, accessed July 2018.

Loatman, Paul."Elmer E. Ellsworth—Citizen Soldier," from an address given May 21, www.mechanicville.com/history/ellsworth/citizensoldier.htm, accessed August 4, 2011.

"Mr. Lincoln's White House Maps," www.mrlincolnswhitehouse.org/washington/ mr-lincolns-white-house-maps/, accessed August 18, 2017.

National Museum of Civil War Medicine. "Embalming and the Civil War," www. civilwarmed.org/embalming1/, accessed February 20, 2016.

National Park Service. "The Lincolns in Springfield 1849-1861," https:// www.nps.gov/liho/learn/historyculture/springfield2.htm, accessed April 10, 2015.

Nelson, Robert K. "Of Monsters, Men—And Topic Modeling", *Opinionator*, May 29, 2011, *The New York Times*, opinionator.blogs.nytimes.com/2011/05/29/of-monsters-men-and-topic-modeling/#more-94157, accessed March 24, 2012.

O'Brien, John A. *President Lincoln in Civil War Washington*, www.lincoln inwashington.com/2012/07/16/he-has-probably-gone-to-mr-sewards-house/, accessed April 28, 2017.

Rothenstein, David S. "Civil War Lost and Found: Lincoln's First Ballroom," blog.historian4hire.net/2011/06/27/inaugural-ballroom/, accessed June 27, 2011.

Scott, Eugene. "Nikki Haley: Confederate flag 'should never have been there,'" CNN, July 10, 2015, www.cnn.com/2015/07/10/politics/nikki-haley-confederate-flag-removal/index.html, accessed July 31, 2018.

Sullivan, Patricia. "Alexandria to take up its Confederate memorials tonight," *Virginia Politics*, September 8, 2015, www.washingtonpost.com/local/virginia-politics/alexandria-to-take-up-its-confederate-memorials-at-council-tonight/2015/09/08/4f02bc0c-562b-11e5-b8c9-944725fcd3b9_story.html?utm_term=.7750e56121ba, accessed August 1, 2018.

Taphophilia.com. "Presidential Funerals," www.taph.com/presidential-burials/presidential-funerals-2.html, accessed June 2015.

USFlag.org. "Flags of the Confederacy: Confederate Stars and Bars," www.usflag.org/confederate.stars.and.bars.html, accessed July 30, 2018.

Weather.gov. "History of Federal Weather Services in Central Illinois," www.weather.gov/ilx/, accessed June 2, 2015.

Whitman, Walt. "O Captain! My Captain!" www.poetryfoundation.org/poems/45474/o-captain-my-captain, accessed September 23, 2018.

Winkle, Kenneth J. "Abraham Lincoln: Self-Made Man," *History Cooperative*, Summer 2000, www.historycooperative.org/journals/jala/21.2/winkle.html, accessed August 2011.

Additional Types of Published Sources

Billings, Grace Bedell to John E. Boos, January 24, 1934, *The Forbes Collection of American Historical Documents, Part Six*, catalogue, New York, May 22, 2007.

Ellsworth, Elmer. "Golden Resolutions," March 9, 1860, published in a variety of newspapers, including the *Urbana* [IL] *Union*, *Saint Louis* [MO] *Republican*, and the *Chicago Tribune*.

The Essex Historical Collection, Salem, MA, Vol. XXV, 1888.

Goodheart, Adam. booktalk transcript at the Library of Congress, accessed October 13, 2017, www.loc.gov/today/cyberlc/transcripts/2011/2011nbf/agoodheart.txt.

Heintzelman, Samuel P. Samuel Peter Heintzelman Papers. Manuscript/Mixed material, Library of Congress, www.loc.gov/loc.mss.ms010067, accessed February 26, 2018.

Harvey, Jerome J. *Occupied City: Portrait of Civil War Alexandria, Virginia*. Alexandria, VA: Alexandria Convention and Visitors Association, 2003.

"Introducing Our Own Authors: Dr. Charles Ingraham Tells Us More of Colonel Ellsworth Whose Life We Have Just Published." *Press Impressions for December*, Chicago: The University of Chicago Press, 1925.

Lincoln, Abraham to Ephraim D. and Phebe Ellsworth, May 25, 1861, Washington D. C., The Huntington Library, Art Collections and Botanical Gardens, Abraham Lincoln Special Collection.

Loatman, Jr., Paul. "Elmer Ellsworth—Citizen Soldier," remarks given in Mechanicville, New York, May 21, 2000, www.mechanicville.com/ history/ ellsworth/citizensoldier.htm.

Lorrequer, Harry. "Letter from the Zouave camp," *New York Leader*, July 7, 1861, dmna.ny.gov/historic/reghist/civil/infantry/11thInf/11thInfCWN.htm, accessed February 12, 2017.

10. Company, National Guard Exhibition Drill at Cozzens' Hotel," July 27, accessed November 1, 2017, 185960chicagoans-entertained-second-company-national-guard.html?pagewanted=all.

"Introducing Our Own Authors: Dr. Charles Ingraham Tells Us More of Colonel Ellsworth Whose Life We Have Just Published." *Press Impressions for December*, Chicago: The University of Chicago Press, 1925.

"U.S. Policy for Individual and Collective Military Training," www.mod.gov.ba/files/ file/dokumenti/defense/trainingpolicy.pdf.

Wasserman, Jerry. *Transnational Cross-dressing, Intercultural Pageantry: Zouave Costume in Performance.* www.inter-disciplinary.net/wp-content/uploads/.../jwassermanpaper. pdf, accessed summer 2011.

Unpublished Sources

Ellsworth, Phebe. "Memoranda—Diary, Letters, and Poem," dictated manuscript, written by Charity Louisa (Steadwell) Mabbitt, New York State Historical Society photostat copy in the collection of the KCWM/LFAC, and original in the collection of the New York Public Library.

"Some Events Connected with the Life of Judith Carter Henry." Unpublished manuscript, Manassas National Battlefield Park, Resource #10, www.cr.nps.gov/nr/twhp/wwwlps/lessons/12manassas/12facts3.htm, accessed July 14, 2012.

Wood, William S. *To the Committee of Arrangements for the RECEPTION OF THE PRESIDENT ELECT* (sic), handbill, Box 2, NPLC/LOC.

Index

281; Elmer Ellsworth and, xiv, 189, 195, 200, 201–202; leadership of, 186, 274; Marshall House flag and, 278, 279; Medal of Honor and, 275; overview of, 272–276; *photo*, 274, 282; recollections of, 170, 192, 277; shooting by, xvi, 224
Browning, Orville, 130, 133
Buchanan, James, xiii, 78, 95, 214, 215
Buckner, Simon Bolivar, 31, 151–152
Buffalo, New York, 138
Bull Run, battle of, 246–260
Burgess, James M., 121–122
Burgesses Corps, 89
Burnet House, 133
Burnett, Edward S., 254–255
Burrell, Dave, 206
Burton, Richard, 70

Cameron, Simon, xiii, 115, 153–154
Campbell's Run, 244–245
Camp Lincoln, xv, 172, 174–175
Camp Sinnissippi, 47–48
Camp Wool, 88
Carnegie, Andrew, 96
Chappel, Alonzo, 208
Charlestown City Guard, 93
Chase, Kate, 267
Chase, Salmon, xiii
Chestnut, James, 160
Chestnut, Mary, 233
Chicago, Illinois, 28–29, 42
Chicago Fire Brigade, 162
Chicago Light Infantry, 105
Chicago National Guard Cadets, 5, 40–43, 47–48, 56, 57–60
Chicago Volunteer Fire Brigade, 58
Chisholm, James, 160
Cincinnati, Ohio, 96–97
City Guard Battalion militias, 95
Civil War, beginning of, 120, 160
Clay, Henry, 15

Cleveland, Michigan, 85
Cleveland, Ohio, 136
Cleveland Light Guards, 85
Clybourn, James A., 35, 77
Coates, Edwin M., 77
Coates, E. F., 195
Colonel Elmer Ellsworth (Randall), 10
"Colonel Scott's Zouave Regiment," 104
Columbus, Ohio, 134–135
command drill, 90
Company A (Illinois Infantry), 104, 186, 188, 251
Company B (Chicago Zouaves), 105
Company E, 186
Company H (4th Virginia Cavalry), 251, 255
Company K (Illinois Infantry), 104
Complete Instructions for the Recruit in the Light Infantry Drill (Ellsworth), 18
Cone, J. E., 35, 54
Conner, Freeman, 77
Cook, Daniel, 42
Cook, John Pope, 41–42, 47, 68, 72, 98
Corliss, John Moore, Jr., 17, 21
Corliss & House, 17, 21
Corning, Erastus, 121
Cregier, John, 237–238, 248, 258
Crimean War, 70
Crowell, J. H., 217
Cummings, Arthur, 252
Currier and Ives, 208
Curtis, Edward, 217
Curtis, Newton, 17
Cutler, William H., 77

Danks, William Newton, 77
Darrow, Clarence, 118
Davis, David, 73, 88, 125
death, memorial responses regarding, 203–207, 208–209
Democratic Party, 111

About the Author:

Meg Groeling is a regular contributor to the popular Emerging Civil War blog. A writer, teacher, and curriculum developer since 1987, Meg has taught at both the elementary and middle school levels for more than thirty years. She graduated from California State University, Long Beach, with a B.A. in liberal studies and has been involved in continuing education for her entire career. Meg received a master's degree from American Public University in military history, with a Civil War emphasis. Her first book, *The Aftermath of Battle: The Burial of the Civil War Dead*, was published in the fall of 2015. Meg lives in Hollister, California, in a lovely 1928 bungalow covered with roses outside and books inside.